THE SOCIOLOGY OF SLAVERY

For
C. L. R. JAMES

The Sociology of Slavery

Black Society in Jamaica, 1655–1838

―――――

With a new Introduction

ORLANDO PATTERSON

polity

First published in 1967 by MacGibbon & Kee Ltd

This edition published in 2022 by Polity Press

Polity Press
65 Bridge Street
Cambridge CB2 1UR, UK

Polity Press
101 Station Landing
Suite 300
Medford, MA 02155, USA

ISBN-13: 978-1-5095-5097-5 (hardback)
ISBN-13: 978-1-5095-5098-2 (paperback)

A catalogue record for this book is available from the British Library.

Library of Congress Control Number: 2021951461

Typeset in 11 on 13pt Plantin MT
by Cheshire Typesetting Ltd, Cuddington, Cheshire
Printed and bound in Great Britain by CPI Group (UK) Ltd, Croydon

The publisher has used its best endeavours to ensure that the URLs for external websites referred to in this book are correct and active at the time of going to press. However, the publisher has no responsibility for the websites and can make no guarantee that a site will remain live or that the content is or will remain appropriate.

Every effort has been made to trace all copyright holders, but if any have been overlooked the publisher will be pleased to include any necessary credits in any subsequent reprint or edition.

For further information on Polity, visit our website: politybooks.com.

CONTENTS

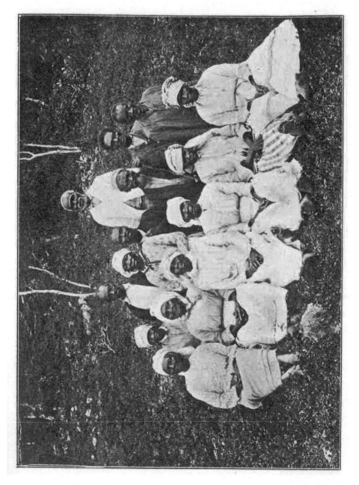

Formerly Enslaved Jamaicans (c 1870s)

Life and Scholarship in the Shadow of Slavery

The Sociology of Slavery was not simply my first scholarly book, but the academic and deeper intellectual as well as sources of all my later works on slavery, race and freedom. The slave plantations and their post-emancipation incarnations have profoundly influenced Jamaican society. For me, their presence could not have been more personal and pervasive. When I was four years old, my mother and I moved to Lionel Town in the centre of one of the island's main sugar-producing areas. The only adequate pre-primary school in the area was located in the church hall of a once elegant Anglican church in a bleak village called the Alley, once known, incredibly, as the Paris of Jamaica in the 18th century, and I was sent to live in the home of a family friend who was a foreman on the Monymusk estate, one of the island's oldest, owned in the mid-18th century by Sir Archibald Grant who also owned a slaving station in West Africa that directly provided the estate with its enslaved. The house was located literally in the midst of the cane fields. A narrow dirt track ran from alongside it through a dark, dirt-poor village of wattle and daub huts, the former habitation of enslaved workers, in which the Indians, who had been brought over from India to replace them, still lived. The emaciated stiff bodies of the men clad in dhoti loincloth, the dull glow of the women's hollowed eyes as they stared back at me and the other Black children, squatting before their rice pots above the wood fire on the ground, left an indelible impression on me. In hushed

[1] My warmest thanks to Professors Loïc Wacquant and Chris Muller for encouraging the publication of this new edition and for their valuable comments on an earlier draft of this introduction. Thanks also to the anonymous readers of the introduction for their very useful comments.

tones, the older children would often tell me: 'Dat's where di slave dem used to live.' We moved to May Pen for my primary school, the then small capital town of Clarendon, once surrounded by sugar plantations and cattle pens: Sevens, Halse Hall, Suttons, Moreland, Amity Hall, New Yarmouth, Parnassus, only a few, like Monymusk, still going strong, most marked by the ruins of great houses shrouded in thorny bush – Bog, Parrins, Carlisle, Paradise, Exeter and Banks. From my childhood I began to wonder what life was like for the enslaved whose violently enforced labour made it all possible, imaginings made vivid by the scary duppy stories, told at dusk, by the older children and grandparents of the ghosts of the enslaved still haunting the eerily hot spaces around the silk cotton trees of the lonely country roads leading from the town.

West Indian history had just begun to find a place amid the imperial history that still dominated the colonial curriculum of my primary school with its *Royal Readers*, as well as my secondary education, focused on British history and literature, and I seized every chance to study it. My very first research project was a study of the Morant Bay rebellion, the revolt of former Jamaica enslaved in 1865 that was ferociously put down by the colonial authorities, savagely aided by the Maroons. It won the national essay prize of the Jamaica History Teachers' association in 1957 and confirmed my decision to study history should I win a scholarship to the recently formed University College of the West Indies. I did win a scholarship to the university, but to my great disbelief, in a typical act of learned imperial arrogance, the Black, Naipaulian mimic men who then ran the university ordered me to major in economics, which was being instituted for the first time in my freshman year and did not have enough applicants, my pleas and those of my distraught high-school history master simply brushed aside. Fortunately, the Economics Department was really an inter-disciplinary group dominated by two eminent social anthropologists, R. T. Smith and M. G. Smith, the sociologist Lloyd Brathwaite, and the demographer George Roberts. All recognized the centrality of history and enslavement for any understanding of the Caribbean. This included the economists of the department, George Cumper and, later, George Beckford. Indeed, Beckford saw the slave plantation and its later developments as so critical for any understanding of West Indian economy that he developed, along with the economist

Lloyd Best, what became known as the 'Plantation Model' of the Caribbean economy and society. In addition to these interdisciplinary scholars, with whom I was later to work in the New World Group of Caribbean intellectuals, I developed strong friendships with fellow students who shared my historical view of Caribbean scholarship, particularly the political economist Norman Girvan and the historian Walter Rodney.

There were, however, other forces that pulled me to an engagement with European thought and culture, both in my study of slavery and on the development of Europe's culture of freedom. I arrived in London to begin my research on slavery in 1962, in what was to be the most exciting decade in the modern cultural history of Britain. I soon became deeply immersed in three networks of friends and fellow intellectuals: the West Indian student community, focused on the West Indian Student Centre in Collingham Gardens, Earls Court; the newly emerged *New Left Review* group that had broken off from the old Oxford New Left; and the literary group of West Indian writers and artists that came to be known as the Caribbean Artists' Movement, founded mainly by the poet-historian Edward Kamau Brathwaite, its first meeting being held at my flat in London.[1] My involvement with the West Indian Students' Union mainly kept alive my engagement with the broader West Indian society, in much the same way that the University of the West Indies (UWI) had earlier done, and my commitment to return to Jamaica to give back and help in its post-colonial development, a necessary pull, in view of the nearly irresistible temptations of intellectual and cultural life in Britain of the sixties.

My involvement with the new *New Left Review* group (which had emerged in 1960 from the merger of E. P. Thompson's *New Reasoner* and Stuart Hall's *Universities and New Left Review*) came not long after the Perry Anderson take-over that basically sidelined Thompson and the older post-communist left that had started it. I became deeply involved with the group, eventually joining its editorial board, through my relationship with Robin Blackburn, whom I met during his freshman year at LSE after he had been sent down from Oxford. I was soon immersed in the many strands of Marxist

---

[1] Anne Walmsley, *The Caribbean Artists Movement 1966–1972: A Literary and Cultural History*, New Beacon Books, 1992.

thought of the period. Although Blackburn was later to write major studies on slavery and abolition, in his early years he showed little interest in the subject. To the degree that slavery was ever mentioned, it was focused exclusively on the Marxian theory of the slave mode of production, on which Perry Anderson was to later write at length.[1] Nonetheless, my later deep involvement with the origins and development of European culture and the role of slavery in the emergence and persistence of its central value, freedom, originated in those intense discussions on the crisis of the left, and the problem of where in the world was Europe going, which preoccupied us in our fortnightly evening sessions. Interestingly, only one member of the circle of intellectuals we cultivated ever expressed any interest in the archival work I was doing on slavery in Jamaica at the time and that was the existential psychologist R. D. Laing, then the rising star of the anti-psychiatry movement who, after one of our meetings when I had vainly raised the subject of the real enslaved of 18th-century Jamaica in contrast to the abstraction of the slave mode of production, pulled me aside and asked what I had learned from my studies about the existential reality of slavery. My answer intrigued him, and I was both surprised and flattered when, a few days later, he invited me to address his experimental group of residential schizophrenic patients and their therapists at Kingsley Hall in Bromley, East London. It was my very first public lecture on slavery, drawing on my dissertation research, my audience, apart from Laing and the other resident psychotherapist, Joseph Berke, being a deeply attentive group of English psychotics, among whom was the then unknown English painter, Mary Barnes who, after the talk, led me by the hand on a guided tour of her grease crayon paintings. Their questions, and the fact that they found the subject so personally engaging, led me to focus more on the problem of the social psychology of slavery that appears in Chapter 6 of *The Sociology of Slavery*.

There was one other important personal experience in England that greatly influenced the writing of *The Sociology of Slavery*.

---

[1] My last contribution to *New Left Review* included a strong critique of one of the most abstruse, though well-received versions of the slave mode of production by Barry Hindness and Paul Hirst, 1975, *Pre-Capitalist Modes of Production*, Routledge. See my 'Slavery in Human History', *New Left Review*, I/117, Sept./Oct. 1979, pp. 31–67.

Not long after we arrived in England, Norman Girvan, Walter Rodney and I received a note from C. L. R James, summoning us to a weekly meeting with him at his London apartment (we never figured out how James came to know of our existence). We obeyed, of course, read every item on the reading list he sent us and, for the better part of a university term, we literally sat at the feet of the great man – there were not enough chairs in his modest flat, but the seating arrangement was symbolically appropriate – and listened to his interpretation of Marxism, with its strongly Trotskyite slant. James, of course, had been a friend of Trotsky, so the three of us were simply awed at the fact that we were getting the true vision of Marxist theory from someone who had got it from the horse's mouth of one of Marxism's founding fathers. Interestingly, James made no attempt to change my approach to the study of slavery in Jamaica, grounded theoretically more in Hobbes than Marx and, indeed, encouraged me to probe as deeply as I could into the lives and mode of survival of the enslaved. His deep interest in Caribbean society superseded any theoretical interest he may have had when discussing my work with me. Never once did he raise the subject of the slave mode of production. He had only recently returned from Trinidad, where he had been deeply involved with the decolonization movement before his final split with Eric Williams and was writing the appendix to the 1963 edition of the *Black Jacobins*,[1] entitled, 'From Toussaint L'Ouverture to Fidel Castro', to which he occasionally referred during our meetings.

The contrast with my New Left associates could not have been greater. We both agreed that, as West Indians, all our problems and cultural distinctiveness originated in slavery and the succeeding colonial situation. At the time, James was also writing one of his great classic studies, *Beyond a Boundary*, on the role of cricket in West Indian culture; his very grounded treatment of the subject was similar to my own approach to Jamaican slavery and underdevelopment. James was also instrumental in the publication of my first novel, *The Children of Sisyphus*, which he recommended to his publisher, without even asking me, after reading the manuscript

[1] C. L. R. James, 1938, 1963, *The Black Jacobins*, New York, Random House, Inc.

that I had nervously left with him after one of our meetings, later writing a long and very favourable review article on it.[1] My admiration, and gratitude for all I had learned from him during those Friday evening listenings, was partly expressed in the dedication of *The Sociology of Slavery* to him.

The Sociology of Slavery was the first book-length study of Jamaican slavery and slave society. It is also among the first studies *in English* to focus in its entirety on the culture, social organization, cultural life and attitudes and modes of resistance of the enslaved, in the New World. There were, of course, many book-length and other studies on Jamaica before, but they were focused mainly on other aspects of the society – its politics, economy, demography, flora and fauna, climate, the white ruling class and so on, or general studies with a chapter on slavery in general. Oddly, even the more recent scholars of Jamaican history who immediately preceded me seemed to have deliberately avoided any direct treatment of the subject. Douglas Hall, for many years chair of history at UWI, wrote his dissertation and most important work, *Free Jamaica*,[2] on the immediate post-emancipation period, the same relatively brief period covered by Philip Curtin[3] in his published dissertation, *Two Jamaicas*. Indeed, with the notable exceptions of C. L. R. James' *Black Jacobins* (first published in 1938), Eric Williams' *The Negro in the Caribbean* (1942)[4] and *Capitalism and Slavery* (1944),[5] and Elsa Goveia's *Slave Society in the British Leeward Islands at the End of the*

[1] C. L. R. James, 1964, 'Rastafari at Home and Abroad', Review of Orlando Patterson, *The Children of Sisyphus*, *New Left Review*, Vol. 1/25.
[2] Douglas Hall, 1959, *Free Jamaica, 1838–1865*. Yale University Press. In 1962, Hall published a very general paper on slavery, in the course of thirteen pages dealing with the socio-economic dilemmas of the planters, the economic effects of emancipation, and the consequences of slavery and post-emancipation society for his day. Hall, 1962, 'Slaves and Slavery in the British West Indies', *Social and Economic Studies*, Vol. 11, No. 4, pp. 305–18. Nearly three decades later, he published a well-edited edition of the Thistlewood diary, crafted in his thorough and understated style, that introduced Caribbean scholars to this important diary.
[3] Philip Curtin, 1968, *Two Jamaicas: The Role of Ideas in a Tropical Colony, 1830–1865*, Praeger.
[4] Eric Williams, 1942, 1970, *The Negro in the Caribbean*, Haskell House.
[5] Eric Williams, 1944, 2021, *Capitalism and Slavery*, University of North Carolina Press.

Eighteenth Century,[1] which appeared two years before *The Sociology of Slavery*, this avoidance of slaving and the enslaved as the *focus* of research, was true of all the English-speaking historians writing on the West Indies. Reference was, of course, made to the enslaved in many of these earlier studies, but rarely to their way of life, and no one had written a book-length study. I drew on the most important of these studies, especially Lowell Joseph Ragatz's *The Fall of the Planter Class in the British Caribbean, 1763–1833*,[2] Frank W. Pitman's *The Development of the British West Indies, 1700–1763*,[3] George Roberts'[4] *Population of Jamaica*, and M. G. Smith's paper on the early 19th-century British Caribbean.[5] The authors of the latter two were my undergraduate teachers, and Smith's paper was of special importance in pointing the way towards how a sociologist would approach the study of slavery. Although he wrote nothing on slavery in Jamaica, another of my teachers, the British anthropologist, Raymond Smith, was important in my study of the enslaved family, since I adapted his theory of the developmental cycle of the household, which he had derived for the anthropologist, Meyer Fortes, in writing about the subject.

It is hard to imagine it now, but before *The Sociology of Slavery*, with the partial exception of Kenneth Stampp, there was not a single book-length study in English focused on the social and cultural practices of the enslaved and their responses to their enslavement, by any professional historian writing on the West Indies and North America. U. B. Phillips, the dominant, white-supremacist historian on U.S. slavery up to the middle of the century, wrote on aspects of enslaved life, especially in his slightly less racist, *Life and Labor in the Old South*,[6] but as part of his wider pro-Southern study of the slave South, as were similar chapters in the broader

[1] Elsa Goveia, 1965, *Slave Society in the British Leeward Islands at the End of the Eighteenth Century*, Yale University Press.

[2] Lowell Joseph Ragatz, 1928, *The Fall of the Planter Class in the British Caribbean, 1763–1833*, The Century Company.

[3] Frank W. Pitman, 2017, *The Development of the British West Indies, 1700–1763*, Yale University Press.

[4] George W. Roberts, 1957, *The Population of Jamaica*, Cambridge University Press.

[5] M. G. Smith, 1965, 'Some Aspects of Social Structure in the British Caribbean about 1820', in his *The Plural Society in the British West Indies*, University of California Press.

[6] U. B. Phillips, 1929, *Life and Labor in the Old South*, Little, Brown.

studies of plantation slavery in Mississippi by Charles Sydnor.[1] A change occurred among white scholars following the civil rights revolution, especially in the revisionist work of Kenneth Stampp,[2] which challenged the prevailing pro-Southern works of U. B. Phillips and others; and there was the important comparative works by Tannenbaum[3] and Klein.[4] While anti-slavery and sympathetic to the enslaved, none of these works by white historians was wholly focused on the life of the enslaved and culture although Stampp's book was exceptional in devoting over a third of the volume to these subjects. Both Tannenbaum's and Klein's works were concerned primarily with the question of the differences between Latin American and U.S. slavery. Stanley Elkins'[5] work, which compared slavery with the Nazi concentration camp in arguing that there was more than a core of truth in the infantilized image of blacks reflected in the slaveholder's Sambo stereotype, was indeed focused on the life and thoughts of the enslaved and, while his comparison with the Nazi concentration camps was not as far off the mark as so many critics claimed, he erred, not so much in identifying similarities in the psychological responses of Jewish inmates and slaves but in his interpretation of the meanings and significance of these behavioural and psychological strategies of the enslaved. The work was published in 1959 and still in vogue when I was researching *The Sociology of Slavery*. Indeed, my critique of the work's basic argument was among the first to be published and became the concluding chapter of Ann J. Lane's collection of critical writings on the Elkins book.[6]

The situation was different among the pre-civil rights era of Black American intellectuals, historians and sociologists, among whom the experience of slavery and its consequences for later Black life was of great importance and figured prominently in their debate with racist scholars in the Jim Crow South. I read many of these Black scholars as an undergraduate, partly at the

---

[1] Charles Sydnor, 1933, *Slavery in Mississippi*, D. Appleton-Century.
[2] Kenneth Stampp, 1956, *The Peculiar Institution*, Knopf-Doubleday.
[3] Frank Tannenbaum, 1946, *Slave and Citizen*, Alfred Knopf.
[4] Herbert Klein, 1967, *Slavery in the Americas: A Comparative Study of Virginia and Cuba*, University of Chicago Press.
[5] Stanley Elkins, 1959, *Slavery*, University of Chicago Press.
[6] Ann J. Lane, 1971, *The Debate Over Slavery*, University of Illinois Press. I will have more to say below on just where Elkins erred.

urging of one of my teachers, Lloyd Brathwaite. A passage from a paper written in 1898 eloquently expressed DuBois' views on what was missing in the study of slavery: that while a great deal had been written on the legal and political aspects of the subject, 'of the slave himself, of his group life and social institutions, of remaining traces of his African tribal life, of his amusements, his conversion to Christianity, his acquiring of the English tongue . . . of his whole reaction against his environment, of all this we hear little or nothing, and would apparently be expected to believe that the Negro arose from the dead in 1863'.[1] Sixty-four years later, that is exactly how I felt about the study of the Jamaican past as I prepared to enter the archives of the British Records Office and British Museum.

Not long after *The Sociology of Slavery* was published, the situation changed dramatically and a tide of scholarly works on Jamaica appeared. These works fall into two broad categories, which may be called *dominion* and *doulotic* studies. Dominion studies are those primarily concerned with the rule and rulers of the island; the nature of its macro-level socio-political system and economy, in the context of which its enslaved, as human capital, are considered; and, in keeping with one common meaning of the term, studies on the island's existence as 'a country that was part of the British empire but had its own government' (Merriam-Webster). Doulotic studies are those mainly concerned with the island's enslaved population, seen from the enslaved's perspective, their demographic development and modes of socio-cultural survival, resistance, and adjustment to the system; the micro-level relations of domination between enslaver and enslaved; the meso-level nature and conflicts within the plantations, pens and other localized units of production, as systems of total domination; and the functioning of slavery as an institutional process.[2]

---

[1] W. E. B. DuBois, 'The Study of the Negro Problems', *Annals of the American Academy of Political and Social Science*, Vol. 11, 1898, cited in J. D. Smith, 'A Different View of Slavery: Black Historians Attack the Proslavery Argument, 1890–1920', *Journal of Negro History*, 1980, Vol. 65, No. 4.

[2] The term comes from the Greek *doulosis*, meaning enslavement, derived from *doulos*, 'slave'. I use the spelling 'doulotic' to distinguish it from the related term 'dulotic' used in social biology for a species of enslaving ants.

Jamaica has been fortunate in having outstanding scholars who have written major works from one or other, or both, of these perspectives. B. W. Higman surely ranks near, or at the top, of scholars who work on West Indian slavery with a special focus on Jamaica, with works from both perspectives. His monumental study of the historical demography of the West Indies serves scholars working from both perspectives and will continue to do so for years to come.[1] For decades, before retiring to Australia, he worked in Jamaica, producing world-class scholarship on Jamaican and West Indian slavery, from his base at the University of the West Indies where he trained generations of West Indian historians. His meso-level work on Montpellier plantation[2] shifts the focus to the doulotic and the 18th century and stands comparison with the Jamaican part of Dunn's masterpiece comparing plantations in Jamaica and Virginia.[3] I hasten to add that I disagree with several findings in Higman's works, especially his revisionist view of the enslaved's familial relations, which was too influenced by U.S. cliometric studies, and his rather too sanguine view of the system as a whole but, having already published these disagreements, there is no need to repeat them here.[4] Approaching Higman's and Dunn's doulotic works in depth and quality are those of Trevor Burnard who has fast become the most prolific student of Jamaican slavery, writing from both perspectives. His study of Thomas Thistlewood's relations with his enslaved workers[5] brings the study of Jamaican slavery down from that of the meso-level unit of the plantation to the micro-level of what Marx called the 'relation of domination', a term I borrowed for my own comparative study of slavery. If there ever were any doubts about the

[1] B. W. Higman, 1984, *Slave Population of the British Caribbean, 1807–1838*, Johns Hopkins University Press.

[2] B. W. Higman, 1998, *Montpelier, Jamaica: A Plantation Community in Slavery and Freedom, 1739–1912*, University Press of the West Indies.

[3] Richard S. Dunn, 2014, *A Tale of Two Plantations: Slave Life and Labor in Jamaica and Virginia*, Harvard University Press.

[4] See Orlando Patterson, 'Recent Studies on Caribbean Slavery and the Slave Trade', *Latin American Research Review*, Vol. 17, No. 3, 1982. For my more detailed critique of Higman's interpretation of the slave family, see my paper: 'Persistence, Continuity, and Change in the Jamaican Working-Class Family', *Journal of Family History*, Vol. 7, No. 2, 1982, pp. 135–61.

[5] Trevor Burnard, 2004, *Mastery, Tyranny, and Desire: Thomas Thistlewood and his Slaves in the Anglo Jamaican World*, University of North Carolina Press.

conclusion I arrived at in *The Sociology of Slavery*, that Jamaican slave society was a Hobbesian state of savage exploitation and, with the possible exception of the enslaved in the Laurion silver mines of ancient Attica, the most brutal in all history, Burnard's probing re-examination[1] of Thistlewood's world has disabused us of them. An impressive body of work is further illuminating the doulotic perspective on the system, a rigorous recent example of which being Justin Robert's[2] comparative study of the kinds and intensities of labour activities and the sickness and mortality rates of the enslaved in Jamaica, Barbados and Virginia, which nicely complement's Dunn's comparative work.

An important and growing number of works have brought sex and gender to the forefront of doulotic studies.[3] *The Sociology of Slavery* was the first modern book on Jamaica, and the second

---

[1] It is interesting that, fifteen years before Burnard's academic block-buster, the Jamaican historian Douglas Hall had produced a valuable edited version of Thistlewood's diary, noted earlier: *In Miserable Slavery: Thomas Thistlewood in Jamaica, 1750–86*, Macmillan Press. Given the explosive nature of the subject and its implications for the study of Jamaican slavery, and slavery in general, Hall's understated editing may have prevented his work from reaching a wider audience. In a later study Hall's detachment from Thistlewood's gross inhumanities may have been taken too far in his admiring discussion of the enslaver's botanic and gardening interests, occasionally referring respectfully to him as 'Mr Thistlewood'. It was a bit odd, like writing about the Marquis de Sade's curious reflections on the literary merits of Matthew 'Monk' Lewis' gothic writings without ever mentioning the fact that he was, well, a sadist. See Douglas Hall, 2001, 'Planters, Farmers and Gardeners in Eighteenth-Century Jamaica,' in B. Moore, B. W. Higman, C. Campbell and P. Bryan, eds, *Slavery, Freedom and Gender: The Dynamics of Caribbean Society*, University of the West Indies Press, pp. 97–114.

[2] Justin Roberts, 2018, *Slavery and the Enlightenment in the British Atlantic, 1750–1807*, Cambridge University Press.

[3] For an assessment, see Hilary Beckles, 'Sex and Gender in the Historiography of Caribbean Slavery', in Verene Shepherd, Bridget Brereton, Barbara Bailey, eds, 1995. *Engendering History: Caribbean Women in Historical Perspective*, Palgrave Macmillan, pp. 111–24. Although primarily on Barbados, his work on enslaved women in that island has important comparative relevance to Jamaica: Beckles, 1989, *Natural Rebels: A Social History of Enslaved Black Women in Barbados*, New Brunswick, N.J.: Rutgers University Press; See also, Marietta Morrissey, 1989, *Slave Women in the New World: Gender Stratification in the Caribbean*, University Press of Kansas; Diana Paton and Pamela Scully, 'Introduction: Gender and Slave Emancipation in Comparative Perspective' in Pamela Scully and Diana Paton, eds, *Gender and Slave Emancipation in the Atlantic World*, Durham, N.C., 2005, pp. 1–34; Barbara Bush, 1990, *Slave Women in Caribbean Society*, Indiana University Press.

(after Goveia) on the West Indies more broadly, to discuss at length the triple exploitation of enslaved women on the plantation – their disproportionate representation in the fields and limited occupational opportunities, the sexual abuse of their bodies, the burdens of reproduction – and their sometimes anti-natalist attitudes as a form of resistance against the system.[1] I wouldn't presume to think that my work influenced the many fine studies on women in Jamaican slavery that followed it,[2] but this I can say: the study of their plight in Jamaica was first explored in *The Sociology of Slavery*. While this emphasis on gender is to be applauded, I am somewhat concerned with the overemphasis of most of these works on the late abolitionist era of slavery. In this regard, the works of Kathleen Wilson,[3] Katie Donington[4] and Diana Paton[5] show that there is no shortage of data for the study of gender in the early 18th-century period of the society. Some authors have also been inclined to defend the sexual virtue and heroism of enslaved women, and their presumed propensity for the nuclear family, as

[1] See *The Sociology of Slavery*, pp. 61, 106–12, 157.

[2] Lucille Mathurin Mair was the pioneer of gender studies of Jamaican and West Indian slavery, on which see her very influential 1974 dissertation, eventually published in 2006 as *A Historical Study of Women in Jamaica, 1655–844*, University of the West Indies Press. Mair drew on *The Sociology of Slavery* in her interesting theory that gender attitudes and the disproportionate use of women in the fields may have retarded technological development on Jamaican slave plantations. See her chapter: 'Women Field Workers in Jamaica during Slavery', in B. Moore, B. W. Higman, C. Campbell and P. Bryan, *Slavery, Freedom and Gender: The Dynamics of Caribbean Society*, 2001, pp. 184–5.
See also Diana Paton, 2004, *No Bond but the Law: Punishment, Race, and Gender in Jamaican State Formation*, Duke University Press. See also Pamela Scully and Diana Paton, eds, 2005, *Gender and Slave Emancipation in the Atlantic World*, Duke University Press; Marietta Morrissey, 1986, 'Women's Work, Family Formation, and Reproduction among Caribbean Slaves', *Review*, Winter, 1986, Vol. 9, No. 3; Sasha Turner, 2019, *Contested Bodies: Pregnancy, Childrearing, and Slavery in Jamaica*, University of Pennsylvania Press; Barbara Bush, 1990, *Slave Women in Caribbean Society, 1650–1838*, Heinemann Publishers; Verene Shepherd, *op. cit.*, p. 2002.

[3] Kathleen Wilson, 2003, *The Island Race: Englishness, Empire and Gender in the Eighteenth Century*, Routledge.

[4] Katie Donington, 2020, *The Bonds of Family: Slavery, Commerce and Culture in the British Atlantic World*, Manchester University Press.

[5] Diana Paton, 2001, 'Punishment, Crime, and the Bodies of Slaves in Eighteenth-Century Jamaica', *Journal of Social History*, Vol. 34, pp. 923–54; as well as her 2012, *Obeah and Other Powers: The Politics of Caribbean Religion and Healing*, Durham, N.C.: Duke University Press.

if their survival under the genocidal and rapine conditions of slave life were not enough.

Rhoda Reddock's bracing Marxist–feminist studies have stoutly challenged this historiographic line.[1] The attempt to impose the Western nuclear family on West Indian working-class women, she shows, has failed, both during and after slavery by missionaries and middle-class do-gooders, and one lesson she draws from her comparative study of Caribbean slavery is that 'Love of motherhood was neither natural nor universal.'[2] The works of Randy M. Brown,[3] mainly on Berbice, of Patricia Mohammed[4] on Jamaica, and of Kamala Kempadoo on the Caribbean,[5] have forcefully advanced this realistic and unsentimental feminist agenda, which recognizes that among poor and working-class Caribbean women from the period of slavery until today, as Kempadoo well puts it: 'Sexuality is strongly linked to survival strategies of making do, as well as to consumption, which in itself is often seen as a prerequisite for survival. It is not always conflated with intimacy or love, nor necessarily, when economically organized, seen to violate boundaries between the public and private.'[6] My work on Jamaican slavery, as well my ethnographic field studies of the Kingston poor in the early 1970s, fully bear this out, and I make no apologies for pointing out that sex work was one of the strategies of survival by enslaved women in the misogynistic nightmare of Jamaican slave society. Slavery was drenched in violence, rape an integral part, and tragically, the violence of the enslaver against the enslaved seeped down like a viper's poison through the veins of the entire system, deep into the relations among the enslaved themselves, especially between older, more advantaged enslaved men and

[1] Rhoda Reddock, 1994, *Women, Labour and Politics in Trinidad and Tobago. A History*, Ian Randle.

[2] Rhoda Reddock, 1985, 'Women and Slavery in the Caribbean: A Feminist Perspective', *Latin American Perspectives*, Vol. 12, No. 1, Latin American Colonial History, pp. 77, 78.

[3] Randy M. Browne, 2017, *Surviving Slavery in the British Caribbean*, University of Pennsylvania Press.

[4] Patricia Mohammed, 2000, '"But Most of All Mi Love Me Browning": The Emergence in Eighteenth and Nineteenth-Century Jamaica of the Mulatto Woman as the Desired', *Feminist Review*, Vol. 65, No. 1, pp. 22–48.

[5] Kamala Kempadoo, 2004, *Sexing the Caribbean: Gender, Race and Sexual Labor*, Routledge.

[6] *Ibid.*

women, intimate violence that we still live with in the West Indies, especially Jamaica, where violence against women, members of the LGBTQ community, and other vulnerable groups, is endemic.

The works of Michael Craton deserve mention in any review of the literature on Jamaican and broader Caribbean slavery, if for no other reason than its prolificity, especially his works on Worthy Park. *The Sociology of Slavery* was the first work to use materials on Worthy Park. I had been told of their existence by a friend who had worked in the offices of the estate and, when I visited it in 1964, I was provided with a box of materials on the enslaved and space to work on them. I had expected more from what my friend had told me, but thankfully made the most of what I had been handed. I was very surprised when I read the announcement of a book on the plantation in late 1969, to be published the following year.[1] I was then a lecturer at the University of the West Indies and a colleague of the distinguished Jamaican economist, George Beckford. We immediately developed a joint research project focusing on the historical development and present socio-economic structure of the plantation, went to Worthy Park and sought permission from the owners to conduct our research. We were flatly denied access to the family papers and most of the archives, although told that we could do what we wanted with the workers.[2] Eight years after the first, dominion-type study, Craton's large doulotic study of the plantation appeared.[3] Craton and Walvin are not to be blamed for the denial of access to us of the estate's papers, which was quite consistent with the racist attitudes of the Jamaican planter class. Although critical of the repeated unctuous posturing towards favoured members of the Caribbean academic community, and several analytic flaws, my review of the work was generally favourable, my judgment being that he was 'not only a first-rate historian

[1] Michael Craton and James Walvin, 1970, *A Jamaican Plantation: The History of Worthy Park, 1670–1970*, University of Toronto Press.

[2] A few years later I conducted a questionnaire-based survey of Worthy Park with a research assistant, along with in-depth interviews of plantation workers, but never analysed the result. Soon after the survey I received a letter from Michael Craton asking me to leave his site alone and find another plantation to study. I gave up the project. The questionnaire materials, which include several network questions, will be deposited with my papers at a yet to be determined library.

[3] Michael Craton, 1978, *Searching for the Invisible Man: Slaves and Plantation Life in Jamaica*, Harvard University Press.

but acute observer of contemporary mores'.[1] Unfortunately, that view had to be changed after it became evident from later works that Craton was a repeatedly dishonest scholar. Sidney Mintz, the eminent, well-tempered Caribbeanist, has upbraided him for his habit of appropriating 'concepts developed and legitimized by other scholars whose works are well known', while citing them for trivial contributions many pages later, as in his appropriation of the Australian anthropologist Peter Wilson's concepts of reputation and respectability in Eastern Caribbean peasant life.[2] Mintz is also unsparing in pointing out Craton's other academic flaws and pretensions in the course of a devastating critique of his book on slave revolts, noting passages that are 'ill-informed or evasive', 'misleading', and the 'insouciant use of concepts unfamiliar to the author'. In another work Craton subjected Mintz himself to this duplicity, prominently entitling a paper on slave revolts 'Proto-Peasant Revolts?' The concept of the Caribbean slave as a proto-peasant was conceived and fully developed by Mintz and well known to Caribbeanists but unlikely to be known to the readers of *Past and Present*, who would only be informed near the end of the paper that Mintz had 'coined' the term without citing the Mintz paper, where it was clearly evident that he had done more than simply 'coined' the term, instead citing a paper Mintz had co-authored with Douglas Hall.[3] Perhaps the most egregious act of academic deceit committed by Craton was his report of my interpretation of the personality of the Jamaican enslaved in their interaction with their enslavers, discussed at length in Chapter 6, Section 5 of *The Sociology of Slavery*. There I pointed out that there was a stereotype of the enslaved known as 'Quashee' in Jamaica, equivalent to the U.S. slaveholders' infantilized stereotype of the African American enslaved, known as 'Sambo', that had recently been made famous, for many infamous, by the American historian Stanley Elkins. My argument, which in one crucial respect was critical of Elkins, was that Quashee, far from reflecting the true

[1] Orlando Patterson, 1982, 'Recent Studies on Caribbean Slavery and The Atlantic Slave Trade', *Latin American Research Review*, Vol. 17, No. 3, pp. 251–75.
[2] Sidney Mintz, 1984, 'More on the Peculiar Institution', *New West Indian Guide/Nieuwe West-Indische Gids*, Vol. 58, No. 3/4, pp. 185–99.
[3] Michael Craton, 1979, 'Proto-Peasant Revolts? The Late Slave Rebellions in the British West Indies, 1816–1832', *Past and Present*, No. 85, pp. 99–125.

nature of the enslaved, was a case of the enslaved 'playing fool to catch wise', in the words of a famous Jamaican proverb and was, in fact, a psychological mode of resistance or what James C. Scott later called a 'weapon of the weak' in a work that correctly cites my view of the subject.[1] Incredibly, Craton reported in one of his papers that: 'Patterson describes the Quashy as a slave who fulfils the masters' degrading stereotype of the Negro; lazy, deceitful, temperamental, childlike if not dog-like' – an interpretation apparently reinforced by the modern Jamaican epithet 'Quashy Fool' for what Englishmen would call 'an ignorant peasant'.[2] This is the exact opposite of my argument, which, as pointed out earlier, was included in a well-known collection of critical works on Elkins![3] What does one make of a scholar who writes many presumably major works yet is so repeatedly dishonest? I leave it to the community of historians of Caribbean slavery to decide.

The Sociology of Slavery concentrated on the sugar plantation sector of Jamaica's slave system and, while no one doubts that sugar dominated the entire economy and social order to the very end, it is a reasonable complaint that the work neglected the sectors of the economy not in sugar, especially those sectors producing coffee, livestock and other produce. The works of Higman,[4] Shepherd[5] and Monteith[6] have greatly illuminated these sectors.

---

[1] See James C. Scott, 1990, *Domination and the Arts of Resistance: Hidden Transcripts*, Yale University Press, p. 24.

[2] Michael Craton, 1974, 'Searching for the Invisible Man: Some of the Problems of Writing on Slave Society in the British West Indies', *Historical Reflections / Réflexions Historiques*, Vol. 1, No. 1, p. 50.

[3] On Elkins, as indicated earlier, I am sympathetic to his comparison of slavery with the Nazi concentration camp. Unlike many critics of Elkins, I also found similarities to the Sambo stereotype in Jamaica, as I did later in other slave societies such as ancient Rome in the slaveholder class's mocking stereotype of Greek slaves as worthless, unmanly and garrulous, or 'Graeculus', well documented in Roman comedy. Where we differ sharply is my interpretation that 'Quashee' and 'Sambo' were deliberately using the stereotype as a subaltern weapon against the slaveholder, as were the Graeculus of ancient Rome. See Orlando Patterson, 1982, *Slavery and Social Death: A Comparative Study*, Harvard University Press, pp. 91, 96–7, 338.

[4] Higman, 1976, *op. cit.*; see also his 1986 'Jamaican Coffee Plantations 1780–1860: A Cartographic Analysis', *Caribbean Geography*, Vol. 2, pp. 73–91; and his 1989 'The Internal Economy of Jamaican Pens, 1760–1890', *Social and Economic Studies*, Vol. 38, No. 1, pp. 61–86.

[5] Verene A. Shepherd, 2009, *Livestock, Sugar and Slavery: Contested Terrain in Colonial Jamaica*, Ian Randle.

[6] Kathleen E. A. Monteith, 2002, 'The Labour Regimen on Jamaican

Higman[1] showed that in 1832 the sugar plantations contributed 58.5 per cent of the island's total income, compared with 12.6 per cent from the coffee plantations and 10.4 per cent from livestock pens.

My reason for not paying more attention to these sectors points to an important division in doulotic studies of slavery in Jamaica, recently highlighted by Burnard,[2] a division based on temporality. There were profound differences between the state of affairs in Jamaica between the century and a half prior to the abolitionist movement leading to the ending of the slave trade in 1807 and what came afterwards. *The Sociology of Slavery* covered the entire period of slavery but was firmly rooted in the classic earlier period of 145 years, fully 80 per cent of the entire period of slavery, for most of which the sugar plantation was indeed predominant and the vast majority of enslaved toiled on them. It was also when the system was at its most ruthless and, as Burnard notes, and I completely agree, 'All of us working on slavery in the period before abolitionism struggle with the realization that enslaved people's lives were miserable and stunted in ways that make it hard to see how Jamaican slaves could have led any sort of lives that held any meaning for them.'[3] Indeed, one may well turn the issue around and question the overwhelming emphasis on the last forty years of slavery by the majority of studies on the subject, not only those on gender as previously noted. This was the period of abolitionist activism, with the planters' backs increasingly up against the wall in an ideological battle that they eventually lost. During this period, in response to the relentless criticisms of the horrors of the system they had created, they desperately tried to ameliorate it. After the ending of the slave trade the amelioration intensified, not simply in response to abolitionist rhetoric, but out of the stark realization by the slaveholders that if they were to procure more enslaved persons, they had to induce them to reproduce. How reasonable is it then, to base one's account of slavery in Jamaica on

Coffee Plantations During Slavery', in Kathleen E. A. Monteith and Glen Richards, eds, *Jamaica in Slavery and Freedom: History, Heritage and Culture*, University of the West Indies Press, pp. 259–73.

[1] Higman, 1976, *op. cit.*, pp. 16–17.

[2] Trevor Burnard, 2020, *Jamaica in the Age of Revolution*, University of Pennsylvania Press, p. 13.

[3] Burnard, 2020, *op. cit.*, p. 14.

this last-gasp period of transition, to the neglect of the previous 80 per cent of the history of the system, which was the classic period of unrestrained wealth-generation based on the merciless exploitation of the enslaved and the protracted genocide of their recruitment, replacement and growth, made possible by the slave trade.[1]

Perhaps not. This is like confining a study of the history of racism and the economic exploitation of blacks in America to the post-civil rights era. And yet, remarkably, the great majority of works on slavery in Jamaica are confined to this period. What accounts for this bias? A clue to the answer is the apocryphal story of the drunkard who lost the keys to his home in the dark but kept looking for them under the streetlight, because that's where the light was. The data on Jamaica during the period of abolition are exceedingly, and temptingly, rich, accounting for the large number of historians of many nationalities attracted to the study of this period of the island's slavery. That's where the light is. Alas, that's not where the keys to most of the horrors are to be found.

Turning to dominion studies, the first post-war study from this perspective focused on the West Indies is Elsa Goveia's pathbreaking work on the British Leeward Islands.[2] Her opening statement on the work is a good definition of what I am calling dominion studies: 'The term "slave society" in the title of this book refers to the whole community based on slavery, including masters and freedmen as well as slaves. My object has been to study the political, economic and social organization of this society and the interrelationships of its component groups and to investigate how it was affected by its dependence on the institution of slavery.' Goveia selected the Leeward Islands because they were among the most 'mature' of the British Caribbean societies and 'analysis of its characteristics sheds light on the characteristics of plantation slavery and of "creole" society of the eighteenth century throughout the islands'.[3] Furthermore, it was Goveia who was first to apply

---

[1] On which see Richard Sheridan, 1965, 'The Wealth of Jamaica in the Eighteenth Century', *Economic History Review,* Vol. 18, pp. 292–311; Richard Sheridan, 1985, *Doctors and Slaves: A Medical and Demographic History of Slavery in the British West Indies,* 1680–1834, Cambridge University Press, Chapters 5–8.

[2] Elsa Goveia, 1965, *Slave Society in the British Leeward Islands at the End of the Eighteenth Century,* Yale University Press.

[3] *Ibid.,* pp. vii, viii.

the concept of creolization, which she did repeatedly throughout the work. Although she contrasted her position with mine in her review of *The Sociology of Slavery*[1] in arguing that the Leeward Islands' slave system was 'highly organized and integrated', our positions were really not that dissimilar, since I am in complete agreement with her that that integration was entirely 'on the basis of racial inequality and subordination of the labouring majority of blacks to the minority of whites'. Our views on the destructive nature of slavery on the familial and sexual lives of the enslaved are identical,[2] and my view that the slave system was best viewed as a collection of largely self-contained plantation units, certainly when viewed from the perspective of the enslaved – the essence of my doulotic approach – is identical to her own verdict that: 'At the end of the eighteenth century each of the plantations . . . was itself a small world, and the field slave was trapped in this world, like a fly in a spider's web.'[3] Our principal difference was that she approached the system from a dominion or macro-level perspective. But there was another: she was writing about the Leeward Islands, whereas I wrote about Jamaica, a larger and much more complex and unequal system, possibly the most pitilessly cruel and exploitative in modern history.

Higman has also written most extensively from the dominion perspective, as have an impressive number of other scholars. As I have already hinted, he somewhat normalizes the role of the white slaveholder class and the slave economic system, especially in his study of the managerial aspect of the plantation regime. His *Plantation Jamaica:1750–1850*[4] is an important and necessary work, but one reads it with some unease, a bit like reading a

[1] Elsa Goveia, 'Slave Society' Review of *The Sociology of Slavery*', *The Times Literary Supplement*, No. 3411, 13th July 1967, p. 622. (The Times Literary Supplement Historical Archive, 1002–2019). Signed reviews were introduced by the TLS only in 1974 and the authors of earlier reviews made available much later, when I became aware of the fact the review was by Goveia. It is unlikely that Goveia would have referred to her own work in a signed review.

[2] Goveia, *op. cit.*, p. 237.

[3] Goveia, *op. cit.*, p. 238.

[4] B. W. Higman, 2005, *Plantation Jamaica: 1750–1850: Capital and Control in a Colonial Economy*, University of the West Indies Press. See also his 1988 work, *Jamaica Surveyed. Jamaica Maps and Plans of the Eighteenth and Nineteenth Centuries*, University of the West Indies Press.

meticulous analysis of the Nazi *Totenkopfverbände*, the SS Death's-Head Battalions that guarded and managed the concentration camps. Like all his other works, it is expertly crafted and thoroughly documented, and he is unsentimental in his approach to the subject, writing in the introduction:

> Their business was exploitation and part of my task is to assess how efficiently they carried out that enterprise. It is only by taking this perspective that it is possible to understand the working of the larger system of plantation economy and the role of enslaved and free workers within the society. The people who did the hard work of the plantations remain essentially voiceless in the narrative, reduced to the tools of capital and themselves literally human capital. It is a harsh story.

Quite so. Nonetheless, other works such as Burnard's are consistently more critical.[1] From the older generation one may single out those of Brathwaite,[2] Sheridan,[3] the Bridenbaughs,[4] Greene[5] and Dunn.[6] It may strike some as odd that I have classified Brathwaite's work as a dominion study but, contrary to the popular view of the work as one focused on the life and culture of the slaves, it is largely devoted to the political, social and economic structure of the society and the role and attitude of the whites: only 59 of the text's 312 pages directly examines the Black population. Brathwaite's work is strongly influenced by Elsa Goveia's study of the Leeward Islands, both in its attempt to interpret Jamaica during the same

---

[1] See in particular his comparative study, with John Garrigus, of Saint-Domingue and Jamaica, which draws out distinctive patterns in both systems, while demonstrating their enormous significance for the economies of France and Britain and, in more general terms, the rise of European capitalism in the 18th century: *The Plantation Machine: Atlantic Capitalism in French Saint-Domingue and British Jamaica*, University of Pennsylvania Press (2016).

[2] Edward Brathwaite, 1971, *The Development of Creole Society in Jamaica, 1770–1820*, Clarendon Press.

[3] Richard Sheridan, 1974, *Sugar and Slavery: An Economic History of the British West Indies*, Johns Hopkins University Press.

[4] Carl and Roberta Bridenbaugh, 1972, *No Peace Beyond the Line: The English in the Caribbean, 1624–1690*, Oxford University Press.

[5] Jack P. Greene, 2016, *Settler Jamaica in the 1750s: A Social Portrait*, University of Virginia Press.

[6] Richard Dunn, 1972, *Sugar and Slaves: The Rise of the Planter Class in the English West Indies, 1624–1713*, University of North Carolina Press.

period of time as a systemic whole, and in his use of the creolization concept, neither of which is sufficiently acknowledged. In any
case, his use of the concept of creolization is problematic in light of
the still pluralistic and 'disunited' state of Jamaica and other West
Indian societies emphasized by Goveia,[1] the failure to distinguish
localization from creolization, and the assumption that creolization entails assimilation and harmony, especially in sexual relations and racial mixing. His extraordinary view that it was 'in the
intimate area of sexual relations' that 'inter-cultural creolization
took place' by engendering a mixed group that helped 'to integrate
the society',[2] would certainly have been rejected by Goveia and,
after the sickening revelations on Thomas Thistlewood[3] whose
cruelty and insatiable sexual sadism Douglas Hall agrees was the
norm in Jamaica,[4] must now be viewed with disbelief. The commonly held view that Brathwaite 'coined and deployed the term
creolization as a theory of Caribbean culture', recently asserted by
Kamugisha, is incorrect and puzzling.[5] The concept was long in
use among linguists, and its extension to Caribbean cultural processes received its definitive theoretical formulation in a 1968 conference at the University of the West Indies (coming after Goveia's
empirical use of the term), described by the Finnish creole scholar
Angela Bartens as 'one of the major events which initiated the era
of modern creolistics',[6] a quarter of whose attendees were social
scientists and historians, myself included, that Brathwaite would
certainly have known about.[7]

[1] Goveia, *op. cit.*, p. 338.
[2] Brathwaite, *op. cit.*, pp. 303–5.
[3] Trevor Burnard, 2004, *Mastery, Tyranny, and Desire: Thomas Thistlewood and his Slaves in the Anglo-American World*, University of North Carolina Press.
[4] Douglas Hall, *In Miserable Slavery: Thomas Thistlewood in Jamaica, 1750–86*, 1989, Macmillan Press, p. xix.
[5] Aaron Kamugisha, 2019, *Beyond Coloniality: Citizenship and Freedom in the Caribbean Intellectual Tradition*, Indiana University Press.
[6] Angela Bartens, 2001, 'The Rocky Road to Education in Creole', *Estudios de Sociolinguistica*, Vol. 2, No. 2, p. 28.
[7] The definitive account of that transformative conference is given by Dell Hymes, one of the founders of sociolinguistics and creole studies, *Items*, Vol. 22, No. 2, 1968. Find it here: https://items.ssrc.org/from-our-archives/pidgini zation-and-creolization-of-languages-their-social-contexts/
On creolization in 17th-century Jamaica, see David Buisseret, 'The Process of Creolization in Seventeenth-Century Jamaica', in David Buisseret and Steven Reinhardt, eds, 2000. Texas A&M University Press, pp. 19–34.

Prominent among earlier scholars who, in critical reaction against the acculturation studies of Herskovits, had clearly articulated a conception of the Caribbean as a space in which creolization was the norm, was Sidney Mintz, who spent a lifetime researching the problem and developing a theoretical framework for understanding it.[1] One prominent creole linguist who has extended her work from language to the socio-cultural domain of what she calls the 'creole space' is Bartens, whose book is an important contribution to the historical sociology of creolization that deserves greater attention among Caribbeanists.[2] Given its roots in the study of language, it is perhaps not surprising that one of the most theoretically sophisticated and empirically informed works on the Jamaican creolization process is by the critically acclaimed British historian of French and Francophone Caribbean literature, Richard D. E. Burton.[3]

Mary Turner's[4] thoroughly documented, well-written work on the island during the same period covered by Brathwaite, paints a more complex, conflict-ridden system from which the religious sphere was not spared. The works of Sheridan, the Bridenbaughs and Dunn are especially valuable in placing Jamaica within its broader West Indian context, the latter two emphasizing the failure of early British Jamaica as a social system.[5] Greene's recent study offers a wealth of information on a wide range of social and economic activities, land use and demographic patterns at an unusual

Buisseret's 'Introduction' to the volume offers one of the clearest and most comprehensive models of the creolization process I know of.

More recently, the theoretical complexities and contradictions of the concept, and the tensions between its usage by linguists, historians and anthropologists, as well as its global applications, have been examined in Charles Stewart, ed., 2016, *Creolization: History, Ethnography, Theory*, Routledge.

[1] On which, see Michael Zeuske, 2011, 'Sidney Mintz: Work, Creolization, Atlanticization', *Review*, Vol. 34, No. 4, pp. 423–8.

[2] Angela Bartens, 1996, *Der kreolische Raum: Geschichte und Gegenwart*, Annales Academiae Scientiarum Finnicae. See the useful review and summary by Stephanie Hackert, 1999, *Journal of Pidgin and Creole Languages*, Vol. 14, No. 1, pp. 171–6.

[3] Richard D. E. Burton, 1977, *Afro-Creole: Power, Opposition, and Play in the Caribbean*, Cornell University Press.

[4] Mary Turner, 1998, *Slaves and Missionaries: The Disintegration of Jamaican Slave Society, 1787–1834*, University Press of the West Indies.

[5] Dunn, 1972, *Sugar and Slaves: The Rise of the Planter Class in the English West Indies*, p. 276.

level of detail, and for the period of the mid-18th century too often neglected in recent studies.[1]

One quaint work on Jamaican slavery by the American historian Vincent Brown,[2] has left me and many historians from the region perplexed. According to Brown, the catastrophic mortality rate in Jamaica for both blacks and whites, far from hardening attitudes towards death, was the source of cultural creation, 'the principal arena of social life and gave rise to its customs'. This is a polished production, well received, but it describes a world unfamiliar to nearly all of us who have closely studied Jamaican slave society. True, there were elaborate funeral rites among the enslaved, mainly adaptations of African mortuary rituals to the exigencies of the plantation dead yards in which death was celebrated, when given the chance, as a return passage to Africa, which I discussed at some length in *The Sociology of Slavery* (pp. 195–207). Brown argues, however, that death and its rituals were central to life and culture at all levels and among all ethno-racial groups in Jamaican slave society. I found no evidence of any such cultural preoccupation in my years of study of Jamaica, nor has any of the many outstanding historians mentioned above who have studied the period over the past century. To the contrary, insofar as the most reliable contemporary observers mention the subject, it was to comment on the callous indifference of the whites of all classes to death and dying. Lady Nugent, one of the most astute observers of the late period, repeatedly expressed distress and astonishment that 'here no one appears to think or feel for those who are suffering from these frightful attacks' (17th August 1801) and, two weeks later, 'that the usual occurrence of a death had taken place. Poor Mr Sandiford had died at 4 o'clock this morning . . . but all around us appeared quite callous', then on the 10th December that same year: 'He disgusted me very much the other day, by making a joke of poor Lord Hugh's death; *but it is a common custom here.*' [emphasis added][3] Thomas Thistlewood in his thirty-six years of living and

---

[1] Greene, 2014, *op. cit.*

[2] Vincent Brown, 2008, *The Reaper's Garden: Death and Power in the World of Atlantic Slavery*, Harvard University Press.

[3] Maria Nugent, *Lady Nugent's Journal of her Residence in Jamaica from 1801 to 1805*, Philip Wright, ed., 1966, Institute of Jamaica: pp. 16, 18, 45. Brown cites the second of these entries without comment.

keeping a diary on life in Jamaica offers not a single instance of any such preoccupation, the death of fellow whites such as the glutton who 'eats as much as four moderate people would do', treated as a matter-of-fact event that he had coming. The novelist Matthew Lewis, who had an extremely keen eye for anything unusual about Jamaican conventions and, as a celebrated gothic novelist, would certainly have been alert to unusual death customs among his fellow whites, comments informatively about the 'African' burial customs, obeah beliefs and ancestor worship of the blacks, but tells us nothing unusual about the whites' responses to death.[1] The response to Lewis' own death is revealing. As the most celebrated slaveholder of his time, one would have expected what Brown describes as 'intense and significant political activity' and familial mourning rituals around his death. Instead, few mourned the rich man's death, the editor of the journal, Judith Terry, commenting: 'Celebrity that he was, his death caused hardly a ripple.'[2] On this we can all agree: Professor Brown has forcefully restated the well-known fact that death was pervasive in Jamaican slave society.

One category of dominion studies concerns the development and role of the coloured or mixed racial group and of manumission in Jamaica, a subject first extensively explored by Goveia in her study of the Leeward Islands. The group was relatively small, but of increasing importance and influence from the late 18th century, attracting the racist venom of the island's most educated and important 18th-century resident, Edward Long.[3] Jamaica's, and other West Indians', odd mix of hypodescent and hyperdescent rules of racial assignment, its notions of whiteness and racial purity combined with the peculiar eventual recognition of legal equality for the more prosperous of the mixed group, and the general 'white bias' of the society that lingers to this day,[4] orig-

[1] Matthew Lewis, 1999, *Journal of a West Indian Proprietor*, edited by Judith Terry. Lewis lightheartedly refers once to his Jamaican ancestors who have 'always had a taste for being well lodged after their decease' (p. 100).

[2] *Journal of a West Indian Proprietor*, p. xiii.

[3] On Edward Long and the free coloureds, see Burnard, 2020, *op. cit.*, Chapters 2 and 5.

[4] The Jamaican sociologist, Fernando Henriques, coined this term, and it still resonates even to this day, reflected in the bizarre recent increase in the use of skin whitening cream even among reggae and dancehall stars. See his *Family and Color in Jamaica*, Eyre & Spottiswoode, 1953. On the sad matter of present-day skin whitening in the island see Rebekah Kebede, with

inates in the interaction of coloured and whites and their joint contempt for blackness, enslaved or not. As the novelist and slave-holder Matthew Lewis perceptively observed: 'nor can the separation of castes in India be more rigidly observed than that of complexional shades among the Creoles'.[1] A peculiar feature of Jamaican slave society, which it shared with its American counterpart, was its hostility to manumission throughout the 17th and 18th centuries. Economist Ronald Finlay and I have shown that manumitted played a critical role in the maintenance and stability of most large-scale slave systems, especially where enslaved outnumbered the slaveholder population, playing important middlemen roles as well as reinforcing feelings of self-degradation among the enslaved.[2] Although Jamaican white slaveholders recognized this, it is typical of the racist vehemence and notions of racial purity that they only reluctantly came to embrace this principle of self-preservation, a problem well explored in Newman's recent study.[3] A substantial literature has emerged on the subject since Goveia and Brathwaite's works.[4] While the strong emphasis on the

Marlon James, 2017, 'Why Black Women in a Predominately Black Culture are still Bleaching their Skin. Investigating deep-rooted ideals in Jamaica', Marie Daire, https://www.marieclaire.com/beauty/a27678/skin-bleaching -epidemic-in-jamaica/

[1] Matthew Lewis, 1999, *Journal of a West Indian Proprietor*, Oxford World Classic, Oxford University Press.

[2] Ronald Finlay, 1975, 'Slavery, Incentives, and Manumission: A Theoretical Model', *Journal of Political Economy* Vol. 83, no. 5, pp. 923–34; Orlando Patterson, 1982/2018. *Slavery and Social Death: A Comparative Study*, Chapters 8–10.

[3] Brooke N. Newman, 2018, *A Dark Inheritance: Blood, Race, and Sex in Colonial Jamaica*, Yale University Press.

[4] Mavis Campbell, 1976, *The Dynamics of Change in a Slave Society: A Sociopolitical History of the Free Coloreds of Jamaica, 1800–1865*, Fairleigh Dickinson University Press; Arnold A. Sio, 1976, 'Race, Colour, and Miscegenation: The Free Coloured of Jamaica and Barbados', *Caribbean Studies*, Vol. 16, No. 1, pp. 5–21; Gad J. Heuman, 1981, *Between Black and White: Race, Politics, and the Free Coloreds in Jamaica, 1792–1865*, Praeger; Daniel Livesay, 2018. *Children of Uncertain Fortune: Mixed-Race Jamaicans in Britain and the Atlantic Family, 1733–1833*, University of North Carolina Press; David B. Ryden, 2018, 'Manumission in Late Eighteenth-Century Jamaica', *New West Indian Guide / Nieuwe West-Indische Gids*, Vol. 92, Nos. 3–4, pp. 211–44; Erin Trahey, 2019, 'Among Her Kinswomen: Legacies of Free Women of Color in Jamaica', *The William and Mary Quarterly*, Vol. 76, No. 2, pp. 257–88; Wilmot Swithin, 2020, 'Free Blacks, Free Coloureds and Freedmen in Jamaican Politics, 1830–1842', *Journal of Caribbean History*, Vol. 54, No. 2, pp. 228–55.

abolitionist period may be justified on the grounds that this was when the group grew substantially in numbers and importance, there is still much to be written on the subject in the early and classic 18th-century periods of the society, as the works of Livesay, Burnard and Newman have clearly demonstrated.[1]

A growing number of first-rate works from younger scholars indicate that the historiography of dominion studies on Jamaica continues to thrive, most notably those by Petley,[2] Ryden,[3] Smith[4] and Graham.[5] A recent trend is to locate Jamaican dominion studies within the broader context of the Atlantic framework of historical scholarship, what has been called the 'Atlanticization' of slavery studies, from which has emerged a vast body of scholarship. Eric Williams' enormously influential work is, of course, the classic study in this area,[6] which has generated a huge literature of critics and defenders.[7] As a comparative historical sociologist I can hardly complain about this development although it is worth bearing in mind the words of one of Jamaica's most eminent historians, Franklin Knight, who cautioned that such studies should never lose sight of the fact that the Caribbean society being studied should steadfastly remain 'the main event'.[8]

---

[1] Livesay, *op. cit.*, 2018; Burnard, *op. cit.*, 2020, 'The Ambiguous Place of Free People in Jamaica', Chapter 5.

[2] Christer Petley, 2009, *Slaveholders in Jamaica: Colonial Society and Culture during the Era of Abolition*, Routledge; also, 2018, *White Fury: A Jamaican Slaveholder and the Age of Revolution*, Oxford University Press.

[3] David Beck Ryden, 2009, *West Indian Slavery and British Abolition, 1783–1807*, Cambridge University Press.

[4] S. D. Smit, 2006, *Slavery, Family, and Gentry Capitalism in the British Atlantic: The World of the Lascelles, 1648–1834*, Cambridge University Press.

[5] Aaron Graham, 2018, 'A Descent into Hellshire: Safety, Security and the End of Slavery in Jamaica, 1819–1820', *Atlantic Studies*, Vol. 17, No. 2. See also his 2019 study: 'Towns, Government, Legislation and the "Police" in Jamaica and the British Atlantic, 1770–1805', *Urban History*, Vol. 47, No.1. Graham's excellent series of papers on the island are building up to what promises to be an exciting dominion volume on the slave system during its last seven decades.

[6] Eric Williams, 1944/2021, *Capitalism and Slavery*, University of North Carolina Press.

[7] See Kenneth Morgan, 2000, *Slavery, Atlantic Trade and the British Economy, 1660–1800*. Also, H. Cateau and S. Carrington, eds, 2000, *Capitalism and Slavery Fifty Years Later. Eric Eustace Williams – A Reassessment of the Man and His Work,* Peter Lang Inc.

[8] Franklin Knight, 2011, *The Caribbean: The Genesis of a Fragmented Nationalism*, Oxford University Press, Introduction.

One fascinating aspect of dominion slave studies is the examination of Jamaica's, and the wider West Indian, role in the formation of British national, gender and familial identities by scholars of British cultural and imperial studies, especially Catherine Hall and her collaborators,[1] Kathleen Wilson,[2] Susan Amussen[3] and Katie Donington.[4] The last three works are of special value in their focus on the 17th and 18th centuries and transgenerational developments, taking temporality seriously in their historical analysis. An important and necessary dimension of these studies are those making the case for reparations in light of what is now acknowledged as a crime against humanity, most notably those of Hilary Beckles and Verene Shepherd.[5]

The studies discussed above have all greatly enriched our knowledge of enslavement in Jamaica and the broader West Indies. However, the single most important development in the study of modern slavery in the Atlantic since the 1960s, with important implications for our understanding of Jamaican slave society, concerns the Atlantic slave trade. Important studies had been published on the trade from the early 1930s,[6] with a surge in the

[1] Catherine Hall, 2002, *Civilizing Subjects: Colony and Metropole in the English Imagination, 1830–1867*, University of Chicago Press; and, with Nicholas Draper, Keith McClelland, Katie Donington and Rachel Lang, 2014, *Legacies of British Slave-Ownership: Colonial Slavery and the Formation of Victorian Britain*, Cambridge University Press.

[2] Kathleen Wilson, 2003, *The Island Race: Englishness, Empire and Gender in the Eighteenth Century*, Routledge.

[3] Susan D. Amussen, 2007, *Caribbean Exchanges: Slavery and the Transformation of English Society, 1640–1700*, University of North Carolina Press.

[4] Katie Donington, 2020, *The Bonds of Family: Slavery, Commerce and Culture in the British Atlantic World*, Manchester University Press.

[5] Hilary McD. Beckles, 2013, *Britain's Black Debt: Reparations for Caribbean Slavery and Native Genocide*, University of the West Indies Press; Verene Shepherd, 2014, 'Jamaica and the Debate over Reparation for Slavery: An Overview', in Catherine Hall, Nicholas Draper and Keith McClelland, eds, *Emancipation and the Remaking of the British Imperial World*, Manchester University Press, Chapter 13, pp. 223–50.

[6] Especially Elizabeth Donnan's monumental four-volume editions of documents on the trade: *Documents Illustrative of the History of the Slave Trade to America, Carnegie Institution of Washington*, 1930–1935. The valuable, although now neglected works of Melville Herskovits, especially *Dahomey: An Ancient West African Kingdom*, 2 Vols., 1938 and *The Myth of the Negro Past* (1941) deserve continued recognition. For an excellent, balanced assessment of

late fifties and sixties, prompted in part by the Civil Rights movement in America and the rise in the study of African history with
the post-war decolonization movements. I made full use of those
earlier works in Chapter 5 of *The Sociology of Slavery*, 'The Tribal
Origins of the Jamaican Slaves'.[1] However, the publication of
Curtin's seminal work, *The Atlantic Slave Trade: A Census*, in 1972,[2]
marked a fundamental turning point in the study of the slave trade,
and of Atlantic History more generally, bringing methodological
rigour and synthetic integration to the subject that overturned
long established views about the nature and extent of the trade.[3]
The most significant of his findings was the point estimate of the
total number of slaves imported to the New World at 9,566,000,
complete with a margin of error of between +9.8 and −16.4 per
cent. This greatly reduced the guestimates that prevailed at the
time, some as high as thirty million transported from Africa. Of
special interest to me were Curtin's estimates of the contribution
of the different regions of Africa to the slave trade, the number
and proportions of slaves who went to the different regions of the
Americas, especially the Caribbean, and the numbers exported
over time. Curtin's work was based entirely on secondary sources,
among which was *The Sociology of Slavery*. Indeed, one of the more
important sections of the book, Chapter 5 on the English slave
trade in the 18th century, relied substantially on *The Sociology of
Slavery* and LePage's *Jamaican Creole*[4] for its main conclusions on

Herskovits and his works, see Jerry Gershenhorn, 2004, *Melville J. Herskovits
and the Racial Politics of Knowledge*, University of Nebraska Press.
    [1] See the notes to Chapter 5.
    [2] Philip Curtin, 1972, *The Atlantic Slave Trade: A Census*, University of
Wisconsin Press.
    [3] For a recent review of scholarship on the trade see Stephen D. Behrendt,
'The Transatlantic Slave Trade', *The Oxford Handbook of Slavery in the
Americas*, edited by Mark M. Smith and Robert L. Paquette.
    The German historian, Michael Zeuske, in a comprehensive historiographical essay, has criticized what he considers an overemphasis on the
hegemonic slaveries of antiquity, Islam and the Americas and appeals for
scholarly engagement with the 'smaller slaveries' of the world, which is precisely what I attempted in *Slavery and Social Death: A Comparative Study*. See
his 'Historiography and Research Problems of Slavery and the Slave Trade
in a Global-Historical Perspective', *International Review of Social History*, Vol.
57, No. 1 (April 2012), pp. 87–111.
    [4] Curtin drew on Chapter 5 of *The Sociology of Slavery*, pp. 113–44, and
on R. B. LePage and David De Camp, 1960, *Jamaican Creole: An Historical
Introduction to Jamaican Creole*, St Martin's Press.

the cross tabulation of the changing ethnic origins of the captives through time.[1] Curtin's work stimulated a flood of studies, which continues to the present. A critical review of the work by Inikori not only pinpointed some of its main limitations but argued, correctly, that Curtin's estimates were too low and required a 'substantial upward revision'.[2]

The next major turning point was the shift towards primary sources and more precise quantification by scholars such as David Eltis, David Richardson, Herbet S. Klein, Henry Gemery, Jan Hogendorn, John Thornton, J. E. Inikori, among many others. The third main development came with the Trans-Atlantic and Intra-Atlantic slave trade databases. This enormously valuable resource, called 'the gold standard of digital humanities', originating in earlier work by Herbert Klein, Jean Mettas, Serge and Michelle Daget and David Richardson, evolved into a single multisource dataset through the joint work of David Eltis, Stephen Behrendt and David Richardson, who received critical support in the formative stage of the project from Harvard's W. E. B. DuBois Institute for Afro-American Research (and later the Harvard Hutchin's Center), with later support from funding agencies and universities, especially Emory where it was located for twenty years after leaving Harvard,[3] and now Rice University, to which it moved in 2021.

There are now 36,000 trans-Atlantic voyages in the database, each of which carried an average of 304 captives. One important correction emerging from the database concerns Curtin's original estimate of 9.5 million Africans transported from Africa. The database indicates that Inikori was correct in his assessment that Curtin had substantially underestimated the extent of the trade: the most recent estimate, based on far better primary sources and careful quantification, is that at least 12,520,000 African captives were forced from Africa for the Americas, with

[1] Curtin, 1972, *The Atlantic Slave Trade*, pp. 130, 158–61. See in particular Table 46, p. 160. summarizing the chapter's findings.

[2] J. I. Inikori, 1976, 'Measuring the Atlantic Slave Trade: An Assessment of Curtin and Anstey', *Journal of African History*, Vol. 17, No. 2, April 1976, pp. 197–223.

[3] I was a founding board member of the DuBois Institute but have long ceased being a formal member. See the history of the project here: https://www.slavevoyages.org/about/about#history/1/en/

a possible upper limit of 15.4 million enslaved, which means that there were between 24 and 62 per cent more enslaved Africans transported than Curtin's point estimate. At the two extremes of these estimates – Curtin's eight million and the current database's 15.4 million – Curtin may have underestimated the traffic by nearly 100 per cent. Since new voyages are being added continuously to the database, the correction is likely to be higher. Staying with the database's lower estimate, of the 12.5 million who left, 10.7 million disembarked mainly in the Americas, with an average of 265 Africans. Some 633 voyages (1.8%) were lost at sea or captured, or experienced some other fate, including slave revolts.[1]

Curtin had already noted that a disproportionate number of slaves landed in the Caribbean. However, for students of West Indian enslavement, and for Jamaica in particular, the database indicates that, in both proportionate and absolute terms, the numbers going to Jamaica were staggering. The new map, from the project's valuable set of Introductory Maps,[2] visually indicates the extraordinary numbers that went to the Caribbean, especially Jamaica, when compared with North America. Having carefully followed the development of the database over the years, I have repeatedly drawn on it to update the estimated numbers going to Jamaica and the regions from which the Africans arriving in the island came.

How do these recent figures compare with my estimates of over 55 years ago? In the first place, far more slaves went to Jamaica than any of us, including Curtin, suspected at the time. I was, however, more concerned with the proportion of slaves contributed by different regions of Africa, given my primary interest in tracing the tribal and cultural origins of the Jamaican enslaved, reflected in the title of Chapter 5. In this regard, apart from the very earliest period, 1655–1700, my proportional estimates have held up reasonably well. In broad terms, I had estimated that during the first half of the period of slavery the single largest group of slaves would have come from what was called the Gold Coast (now Ghana), the

[1] See https://slavevoyages.org/voyage/about#methodology/coverage-of-the-slave-trade/1/en/

[2] See Introductory Maps: https://slavevoyages.org/voyage/maps#introductory/

Table 0. Number of Slaves Disembarked in Jamaica from Embarkation Regions of Africa, 1601–1840

Years	Senegambia	Sierra Leone	Windward Coast	Gold Coast	Bight of Benin	Bight of Biafra	W. Central Africa	S.E. Africa	Total
1601–1610	NA	NA	NA	NA	NA	NA	97	0	97
1651–1660	NA	NA	NA	NA	NA	94	0	0	94
1661–1670	0	0	0	0	1,090	6,025	632	4,392	12,139
1671–1680	273	0	0	3,357	3,845	3,316	1,437	2,262	14,490
1681–1690	1,389	177	0	734	12,583	4,699	8,878	199	28,659
1691–1700	5,814	697	0	3,599	7,848	7,411	10,255	0	35,624
1701–1710	2,934	382	194	21,006	17,837	1,269	10,327	0	53,949
1711–1720	1,574	479	0	27,994	16,052	829	3,053	1,462	51,443
1721–1730	3,284	595	383	32,424	18,033	8,613	12,135	0	75,467
1731–1740	1,017	213	1,914	23,718	3,264	13,548	28,693	0	72,367
1741–1750	3,614	3,653	1,080	15,461	2,103	30,235	13,831	0	69,977
1751–1760	2,573	1,992	8,557	29,927	6,221	22,239	13,348	0	84,857
1761–1770	998	4,419	8,937	29,281	9,725	21,942	5,986	0	81,288
1771–1780	2,930	7,521	8,847	37,826	11,605	33,663	3,655	0	106,047
1781–1790	1,386	2,792	3,417	39,991	8,122	37,723	3,753	0	97,184
1791–1800	916	8,217	5,463	22,073	6,509	72,147	49,300	0	164,625
1801–1810	561	1,469	2,261	14,185	3,273	32,846	14,305	0	68,900
1831–1840	450	1,708	0	0	0	0	232	0	2,390
Totals	29,713	34,314	41,053	301,576	128,110	296,599	179,917	8,315	1,019,597

Table composed by author from *Trans-Atlantic Slave Trade Data Base*, https://www.slavevoyages.org/assessment/estimates

second largest from the Slave Coast and the Bight of Benin (now Nigeria), and that during most of the second half of the eighteenth century the largest contingent came from Nigeria, but that 'during the last seventeen years of the trade there was a striking reappearance of slaves from Southwestern Africa, particularly from the region of the Congo' (p. 144). This is broadly what the Atlantic database shows, although the decennial estimates differed, especially during the 17th century.

One pleasant surprise is the degree to which slaves from Ghana dominated the period between 1700 and 1740. I had argued, along with the creole linguists, that this was the period in which the creole language and Afro-Jamaican culture was at its most formative stage and the major presence of slaves from Ghana during this time would have meant that their impact would remain lasting, even if their numbers were later surpassed by enslaved persons from Nigeria. This argument is now strengthened.

However, not everything went my way with these latest data. The biggest surprise is the fact that during the 17th century 6,853 of the Jamaican enslaved came from South East Africa! No one saw anything like this during the 20th century. Indeed, it was considered a near certainty that hardly anyone came from South East Africa to the islands, or to North America (what the Portuguese slavers were up to in South America and Southern Africa was anybody's guess at that time). That clearly was not the case. However, they were soon overwhelmed by slaves from West Africa and there is no trace of their cultures or languages in the creole culture of Jamaica, then or now.

In the next section I will return to these latest findings on the demographic history of Jamaica and their startling implication that the history of enslavement in the island was one of protracted or slow-moving genocide on a scale that approaches the Jewish holocaust in Nazi Germany.

The Sociology of Slavery was the work that launched my career as a historical sociologist. As such, beyond the personal desire, rooted in my upbringing and history, to understand what had produced me and my society, it was motivated by an important theoretical problem in sociology that had been posed by the leading sociologist of my youth, Talcott Parsons, which was: how is society possible, or more basically, how does social order come about?[1] For Parsons, that problem was first explored explicitly by Hobbes, who in *Leviathan*[2] famously posed the problem with his depiction of the state of nature as one of war of all against all, in which there was 'continual fear, and danger of violent death' and life was 'solitary, poor, nasty, brutish and short', the solution to which was submission to the absolute authority of the state or Leviathan. Parsons rejected Hobbes' solution in favour of his normative theory of action in which individuals come to accept the demands of social life through their internalization of cultural norms.[3] Even as an undergraduate forced to imbibe this functionalist dogma, I had developed deep scepticism about the Parsonian solution. It was evident to me then that this simply begged the question: yes, order is possible because of internalized culture, and I have subsequently spent a good deal of intellectual effort trying to figure out how culture persists,[4] but where did this culture come from?

Parsons did have the salutary effect of leading me to Hobbes, whose *Leviathan* I read as avidly as Camus and Marx during my final undergraduate year. At the LSE Sociology department where I arrived in the fall of 1962, I had to justify why my thesis was not going to be merely another history of 'facts and more damn facts' to my doctoral supervisor, David Glass, Britain's most eminent demographer. Hobbes, as is well known, had stated that slavery was a clear case of a state of nature, his views on the subject informed by ancient classical slavery. My answer was that Jamaican slavery came closest to an existentially real case study

---

[1] T. Parsons' first explicit exploration of the problem in Hobbesian terms was in his foundational work, 1937, *The Structure of Social Action*, The Free Press, pp. 89–102. He elaborated on it in his 1951 work, *The Social System*, Harper and Row, pp. 36–45.

[2] Thomas Hobbes, *Leviathan: Or the Matter, Forme and Power of a Commonwealth* (1651) Oxford University Press (2012).

[3] For one of many discussions on this issue see, D. Lockwood, 1956. 'The Social System,' *British Journal of Sociology*, Vol. 7, pp. 134–6. This was one of the works that influenced my own appraisal of the 'problem'. See also, Desmond Ellis, 1971, 'The Hobbesian Problem of Order: A Critical Appraisal of the Normative Solution', *American Sociological Review*, Vol. 36, No. 4, pp. 692–703.

[4] See for example, Orlando Patterson, 'Culture and Continuity: Causal Structures in Socio-Cultural Persistence', in Roger Friedland and John Mohr, eds, 2004. *Matters of Culture: Cultural Sociology in Practice*, Cambridge University Press, pp. 71–109.

of a society in which life was indeed nasty, brutish and short and, with its endless series of revolts by the enslaved, racial and ethnic divisions, rapes, suicides, homicides, gibbeting, bilboeing, flight, and merciless use of the whip, a state of war of all against all. The interesting thing about Hobbes, I pointed out, was that he imagined this state of nature to have existed not simply in the condition of preliterate societies (those imagined 'savage people in many places of America') but in the descent of civilized people back into this savage state. He had in mind the English Civil War. North America, like Barbados was still mainly British white colonies of settlement when the *Leviathan* was published (1651) and Jamaica was not captured by the British until four years after this. Nonetheless, I argued that a far better case study was 18th-century Jamaica, in which civilized Britons, after a few weeks' sojourn, erupted into near complete savagery in their ruthless relations of domination with the enslaved, in the course of which, as Dunn would later write, they 'lived fast, spent recklessly, played desperately and died young',[1] which Hobbes would, in all likelihood, have agreed came close to his imagined state of declension to warring savagery.[2] My thesis topic was accepted, although it helped that no one at LSE thought much of Talcott Parsons, in spite of his pre-eminence in America and Germany. What I wrote in the preface to the first edition was the gist of my thesis statement: 'Few systems indeed have ever come closer to the brink of the Hobbesian state of nature and, as such, the sociologist researching this society is faced with the fascinating situation of examining on a concrete level the most basic question of his discipline.'[3] Nonetheless, the system did persist, for all the savagery, for 183 years, so the research problem that naturally followed from this was: how was such a system able to survive for all that time? In answering this theoretical question, I would also be addressing the even more important substantive problem that had troubled me from my childhood, and so intrigued R. D. Laing and his patients: what

[1] Richard Dunn, 1972, *Sugar and Slaves*, pp. xiii–xv.
[2] Fifty years after *The Sociology of Slavery*, Trevor Burnard in his *Jamaica in the Age of Revolution* pp. 28–30, has rediscovered the theoretical significance of Hobbes for an understanding of Jamaican slave society. What took so long?
[3] *The Sociology of Slavery*, p. 10.

was it really like for my ancestors? How did they survive the long ordeal of British slavery?

I did address this issue in the penultimate chapter on resistance (see especially pp. 280–3) and considered the detailed account in the book as a whole to be all the answer that was needed, but, with hindsight, perhaps it should have been spelled out more explicitly. The simple answer to the theoretical question is that Hobbes was right. Might, a monopoly of the superior instruments of violence, always prevails, and this might the Hobbesian retro-savages who ruled the island had to their great advantage. As Elsa Goveia had earlier observed of the Leeward Islands,[1] and Burnard much later of Jamaica: 'White Jamaicans survived because they mastered the real and symbolic instruments of violence. And power in the Caribbean is closely connected with trauma.'[2] However, Hobbes' conception of the Leviathan was not one solely of raw power. People, by virtue of being rational beings, he argued, recognized as a practical 'law of nature' that 'peace is good and therefore also the way or means of peace are good', which led them to form a covenant with each other to obey a common authority, a Leviathan, established through what he called 'sovereignty by institutions', that ensured peace, effective government and civilized living. Raw power that fails to ensure peace forfeits the obligation to obey and is the limit Hobbes placed on the Leviathan (some commentators think, contradictorily). My gloss on Hobbes' theory is that Jamaican slave society, while it used the monopoly of might to ensure its genocidal and exploitative rule and prevent successful revolt, it never solidified its rule through 'sovereignty by institutions' and hence never won the obligation to obey from the enslaved population.[3] As Jimmy, the 'very impudent' Ashanti

---

[1] Goveia, 1965, *op. cit.*, pp. 94–5.

[2] Burnard, 2020, *op. cit.*, p. 19.

[3] Here is where Goveia and I differ. She concluded that the whites 'had all the authority and prestige of an established elite, accustomed to manipulate and overawe the lower classes they governed', *op. cit.*, p. 94. However, our difference is due to the difference in the societies we studied. Jamaica was different from the Leeward Islands in this respect, as it was from Barbados which, I have recently argued, did develop rule based on both force and effective Hobbesian 'sovereignty by institutions' in contrast with Jamaica where the institutions existed but did not quite work, certainly not for the Black population. See Orlando Patterson, 2019. *The Confounding Island: Jamaica and the Postcolonial Predicament*, Harvard University Press, Chapter 1.

enslaved by Thistlewood, told him to his face in 1771: 'If this be living he did not care whether he lived or died.'[1] I therefore interpreted the slaveholding class as a proto-Leviathan ruling over a sociological nightmare of doulotic capitalism, brutality, resentment and instability, held together just enough by brute force to produce enormous wealth for a few, the most powerful of whom lived in absentee safety and luxury, the majority biding their time in a system where life remained nasty, brutish and short. There was no better expression of this ruling-class degeneracy than the casualness with which sex, venereal disease and death were viewed, as indicated earlier.

In the absence of any sense of voluntary obligation to obey, resentment and resistance was endemic. Jamaica, in fact, had the highest record of doulotic resistance in the Americas, and possibly in all history, and the last chapter of the work examined this extraordinary record, which I later expanded in a lengthy paper on Jamaican doulotic revolts, one of the two main sequels to *The Sociology of Slavery*.[2] It has been said repeatedly that the great Haitian revolt of the enslaved was the first and only successful such revolt in human history. More recently, one of the island's many doulotic rebellions, known as Tacky's revolt, has been hailed as the greatest of the island's many rebellions.[3] Both these statements are incorrect. As I argued in the work's final chapter, and at far greater length in my paper on doulotic revolts, the British conquest of Jamaica in 1655 was followed by a long series of *interconnected* revolts of the enslaved, known collectively as the First Maroon War, that lasted from 1656 until 1739. Collectively, this was, on several occasions, a

[1] I was to read this years later in Douglas Hall's edition of the Thistlewood diary, first published in 1989: *In Miserable Slavery: Thomas Thistlewood in Jamaica, 1750–86*, p. 204. However, my interpretation in the early 1960s of the archival and contemporary evidence on Jamaica slavery left me in no doubt that this was how many of the enslaved felt and that, apart from the Black and coloured *kapos* on the plantation, the typical Black field worker had little or no respect for the whites or freed Blacks. *Sociology of Slavery*, pp. 91–2.

[2] Orlando Patterson, 1970, 'Slavery and Slave Revolts: A Socio-Historical Analysis of the First Maroon War, 1655–1740', *Social and Economic Studies*, Vol. 19, No. 3, pp. 289–325. The other being the literary sequel, my novel, *Die the Long Day*, William Morrow, 1972.

[3] Vincent Brown, 2020, *Tacky's Revolt: The Story of an Atlantic Slave War*, Harvard University Press.

far greater threat to the Jamaican slave system than Tacky's revolt. There has been a misguided attempt by some historians to view the First Maroon War as something separate from revolts by the enslaved, especially by Michael Craton, whose work on the subject is a compendium of facts on rebellions in the West Indies with a muddled attempt to explain them,[1] and even Burnard errs in this assumption, claiming that: 'In terms of its shock to the imperial system, only the American Revolution surpassed Tacky's War in the eighteenth century.'[2] My close examination of the record of earlier revolts shows this to be flatly not the case. The Maroon communities were constantly sourced by runaways and rebels from the plantations who were inspired to revolt by their presence, even after their treacherous siding with the whites against future rebellions, as Thistlewood's entry in his diary of 1st August 1760, in the midst of Tacky's revolt, makes clear: 'Dr Miller says the rebels give out they will . . . fire all the plantations they can, till they force the whites *to give them free like Cudjoe's Negroes.*' [emphasis added][3] I document at some length the interaction between the enslaved and the guerrilla encampments. Making a hard and fast distinction between enslaved and Maroon rebellions during this period is as spurious as sharply distinguishing between the Viet Cong guerrilla movement and Ho Chi Minh's national liberation front in the Vietnamese wars against the French and Americans.[4] There is no doubt that these interconnected revolts posed a far greater threat to white rule than Tacky's revolt ever did. Indeed, the rebels repeatedly forced the whites to abandon plantations in the frontier regions that the planters badly wanted to establish, since land on

---

[1] Michael Craton, 2009, Testing *the Chains: Resistance to Slavery in the British West Indies*, Cornell University Press. See Sidney Mintz's searing critique: 'More on the Peculiar Institution', *New West Indian Guide / Nieuwe West-Indische Gids*, Vol. 58 (1984), no: 3/4, Leiden, 185–91.

[2] Burnard, *Jamaica in the Age of Revolution*, p. 170.

[3] Hall, 1989, *In Miserable Slavery: Thomas Thistlewood in Jamaica, 1750–86*, p. 110.

[4] The situation was quite different during the 1790s when the Second Maroon War broke out. By then the slaves had come to see the Maroons as traitors not to be trusted and with whom they would have no dealings. See David Geggus, 1987, 'The Enigma of Jamaica in the 1790s. New Light on the Causes of Slave Rebellions', *William and Mary Quarterly*, Vol. 44, No. 2, pp. 274–99.

the southern coast had been completely taken up.[1] Significantly, in all the reports of the governors writing on the deteriorating situation, and in the frantic deliberations of the Legislature on the crisis, their references were *always* to 'the bad success of the parties sent out against *the slaves in rebellion*' [emphasis added].[2] In the end, the slaveholders did something quite remarkable: at the suggestion of the British government they swallowed their pride, sued for peace, and signed a treaty that granted the rebels full sovereignty over their territory as a state within a state. That was victory! It had never happened before in any known pre-existing slave society, although enslavers were to offer terms after this in other slave societies, though nothing as complete and lastingly recognized as this.[3] Hence it deserves the description as the first successful revolt of the enslaved in history. Tacky's revolt certainly frightened the whites, but that was all. It never came close to a threat to the system of slavery, and ended in disaster and carnage for the rebels, along with hundreds of innocent enslaved and, as Trevor Burnard recently noted,[4] was followed immediately by a doubling down by the British slaveholders in their viciousness, as well as the spectacular rise of the 18th-century economy to heights that saw this small island with per capita incomes that far exceeded those of North America. By the 1790s, although Jamaica's enslaved were well aware of the Haitian revolution, they indicated no signs of following suit (though this was to change during the 19th century), for the simple reason that the proto-Leviathan power of the whites was so overwhelming. As Geggus points out: 'As always, the brutality and humiliations of bondage had to be weighed against the risks of resistance. In the absence of circumstances realistically favouring rebellion, the enslaved in Jamaica and many other places simply took pride, it seems, in what was happening in the French colony and showed their awareness by what whites everywhere

---

[1] Patterson, 'Slavery and Slave Revolts,' pp. 301, 304.
[2] *Ibid.*, p. 305.
[3] Barbara Kopytoff, 1978, 'The Early Political Development of Jamaican Maroon Societies', *William and Mary Quarterly*, Vol. 35, No. 2, pp. 287–307; Richard Hart, 1950, 'Cudjoe and the First Maroon War in Jamaica', *Caribbean Historical Review*, Vol. 1, No. 4, pp. 46–79; Philip Wright, 1970, 'War and Peace with the Maroons, 1730–1739', *Caribbean Quarterly*, 16: 5–27.
[4] Burford, 2020, *op. cit.*, Chapter 4.

called "insolence".[1] Tacky's revolt was also inconsequential, both in terms of white dread and its consequences, when compared with Jamaica's other great doulotic revolt, that of the Baptist War led by Daddy Samuel Sharpe in 1831, which had a decisive influence on the British Parliament's decision to pass the act abolishing slavery, the revolt meticulously examined in Tom Zoellner's beautifully written recent study.[2]

So, how did the system not only survive this and the other revolts that followed, but thrived to unprecedented heights of economic success throughout the 18th century. One reason for the success of the whites during and after Tacky's revolt, after coming so close to disaster in the First Maroon War, was one clause in the treaty they signed with Cudjoe, the leader of the rebels, in 1739, who agreed to return all enslaved runaways and aid the colonialists in all future revolts. And they did, starting with Tacky, who was felled by the bullet of a Maroon marksman. Cudjoe's betrayal had tragic consequences for all future resistance. It was an act of monumental betrayal, a case of snatching treachery from the jaws of heroism. Jamaica's enslaved continued to rebel throughout the period of slavery at a rate greater than any other known slave system. However, for the entire period of slavery after 1739 the treachery of the Maroons meant that all future revolts were doomed to failure, as were most acts of that other main form of resistance, running away, the Maroons being paid a bounty for returning them.[3] In an admirable paper, Kathleen Wilson has suggested that the Maroons 'engaged in a double-edge performance of freedom', in Jamaican slave society.[4]

[1] Geggus, *op. cit.*, p. 299.

[2] Tom Zoellner, *Island on Fire: The Revolt that Ended Slavery in the British Empire*, Harvard University Press, 2020.

[3] Jamaican historians and nationalists, especially those searching for what Black American historians sometimes call 'a usable past', have had real problems dealing with the Maroons. We would dearly love to celebrate their triumph over the Jamaican slaveholders and British imperial soldiers in 1739, but their subsequent record of treachery and bounty-hunting perfidy make this impossible. I remember my reaction, as a 17-year-old doing my first archival research at the Institute of Jamaica, to the records of their out-of-control butchery of rebels and innocent peasants in the Morant Bay rebellion of 1865. I cried.

[4] Kathleen Wilson, 2009, 'The Performance of Freedom: Maroons and the Colonial Order in Eighteenth-Century Jamaica and the Atlantic Sound', *The William and Mary Quarterly*, 3rd Series, Vol. 66, No. 1 (Jan. 2009), p. 55.

By the late 18th century, however, they had ceased to be ambiguous role models for the enslaved. The last and greatest slave revolt would be inspired by secular ideas picked from the discarded newspapers of the enslavers and the spirit of liberation buried in Christianity.[1]

Behind the Maroon betrayal was an important tactic of the slaveholder proto-Leviathan of which Hobbes would have fully approved: divide and rule, a tactic also emphasized by Goveia.[2] The colonialists deployed it with devastating effectiveness against the enslaved. They did so in buying and distributing captives from different tribes on the plantations and encouraging their traditional hostilities; in encouraging the division between creole or locally born and those brought from Africa who, from the early 18th century were being contemptuously derided as 'salt-water-neagas' and 'Guinea-birds' by the creoles; in the division between skilled/ elite and gang enslaved; between house slave and field enslaved; between dark skin, sambo skin, mulatto skin, mustee skin, and mustifino near-but-not-quite-there white skin; between men and women; between men and men over women; between women and women over men; between the faithful hoping for favour and freedom who betrayed the rebels plotting revolts running away and poisonings. In his superb recent study, Christer Petley documents how Simon Taylor, the richest planter in Jamaica of his day (the late 1700s) deftly divided the 2248 enslaved on his four plantations and eight pens, balancing one set against another by which means he exercised near perfect control.[3]

The system also survived because the enslaved were able to eke out social and cultural spaces in those areas that were irrelevant to the interests of the whites. In the few hours between work and sleep, on the provision grounds where they were made to feed themselves, precariously,[4] and in the Sunday markets, and the

---

[1] Zoellner, *op. cit.*, pp. 24–34.

[2] Goveia, *op. cit.*, p. 95.

[3] Christer Petley, 2018, *White Fury: A Jamaican Slaveholder and the Age of Revolution*, Oxford University Press, p. 60.

[4] The provision ground system has been called the foundation for a 'proto-peasantry' by Mintz, as noted earlier and it was, indeed, cherished by the slaves in allowing some respite from the surveillance of the slaveholders, but one should be careful not to miss the fact that it was another element of exploitation. The system, in fact, did not quite work in that the slaves were

saturnalia of Christmas, the enslaved welded from the fragments of African culture, the exegeses of the Caribbean environment, and the scraps of white culture forced upon them, the beginnings of Afro-Jamaican creole culture. *Most* of *The Sociology of Slavery* was devoted to these creole cultural constructions – a point that must be emphasized in view of those who have ignorantly claimed that I have neglected the life, real death and agency of the enslaved – and this was in many ways its most important substantive contribution, especially the search for the tribal origins of the Jamaicans (now updated in Table 1, above) and the African roots of their religious, witchcraft and obeah beliefs, their celebratory death rituals, their music, dances, seasonal festivals, and their Afro-Jamaican dietary and agricultural practices. The work, as indicated earlier, also examined sex and family life under conditions of pervasive physical terror, the spectre of starvation, and extreme sexual violence from both the whites and more privileged enslaved lackeys. The book, in fact, initiated the study of Afro-Jamaican social and cultural creolization, drawing on the work of earlier historical ethnography of the broader Caribbean,[1] and of Africa, such as those

chronically undernourished, and many lived on the verge of starvation with the risk of outright famine and mass starvation when hurricanes, drought and wars struck. See *The Sociology of Slavery*, pp. 216–18. Kenneth Kiple, 1984, *The Caribbean Slave: A biological History*, Cambridge University Press, pp. 66–70. See also, Richard B. Sheridan, 1976. 'The crisis of slave subsistence in the British West Indies during and after the American Revolution,' *William and Mary Quarterly*, Vol. 33, No. 4, pp. 615–41.

[1] Especially the work of my former undergraduate teacher, M. G. Smith, not only his writings on West Indian pluralism, cited earlier, but other works such as his 1960 publication: *Government in Zazzau, 1800–1950*, an early model of historical sociology for me; *West Indian Family Structure*, 1962, Research Institute for the Study of Man; *The Ras Tafari Movement in Kingston, Jamaica, 1960* (with R. Augier and R. M. Nettleford), Institute of Social and Economic Research.

Other influential early studies include: the classic symposium edited by Vera Rubin, 1960, *Caribbean Studies: A Symposium*, Institute of Social and Economic Research; Raymond Smith, 1956, *The Negro Family in British Guiana. Family Structure and Social Status in the Villages*, Routledge; Sidney Mintz, 1959a, 'The Plantation as a Socio-Cultural Type', in *Plantation Systems of the New World*, Vera Rubin, ed., pp. 42–53, Washington, DC: Pan-American Union, 1959b, 'Labor and Sugar in Puerto Rico and in Jamaica, 1800–1850', in *Comparative Studies in Society and History*, Vol. 1, No. 3, pp. 273–81; 1966, 'The Caribbean as a Socio-Cultural Area', in *Cahiers d'Histoire Mondiale*, Vol. 9, pp. 912–37; Melville Herskovits, 1941, *The Myth of the Negro Past*, Harper & Brothers; 1937, *Life in a Haitian Valley*, Knopf.

by Herskovits, Mintz and Murdock, a process that I theorized in later works building on this baseline study.[1]

In the final analysis, the simplest explanation is, as Hobbes pointed out, that most people 'shun death'. And death was everywhere in Jamaican slave society as I was among the first to show both in *The Sociology of Slavery* and its literary sequel, *Die the Long Day*[2] – the physical death they tried to shun, the social death that they could not. I have repeatedly used the term protracted or slow-moving genocide to explain the demographic and social situation of the Black population of Jamaica during the period of slavery. This is not a metaphor. With the data from the Atlantic Slave trade database now available, it is possible to calculate more precisely the real death toll of Jamaican slavery by using a simple counterfactual strategy.

To do so, what we need is another suitably distinct slave society that shows us what might have been possible – a counterfactual – had the British proto-Leviathan in Jamaica not pursued the Hobbesian demographic strategy of buying, mercilessly over-exploiting and replacing their enslaved from the slave trade. The demographic experience of the enslaved in North America provides just such a counterfactual case.[3] American slaveholders bar-

---

[1] On my theory of segmentary and synthetic creolization see 'Context and Choice in Ethnic Allegiance: A Theoretical Framework and Caribbean Case Study', in Nathan Glazer and Patrick Moynihan, eds, 1975, *Ethnicity: Theory and Experience*, Harvard University Press, pp. 316–19. On the processes of cultural transmission and adaptation of African beliefs and values, see Orlando Patterson, 1976, 'From Endo-deme to Matri-deme: An Interpretation of the Development of Kinship and Social Organization among the Slaves of Jamaica, 1655–1830', in Samuel Proctor, *Eighteenth Century Florida and the Caribbean*, University Presses of Florida, pp. 50–9. See also 'Persistence, Continuity and Change in the Jamaican Working Class Family', *Journal of Family History* (1981), pp. 135–61.

[2] Orlando Patterson, 1972, *Die the Long Day*. William Morrow. See Janelle Rodrigues' probing recent analysis of my treatment of death and mourning in this novel, 'Myal, Death and Mourning in Orlando Patterson's *Die the Long Day*', *Cultural Dynamics*, June, 2021, pp. 1–17, https://doi.org/10.1177/09213740211011193

[3] The striking differences in the demographic patterns of North America and the West Indies were remarked on from the late 18th century and used in abolitionist advocacy. See B. W. Higman, 1984, *Slave Populations of the British Caribbean, 1807–1834*, pp. 305–6. It was noted by W. E. B. DuBois in his *Black Reconstruction in America 1860–1880*, Russell & Russell, 1935, p. 4. Philip Curtin drew closer attention to it in his 1969 work, *The Atlantic Slave Trade: A Census*, University of Wisconsin Press, pp. 88–91; as did Robert Fogel

gained from early on that it made more sense to reproduce their enslaved population than rely entirely on the slave trade, and by the early 18th century they had succeeded in doing so, the creole enslaved population well in excess of the Africans by that time. To be sure, they were no angels for, as Tadman has shown, this choice was made easier for them by virtue of the fact that the crops from which they made their wealth was not sugar, that, indeed, where they were sugar planters, as in Louisiana, they were just as inhumanly vicious as their Jamaican counterpart, with similarly lethal demographic consequences.[1] Richard Dunn has given us an indelible meso-level demographic analysis of these 'two radically different slave systems in action', wherein the Jamaican planters treated the enslaved 'as disposable cogs in a machine: importing slaves from Africa, working them too hard, feeding them too little, exposing them to debilitating disease, and routinely importing new Africans to replace those who died', in contrast with the demographic growth of the enslaved in Virginia.[2]

Two arguments against this counterfactual strategy must be considered. The first, that environmental and epidemiological factors prevented such a reproductive approach by the Jamaican planters, can be dismissed with one word: Barbados – with a very similar West Indian environment, which was so successful at reproduction that it was capable of providing other eastern Caribbean islands with enslaved and ex-enslaved before and after abolition; indeed, there were even concerns among some Barbadian planters that their small island risked overpopulation.[3] Furthermore, it appears that the disease environment of the U.S. South was not that much better for the enslaved than that which prevailed in Jamaica, reflected in the fact that mortality rates were not very different, although there is some question about

and Stanley Engerman, in their 1974 study, *Time on the Cross*, W. W. Norton, p. 25.
    [1] Michael Tadman, 2000, 'The Demographic Cost of Sugar: Debates on Slave Societies and Natural Increase in the Americas', *American Historical Review*, Vol. 105, No. 5, pp. 1534–75.
    [2] Richard S. Dunn, 2014, *A Tale of Two Plantations: Slave Life and Labor in Jamaica and Virginia*, Harvard University Press, p. 73.
    [3] B. W. Higman, 1984, *Slave Populations of the British Caribbean, 1807–1834*, Johns Hopkins University Press, pp. 304–7; 375–7. See also Kenneth K. Kiple, 1984, *The Caribbean Slave: A Biological History*, Cambridge University Press, pp. 105–6.

this.[1] The second argument, that the American slaveholders were both more willing and better able to feed their enslaved because of their large farming community does not hold up. Tadman has shown that there were huge mortality differences between blacks and whites and that the more favourable reproduction rate of American blacks to those in the Caribbean came at great cost to the former. In other words, it was not all that costly to American planters to ensure the much greater reproduction of the enslaved. The difference is explained in terms of the extremely exploitative demands of the sugar plantation system, where more profits could be made by relying on the slave trade both to increase the population and provide more males than females. Furthermore, as many works have now shown, Jamaica was an integral part of the Atlantic economic system for the entire period of slavery and bought much of its staples and food from America. Additionally, profit margins in Jamaica far exceeded those of the American slave South. From Burnard's calculations, in the late 18th century the wealth of Southern planters 'paled beside that of Jamaica', and 'the average White in Jamaica was 36.6 times as wealthy as the average White in the Thirteen Colonies'.[2] Therefore, had they so desired, the Jamaican planters could easily have bought more food and other necessities to pursue a successful reproductive strategy, as Barbadian slaveholders successfully did, instead of overworking and underfeeding them.[3] On the evidence of the planters themselves, the cost of rearing an enslaved person to the age of fourteen in 1831–2, was not much higher in Jamaica than Barbados: 112 sterling, compared to 109 sterling in Barbados, much lower than

[1] Robert W. Fogel and Stanley L. Engerman, 1979, 'Recent Findings in the Study of Slave Demography and Family Structure', *Sociology and Social Research*, Vol. 63, pp. 567–8. Michael Tadman, however, has challenged the view that mortality rates in the two regions were not far apart, as has Higman. See Tadman, 2000, 'The Demographic Cost of Sugar: Debates on Slave Societies and Natural Increase in the Americas', *American Historical Review*, Vol. 105, No. 5, p. 1558.

[2] T. G. Burnard, 2001, 'Prodigious Riches': The Wealth of Jamaica before the American Revolution', *Economic History Review*, Vol. 54, No. 3, pp. 519–20.

[3] R. B. Sheridan, 1965, 'The Wealth of Jamaica in the Eighteenth Century', *Economic History Review*, Vol. 18, No. 2, pp. 292, 311. Burnard, 2001, *op. cit.*, found that Sheridan greatly underestimated the island's wealth.

other slave colonies such as Trinidad, where it was 162 sterling.[1] Given that Jamaica is over 25 times the size of Barbados, with far more resources complementing the plantation system than in mono-crop Barbados (cattle pens, numerous rivers for irrigation and mill-power, protected harbours, relatively abundant forests, several commercial centres, and its large export-oriented coffee sector, which very likely exercised a positive joint demand for the dominant sugar crop, given that consumption of the former strongly activated the need to consume the latter in the British and American markets), with a more rational, less blindly exploitative strategy, it could easily have far exceeded Barbados', and replicated America's reproductive performance.[2] Instead, planter economic calculations resulted in a slave system where 'the lives of the enslaved population in Jamaica were the most miserable in the Atlantic World, especially in the first half of the eighteenth century, when ... the great majority of slaves were traumatized, brutalized and alienated migrants from Africa'.[3]

It must be concluded, then, that the demographic strategy of the Jamaican slaveholder was one of clear choice. As the demographic historian Kenneth Kiple notes, 'as long as a master had control over a slave's life, he controlled to a large extent what he consumed', and obviously his physical survival.[4] As I was among the first to point out,[5] and Kiple later specified at length, Jamaican slaves spent their lives hungry and malnourished, on the verge of starvation, with numerous nutritional diseases resulting in endemic bone and dental problems, debilitating mood swings, pellagra, beriberi due to widespread thiamine deficiency, dropsy, dirt-eating, which was a desperate response to calcium and other mineral deficiencies, all of which weighed especially hard on children, whom 'malnutrition tormented twice, working much of its

---

[1] Douglas Hall, 1962, 'Slaves and Slavery in the British West Indies', *Social and Economic Studies*, Vol. 11, No. 4, p. 307.

[2] Tadman, *op. cit.*, it should be noted, argues that the diet of U.S. slaves may not even have been the cause of their exceptional rates of natural increase, p. 1559. This, however, is controversial.

[3] Trevor Burnard and John Garrigus, 2016, *The Plantation Machine*, p. 38.

[4] For a detailed examination of the contrasting demographic strategies of U.S. and Jamaican slaveholders, see Kenneth Kiple, *op. cit.*, pp. 104–19.

[5] *The Sociology of Slavery*, pp. 94–112. Building on the pioneer work of George Roberts, 1957, *The Population of Jamaica*, Cambridge University Press, especially Chapters 6–8.

debilitating and often deadly effects through poor maternal nutrition before even touching the child via his own nutritional intake'.[1]

One final argument against this conclusion needs attention, given the academic distinction of its authors. Stanley Engerman and Herbert Klein[2] have argued that it was not conditions in the Caribbean, especially Jamaica, or planter attitudes, that accounted for the failure of the Jamaican population to reproduce. They claim that mortality rates in the U.S. were similar to those of Jamaica and that fertility rates largely account for the demographic difference. The crucial factor explaining these fertility differences were the distinctive lactation practices of the Africans brought over to Jamaica, its key feature being prolonged breast-feeding. Because Africans constituted a much larger proportion of the Jamaican population throughout the period of slavery than of the U.S. Black population, they argue, this factor largely explains the huge difference in survival and reproduction rates. In simple terms, an African cultural pattern is to be blamed for the demographic disaster in Jamaica, not the attitudes of the planters or their brutal treatment of the enslaved. There are numerous problems with this argument, beginning with the quality of their data, leading the authors to admit in the end that it is 'highly speculative'. One major hurdle is Barbados, which, with similar lactation practices as Jamaica, had a rate of reproduction more like America's.[3] Another was the severe understatement of infant deaths in the registration data on which they relied,[4] which leads one to question whether Jamaican and U.S. mortality rates were that similar. Furthermore, as Kiple has pointed out, while the fat and protein quality of the milk of lactating African women is lower than in the U.S., studies have shown that prolonged breast feeding offered the best chance of survival for the child since 'it at least contains a high-quality protein that the child will be without when he is finally weaned'.[5] Thus, far from accounting for the

[1] Kiple, *ibid.*, p. 103.
[2] H. Klein and S. Engerman, 1978, 'Fertility Differentials between Slaves in the United States and the British West Indies', *William & Mary Quarterly*, Vol. 35, No. 2, pp. 357–74.
[3] For one explanation for the 'anomaly' of Barbados, see Michael Tadman, *op. cit.*, p. 1565.
[4] See Higman, 1984, *Slave Populations of the British Caribbean*, p. 314.
[5] Kiple, *op. cit.*, p. 34.

lower rate of reproduction, the lactation practices of Jamaican enslaved women may well have prevented a disastrous situation from being even more catastrophic by delaying the moment when the enslaved child was weaned into the deathly environment of malnutrition and planter indifference, if not downright hostility, throughout the period of the slave trade. Slave women may also well have prolonged lactation as a form of birth control to prevent bringing children into the horrors of the plantation, and to provide opportunities for relief from the dawn to dusk burden of field labour, not to mention the sexual predation of the whites and slave drivers. Verene Shepherd referred to this as the enslaved women's effort to free their 'enchained wombs'.[1] Not considered, too, is the fact that sexual assault was a source of chronic venereal diseases, causing widespread sterility. On Thistlewood's estate, almost every woman of childbearing age had gonorrhea, Africans infected within days of arrival in the island[2] and there is every reason to believe that this was the case throughout the island. It is now established medical fact that, among women, untreated gonorrhea causes pelvic inflammatory disease that permanently damages the reproductive system, leading to infertility, in addition to stillbirth or miscarriage.[3] It also causes epididymitis in men which also leads to infertility. Kenneth Morgan, in an otherwise sound piece, has played this down, confounding it with the spurious issue of slave women's morality.[4] The real issue, however, was the chronic raping of enslaved women. As Burnard correctly points out: 'White men molested slave women in part because they could do so without fear of social consequence and in part because they constantly needed to show slaves the extent of their dominance. The institutional dominance of white men had to be translated into personal dominance.'[5] In doing so they rapidly spread the more virulent strain of gonorrhea they

---

[1] Verene A. Shepherd, 2002, 'Petticoat Rebellion?': The Black Woman's Body and Voice in the Struggles for Freedom in Colonial Jamaica', *In the Shadow of the Plantation: Caribbean History, and Legacy*, ed. Alvin O. Thompson, p. 24.

[2] On which, see Hall, 1989, *In Miserable Slavery*, p. 135.

[3] Richard S. Dunn, *A Tale of Two Plantations*, pp. 161–3.

[4] Kenneth Morgan, 2006. 'Slave Women and Reproduction in Jamaica, c1776–1834', *History* 91(302): 231–53.

[5] Trevor Burnard, 2004, *Mastery, Tyranny, and Desire*, pp. 156–62.

brought from Europe, to the detriment of the fertility of enslaved women.

Another kind of evidence demolishes this attempt to blame African lactation practices for Jamaica's demographic disaster. Tadman[1] has shown that in the Louisiana sugar belt of the slave South, where the lactation practices of the enslaved were similar to those of other North American enslaved as well as their white enslavers, a similar pattern of massive demographic decline is found, resulting from the same combination of inhumane treatment and imbalanced sex-ratios. The horrendous overworking of women on the Louisiana cane fields reduced their fertility, reinforcing Dunn's argument that 'the sugar labor performed by the Mesopotamia women [of Jamaica] in their prime childbearing years was the main cause of their low birthrate'.[2] This heavy toll on fertility, argues Tadman, combined with the ability to replace the dead by buying a male-dominated workforce from the older slave states, was the lethal combination accounting for the catastrophic demographic decline of the Jamaican population, not African lactation practices, not even yellow fever.[3]

Perhaps the strongest evidence that it was the peculiar savagery of the condition of enslavement in Jamaica that most accounts for the demographic decline is how swiftly the Jamaican population began to reproduce almost immediately after abolition, in spite of persisting African-type lactation practices among the formerly enslaved African and creole blacks (who had similar practices) and has never stopped growing.[4] Ironically, recent studies have shown that the decline of traditional breast-feeding practices among Jamaican and other West Indian peasant and urban working-class women since the 1950s, and their replacement with commercially promoted infant formulas, has led to a disastrous *increase* in infant malnutrition, illnesses and mortality.[5]

[1] Michael Tadman, 2000, 'The Demographic Cost of Sugar: Debates on Slave Societies and Natural Increase in the Americas', *American Historical Review*, Vol. 105, No. 5, pp. 1534–75, 1555, 1561.
[2] Dunn, *A Tale of Two Plantations*, pp. 163–4.
[3] Tadman, *op. cit.*, pp. 1538, 1543.
[4] See George Roberts, 1957, *The Population of Jamaica*, Cambridge University Press, pp. 42–5.
[5] Thomas J. Marchione, 1980, 'A History of Breast-Feeding Practices in the English-Speaking Caribbean in the Twentieth Century', *Food*

This being so, consider Figures 1 and 2. Figure 1 shows the relative percentage of slaves taken to Jamaica and the North American mainland by decade between 1651 and 1830. Between 1651 and 1660, North America received far more slaves than Jamaica. In 1655 Jamaica was taken by the British from the Spanish and, instantly, everything changed. Between five and ten times more slaves were delivered to Jamaica than to North America during the six decades after 1660, and the last three decades of the 18th century and more than twice as many in the middle decades in between. Figure 2 shows the cumulative effect in absolute numbers: between 1650 and 1830, a total of 1,017,109 Africans were disembarked in Jamaica, while only 388,233 were taken to North America.[1] However, in 1830 there were 2,009,048 enslaved in America and, including free blacks, some 2,328,642 Black souls. At that time, there were only 319,074 enslaved in Jamaica and, all told, 359,147 people of some Black ancestry.

What this astonishing difference amounts to is this: had Africans and their descendants experienced the same rate of increase in Jamaica as had occurred in North America, the theoretically possible 1830 enslaved population in the island would have been 5,262,522 and its total Black population (including free coloured or people of mixed ancestry) would have been 6,100,620. Taking account of the 359,147 survivors in 1830, and using North American slavery as a counterfactual yardstick, we must conclude that there were 5,741,473 missing Black Jamaicans in 1830, which is a measure of British protracted genocide of Black people in the island between 1655 and 1830. To express this in the stronger causal terms of a counterfactual conditional: had it not been for the distinctive features of Jamaican slavery, 5,741,473 Jamaican lives would not have been lost. (My estimate, I hasten to add, is confined to the

and Nutrition Bulletin, Vol. 2, No. 2, The United Nations University, pp. 1–11.
[1] The striking differences in the demographic patterns of North America and the West Indies were remarked on from the late 18th century and used in abolitionist advocacy. See B. W. Higman, 1984, *Slave Populations of the British Caribbean, 1807–1834*, pp. 305–6. It was noted by W. E. B. DuBois in his *Black Reconstruction in America 1860–1880*, Russell & Russell (1935), p. 4. Philip Curtin drew closer attention to it in his 1969 work, *The Atlantic Slave Trade: A Census*, University of Wisconsin Press, pp. 88–91; as did Robert Fogel and Stanley Engerman in their 1974 study, *Time on the Cross*, W. W. Norton, p. 25.

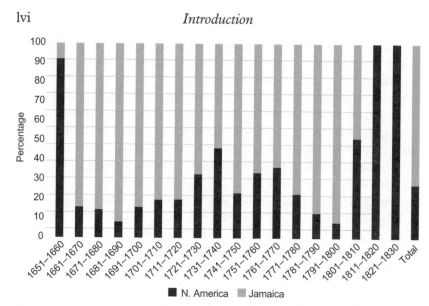

Figure 1. Relative Percentages of Slaves Disembarked in Jamaica and North America

Figure 2. A Counterfactual Picture of Jamaican Genocide: Jamaican & North American Slavery Compared, 1650–1830

Graphs composed by author from Trans-Atlantic Slave Trade Database, https://www.slavevoyages.org/assessment/estimates

Jamaican enslaved population, both the Africans brought there and their descendants, with no implications for African lives lost in Africa.)[1] This figure, we might note, is not much smaller than the six million Jews eliminated in the Nazi holocaust. Jamaican slavery, we conclude, was a clear case of genocide.

To be sure, there are varieties of genocide.[2] The British genocide of Blacks in Jamaica took place over 183 years rather than the twelve years of the Nazi holocaust and 2–4 years of the Ottoman genocide of at least 1.1 million Armenians between 1915 and 1919. This suggests a distinction between protracted or slow-moving and concentrated genocide. Several scholars have drawn attention to the differences and similarities between slavery and the Jewish genocide 'without lapsing into facile equation or producing crude hierarchies of suffering', as A. Dirk Moses aptly puts it.[3] Some, such as Drescher and Hirsch have emphasized the differences.[4] Others, without underplaying the differences, have pointed to similarities, several drawing on my concept of social death in addressing the parallels. In her definitive study of life in Nazi Germany, Kaplan repeatedly describes the pre-destruction period leading up to the death camps as a condition of social death for the Jews living in Germany: 'In the 1930s Nazi Germany succeeded in enforcing social death on its Jews – excommunicating them, subjecting them to inferior status, and relegating them to a perpetual state of dishonour.'[5] Daniel Goldhagen, writing about the same

---

[1] The question of the demographic impact of the Atlantic slave trade on West Africa is a thorny one, which this argument carefully avoids. See Patrick Manning, 'The Slave Trade: The Formal Demography of a Global System', in J. I. Inikori and S. Engerman, eds, 1992, *The Atlantic Slave Trade: Effects on Economies, Societies and Peoples in Africa, the Americas and Europe*, Duke University Press, pp. 117–41.

[2] On which, see Alan S. Rosenbaum, ed., 1996, *Is the Holocaust Unique?: Perspectives on Comparative Genocide*, Westview Press. And more recently Donald Bloxham and Dirk Moses, eds, 2010, *The Oxford Handbook of Genocide Studies*, Oxford University Press, especially parts 3 and 4.

[3] A. Dirk Moses, 2008, 'The Fate of Blacks and Jews: A Response to Jeffrey Herf', *Journal of Genocide Research*, Vol. 10, No. 2, p. 275.

[4] Jeffrey Herf, 'Comparative Perspectives on Anti-Semitism, Radical Anti-Semitism in the Holocaust and American White Racism', *Journal of Genocide Research*, Vol. 9, No. 4, 2007, pp. 575–600; Seymour Drescher, 'The Atlantic Slave Trade and the Holocaust: A Comparative Analysis', in Rosenbaum, *op. cit.*, pp. 65–85.

[5] Marion A. Kaplan, 1998, *Between Dignity and Despair: Jewish Life in Nazi Germany*, p. 288. See also pp. 5, 9, 34–6, 150–60, 166, 173–9, 184–200, 299.

time, made a similar point, arguing that while German Jews were indeed totally dominated, natally alienated and dishonoured, the distinctive features of social death, the critical distinction lay in the fact that the slaveholder found value in the body of the enslaved, while the Nazi terrorist sought the elimination of Jewish bodies.[1] More recently, Claudia Card has argued that my concept of social death is 'central to the evil of genocide (whether the genocide is homicidal or primarily cultural)' and that it is what 'distinguishes genocide from other mass murders'.[2] Card focuses on the fact that a people's social identity, based on their distinctive way of life, is what gives meaning to their existence, and destroying this is what most critically defines genocide: 'Social vitality exists through relationships, contemporary and intergenerational, that create an identity that gives meaning to life. Major loss of social vitality is a loss of identity and consequently a serious loss of meaning for one's existence. Putting social death at the centre takes the focus off individual choice, individual goals, individual careers and body counts, and puts it on relationships that create community and set the context that gives meaning to choices and goals.'[3] In making this philosophical move, Card was actually returning to the pioneering student of the subject, Raphael Lemkin, who coined the term 'genocide', and for whom 'the destruction of cultural symbols is genocide', as well as actions that 'menace the existence of the social group which exists by virtue of its common culture'. It also, of course, involved 'the criminal intent to destroy or cripple permanently a human group'.[4] The fact that it does not do so completely does not make it any less genocidal, since 'Lemkin made clear that total extermination was not necessary for genocide to occur.'[5] Some Jews survived. Some Jamaicans survived.

From all this, it is clear that what happened in Jamaica between 1655 and 1838 was genocide in every sense of the term, for what

[1] Daniel J. Goldhagen, 1997, *Hitler's Willing Executioners: Ordinary Germans and the Holocaust*, Knopf, pp. 168–9.

[2] Claudia Card, 2003, 'Genocide and Social Death', *Hypatia*, Vol. 18, No. 1, Feminist Philosophy and the Problem of Evil, pp. 63–79.

[3] Card, *ibid.*, p. 63.

[4] A. Dirk Moses, 'Raphael Lemkin, Culture, and the Concept of Genocide', in Donald Bloxham and A. Dirk Moses, eds, *The Oxford Handbook of Genocide Studies*, pp. 21, 25.

[5] *Ibid.*, p. 21.

we find is both ethno-cultural destruction, physical brutalization and the denial of existence to 5,741,473 souls. While both were genocide, there are three differences between the Nazi and the Jamaican holocaust. The first is temporal, the fact that the Jewish social death lasted for twelve years (1933 to 1945) while that of Jamaicans lasted for 183 years of deracination, the loss of connection with their past, of any recognized sense of any rights in or belonging to the land of their birth, to their own children and parents, to their very selves and bodies. The second, already mentioned, that the Jewish physical elimination was concentrated over a short period of four years, while that of Jamaicans lasted for 183 years in the drip, drip, drip of shortened lives and curtailed fertility, so tortured and degraded that death was vociferously celebrated as 'a welcome relief from the calamities of life and a passport to the never-to-be-forgotten scenes of their nativity'.[1] The third concerns the nature of the elimination, and is likely the most contentious: in the case of the Jews, actual living bodies were destroyed; in the case of the Jamaicans, in addition to the abbreviated lives and outright individual murders, mass executions and suicides, potential living bodies were preventively destroyed – lives that would almost certainly have happened, should by any and all human standards have eventuated, under the quite reasonable counterfactual condition. The absence of these 5,741,473 Jamaican lives is not a hypothetical. It was a deliberate curtailment. Like female gendercide, the deliberate preventive obliteration of up to 117 million females mainly through sex-selective termination of pregnancies,[2] it was a crime against humanity. The comparison with gendercide

[1] James M. Phillippo, 1843, *Jamaica: Its Past and Present State*, James M. Campbell & Co. p. 95. He also notes that 'suicide was awfully prevalent', p. 97.
[2] The term was coined by Mary Anne Warren in her 1985 study, *Gendercide: The Implications of Sex Selection*, Roman & Allanfield. It was estimated at 100 million by the *Economist* in 2010 and by Nobel laureate economist Amartya Sen at 117 million in 2015. https://www.thenews.com.pk/latest/4182-amartya-sen-suggests-solutions-to-gendercide; *Economist*, 6th March 2010: https://www.economist.com/leaders/2010/03/04/gendercide.
Note that the term refers to 'the deliberate extermination of persons of a particular sex (or gender)' and includes males, as in the Serbian sex-selective massacre of ethnic-Albanian men in 1999, or the Stalinist purges. However, my focus is on female gendercide, which more approximates the genocidal missing bodies of Jamaican slave society, since the vast majority of the 117 female victims of gendercide are 'missing' persons not allowed an existence because of their gender.

is clarifying in that it emphasizes the fact that genocide need
not involve deliberate killings, actual bodies, or concerted mass
murder (although these frequently happened in Jamaica, especially after real and attempted plots of rebellion, as well as in gendercide with infanticide). As Warren points out: 'not all instances
of genocide involve direct or deliberate killing. Deaths or cultural
disintegration deliberately or negligently brought about through
starvation, disease or neglect may also be genocidal. Indeed, some
acts of genocide *do not involve any deaths at all, but rather consist in
the wrongful denial of the right to reproduce.*' [emphasis added][1] To
repeat, for 183 years, Jamaicans had their ancestral memories, and
traditional cultures destroyed, their actual lives ravaged, ruthlessly
exploited and severely shortened, their familial bonds shattered,
their bodies casually raped with impunity and infected with life-
shortening diseases, their reproductive rights denied, leading to
the accumulation of 5,741,473 missing persons. One can think of
few more heinous cases of a crime against humanity.

When British slavery was finally abolished in 1838, Jamaicans, as
we have noted, had experienced it for 183 years. I write this introduction in 2021, exactly 183 years after the abolition. The island
has never fully recovered from the uniquely violent decimation of
that first half of its history. 'One of the characteristics of traumatic
memory', Dan Stone has written, 'is that it cannot be suppressed
at will', and societies remain scarred long after its experience.[2] The
Prime Minister of Jamaica, the Most Honourable Andrew Holness,
in his 2021 Emancipation Day speech commemorating the abolition of slavery in the island, noted the facts that it has been 183
years since abolition, and the role that the last great rebellion of the
enslaved, led by National Hero, the Rt Excellent Samuel Sharpe,[3]
played in helping to bring it about. But then he added something
with which his entire nation would have somberly agreed: *'The use*

---

[1] Mary Ann Warren, *Gendercide*, cited in Adam Jones, 2000, 'Gendercide
and Genocide', *Journal of Genocide Research*, Vol. 2, No. 2, pp. 185–211.

[2] Dan Stone, 'Genocide and Memory', in Donald Bloxham and A. Dirk
Moses, eds, *The Oxford Handbook of Genocide Studies*, pp. 102, 114.

[3] Sharpe was proclaimed a National Hero of Jamaica in 1975. A Teacher's
College in Montego Bay is named after him, and a memorial erected in that
city, the main urban site of the revolution, in his honor. His image graces the
Jamaican $50 bill.

of violence has followed us from our history.[1] Today, Jamaica remains one of the most violent nations on earth, as it was in the eighteenth century, with a homicide rate that places it in the top five of all nations, and a rate of femicide, the murder of women, consistently at the very top of the world's nations.[2] The dead yards of the nation's slums[3] bear ghoulish witness to the plantation dead yards of that first half of its existence.[4] For Jamaica, 'the politics of postgenocidal memories are matters of life and death'.[5]

That first half of our history has never been fully told. If the truth be known, it can never be fully known. Genocide, fast or slow moving, is unknowable. Unimaginable. We try as historians and sociologists to fathom and feel its horror, its sorrow, its unrelenting grief, its preternatural evil. But in its hollowing banality,[6] it defies all understanding. Having reached the limits of historical and sociological understanding I tried to imagine that first half of our past in the literary sequel to *The Sociology of Slavery*, my novel, *Die the Long Day*,[7] which drew on the materials I had collected for the earlier work to re-create a day of death and celebratory mourning on an 18th-century slave plantation. During the mourning for the murdered heroine (butchered by the Maroons at the request of the white overseer), an old Fanti woman, slightly crazed, wanders amidst the mourners, repeatedly wailing in a voice as dark as death, a dirge that was all she had remembered from her deracinated African past. It went like this:

---

[1] Emancipation Day 2021 Message by Prime Minister, the Most Honorable Andrew Holness, ON, PC, MP, 1st August 2021. Jamaica Information Service. https://jis.gov.jm/speeches/emancipation-day-2021-me ssage-by-prime-minister-the-most-hon-andrew-holness-on-pc-mp/

[2] The U.N. *Global Study of Homicide*, 2019.

[3] Ian Thomson, 2011, *The Dead Yard: A Story of Modern Jamaica*, Nation Books.

[4] For a more historically grounded reflection on the historical roots of contemporary violence in Jamaica, see Michele Lemonius, 2017, 'Deviously Ingenious': British Colonialism in Jamaica', *Peace Research*, Vol. 49, No. 2, pp. 79–103.

[5] Dan Stone, *op. cit.*, p. 115.

[6] I echo here Hannah Arendt, 1963, *New Yorker* essay, 'Eichmann in Jerusalem: A Report on the Banality of Evil', by which she meant the normalization of wickedness, which is about as apt a description of Jamaican slave society as I can think of.

[7] Orlando Patterson, 1972, *Die the Long Day*, William Morrow.

Do not say anything,
O Mother, Sister,
Do not say anything.
For anything you say, will be too much,
And nothing you say, will be enough.

Orlando Patterson,
Harvard University

JAMAICA, and the other West Indian Islands, are unique in World history in that they present one of the rare cases of a human society being artificially created for the satisfaction of one clearly defined goal: that of making money through the production of sugar. In 1655 both the British masters and their slaves, who were later to come in such vast numbers, were total strangers to the land upon which they were destined to build a completely new society. The vast majority of the people who were to mould this society came against their will. This was true not only of the slaves, but of the large numbers of Irish, Welsh, Scots and English, who, coming originally as indentured servants and, later, under the pressure of economic deprivation, were as much the victims of the capitalist exploiters of England as were the bewildered tribesmen of Africa whose labour they were to supervise.

And of those whites who came to the colony with the high hopes of quickly making their fortunes and returning home many indeed were to spend the rest of their days bemoaning their foolhardiness. For Jamaican slave society was no place for the poor, ambitious pioneer. After the first fifty hectic years of indecision during which an unscrupulous few may have fulfilled their dreams, Jamaica developed into what it would remain for the rest of the period of slavery: a monstrous distortion of human society. It was not just the physical cruelty of the system that made it so perverse, for in this the society was hardly unique. What marks it out is the astonishing neglect and distortion of almost every one of the basic prerequisites of normal human living. This was a society in which clergymen were the 'most finished debauchees' in the land; in which the institution of marriage was officially condemned among both masters and slaves; in which the family was unthinkable to the vast majority of the population and promiscuity the norm; in which education was seen as an absolute waste of time and teachers shunned like the plague; in which the legal system was quite deliberately a travesty of anything that could be called justice; and in which all forms of refinements, of art, of folkways, were either absent or in a state of total disintegration. Only a small proportion of whites who monopolized almost all the fertile land in the island, benefited from the system. And these, no sooner had they secured their fortunes, abandoned the land which the production of their own wealth had made unbearable to live in, for the comforts of the mother country.

The question which one inevitably asks on confronting this unnatural situation is how was it that it managed not to fall into total anarchy? How was such a system able to survive for nearly two centuries? This work is an attempt to answer this question. Posed in this way, it is clear that while the data employed is largely historical, the treatment of the subject is, of necessity, sociological. The society during the period of slavery presents a remarkable case study of the nature of social values and of social change. More important, it is of marked relevance to the fundamental sociological problem of social order and control. Few systems indeed have ever come closer to the brink of the Hobbesian state of nature and, as such, the sociologist researching this society is faced with the fascinating situation of examining on a concrete level the most basic question of his discipline; one which, nearly always, has been posed in the most abstract of terms.

But this is not to say that the work is intended solely for sociologists. On the contrary, it is hoped that it will fill a vital gap in the history of Jamaica and the other English speaking West Indian Islands. So far, with a few noteworthy exceptions, the historiography of the West Indies has developed in two directions. On the one hand there are the large number of works by scholars of imperial history to whom the islands are of significance only in so far as they represented the platform upon which the European powers thrashed out their imperial differences. On the other hand, there are the scholarly, though often tedious works of those historians who have concentrated almost exclusively on the constitutional development of the islands.

It is easy to understand why the historians of the colonizing society and those of the local white plantocratic and settler élite should have so narrowed their perspectives. As Fannon so rightly observes: 'The settler makes history and is conscious of making it. And because he constantly refers to the history of his mother country, he clearly indicates that he himself is the extension of that mother-country. Thus the history which he writes is not the history of the country which he plunders but the history of his own nation in regard to all that she skims off, all that she violates and starves'. Thus, one looks in vain throughout the volumes of the *Jamaican Historical Review* for any paper of significance on the negro population of the island, (which, since 1700 always constituted more than 90 per cent of the total population) either during slavery or afterwards.

Nor is it difficult to understand why this tradition should have been so faithfully preserved by the recently emerged bourgeois intelligentsia of the formerly enslaved negro population. This is merely an indication of the effectiveness of the process of mystification which has had three-hundred years of British colonial rule within which to consolidate and impose its crippling influence.

This is the first attempt therefore, to analyse, in all its aspects, the nature of the society which existed during slavery in Jamaica, and in particular, to concentrate on the mass of the Negro people whose labour, whose skills, whose suffering and whose perseverance and, at times, defiance, managed to maintain the system, without breaking – like the Arawaks under their Spanish masters before them – under its yoke.

This work is a revised version of a doctoral thesis which was written at the London School of Economics under the supervision of Professor David Glass. It is difficult to over-estimate the debt I owe to Professor Glass; the guidance, encouragement and criticisms which he made throughout the various stages of the writing of the original manuscript were invaluable. I am, of course, entirely responsible for whatever inelegance of style or misinterpretation of data that may exist in the final version.

I must also acknowledge my gratitude to the librarians and attendants of both the Manuscript Department and the Reading Room of the British Museum; to the officials and attendants of the Public Records Office, London; to the Librarian of the Royal Commonwealth Society; to the Secretary of the Library of the West India Committee, London; and to the Librarian and attendants of the London School of Economics. Thanks are also due to the Librarian and attendants of the Institute of Jamaica; to the Archivist of the Jamaica Archives; to the Librarian and attendants of the University of the West Indies, Jamaica; and to Mr Pat Rousseau, The Accountant and Manager of Worthy Park Estate, Jamaica, who not only arranged for me to read the private historical documents of the Estate, but very kindly provided me with a guide to the slave ruins of the plantation. To Mrs Leonie Amiel and Miss Kathrin Phillips who typed, respectively, the original and revised versions of this work, my warmest thanks.

During the three years in which I carried out the research for this work I was supported by the Commonwealth Scholarship Commission. It is hardly necessary to state that without their assistance this work would not have been possible. I would also like to thank the British Council for the kindness and efficiency with which they performed their functions as representatives of the Commonwealth Scholarship Commission.

Finally, for her unflinching patience, interest and encouragement, and for the innumerable valuable suggestions relating to all aspects of this work, and in particular, for her elucidation of the more esoteric aspects of African kinship systems, I am greatly thankful to my wife.

THE SOCIOLOGY OF SLAVERY

CHAPTER I

The Masters:
An Overall View of Slavery

WHEN the British captured Jamaica in 1655, its historical slate was, in all practical senses, wiped completely clean. The island was discovered by Columbus in 1494, and between then and 1655, the Spaniards with the ruthless cruelty that characterized their treatment of the indigenous Indian peoples,[1] had wiped out the entire native population, only seventy-four remaining in 1611.[2] Lacking the all-important mineral resources which they valued so highly, the Spaniards largely neglected the island; and apart from the export of hides, the small white population, reduced through emigration, diseases and physical degeneration caused by incestuous inbreeding, to no more than 696 souls,[3] existed on a subsistence economy in which they 'passed their days in gloomy langour, enfeebled by sloth and depressed by poverty'.[4]

An examination of the lives of the slaves must begin with an understanding of the socio-economic order of their masters since, within this wider framework the slaves were merely one element albeit the most important, in the total structure and functioning of the slave system. Our analysis of the system will be divided into three sections. The first deals with the growth and structure of the economic base of the society; the second examines its political structure and growth; and the third discusses the nature of the white community.

[1] See Bartolome De Las Casas, *The Tears of the Indians*, etc, (1656) also, L. Hank, *Bartolome De Las Casas: An Interpretation*, pp. 56–60.
[2] The Abbot of Jamaica to the King of Spain, July 1611, in F. Cundall and J. L. Fietersz, *Jamaica Under the Spaniards*, pp. 34–5.
[3] *Ibid.* There were also 558 Negro slaves and 107 free Negroes. In 1655 there were only 450 men capable of bearing arms, *ibid.*, p. 50.
[4] B. Edwards, *The History of the British Colonies in the West Indies*, Vol. 1, Bk. 2, p. 198. (1801–7.)

THE DEVELOPMENT OF JAMAICA, 1655–1834

Jamaica's development during this period falls into three phases. First, the early period between 1655 and 1700 including the capture and early attempts at settling the island; secondly, the period between 1700 and 1774, which marks the development of large-scale agriculture and the golden period of prosperity; and thirdly, the period between 1774 and 1834 which saw the gradual decline and eventual collapse of the system.

A. 1655–1700 Jamaica was captured, after a disastrous attempt at taking Santo Domingo, as part of Cromwell's 'grand design' against the Spaniards in the New World, and for the first seven years of the English occupation the island was ruled under military government. Only the extreme apathy of the Spaniards to the fate of the island can explain how the English managed to keep it, for the soldiers who formed the bulk of the conquering army were among the most ill-equipped imaginable. Three thousand of them came originally from England, another 5,000 from the Leeward Islands and from Barbados.

Of the planters Venables wrote that they were 'the most profane, debauched persons that we ever saw, Scorners of Religion and . . . so loose as not to be kept under discipline',[1] and later, from his confinement in the Tower he also condemned the soldiers who left from England as 'a rascally rabble of raw and inexperienced men'.[2] The commanders, however, were just as incompetent as their soldiers, both Penn and Venables being continually at loggerheads. In a letter to his brother one of the conquering soldiers complained that most of those who came originally from England 'were apprentices that ran from their masters and others that come out of Bridewell or one Goal or another' and further that the expedition had 'a great many bad commanders as well as bad soldiers'.[3] The island fared badly in these early military years. Although in 1656 there was still 'a very great store of Horses, Bulls, Cows and Hogs'

---

[1] 'The Narrative of General Venables', B.M. Add. MSS. 11410.
[2] *Interesting Tracts Relating to Jamaica*, p. 91.
[3] Letter of Danil How, Add. MSS. 11410.

in the island,[1] by the fourth year of the occupation they had almost all been massacred. The soldiers had refused to plant, depending mainly on the cattle, and when these became scarce there was general famine and starvation. Tropical fever also played havoc with the small population; seven hundred soldiers dying in one week during the first year of occupation.[2] Only the capable leadership of D'Oyley – who, however, 'neither loved, encouraged, nor understood Planting'[3] – averted general mutiny as the soldiers all dreaded the prospect of settling in the island which they viewed, understandably, as a graveyard.

After his initial disappointment over the bungling of his plans by his commanders, Cromwell decided to make the best of what he had and set about peopling the island. Civil government was established in 1661 and various proclamations were issued encouraging people to settle there.[4] On the whole these attempts met with little success. Colonel Stokes of Nevis came with 1,800 settlers in 1656 and 500 men also arrived with their families from the Bermudas, but by 1660 'not 80' of them remained.[5] The remaining soldiers were disbanded and encouraged to set up plantations. Later, convicts and indentured servants were sent over[6] and a few religious groups, including Quakers and Huguenots took advantage of the favourable conditions offered them there.

Until about 1670 the majority of the settlers 'were old West Indians'[7] from Barbados and other eastern Caribbean islands, although the principal Barbadian planters strongly resented this drain on their manpower and were 'very averse from anything to the good of Jamaica'.[8]

Among those migrating from Barbados were a few wealthy and experienced planters, the most important being Modyford, who was later to play a significant part in the early civil administration of the colony. Two groups of settlers also came from Surinam, the last

[1] Anon: *A True Description of Jamaica*, 1657, p. 2.
[2] Sedgwick to Whitehall, C.O.I/32.
[3] T. Malthus, *The Present State of Jamaica*, 1683, p. 34.
[4] Anon: *The Colonization of Jamaica: Proclamations, Commissions, etc. Relating to the Planting and Settling of Jamaica*. 1792.
[5] 'The Relation of Col. D'Oyley' Add. MSS. 11410, f. 16–17.
[6] See C.S.P. 1661–1668; esp. Nos. 292 and 350.
[7] E. Hickerighill, *Jamaica Viewed*, 1660.
[8] C.S.P. America and W.I. 1661–1668, No. 186.

group, about 1,230, coming in 1675.[1] Later a contingent of Jews arrived from Surinam after successfully petitioning the King against a blatant act of discrimination intended to keep them from migrating.[2] This emigration of settlers from the eastern Caribbean had ceased by the last decade or so of the seventeenth century, for Sir Hans Sloane, who visited the island around that time, found the white inhabitants 'for the most part Europeans'.[3] Attempts at peopling the island with whites already seemed doomed to failure. Governor Lynch wrote that in 1660 there were, 'by report', some 2,200 soldiers and planters and about the same number of merchants and settlers in the island.[4] But this was likely to have been a gross over-estimate, for in 1662 a census stated that there were 2,600 men, 645 women and 408 children.[5] Two years later the white population was estimated at 3,150 and in 1773 at 7,768 with 9,504 slaves and 800 seamen.[6] Two years later, Cranefield's estimate revealed a fall in the population[7] and after 1677 this decline became even more pronounced. Then came the spectacular earthquake of 1692, which wrecked not only Port Royal, but the entire island. Mortality and emigration after the earthquake resulted in an even greater decline, which continued until 1739.

The failure of the white population to expand during this first phase of the island's history is due primarily to certain basic economic factors to which we must now turn our attention. The first half of this phase of Jamaica's development was dominated by the activities of the Buccaneers and Privateers (the difference between them being only that the latter had a royal commission) whose exploits are too well known for us to repeat here. Governor Mody-ford greatly encouraged these sailors and was a great friend of the famous Sir Henry Morgan who, later, was himself to rise to the post of Lieutenant Governor.[8] A considerable amount of money was brought into the island by the plunders of these men and between 1664 and 1688 the island enjoyed a wave of commercial prosperity;

[1] C.S.P. 1675, No. 675, vii; No. 504.
[2] *Ibid.* No. 675, 808, 818, 504.
[3] Sir Hans Sloane, *Voyage to Jamaica with The Natural History of Jamaica,* Intro. 1707–25.
[4] C.O.I/14.   [5] Add. MSS. 11410, B.M. f. 12.
[6] See Appendix to *Journals of the Jamaica House of Assembly,* Vol. I.
[7] His estimate was 5,500; 'Situation . . . of Jamaica' C.O. 138/2.
[8] E. A. Cruikshank, *The Life of Sir Henry Morgan,* 1935.

but it is doubtful whether this prosperity benefited the colony very much in terms of its long-run development. In 1670 the British government began to take measures to curb the activities of the Buccaneers especially since it was made a condition of peace with Spain. Lord Vaughan in 1675 echoed the view of many of the more responsible settlers when he wrote that privateering was the 'only enemy of planting'.[1] Lynch also emphasized the fact that these buccaneers were a menace to trade as well as settlement since they encouraged many of the servants to 'run away (and) turn Pirates'.[2]

Secondly, during this first phase, an early, initially successful, attempt at establishing a diversified farming economy finally came to nothing by the end of the century. A report on the island in 1660 stated that the main commodities produced were sugar, cocoa, cotton, dyewood, salt, pepper, pimento, drugs and cochineal.[3] Modyford's first 'view' of the island in 1664 is more informative. He tells us that most of the old soldiers had become hunters of wild boar which they prepared and sold to the merchants in the towns at a profit ranging between 15 per cent and 25 per cent:

> with the profit some of them buy servants and slaves and begin to settle brave plantations; others, like idle fellows, drink all out; but now the hunting begins to abate, more have settled land than ever, for that there is scarce any place near the sea but is settled, and many are gone into the mountains . . .[4]

Modyford also listed a much wider range of commodities produced by the island and prematurely painted a promising future for the small cultivator.

A report of 1670 gives more details concerning the relative importance of the different commodities. There were fifty seven sugar works producing yearly 1,710 thousandweights of sugar; forty seven cocoa walks yielding 188,000 lbs of nuts, and many more, the report added, were being planted. There were also forty nine indigo works; three salt ponds of over 4,000 acres yielding 10,000 bushels and 'capable of much more'. The mountains were said to be 'full of pimento'; cattle had increased over the past six years from 60 to 6,000 heads; and there were various other commodities, all

---

[1] C.O. 138/3.   [2] C.O. 138/4.   [3] C.O.I/14.
[4] Modyford, '*A View of the Condition of Jamaica*', *Journal of the House of Assembly*, Jamaica, Vol. I, Appendix.

thriving.[1] In his observations on the island in 1675 Cranefield noted a 'great forwardness' in the production of sugar. But he also noted that cocoa, the small farmer's crop, had increased rapidly on the north side of the island over the past five years.[2] Three years later, a published account of the island stated that cocoa was 'the principal and most beneficial commodity of the Isle' there being about sixty walks and their produce were in 'great demand'.[3] The author then gave a valuable estimate of the costs of establishing a cocoa walk of between five and six hundred acres. With six Negroes, four white servants (including their passage and diet for a year) the service of an overseer for one year, and an adequate supply of cattle the total cost would amount to only £275 5s 0d[4]. Compared with this, a sugar estate, which as early as 1672 was described as being more like a 'small town or village'[5] averaged about 1,000 acres in size and cost between £4,488[6] and £5,000[7] to establish. Further, the profit on such estates – about £1,000 per annum – would not start coming in until the fourth year.

We understand why it is then that when, toward the end of the seventeenth century, a mysterious plant disease wiped out almost all the cocoa plants in the island, the consequence was an immediate falling off of the settlement of the colony. In addition to this disease, between 1689 and the end of the first decade of the 18th century, the island was plagued with a series of disastrous natural calamities. The first was a vicious hurricane in 1698 which wiped out many plants and buildings. Then in 1692 came the famous earthquake which ranks as one of the worst in modern history. Three-quarters of the entire town of Port Royal went under the sea taking with it most of the inhabitants.[8] Concern with the horrors of Port Royal often leads historians to neglect the fact that the earthquake had disastrous consequences for the rest of the island as well. Barham

---

[1] Appendix, *Journal of the House of Assembly, Jamaica*, Vol. I.
[2] Cranefield, 'Observations on the Present State of Jamaica', C.O. 138/2.
[3] R. Blome, *Description of Jamaica*, 1678, p. 4.
[4] *Ibid.* pp. 7–9.
[5] T. Trapham, *A Discourse of . . . Jamaica*, 1679, p. 26.
[6] See Thomas Lynch to Lord Arlington, MSS. 11410.
[7] Lord Vaughan to Secy. of Trade etc. C.O. 138/3.
[8] For several first-hand accounts of this incident see Barham's MS history of the island, 1722: Sloane MSS. 3918, B.M. f. 161–174. See also T. Parkhurst, *The Truest . . . Account of the late Earthquake in Jamaica*, 1693.

wrote that there was 'not a house standing at Passage Fort, but one at Liguanea and none at St. Jago except a few low houses built by the wary Spaniards'.[1] And the governor wrote in his despatch that:

> In the space of two Minutes all the Churches, Dwelling houses and sugar works of the whole island were thrown down, two third of Port Royal swallowed up by the Sea all its forts and Fortifications demolished and great part of its inhabitants either knockt on the head or drown'd.[2]

Still worse was the ensuing pestilence which took even more lives than the earthquake.

Not long after this disaster came another in the form of a French invasion of the island. In 1694 Du Casse and his fleet, for an entire month, plundered the northern and eastern coasts of the island which were exactly the areas containing most of the smaller settlers. Over 1,300 Negroes were taken and a great amount of other bounty.[3]

Conditions on the island were now desperate. Beeston wrote home that:

> We want all necessaries and ships to carry away Produce of the Country, for that if this war hold much longer these colonies must come to nothing; for no people come on, many dye, some gett away for fear, others who are in debt and many press into the King's ships which also frighten away others, and by many ways decrease which disheartens those that have interest, and cause them to talk of removing.[4]

In 1695 the white population was estimated at 2,440; the next year at 1,390. Even the privateers and seamen, Beeston wrote in despair, had begun to desert the island. The French invasion was also accompanied by several slave uprisings which also discouraged many settlers.[5]

The extremely high cost of living was another factor driving many of the smaller settlers away from the colony. Beeston attributed this to the scarcity of supplies from the North American colonies due to the war.[6] But long before this war many had complained

---

[1] *Ibid.* [2] Beeston to Board of Trade, C.O. 138/7.
[3] See Gardner, *History of Jamaica*, p. 103. (1873).
[4] Beeston to Board of Trade – C.O.138/9.
[5] See Ch. 9 below. [6] Beeston *op. cit.*

of the astonishingly high cost of living in the island. In 1687 Francis Crow wrote home that 'this is one of the most expensive, dear places in the known world, for all manner of provisions.'[1] Even earlier, in 1671, Lynch had complained that 'provisions are so horribly dear and scarce to newcomers and those who have no plantations that they need nothing else to discourage them'[2] attributing the inflation to the presence of the Privateers at Port Royal. In 1707 Richard Tabor wrote home of 'the difficulties of living here' and of 'how little a way a large summe of money will goe toward the purchasing even the necessities of life.'[3]

Another significant economic element of this first phase was that, going hand in hand with the official policy of encouraging small settlers and diversified farming, were the attempts of many of the larger planters to monopolise most of the available land and thus keep out these smaller settlers. As early as 1669 John Styles reported that after 1667:

> The old soldiers, who call themselves the conquerors of the land, took advantage of the Dutch Wars to work upon pretending danger to destroy their neighbours and keep up their own boundless tyrannical power under pretence of carefulness.[4]

Martial law, he tells us, was declared in the island and many people were obliged to travel twenty or thirty miles to keep guard without any security to their families who they left at home. He complained also of rigged elections and of widespread corruption in the law courts, and adds:

> This was the first destruction of small settlements and the hindrance of greater and many were forced to sell their plantations to their Lords and Masters for what they could get or else run from them and leave all.[5]

Equally corrupt monopolistic practices also resulted from the scarcity of competent and honest surveyors, and several estates

---

[1] The Ja. Historical Review, Vol. 3 No. 2, p. 54.
[2] Lynch to Lord Arlington, Add. MSS. 11410, B.M.
[3] 'As to the State of Jamaica in 1707' in *The Jour. of Negro History*, Vol. 27, 1942.
[4] J. Style to Secy. Sir William Morrice: C.S.P. 1669–74, No. 7.
[5] *Ibid.*

were 'smothered from the right heirs and . . . enjoyed by strangers.'[1] Lynch observed in 1671, that the great number of African slaves and the large estates, the major part of the land of which remained idle, had together driven away the small settler, making white labour both dear and scarce.[2]

Thus less than two decades after the occupation of the island we begin to detect tendencies toward monopolization which later were to prove disastrous in terms of making the island a 'colonie de peoplement'. The series of natural and political calamities which the island experienced at the end of the seventeenth century seemed to have played right into the hands of these monopolists. By the opening of the eighteenth century Jamaica had entered an entirely new phase of development, that of a large-scale, largely mono-crop agricultural system.

B. 1700–1774 The monopolistic elements latent in seventeenth century British-occupied Jamaica became manifest during the eighteenth century. Although attempts at peopling the island were never entirely given up until the mid-eighteenth century, it is clear that such attempts were largely stimulated by the fear of internal rebellion by the slaves rather than out of any genuine desire to increase the white population of the island.[3]

Jamaica's recovery after the bleak years of the early 1680s, on the basis of the new large-scale sugar system, was phenomenal. In 1739, when the golden age of prosperity may be said to have begun (and the white population somewhere between 7,000 and 8,000) the export of sugar amounted to 33,155 hogsheads, of 14 cwt each.[4] In 1764, with the white population at 9,640, exports from the island were approximately 35,000 hogsheads of sugar and 10,000 puncheons of rum (in addition, of course to other articles).[5] In 1768, when the white population was estimated at 17,000, a total of 55,761 hogsheads of sugar at 16 cwt each was being exported, in addition to 15,551 puncheons of rum, 201,960 gallons of molasses (all to North

[1] B. Corbett, Sloane MSS. 4020, f. 22–23. *A Memorial of . . . Ja.* 1670–73.
[2] Lynch to Arlington, B.M. Add. MSS. 11410.
[3] Gardner, *op. cit.* p. 159. For accounts of attempts at peopling the island with whites see, Spurdle, *Early W.I. Govts.*; also, Pitman, *The Development of the B.W.I.*, 1917, ch. 5.
[4] Bryan Edwards, *op. cit.* Vol. I, p. 302.
[5] *Ibid.*

America) and substantial quantities of other commodities.[1] And at the peak of its prosperity in 1774, 78,304 hogsheads of sugar, 26,074 puncheons of rum and 1,020 hogsheads of molasses were being exported. Sugar, pimento, coffee, hides, wood and even some cotton made up the rest of the export figures.

Accompanying this massive increase in productivity was, of course, an even greater rate of increase of the slave population which, long before the end of the seventeenth century, had replaced white servants as the mainstay of the island's labour force.[2]

The Jamaican slave economy during this and the ensuing phase of decline, was based on an elaborate but never completely successful commercial system: the well known triangular trade spanning the three continents of Europe, Africa and America. Ships, fitted out by English merchants, sailed to Africa where slaves were bought in exchange for goods which were often of very little value in England. The slaves were taken to the English possessions in the New World where they were sold in return for the goods produced in the different areas. These were then taken to Britain where they were sold again at a profit. It is not difficult to imagine what enormous wealth this trade, with its three distinct margins of profit, brought to the English merchants engaged in it. Eric Williams has ably demonstrated how the wealth accumulated from the trade greatly contributed to the development of commercial, and later industrial capitalism in Britain.[3] In addition to the triangular trade the islands traded directly with the American mainland colonies from which they derived most of their essential plantation stores and, especially in the case of the Eastern Caribbean, most of their food provisions. It has also been suggested that, as in the trade with Britain, the West Indian merchant played an increasingly passive role in their two way trade with the North American colonies and also contributed substantially to the capital formation of the New England states.[4] The economic realities of the 18th century, however, made the triangular trade in the way Whitehall conceived of it, little more than a wishful model. First, there was the fact that the American colonies were permitted to trade directly with foreign colonies in

---

[1] Bryon Edwards, *op cit.* Vol 1, p. 303
[2] See chapter on Slave Population below.
[3] Eric Williams, *Capitalism and Slavery,* pp. 176–7. (1964).
[4] R. Pares: *Yankees and Creoles,* pp. 11, 161–3.

the New World. Since these colonies, especially those of the French, produced their sugar at a much cheaper rate than the British West Indians, they were able to undersell them in the world market. The Americans therefore refused to take sugar in return for the goods they supplied the British growers, but instead demanded payment in cash with which they bought their sugar from the French islands.[1] This unfavourable balance of payment situation led to a considerable amount of specie being drained from the financial resources of Jamaica and the other British islands to which Britain responded, in favour of the West Indies, by passing the famous molasses acts, the only real consequence of which was further stimulation of revolutionary fervour in America and widespread illicit trading.[2]

Secondly, Jamaica carried on quite extensive trade with the Spanish colonies. This was partly a reflection of the scarcity of money in the island.[3] Almost all the currency used by Jamaicans during the period of slavery came from the Spaniards through the latter's trade for slaves and English manufactures with the island.[4] Between 1750 and the end of the eighteenth century the amount of currency available in Jamaica varied considerably, depending on the state of the Spanish trade. When this trade was low, the position of the West Indian planter could be very embarrassing, as a creditor who wished to seize his property could easily do so by foreclosing on him. So desperate was the shortage of currency at times that sugar was declared legal tender; but since the legal rate at which sugar exchanged for other goods was often greater than its market price, this solution was strongly opposed by creditors.[5]

Thirdly, by the middle of the eighteenth century, many of the ships from Africa refused to take West Indian sugar in return for their slave cargoes, but demanded cash instead. With this money they then bought, illegally, the cheaper sugar to be had from the French islands which they brought into England at the preferential rate of the British grown sugar.[6] From now on ships were sent in

---

[1] Pitman, *op. cit.*, p. 138.　　[2] Pitman, *op. cit.*, Ch. 2.

[3] See, Anon. *The State of the Island of Jamaica Chiefly in Relation to Commerce, etc. 1726*, pp. 33–34.

[4] Pitman, *op. cit.*, p. 147.

[5] *Ibid.* p. 139.

[6] L. Ragatz, *The Fall of the Planter Class in the British Caribbean, 1763–1833.* (1928) p. 89; also Pitman, *op. cit.*, p. 242.

ballast from England to bring home the sugar grown in the British colonies.

Before coming to the final phase of the slave economy, note must be taken of the credit facilities of the West Indian planters. Originally these creditors were quite distinct from the planting interests, simply advancing them capital as they would to any other group of investors. During the course of the eighteenth century, however, many of the wealthy absentee planters themselves became merchants and creditors; and at the same time, many of the original merchants came into possession of Jamaican and other West Indian estates by the foreclosure of their mortgages on indebted planters. The result was that 'the interests of the planters and the mercantile element . . . tended to become one and inseparable'.[1] Soon many merchant houses became exclusively concerned with West India business, with these basic consequences.

First, it meant that the relationship soon became permanent. The merchants' hands were as much tied in the affairs of the colonies as the planters'. One result of this was that the wealthy absentee sector of the latter combined with the former to form the powerful West India interest in England, whose combined lobbying strength was greater than any other interest group during the last half of the eighteenth century.[2] The second consequence of this relationship was the ease with which credit could be procured and the ensuing waste and extravagance this entailed. Easy money led to rampant speculation and foolhardy ventures culminating in the perverse ethic that debt was a mark of distinction.[3] Thirdly, this relationship was almost a closed one and could be entered only through inheritance or through the expenditure of vast outlays of capital. The middle-sized farmers in Jamaica had to depend on local credit which was often very dear. Browne, who visited the island a little after the mid-eighteenth century, claimed that 'one half' of the settlers, as the middle range planters were called, were in debt which 'they find no easy matter to discharge.' Creditors also obliged the settlers to use excessively expensive freighting, shipping and sales facilities which they offered.[4] Thus, the wealthy and largely

[1] Ragatz, *op. cit.*, pp. 93, 100–101.
[2] See Ragatz, *op. cit.*, pp. 93–94. Also Eric Williams, *op. cit.*, p. 96.
[3] Ragatz, *op. cit.*, p. 10.
[4] P. Browne, *The Civil & Natural History of Jamaica.* 1789, p. 23.

absentee owners consolidated their position to the exclusion of smaller settlers and to their own eventual disaster.

C. 1774–1834   Bryan Edwards rightly chose 1774 as 'the meridian' of Jamaica's prosperity as it is from this time that the island began its gradual decline. The starting point of this collapse was the American Revolution, the major consequence of which was the cutting off of the main source of most of the capital goods needed on the plantations. This, in turn, led to an increase in their cost of production which – coming at a time when more cheaply produced foreign grown sugar was flooding the world market – proved disastrous. In addition an important market was lost in the American colonies which, until 1774, bought most of the molasses exported from the island.[1]

Secondly, the island had hardly recovered from the blow of the American Revolution when it experienced a series of natural calamities bearing a freakish parallel to those at the end of the seventeenth century. Between 1780 and 1786 five hurricanes spread 'ruin and desolation' throughout the island. Jamaica had been more fortunate than the other islands in that her slave population was largely responsible for feeding itself.[2] But coming at exactly the time when food supplies were not available from America, these hurricanes resulted in famine and widespread starvation in which between 15,000[3] and 16,000[4] Negroes died.

Although the island made a remarkable recovery in terms of production by 1790, calamities of another sort were awaiting it. To meet her increasing war expenses, the duties on goods imported into Britain were increased. Before the revolution the charge on muscovado sugar, per cwt, entering Britain was 6s9/10; by 1782 it was 12s2/5.[5] Insurance and freight charges also soared. At the outbreak of the war with France all these rates went up once again. In 1806 the duty on sugar entering Britain was 61.7 per cent of its wholesale price,[6] and with the slump in prices in 1822 the price of sugar went below its costs and duties.

---

[1] Edwards, Vol. I. p. 305. For detailed discussion on the effects of the American Revolution, see Ragatz, Ch. 5: and Williams, Ch. 6.

[2] See Ch. 8 below.

[3] Edwards, Vol. I. pp. 234–35; also, Report of Fuller *et al*, R.T. 6: 10, f. 43.

[4] Anon, 'Notes in the Defence of the British Colonies'. *The Jamaica Journal*, Vol. 2, No. 2.

[5] Ragatz, *op. cit.*, p. 164.   [6] *Ibid*, p. 297.

A fourth factor leading to the collapse of the Jamaican economy was the abolition movement. The nature and development of this movement is too well known for us to give any detailed account here. The net result of the abolition of the slave trade was a drastic curtailment of the labour force which depended on an unlimited supply of Africans to replace those who were so rapidly destroyed by the system and who were unable to reproduce themselves.[1] With the abolition of their labour supply the wastefulness and inefficiency of the Jamaican plantation system stood exposed. Hasty and unsuccessful measures were taken to encourage the slaves to reproduce themselves. Many plantations were unable to continue and were simply abandoned; or, unable to produce the necessary amount of sugar to cover their debts, were foreclosed upon.[2]

Fifthly, the slave plantations began to face competition from various sources. The more efficiently produced foreign-grown sugar, especially that of Brazil, the French islands and Cuba, ousted that of the old West Indian islands from the continental market.[3] Another source of competition was the East India company which was rapidly opening up the newly planted lands of the Indian ocean and exploiting the unlimited supplies of cheap (and often forced) labour to be had there. As their interests grew, they increasingly lobbied for an equalization of tariffs, finally succeeding in 1837.

The third source of competition for Jamaica and the other old West Indian colonies came from the newly ceded British possessions in the Caribbean such as Trinidad and Demarara. These regions were able to produce at a much cheaper rate, largely because their soil was virgin and more fertile. What was even worse, they flooded the already saturated British market with more sugar.

The net result of all this was a collapse in the price of sugar reaching its lowest point in 1822 when the market price of $27s7\frac{1}{4}$ was much below the average cost of production. The prices of other commodities supplied by the island, such as coffee – the production of which had rapidly increased in Jamaica since 1774[4] – also slumped.

The final blow to the slave economy came with emancipation. This movement succeeded the earlier abolition movement and was

[1] See Ch. 4 below.   [2] Ragatz, *op. cit.*, p. 308.
[3] *Ibid.*, p. 337; Williams, *op. cit.*, p. 122–23.
[4] Edwards, Bk. 2, Appendix 2, p. 315.

officially inaugurated in 1823 with the founding of the 'Society for the Mitigation and Gradual Abolition of Slavery throughout the British Commonwealth'. Again, while the importance of humanitarian factors cannot be underestimated, the significance of economic forces must be clearly understood.[1] The abolition of slavery in 1834 was simply the official seal of ruin on a system that had already collapsed.

SECTION 2

POLITICAL DEVELOPMENT AND STRUCTURE

In July 1661 the Council for Foreign Plantations proposed to the King that in order to promote civil government in Jamaica and to make conditions more favourable for settlement, the island should be governed by the same laws as those of England. The proclamation of 1661, however, while observing that settlers should have 'the same privileges to all intents and purposes as our free-born subjects of England' was careful not to mention that the laws of England were in practice there and it made its intention quite clear over the next twenty years by constantly turning down the numerous attempts of the Assembly of Jamaica to declare 'the laws of England in force in this Island'.[2]

From its earliest meetings it became clear that the Jamaican Assembly saw itself as the local prototype of the English House of Commons. Quickly it asserted its rights of jurisdiction over all its members, over all who infringed on its privileges and its freedom of speech, and by 1675 had 'established its independence of the Governor and Council in its internal affairs, and it had obtained the privileges without which no representative Assembly could be effective'.[3] From this point until 1677 the Assembly continued to challenge the prerogative of the Crown. It not only refused to pass a permanent revenue bill (something similar to the Barbadian 4½ per cent tax) which was the main bone of contention – but declared that all money granted was to be used in the island.[4]

[1] Williams, *Capitalism and Slavery*, esp. Chs. 9, 10 and 11.
[2] A. M. Whitsun, *The Constitutional Development of Jamaica*, 1929, Ch. 1, pp. 15–19.
[3] Whitsun, *op. cit.*, p. 48; also, E. Long, *History of Jamaica*, Vol. I. p. 56.
[4] For a useful analysis of Jamaica's constitutional development between 1660 and 1700, see A. P. Thornton, *West India Policy Under the Restoration*.

In 1677 the Lords of Trade decided that it was time to assert their authority. Poyning's law, by which Ireland was ruled, and which declared that no assembly should be called without the king's permission or any law passed without his consent, was to be applied to Jamaica.[1] In addition, it was arbitrarily decreed that the Assembly should pass a permanent revenue bill. These were the two main instructions received by Carlysle on taking up the governorship of the island. As one would imagine a constitutional crisis ensued when 'the Assembly rejected the new constitution with indignation'.[2] Samuel Long, who had been deprived of all his offices by Carlysle,[3] went to England and successfully pleaded the case of his fellow Jamaicans, convincing the Lords of the impossibility – through sheer distance alone – of implementing Poyning's law in the island. The Lords gave way and Carlysle was recalled. In return for a seven years revenue bill and another which promised the perpetual payment of the Governor's salary, the island was granted the legislative powers it had formerly assumed.

But Whitehall continued its efforts to get a permanent revenue bill from the island legislature. Between 1680 and 1684 another constitutional struggle ensued along the same lines as the first ending with a compromise in which a twenty-one years revenue bill was granted in return for the confirmation of the laws of the Assembly.[4] The struggle for a permanent revenue continued between 1684 and 1728 during which period, as Whitsun points out:

> It is sufficient to say that a meeting of the Assembly meant a repetition of the arguments, the quarrels and the ill-feelings of the sessions of 1703. The Assembly continued to dispute the Council's right to amend money bills, to grant additional supplies for three, six, or twelve months only, to tack other acts or clauses to these supply bills, and to appoint officers, to receive and disburse the money so raised.[5]

[1] See Edwards, Bk. 2, p. 221; Bridges, *The History of Jamaica*, Vol. I. pp. 284–88.

[2] Edwards, Vol. I. Bk. 2, p. 222.

[3] Long founded an important family in Jamaica. See Howard, *The Longs of Jamaica and Hampton Lodge*, Vol. 1, pp. 23–44.

[4] Edwards, *The Constitutional Development of Jamaica*, Appendix to Vol. I, Bk. 2.

[5] Whitsun, *op. cit.*, p. 142.

Finally, in 1728 a bill granting a perpetual revenue was passed in return for the confirmation of all the laws and privileges of the island. A total sum of £8,000 annually was granted to the King, but this was made up largely of money already granted in the form of quit rents, fines, and import duties on wine and a few other articles.[1] Whitsun has summed up this conflict as 'the clash of two fundamental principles, centralization against local 'autonomy', in which the former was defeated.[2]

Let us now examine, briefly, the structure and functioning of the government of the island during the eighteenth and early nineteenth centuries. At the head of the government was the Governor, charged with the royal prerogative. Invariably, during the eighteenth century the governors of Jamaica were drawn from two sources in England: the army and parliament.[3] He authorized the convoking, adjourning, proroguing and dissolving of the Assembly and he had a negative vote in all bills proposed by them. He established courts and appointed judges and had the power to pardon and reprieve. He was, in theory, the dispenser of all offices and privileges in the island and established the fees for them. He was also in complete control of the Church and Militia.[4]

The Council, which consisted of twelve members nominated by Whitehall on the recommendations of the Governor, performed a dual function. First, it acted as an advisory body to the Governor and, as such, possessed an executive function; and secondly, it operated as an upper house in the legislature of the island.[5]

The island was divided into several precincts within which J.Ps. tried petty offences and suits in Quarter Sessions. More important cases were tried by the Chief Justice and his associates. After 1758 a Supreme Court, held in Spanish Town, the capital, and two courts of assize were set up. The Governor and Council formed the island's court of appeal.[6] There were many lucrative offices to be had in Jamaica during the period of slavery. Officially, the Governor was given the sole right to appoint all civil, judicial and military offices in the island. During the course of the seventeenth and eighteenth

---

[1] *Ibid.* pp. 152–3; *Journals,* Vol. 2, pp. 620–99; C.O. 137/17, f. 40.
[2] Whitsun, *op. cit.* pp. 166–7.
[3] Metcalf, *Royal Govt. & Political Conflict in Jamaica,* 1728–1823, pp. 229–30.
[4] Leslie, *A New History of Jamaica,* 1740 p. 301; Long, *op. cit.*
[5] Spurdle, *Early West Indian Government,* 1962 pp. 29–30.
[6] *Ibid.* p. 52.

centuries, however, this prerogative was infringed upon by three parties. First, the King by letters patent assumed the right to appoint several of the most lucrative posts in the island, such as the Island Secretary, the Provost Marshal and the Surveyor General. Not only did these appointees generally remain absent and 'farm' out their appointments to deputies; but these deputies themselves further 'farmed' out their appointments to sub-deputies.[1] Long wrote an extended and scathing attack on this 'scene of iniquity' and claimed that he could 'find no terms sufficiently expressive of such complicated treachery and wickedness'.[2] Several attempts were made by both the Governors and Legislatures of the island to restrain this extremely inefficient system, first in 1699, then in 1711 and again in 1715, but all the acts in this respect were disallowed by the King and an order of the Board of Trade of 1699 requiring patentees to take up residence in the island was allowed to become a dead letter.[3]

Secondly, certain offices came to be appointed by the respective English administrative departments. These were: the local comptroller and collector of customs, who was appointed by the English Commissioners of Customs; the local postmaster general, who was appointed by his English counterpart; and the Judge, Advocate General and Registrar of the Court of Vice-Admiralty.[4] Thirdly, the Assembly, the *bête noire* of all Jamaican governors during the seventeenth and eighteenth centuries,[5] assumed the right to appoint certain offices which were originally the preserve of the governor, for example, it appointed its own servants and the important office of the agent of the island in England. Nonetheless, the Governor still had a wide range of offices at his disposal which he could dispose of as he pleased. These included the majority of judicial posts; all military offices; and a variety of miscellaneous posts.[6]

Finally, there was the militia in which all fit males from fifteen to sixty years of age were required to participate. In the early years of the island, when, as one historian puts it, 'Jamaica regarded itself as a floating cruiser in a Spanish sea,'[7] the constant fear of attack

---

[1] Long, *History of Jamaica*, Vol. I, p. 49.
[2] *Ibid.* Vol. I. p. 89.
[3] Spurdle, *op. cit.*, pp. 200–202; Long, Vol. I. p. 80.
[4] Spurdle, p. 203.   [5] Metcalf, *op. cit.* p. 235.
[6] *Ibid.*, p. 208–9   [7] Thornton, *op. cit.*, p. 251.

by either the French or Spaniards resulted in a very efficient militia. But this efficiency fell off during the eighteenth century, for which Long gave three reasons. First, the introduction of regular troops in the island, which encouraged a false sense of security among the white population and led to a decline in militia attendance and discipline. Secondly, 'the absence of many gentlemen of fortune, who choose to reside in Great Britain, and whose personal influence might tend much to revive and support martial spirit among the inhabitants'. And thirdly, the 'indiscreet commissioning of un-qualified and mean persons to be officers.'[1] An even greater evil were the 'reformed officers' – commissioned officers who had re-signed, but who, through an act of the Assembly, could not be forced to serve in an inferior position in any regiment should their services be needed again. Thus there was a large body of qualified and relatively able soldiers who were not expected to perform militia duties.

SECTION 3
THE WHITE SOCIETY DURING SLAVERY

The basic and dominating element in Jamaican slave society was that of absenteeism. This element was central to the whole social order and was in some way related to almost every other aspect of the society. So central was it indeed, and so much was it the root of all the evils of the system, that we may describe the white Jamaican community as an absentee society. A rigorous distinction must be drawn between structural causes and consequences of absenteeism and its historical causes, the reason being that once absenteeism had fully emerged it consolidated itself, and its own evil effects were the very causes of its continuation.

The origins of absenteeism in Jamaica are best understood in terms of a comparison with another colonial society, also based on slavery, in which it did not exist. Pitman has pointed out that one significant difference between the founding of the American colonies and the West Indies was the fact that the original settlers of the former were religiously motivated while in the latter the religious motive was almost insignificant. He points out also, that religion had the effect of turning migration into an 'exodus', breaking all

[1] Long, Vol. I. p. 123.

ties with the mother country.[1] The extremely materialistic basis of Jamaica's foundation – a 'state enterprise', as Pares observes[2] – made it the direct opposite of the American situation.

Pitman further asserts that the differing social background of the early founders of New England and the West Indies – the former being largely of the non-conformist, radical sector of British society, and the latter mainly of the gentry and upper-middle class – resulted in the early upsurge of republicanism in America and its absence in the West Indies.[3] The data, however, do not lend support to this assertion in the case of Jamaica. First, there is no reason to believe that the influential early settlers of the island were of the English gentry, and secondly, as in the case of America, strong republican feelings were in evidence during the early period of Jamaica's development. The first point we shall examine in more detail later; as to the second, we only have to refer back to the earlier discussion on the constitutional struggles of the island to see that strong republican sentiments were in evidence among the early residents of the island. By 1700 local patriotism was so pronounced among the early settlers, and their children who became known as the 'creole party', that on several occasions they attempted to exclude English-born persons from filling posts in the island and even went as far as declaring that they 'will not allow themselves to be called Englishmen'.[4]

Why did this early local patriotism fail to develop? What became of these early, independent, strong-willed settlers? It is in answering this question that we come to the heart of the matter and establish the central reason for absenteeism in the island. The answer is to be found in the new economic system which emerged in Jamaica after the beginning of the eighteenth century. This change we have already discussed.

Those few Jamaicans of the early period who were of the British upper-middle class were the first to return home, having restored their fortunes. As the century progressed the early settlers who had monopolized most of the land and had made their fortunes began sending their children to England to be educated and few of them

---

[1] Pitman, *op. cit.*, pp. 1–2.
[2] Pares, 'Merchants and Planters', *Econ. History Review Supplement*, 4.
[3] Pitman, *op. cit.*, p. 2.
[4] C.S.P. 1706–1708 Nos. 616 and 1423.

returned. By the middle of the eighteenth century 300 children a year were leaving Jamaica for England.[1] The system of primogeniture also led to an increase in absenteeism. Younger children were often provided for by annuities charged against the estate. These children never had any first hand connection with the source of their income and cared even less about it. When, as so often happened, a younger brother inherited from his deceased elder kin, the estate came to be owned by someone who had never seen his property and had little intention of doing so.[2]

We derive a very good estimate of the extent of absenteeism and the degree to which inheritance worsened the situation, by analysing an abstract of wills relating to Jamaican estates between 1625 and 1792.[3] Of the 307 wills actually abstracted (312 are listed but five are missing) 142 of the testators were resident in England at the time they made their wills, while only 133 were resident in Jamaica. Interestingly, fifty two of the 142 English-based testators were residing in London, while the second largest group from a single area came from Bristol. Fourteen of the testators made their wills just before going to Jamaica: one of these claimed that he was formerly of Jamaica and now residing in England but 'shortly bound back' for Jamaica. Another, George Osborne, is a little more revealing. He too was formerly of Jamaica and had been residing in England but he was now (1711) 'intending speedily on a voyage to Jamaica to take care of his estate there'.[4] Quite possibly he had experienced the disastrous consequences of having his estate supervised by an incompetent overseer. Several of the testators in England claimed that they were 'bound for Jamaica, there to reside sometime'. Of those residing in England, thirty claimed that they were 'formerly of Jamaica' but 'now residing in England'. Between 1625 and 1750 there were twenty one such testators. In the last forty two years of the period of the wills there was a rapid proportional increase, nineteen of the testators 'formerly of Jamaica' now residing in England. On the other hand, only four persons were residing in Jamaica who were formerly of England before 1750 and only one such after 1750. This certainly indicates the large

---

[1] Ragatz, *Absentee Landlordism in the British Caribbean 1750–1833*, p. 4.
[2] *Ibid.*
[3] Abstract of Wills Relating to Jamaica, 1625–1792. Add. MS. 34181.
[4] *Ibid.*

numbers who left Jamaica for England in relation to the few who made the opposite voyage.

It seems as if almost all widows of Jamaican husbands left for England soon after their husband's death. All seven of the testators who were widows and residing in England at the time of making their wills claimed that they were 'formerly of Jamaica' during the lifetime of their spouse. Of the rest of the wills, one testator was 'bound shortly for England' from Jamaica; two were resident in Ireland; one in France; five were either in the Army or Navy and the residence of nine was not made clear by the abstracts.[1]

Even more revealing are the contents of these wills. The Jamaican estates went, in almost every case, to relatives in England. One can easily imagine that these inheritors, having no intimate link with the island and perhaps unwilling to give up their particular course of life, would gladly settle for an attorney in the island to supervise his or her estate, thus adding to the number of absentee owners.

Before we go on to discuss the consequences of absenteeism some further estimate of its magnitude must be given. Unfortunately, while many writers remarked on the subject, few gave any figures concerning it. Among the few is Edward Long who categorized the white population of the island in 1774 as follows:[2]

Given number of settled and resident white inhabitants at medium	17,000
Transients or unskilled whites	500
Soldiers and Seamen resident; at an average, about	3,000
Annuitants and Proprietors Non-Resident	2,000
	22,500

Long had earlier estimated the proportion of white servants or non-proprietors at one-third of the total white population. Approximately 11,334 of the resident white population, therefore, would be proprietors while approximately 5,666 of them would be non-proprietors. Thus, approximately one-sixth of the Jamaican proprietors in 1774 were absentee. The full import of this figure is

[1] *Ibid.*
[2] E. Long, Vol. I, Bk. 2, Ch. 2.

not appreciated, however, until it is understood that this one-sixth of the proprietors owned most of the property and slaves in the island.

The extent of this monopolization by the wealthiest group can be examined by a brief survey of the available data concerning ownership of slaves. From the Vestry Minutes of St. Catherine relating to the period between 1799 and 1807 we gather that in 1804 there were 6,791 slaves in the parish owned by 382 masters. An analysis of the frequency distribution of the slaves among the masters' population reveals, however, that ownership was skewed heavily in favour of a few wealthy masters at the upper end of the curve. Thus, the number of masters owning between one and nineteen slaves were 252; the number owning between twenty and thirty nine slaves was 67; between forty and fifty nine slaves, twenty three owners; and between sixty and seventy nine slaves there were twelve owners. At the other end of the frequency distribution we find that six masters or approximately 1.7 per cent of the entire master population owned over one-sixth of all the slaves and the majority of the slaves (3,870) were owned by approximately 8 per cent of the masters. And this, despite the fact that St Catherine, containing the relatively large town of St Jago de la Vega, was weighted heavily on the side of the small proprietors.[1] An examination of the *Jamaica Almanacks* revealed that throughout the last quarter of the eighteenth and early nineteenth centuries less than 5 per cent of wealthiest proprietors owned the great majority of the property and the slaves in each parish.[2]

By the nineteenth century, when the plantation system began to collapse, a large number of indebted estates were foreclosed upon by English creditors who had no interest whatever in residing in the island. An observer, writing 16 years after the abolition of slavery, claimed that the foreclosure of mortgages led to an even greater number of absentee owners, so that nine-tenths of all the land under cultivation in the island before emancipation was owned by absentees.[3]

---

[1] St. Catherine Vestry Minutes, MSS., Records Office, Jamaica.

[2] See the *Jamaica Almanacks*, 1751–1833; see also, Slave Compensation Claims, Jamaica in BPP. XLVIII (215).

[3] J. Bigledow, *Jamaica in 1850: or the effects of 16 years of freedom on a Slave Colony*, p. 79.

It is reasonable to conclude therefore, that since about the middle of the eighteenth century, while the majority of land and slave owners may have been resident, the distribution of the slaves and other property of the island was skewed so heavily in favour of a few wealthy proprietors, most of whom resided in England, that most of the slaves and property can be said to have been owned by absentee landlords.

Let us now consider the consequences of absenteeism for Jamaica. Its most striking effect was the fact that the island was drained of the very people it needed for leadership in all aspects of life. From the beginning to the very end of slavery, the governors of the island frequently wrote to Whitehall complaining that they were unable to find suitable men to fill the council and other important offices. In 1696, for example, Lieutenant Governor Beeston was so short of qualified men that one of the Councillors, who had been expelled from his position because of treasonable association with the French, had to be reinstated, the Governor explaining to the Lords that 'there are not men enough of parts and integrity left in the country to discharge those greater trusts'.[1] Often Beeston could not even get the required quorum of seven members, since the incompetent few who were necessary to make up the quorum often chose deliberately to hold up the processes of government by refusing to answer their summonses.

One hundred and thirty-eight years later, during the apprenticeship period, the Marquis of Sligo, who was then Governor, wrote of the Council that they were:

> a sad set indeed with some exceptions. Several have been put in merely for the protection of their persons being overwhelmed with debt . . . would that I could find an opportunity of getting rid of them . . . Their poverty and inefficiency is a matter of public notoriety, they have no influence, they enjoy no respect, and reduce the character of the body to such a degree that it is hardly considered of the legislature at all.[2]

We have already quoted Long's remarks to the effect that the inefficiency of the Militia was due to the absence of the most capable

[1] C.O. 138/9.
[2] The Sligo Papers: Private Letters of a Governor of Jamaica, MSS. Institute of Jamaica.

proprietors of the island. The Rector of Kingston, in a letter to the Bishop of London, claimed that there were not six families which could be 'described as gentlemen on the whole island', 'they have no maxims of Church or State but what are absolutely anarchical'. The acting governor himself was formerly apprenticed to a shop-keeper. One of the leading planters, Peter Beckford, started off life with three slaves, as hunter and horse-catcher. So did the father of another important planter, Colonel Sale. Nepotism was rife, relations of influential planters, 'let them be never so worthless, are put into all the honourable and profitable posts'.[1]

Absenteeism was also the cause of the gross lack of proper educa-tion in the island. The leaders of the white community viewed the matter of establishing schools with utter contempt. Leslie wrote of the island in the 1720s that 'learning is here at the lowest Ebb'. Although several large donations had been made toward the building of schools, few of them found fruition. The occupation of teacher was 'looked upon as contemptible, and no Gentleman keeps com-pany with one of that character'. A few wealthy planters sent their children to be educated in England, but the majority remained semi-literate and were 'the common butt of every conversation'.[2] This lack of education and the complacency of the leading planters in regard to it, was, in turn, one of the main factors intensifying absenteeism, Long observing in 1774 that 'this lack of educational facilities in the island was one of the principal impediments to its effectual settlement'[3]. Most of the children of the wealthy planters sent to England to be educated never returned. The few who did lived to regret it dearly. Most revealing is a letter written by the daughter of a wealthy resident planter not long after her return from England, where she had attained an 'accomplished' education. To the *Jamaica Magazine* she wrote that 'the infinite causes of disgust and vexation' she now experienced in her 'living death' could 'fill a volume'. She wrote further:

> Need I tell you how many dull and cheerless moments I am doomed to lead in the absence of those dear amusements which have so enchanted me on the other side of the Atlantic; the houses,

---

[1] William May, *Jamaica: Description of the Principal Persons there about 1720, Sir Nicholas Lawes, Governor*; Caribbeana, Vol. 3.
[2] C. Leslie, *A New History of Jamaica*, p. 36.
[3] Long, *History of Jamaica*, Vol. 2, p. 246.

servants and society, the dull routine of life, all disappointed and vexed me.[1]

She complained also that at the balls she attended she was neglected by the few tolerable men available because of her superior education and 'dignified air'. Eventually she married a wealthy planter whom she soon came to despise, finding him 'barbarous' and 'dictatorial', the life of retirement, confinement and drudgery he obliged her to live being 'more intolerable than that of one of his slaves'.[2]

The absence of the most educated and civilized members of the society also led to a complete breakdown of religion and morality among the resident whites since the local leaders were among the most profligate people imaginable. What was worse, the clergymen themselves were often among the most immoral in the island and the established Anglican church in Jamaica represents, perhaps, the most disgraceful episode in the history of that institution. In 1671 Lynch wrote that 'the condition of the Church be so low and the Number of the Ministers here so few that they are not worth taking notice of'.[3] Less than two decades later Francis Crow found the island full of 'sin'.[4] About the same time that William May was writing home to the Bishop of London concerning the incompetence and immorality of the leading inhabitants, Leslie felt obliged to give 'a dismal account' of the 'Church Affairs of the Island'. He found the Clergy 'of a character so vile' as to be unmentionable and concluded that 'they are generally the most finished of our Debauchers'.[5] Despite his strongly pro-Jamaican sentiments, Long had to admit that 'the cloth has suffered disgrace and contempt from the actions of a few'.[6] Other writers were even less generous. An article in the *Jamaica Magazine* of July, 1813 commented on the lamentable state of religion in the island, the greater part of the blame being placed on the clergymen who were described as 'selfish and mercenary' and condemned their 'cold indifference' to the moral state of the island.[7] It was well known that unsuccessful overseers with the right contacts could procure a living as a clergyman. The Reverend

---

[1] The *Jamaica Magazine*, Vol. 4; 1813. Letter signed 'Mellisa'.
[2] *Ibid.*
[3] Add. MSS. 11410, 'Papers relating to the W.I. 1654–1662'.
[4] The Ja. Hist. Review, Vol. 3, No 2, p.53.
[5] Leslie, *op. cit.*, 1740, p. 303.
[6] Long, *op. cit.*, Vol. 2, p. 283.
[7] The *Jamaica Magazine*, Vol. 3 July 1813.

David King observed that 'Holy orders were readily given to men who were imperfectly educated and of indifferent moral character'.[1] and another minister, himself the son of a Jamaican planter, bemoaned the fact that 'the clerical office in Jamaica was a sort of dernier resort to men who had not succeeded in other professions'.[2]

A very interesting explanation of the laxity in morals, which supports our view that absenteeism was central to most of the evils of the society, is given by Thomas Jelly who makes the important observation that the white population had a high mortality rate leading to a high turnover, most of the new recruits coming from Britain. This, he asserts, was 'productive of many evils'. First, men seeking a quick fortune could hardly be expected to concern themselves very much with the moral state of a society to which they felt little commitment; and secondly, 'the continued influx of strangers' tended 'to prevent anything like settled habits of morality or order.'[3]

This lack of religion and moral sanctions was partly responsible for a fourth characteristic of the Jamaican white community: the almost complete breakdown of the institutions of marriage and the family. This breakdown was also in part the result of the fact that there were so few women available. One of the most striking features of Jamaican slave society was 'the almost total absence of female society'.[4] The few available white women were usually the daughters of the small élite of wealthy resident planters and were accessible only to other members of the creole élite:[5] One can easily sympathize with the disillusionment of a young Scottish book-keeper who complained bitterly of his 'forlorn situation' in which he was 'utterly debarred from the society of the decent and the virtues of the other sex'.[6] Not that the few available white women were all that desirable. As we have already noted, few of the educated women returned. Those who were not educated in England usually received a poor private education by tutors specially hired for the purpose.[7] The general picture one gathers of these women is, as Stewart expressed it, that they had 'much of the quashee', an implication

---

[1] D. King, *The State and Prospects of Jamaica, 1850*, p. 79.
[2] J. Riland, *Memoirs of a West Indian Planter*, 1827. p. 106.
[3] Thomas Jelly, *Remarks on the Condition of the Whites and Free Coloured Inhabitants of Jamaica*, 1826, p. 8.
[4] *Ibid.*, p. 10.   [5] *Ibid.*, p. 11.
[6] Letter to the *Jamaica Magazine*, July 1812, sgn. Venis.
[7] See Stewart, *An Account of Jamaica*, 1808, pp. 165–171.

that they were little more enlightened than their slaves. Lady Nugent frequently had cause to bemoan their imbecility, entering on one occasion in her Journal that 'Mrs C is a perfect Creole, says little, and drawls out that little, and has not an idea beyond her pen'.[1]

But the scarcity of white women was only one of many reasons accounting for the lack of marriage and the family. On most estates in the island marriage was forbidden to the white employees, few attorneys being disposed to employ a man with such an encumbrance.[2] While marriage was proscribed, promiscuity with black or coloured women was positively sanctioned. Henry Coor, a millwright and slave owner in the island between 1759 and 1774 said that, 'It was the greatest disgrace for a white man not to cohabit with some woman or other'.[3]

The sexual exploitation of female slaves by white men was the most disgraceful and iniquitous aspect of Jamaican slave society. Rape and the seduction of infant slaves; the ravishing of the common law wives of the male slaves under threat of punishment, and outright sadism often involving the most heinous forms of sexual torture[4] were the order of the day. It was common practice for a white man visiting a plantation to be offered a slave girl for the night.[5] Moreton tells us that many of the white employees on the estate had a rotation system whereby they seduced every desirable female on the plantation over and over again. He also informs us of the practice of many of the attorneys who made a grand annual tour of the estates under their supervision with a large retinue of friends remaining at each estate for a number of days during which there were indescribable scenes of debauchery, the female slaves being primed in advance of their coming.[6]

Recreational facilities were also limited. Racing, gambling, dancing, gossiping, drinking and visitations – often elaborate affairs including the entire household, slaves, pets and all – lasting weeks, sometimes months, were the usual.[7] Occasionally, foreign theatrical

[1] Cundall, *The Journal of Lady Nugent*, p. 72.
[2] B. Mahon, *Jamaica Plantership*. See also, pp. 173, 216
[3] Evidence of Henry Coor, Select Committee on Slave Trade 1790–91.
[4] For a particularly lurid description of such sadistic practices see the evidence of Hercules Ross, 1790–91.
[5] Evidence of C. H. Williams, Report from the Select Committee on the Extinction of Slavery. BPP XX, 1831–32.
[6] Moreton, *Manners and Customs* . . ., pp. 77–78.
[7] See Stewart, Account, pp. 175–184.

groups visited the island. During the early nineteenth century several members of the Jewish community formed an amateur theatrical company whose performance Monk Lewis found not unpleasant. Theatrical efforts, however, whether foreign or local, were often financial failures. The entries for August 6th and 9th, 1788 of the *Jamaica Gazette*, are very revealing in this respect. On August 6th there was a performance of an opera, *Inkle and Yarico* which the reporter claimed was poorly attended. The next week, however, a ball was held in the very same theatre which was packed to capacity – 'upwards of 120' ladies being there and a much larger number of 'gentlemen'. The description of this ball was typical of the vulgar display of wealth and gaudy ostentation which characterized the wealthier section of the society.[1]

But perhaps the most disastrous consequences of absenteeism were to be found in the gross mismanagement of the economic affairs of the island.[2] As early as 1707 the friend of an absentee owner wrote to him describing the hopeless mismanagement of his estates where 'all things' were 'in disorder, the whole works a pot of nastiness and in general out of repair'.[3] In 1774 Long explained how it was impossible for one attorney to properly supervise the many absentee-owned estates for which he acted as agent. The result was that the management of the estate was left almost entirely to the overseers who, being paid on a commission basis, forced the slaves to work far beyond their strength and generally depleted the capital of the estate in order to procure high annual returns.[4] When Mahon wrote his account during the last decades of slavery, conditions had not changed except for the worse. He speaks of the 'wanton destruction of the property of absentee proprietors . . . which had been but too common at all other periods amongst agents and overseers'. He described the neglect of capital equipment in the wasteful drive to increase output:

No attention is paid to fences, to the clearing of pasture lands, or to the repairs of the buildings. Large cane fields are planted without manure; weeds are seen luxuriating in the midst of the

---

[1] 'The *Jamaica Gazette*', No. 64 & 65, 1788.
[2] The same was true of absentee estates in the U.S. See Phillips, *American Negro Slavery*, pp. 250–51.
[3] H. M. Howard, *The Longs of Jamaica and Hampton Lodge*, Vol. 1, p. 46.
[4] Long, *op. cit.*, Vol. 2, p. 406. Cf. Phillips, *op. cit.*, pp. 279–283.

canes as they grow up and all classes, old and young, are out at work, under the scourge of the lash, from four in the morning until after dark at night.[1]

At this rate, we are further informed, in eight years the entire capital outlay of the estate is depleted. Bigledow also noted that absenteeism 'by which the island is cursed' meant that most of the returns to the estates went abroad resulting in almost no re-investment and a drain on the island's foreign exchange which was disastrous for an economy so heavily dependent on foreign supplies.[2]

But the people who suffered most from the neglect and inefficient management due to absenteeism were, of course, the slaves – whether we view them from the point of view of capital equipment or as suffering human beings. Captain Thomas Wilson said that 'It was generally understood where Planters resided themselves, their Slaves were better taken care of than under the direction of Overseers'.[3] Another witness, Dr Jackson, who was in Jamaica between 1774 and 1778 said much the same. And Henry Coor further informed the Select Committee that:

> It was more the object of the overseers to work the Slaves out, and trust for supplies from Africa; because I have heard many of the overseers say, 'I have made my employer 20, 30 or 40 more hogsheads per year than any of my predecessors ever did; and though I have killed 30 or 40 Negroes per year more, yet the produce had been more than adequate to that loss.'[4]

Nor could the slave, as Coor further remarked, expect any relief from the attorney since the latter, too, had a vested interest in exploiting the assets of the owner to its fullest, being paid on a commission basis. Several of the governors of the island attributed the frequent slave revolts of the island to the ill-use resulting from absenteeism[5] and the Jamaican Assembly in an address to the Crown in 1750, expressed much the same view.[6]

We shall conclude our discussion on the social structure of the

[1] Mahon, *op. cit.* pp. 143–144.   [2] Bigledow, *op. cit.*, p. 82.
[3] Minutes of Evidence ... 1790–91.
[4] *Ibid.*
[5] See for example, Governor Hamilton to the Board of Trade, 1715: C.O. 137/11.
[6] C.O. 137/25; 1750.

white community by an examination of the regional and social origins of its members and the stratificatory system which existed during the slave period. As we have seen, the early settlers of the island came mainly from Barbados and other parts of the Eastern Caribbean. Father Williams has argued that most of these Barbadians came originally from Ireland, but his grounds for such assertions are rather weak.[1] There is more plausibility in the view that the admittedly large Irish sector of the white population during the 18th century came directly from Ireland, and not via Barbados, as Williams tried to argue.

One clue to the regional origins of the white population during the seventeenth century is to be found in the names of persons whose wills were registered in Jamaica previous to 1700.[2] Of the 1,862 names listed, eighty-nine were characteristically Welsh (e.g., Peter Pugh, Philip Pendry, Evance Rice and Henry Morgan[3]), eighteen Irish, seventeen Scottish and the remaining 1,738 English.

The danger of too much reliance on this kind of data should be obvious. Yet they are not contradicted by other relevant data. In 1675, Cranefield observed that during the past three to four years no immigrant came from Scotland, about 500 from Ireland and between 1,200 and 1,400 from England.[4] This situation had changed very much by 1729. In that year Governor Hunter wrote to the Council of Trade that the greater part of the militia and, as such, of the white population were 'native Irish'.[5] By this time, too, many Scotsmen were being introduced into the island so that by the 1760s, Long was able to write that they made up as much as a third of the entire white population.[6] In 1788 an observer remarked that 'of the Europeans the Scots are most numerous'.[7] The same writer also tells us that most of the English minority came from London, Plymouth, Bristol, Liverpool and Lancaster.[8] It is noticeable that the free coloured and many of the creole slaves who consciously sought to

---

[1] J. J. Williams *From Whence the Black Irish of Jamaica?* 1932.
[2] Add. MSS. 21, 931.
[3] The famous Buccaneer who is known to have been of Welsh extraction, see E. A. Cruickshank, *The Life of Sir Henry Morgan*, Ch. 1.
[4] Cranefield, *Observations on the Present State of Jamaica*, C.O. 138/2.
[5] Hunter to the Board of Trade, 1729: C.S.P. 1728–1729, No. 895.
[6] Long, *op. cit.*, Vol. 2, pp. 86–87.
[7] Marsden, *An Account of the Island of Jamaica*, (1788), p. 7.
[8] *Ibid.*

assimilate the culture of the whites tended to imbibe Scottish customs, especially in the area of recreation.[1]

We must now examine the social stratification of the white society. During the seventeenth century there were only two classes, Masters and Servants. The Masters were made up largely of the 'old soldiers' who by various dubious means had monopolized most of the best land in the island. It is the common view that the leading members of early Jamaican white society came from the gentry and upper-middle class sectors of English society. The data do not support such a conclusion. While it is true that a few of the founders of the colony came from among the officers of the conquering army – for example, John Ellis, who was an officer in Venables' army – and a few of the important immigrants coming in this early period were derived from the British gentry, for example, John Bathurst and Sir Thomas Modyford,[2] there is reason to believe that the majority of the master class during the seventeenth century came from among the conquering private soldiers and from immigrants of humble origins. We have already quoted John Styles on this subject. Styles' account of the officers of the conquering army who monopolized much of the land makes them out to be anything but of the British gentry, rather that they were generally illiterate and 'all trained up from boys in rebellion and murder'.[3] Francis Crow's opinion of the white population in 1678, 'even of the better sort' would also indicate lower class, or at the most petty-bourgeoise origins.[4] And we have already quoted William May's impression of the origins of the founders and leading members of the colony.

It was these men who employed the indentured servants and convicts sent out to the island during the seventeenth and first half of the eighteenth century.[5] Their treatment of this white lower class was almost as barbarous as their treatment of the Negro slaves, indeed worse, since their tyranny was only temporary. The laws concerning them were almost as severe as those relating to the slaves[6] and when their service was completed they had little en-

---

[1] See Chapter below on Recreation of Slaves.
[2] W. A. Feurtado, *Official and Other Personages of Jamaica, 1655–1790.*
[3] Letter of John Style to Secy. Morrice, C.S.P. 1669–74, No. 7.
[4] Letter of Francis Crow, *op. cit.*
[5] See A. E. Smith, *Colonists in Bondage,* pp. 101–102, 113, 360.
[6] See Act of 1673 'for the good governing of Servants', C.O. 139/3.

couragement to remain on the island. Beeston wrote in 1695 that:

> There is no encouragement given to white servants when their
> time is expired, for they have only 40s given to them for all their
> services and no other inducement to stay in the island . . . They
> are domineered over and used like dogs, and this in time will
> undoubtedly drive away all the commonality of the white people
> and leave the island in a deplorable condition . . .[1]

In the meantime 'many of the planters that are left are not only
grown free from debt since I came here but rich and have stocks of
money by them'.[2] By the end of the first decade of the eighteenth
century, as we have already noted, the wealthy ruling class of
planters had consolidated their position in the island and had 'little
intention of settling the same'.[3] By this time, however, the absentee
movement had begun and all the attempts at peopling the island
had failed miserably. Hamilton wrote of this failure, that it was due
to:

> A want of that publick spirit and due regard to future advantage
> and posterity, so necessary for the good of the whole, which in
> some measure I conceive may be attributed to the general inclina-
> tion of the inhabitants, natives as well as others, sooner or later
> to go home, as their fraise is, most people with that thought,
> their present interest is cheefly consider'd the better enable the
> prosecution of that design.[4]

The result of this scarcity of people in the white community was
a mitigation in the severity with which servants had been treated.
During the 1720s Leslie found that 'servants who behave well,
are respected and encouraged'. They had the same diet as their
masters, wore good clothes, were allowed a horse, and, on occasions,
were attended by a Negro boy. But those who were 'stupid and
roguish' were badly treated, often placed in the stock and beaten
severely and on the expiration of their indenture found it difficult
to be employed.[5]

[1] C.S.P. 1693–1696.
[2] Beeston to Blathwayt, C.S.P. 1696–97, No. 768.
[3] Hamilton to Board of Trade, C.S.P. 1714–15, No. 558. See also C.S.P.
1733, No. 463.
[4] Hamilton to Board of Trade, C.S.P. 1714–15, No. 588.
[5] Leslie, *op. cit.*, pp. 304–305.

The white population ten years after Leslie first published his 'Account' was calculated from the tax rolls by Governor Hunter at 7,148. Of these, 3,009 were white male servants and 948 female servants. The number of white children was given at 1,484.[1] This group of white employees, approximately half of the entire white population, was predominantly Irish and apparently there was no love lost between them and their English employers. In 1729, when there was the fear of a Spanish invasion, Governor Hunter wrote to Whitehall that:

> Our Militia consists cheefly of hir'd or indented servants and these for much the greatest part of the native Irish by their backwardnesse, mutinys and desertion damp'd or rather destroyed the hopes I had of their assistance in the defence of the country.[2]

The next year a fine of £50 was imposed on Captains importing Irishmen, who were not Protestants, to the island.[3] In 1737 the white population was estimated at 8,000 and among them 'not above 1,000 are masters of families or have any property'.[4]

By the 1760s the society had been finally moulded and the class structure Long described remained unchanged for the rest of the period of slavery. The original Scottish and Irish servants, and their descendants were already dominating the senior positions of the community, more and more so as the wealthy English planters left the island to become absentee owners. Thus by this time Jamaica had a dual élite system: one, an absentee élite, predominantly English, who lived in splendour in England and who formed there a part of the powerful West India interest; and the other a resident plantocratic élite which was predominantly Celtic in origin.

Among the local plantocracy were the few wealthy resident planters, the wealthy attorneys, some of whom supervised as many as forty estates, and the holders of high office, both civil and military. This élite was partly centred on the Governor[5] but there was always a strong anti-English faction among the creole white élite, especially

---

[1] C.S.P. 1730, No. 112 & 627; i.
[2] Hunter to Board of Trade, C.S.P. 1728–29, No. 1055.
[3] C.S.P. 1730, Nos, 317, 501.
[4] Trelawney to Newcastle, C.S.P. 1737, No. 379; i.
[5] See *The Journal of Lady Nugent*, ed. Cundall.

during the first two decades of the eighteenth century.[1] A nineteenth century writer informs us that there were two sections in the white élite known as 'the King's House Party' and the 'Country party'. The former consisted mainly of the Governor and the senior administrators; the latter, mainly of the wealthy creole proprietors.[2] The latter often criticized the former for their exorbitant fees and salaries; and during the amelioration period they attacked the King's house party for their supposed pro-emancipation leanings. On occasions, however, there was intense rivalry between the Governor and other senior members of the 'expatriate élite' such as the admiral.[3]

Next, there was a middle class group made up of merchants, professionals, middle sized farmers – mainly producing such crops as coffee and indigo – the more prosperous 'jobbers' or owners of slave-gangs, clerks who worked in the towns and the owners of other 'middle-sized property'. Finally, there was the stratum made up of the overseers, book-keepers and other white servants; the lower ranks of soldiers – and there were always at least two regiments in the island throughout most of the eighteenth century – sailors, and other transient whites. At the top of this group were the overseers, the more successful of whom could expect an attorneyship in due course. This was the group which had the most direct contact with the slaves and, as we have already seen, was most given to their gross ill-treatment.

Not all of the white lower class, however, held supervisory positions over the slaves and the contact between these two groups was not always that of super-ordination and sub-ordination. In the earlier days of indentured servants Leslie wrote of them that:

> The great thing which ruins most of these unfortunate Fellows, is the combining with the Negroes, who tell them many plausible stories, to engage them to betray their Trust.[4]

Long expressed much the same sentiments about many of these lower class whites. 'Many of these menial servants' he wrote, 'who

---

[1] See *The Groans of Jamaica, etc.* 1714. Anon.

[2] J. Bigleddw, *op. cit.*, pp. 45–52.

[3] See, for example, *A Letter from a Friend at Jamaica giving an Impartial Account of the Violent Proceedings of the Faction in that Island, 1746.*

[4] Leslie, *op. cit.*, p. 304.

are retained for the sake of saving a deficiency, are the very dregs of the three kingdoms'; further they caused disturbances on the plantations by seducing the 'wives' of the slaves and were held in contempt by the 'better sort' of slaves who 'heartily despise them'.[1] The relationship with sailors marked the only area in Jamaican slave society where there was any degree of equality between whites and blacks. Of this relationship Kelly wrote that 'sailors and Negroes are ever on the most amicable terms'; there was much 'mutual confidence and familiarity' between them and 'in the presence of the sailor, the Negro feels a man'.[2]

But class distinctions were not rigid among the local whites. Their character was most striking in its spirit of independence and 'a display of conscious equality throughout all ranks of life'.[3] Paradoxically, this character trait was largely produced by slavery itself, for as Edwards recognized, in such a system there are really only two classes: the masters and the slaves.[4] Allied to their spirit of independence and equality was an apparent openness and generosity which was more the reflection of a vulgar ostentation than of any genuine altruism, of which there was hardly any, as evinced by their refusal to subscribe to public facilities even when it was ultimately for their own good. This was itself indicative of what was perhaps their worst quality – a smug, senseless involvement purely with 'immediate interest', which is 'all most of them mind at present'.[5] It was this quality, itself the product of the fragmentary absentee society in which they were brought up or had to adjust to, which was primarily responsible for the pathetic lack of foresight in social, political and economic matters that we have discussed above. And it was Corbett, writing at the time of their greatest prosperity, who was perspicacious enough to identify this quality. Speaking of the refusal of the planters to protect themselves even in the face of a possible rebellion of the slaves, he wrote:

> To what, I say, can we attribute this, to indolence in some, and perhaps Stupidity in others; but in far the greatest Part 'tis owing to a narrow Selfishness, and total Unconcern for every Thing

[1] Long, *op. cit.*, Bk. 2, p. 289.
[2] James Kelly, *Voyage to Jamaica*, pp. 29–30. (1838)
[3] B. Edwards, *op. cit.*, Vol. 2, p. 7.
[4] *Ibid.*, p. 8.
[5] C. Corbett, *Essay Concerning Slavery.*

that doth not regard their immediate interest. Many see symptom of a country Approaching to its Ruin, but they fancy it may last their Time, and they may sell out and get home first, and what comes afterwards they care not. They dont desire any thing to be mended, oppose every Scheme, cannot bear to hear any propos'd which may cause examination into our real Condition, the Weakness of which being discovered might hurt the present Price of Estates; so all is well they cry, 'till they have sold and realized.[1]

Thus we are led back to what was central to the entire system: absenteeism.

CONCLUSION

Our analysis of what was central to the organization and functioning of Jamaican slave society has demonstrated the inherent contradictions of the system. Its completely materialistic basis – both in origins and structure – eventually consolidated into a largely monocrop economy in which the major produce, sugar, was grown and manufactured on large plantations, the ownership of which was concentrated in the hands of a few planters, most of whom were absent. Absenteeism, in turn, robbed the society of its most responsible and able members with disastrous consequences for the economy and for the society as a whole. Finally, by the last four decades of slavery, the system had become so incompetent and inefficient that when the artificially imposed protections of the mother country were removed it rapidly collapsed.

[1] Corbett, *op. cit.*

CHAPTER II

The Slave Plantation

ITS SOCIO-ECONOMIC STRUCTURE

HAVING taken a macro-sociological view of Jamaican slave society, we must now discuss the units of production on which this society was based. These were the plantations, and from the point of view of the slaves it is this unit which was of the greatest importance since it determined most of their activities. Our attention will be centred primarily on the sugar plantation, for the great majority of the slaves were to be found on them. Furthermore, we shall be examining this type of plantation at the time when it reached its peak of development, that is, the post-1739 period.

SECTION I
DESCRIPTION AND ESTIMATED COSTS OF THE PLANTATION WORKS

The Jamaican planters usually spoke of two types of estates – 'planting estates' and 'dry weather estates'. The planting estates were those situated in the mountains where the soil was usually rocky and suitable to what Mahon called 'the old mode of cultivation'. The canes had to be replanted often and returns were relatively poor. Dry weather estates were those on the plains bordering the coastline, were well suited to sugar cultivation, and gave relatively high returns.[1]

Edwards wrote of the sugar plantation that:

The business of sugar planting is a sort of adventure in which the man that engages, must engage deeply. There is no medium, and very seldom the possibility of retreat . . . it requires a capital of

Mahon, *op. cit.*, p. 247-250.

no less than thirty thousand pounds sterling to embark in this employment with a fair prospect of advantage.[1]

Of the estate lands, a third was usually allocated to the growing of canes, and in some cases, corn: another third was usually given over to pasturage and provision grounds: and the rest to woodland which was used both as a reserve in the event of expansion, and as a source of timber. We get an idea of the relationship between the size, number of Negroes and output of a sugar estate from the following table:

TABLE I : OUTPUT AND NUMBER OF NEGROES ON ELEVEN ESTATES[2]

Name of Estate	Acreage	No. of Negroes	Hogs. of Sugar	Puns. of Rum
Mesopotamia (flat)	2,600	310	315	230
Grange (hilly)	1,500	175	165	70
Glenelflay	1,800	230	110	80
Caladeonia	300	180	75	45
Bluecastle	1,800	245	240	140
Blackheath	1,100	110	180	80
Mounteagle	1,000	165	160	80
Spring Garden	2,600	250	165	90
Green River	1,000	240	240	115
Richmond Vale	700	220	155	80
Providence	1,000	106	110	75
Forest	2,000	180	—	—

To facilitate our description of the buildings on the estate we have enclosed a picture of Roehampton which, while it was one of the better constructed estates, nonetheless gives a reasonably good impression of the general layout of the buildings and their relationship to one another. The Proprietor's House or Great House as it was usually called, was the main residence of the whites. If the owner was resident and had a family he would occupy this building and provide other accommodation for the rest of the whites. The

[1] Edwards, *op. cit.*, Vol. 2, p. 290.
[2] Evidence of J. Wedderburn, *op. cit.*, 1790–1791.

architecture of these buildings had little merit. They were constructed of roughly cut stones and wood; the rooms were extremely
large, centred on an enormous hall and the furniture 'generally
plain but genteel'.[1]

The huts of the Negroes were either built in straight rows, as on
Roehampton, or in clusters.[2] Seen from afar, they sometimes appeared very picturesque, 'resembling' at that distance, 'so many villages
of bee-hives, thatched almost to the ground, and over-shadowed by
groves of tall cocoa-nut trees, whose tops, like branches of ostrich
feathers, appeared like umbrellas above them'.[3] But while pleasant
from afar, they turned out to be quite miserable hovels on closer
inspection.[4] The slave village was usually near a river or spring,[5]
thus facilitating the procurement of water. The huts were built on
the African pattern. In the words of one pro-slavery writer, 'The
groundwork of all Negro habitations in Jamaica was as in Sierra
Leone, the Negro huts of Africa . . .'[6] These huts, which had no
floors, were made of wattle and daub; were between fifteen and
twenty feet in length;[7] and from about fourteen feet wide;[8] the
roof was covered either with dried guinea grass or palmetto thatch
or the long-mountain thatch or, occasionally with cane tops.[9] Most
of these huts were divided into two rooms, although many remained
undivided and a few divided into as many as three rooms; the
number of rooms being usually an index of the prosperity and
status of the slaves.[10] On several estates the head Negroes had
separate and better quarters and sometimes their higher status was
indicated by the proximity of their huts to the overseer's residence.
On one estate, for example, the head driver and head cooper lived
only two hundred yards from the overseer while the rest of the
slaves lived a half a mile away.[11] The distance between each hut

[1] Stewart, *An Account of Jamaica*, 1807, pp. 14, 186.
[2] Beckford, *Account of Jamaica*, 1790, Vol. 2, p. 20.
[3] James Kelly, *op. cit.*, p. 12.
[4] Phillippo, *op. cit.*, (1843), p. 216.
[5] Edwards, *op. cit.*, Vol. 2, Bk. 5, Ch. 3.
[6] Anon, 'Notes in Defence . . .', *The Jamaica Journal*, Vol. 2, No. 1.
[7] Edwards, *op. cit.*, Bk. 5, Ch. 3.
[8] Barclay, *A Practical View of Slavery*, p. 313.
[9] *Ibid.*
[10] Evidence of Taylor: Report . . . on the Extinction of Slavery etc. 1831–32, BPP XX.
[11] *Report on the Trial of Fourteen Negroes*, 1824.

was usually no more than 24 feet.[1] Furnishing was very poor: 'a few wooden bowls and calabashes, a water-jug, a wooden mortar for pounding their Indian corn, and an iron pot for boiling the farrago of vegetable ingredients which composed their daily meal, composed almost all their furniture'.[2] Sometimes a crude bed was constructed out of a raised platform on which a mat made of plantain thrash was placed; but most slaves slept on the ground.

The mill (see 5) for grinding the cane so as to extract the juice was one of the most important pieces of equipment on the estate. The source of power could be water, cattle or wind. Water was the most efficient source but not always available and required a considerable capital outlay. Cattle was reliable and relatively cheap, and therefore the most commonly employed, but tended to be slow. Wind was cheap, and at times, could be very efficient, but was not always reliable. In 1768 there were 648 sugar estates on the island and of these 369 were equipped with cattle mills; 235 with water-mills and 44 with windmills.[3]

The boiling-house and curing (or cooling) house were situated near the mill (see 6). Large estates had up to seven coppers, decreasing in size after the first two which were called the 'St Hild's Coppers'. Each of the furnaces had a slave attending it. So did the coppers, the attendants constantly stirring the boiling liquid with long ladles. As soon as the syrup crystallized it was poured into wooden coolers and later taken to the hogsheads in the adjoining building, known as the cooling house. The process of 'potting' the sugar then took place, that is, the molasses was drained from the hogshead through plantain suckers stuck into them. The dunder or skimmings from the cane juice and the refuse from the first two coppers were then led to the still house as well as the molasses.[4] In the still house or distillery (see 7) the rum was made. The most prominent features of this building were '10 deep square cisterns of wood sunk in clay hard beat down where the ingredients for making the rum are put' and allowed to ferment for about ten days.[5]

The trash house was used for keeping the refuse from the mills

[1] Report on the Trial of Fourteen Negroes, 1824.

[2] Phillippo, *op. cit.*, p. 217.

[3] Ragatz, *Statistics for the Study of Br. Caribbean Econ. History, 1763–1833,* p. 5.

[4] Marsden, *An Account of the Island of Jamaica,* 1788, pp. 26–27.

[5] *Ibid.,* pp. 27–28.

and supplied the fuel (in addition to wood) that heated the boilers.
The cattle yard and pen were vital not only for keeping the cattle
but for supplying the necessary manure to the cane fields. Sometimes they were situated in one part of the estate; at other times they
were portable and moved from one part of the field to the next,
thus facilitating the manuring of the soil.

The so-called hospital was more appropriately called a 'hot-
house' by the Negroes. In addition to the room for sick Negroes,
it also contained a room for mothers during their period of confinement, another for slaves suffering solitary confinement, room for
the doctor and one or more storerooms where some goods belonging to the plantation were kept.[1] Other buildings usually
found on most large estates were: a mule stable with a corn loft
above it; sheds for the carts and waggons; and the shops of the
various tradesmen.

SECTION 2

THE PERSONNEL

(i) *The Whites* The law required that for the first ten Negroes on
any estate there should be two white persons and that for every ten
Negroes thereafter there should be one white man.[2] By the end of
the first half of the eighteenth century, however, this law was universally broken and the fines paid for breaking it came to be regarded more as a form of revenue than as punitive fines. Thus,
on the thirty-eight estates listed in St David's parish in 1794 there
were 2,685 Negroes and only 92 whites, or approximately one white
to every twenty-nine Negroes.[3] The nine estates listed which had
more than 100 Negroes had an average of five whites each on them.
Among these five whites would be an overseer, two or three book-
keepers and one or two skilled workmen.

The overseer was the manager of the estate in the absence of
the owner; he was responsible only to the attorney who acted as the
agent for the owner and had nothing to do with the running of the
estate. He supervised the white staff on the estate and gave the order

[1] Edwards, *op. cit.*, Vol. 2, p. 294.
[2] Acts of Jamaica, C.O. 139/3.
[3] From the St. David's Deficiency List, St. David's Vestry Minutes, 1784–
1793, Jamaica Archives.

for each day's quota of work. On most estates he took the daily roll-call of the slaves and visited the sick Negroes in the hot-house, mainly to ensure that they were not simply evading work. During the day he rode over the entire estate to keep a general eye on its operations, and, during crop, constantly checked on the quality of the sugar and rum being produced. He also supervised the running of the great house although his authority was, here, usually only formal.

Most estates had two book-keepers, whose occupation was anything but keeping books. Outside the crop season they alternated between supervising the Negroes in the field and keeping the keys for the stores. During crop they alternated between attending the boiling house and the still house, often resting only six hours in the day. They earned, on average, about £40 per annum.

(ii) *The Slaves: Their Social and Economic Divisions.* It was characteristic of slavery, as of all systems of total domination that almost all the criteria for social and economic divisions within the enslaved group were defined by the enslaving group. That is, social stratification and the division of labour among the slaves were functions of their socio-economic relation to the white group. It is our task to demonstrate this proposition. However, we have chosen to anticipate the outcome of our discussion in order to explain why social status among the slaves has to be considered in terms of their economic functions and not as part of their internal patterns of behaviour.

The common view concerning social divisions among the slaves held both by contemporary and modern historians is that the household slaves formed a kind of slave aristocracy opposed to the field Negroes who, it is claimed, envied the lot of the former. This viewpoint is both crude and erroneous. As Stevens pointed out:

> It has been the common lot of agricultural slaves to endure more labour than other bondsmen; it has, on the other hand, been their privilege, not only to be less exposed than domestics, to the personal caprice and ill-temper of a master, but to have a far greater stability of situation, and a surer possession of their families and of the property they have been permitted to acquire.[1]

Henry Coor said that, 'I have heard many of them say that they

[1] Stevens, J. *The State Called Slavery . . .*, Vol. 1, Ch. 3. Sec. 9.

would rather continue under the hardship of the field, than be what is there called a House Negro'.[1] White women in the slave colonies tended to be more sadistic than their male counterparts and where their authority reigned in the household the slaves were constantly at their mercy. Davidson recalled seeing domestics doing needlework in front of their mistresses with thumb screws on their left thumb.[2] Beckford found that the slaves regarded domestic service as being more honourable and the field as more independent and 'never knew a negro who would not willingly forego the comforts of the house (which service a constant attendance) to be sure of the hours of accustomed leisure'.[3]

A more fruitful distinction among the slaves would be, first, a threefold vertical division between domestics, skilled workers, and field Negroes; and secondly, a horizontal division within each of these groups. To begin with the domestics, the number of these slaves was notoriously high in Jamaica, Corbett referring during the mid-eighteenth century, to those whites who kept twenty to thirty domestics 'to do what may well be done by 5 or 6'.[4] A few years later Long complained of 'too numerous a tribe of domestic servants' stating further that 'from twenty to forty servants is nothing unusual'. He gave the following example of a resident planter's household:

> 1 Butler; 1 Coachman; 1 postilion; 1 helper; 1 cook; 1 assistant cook; 2 footmen or waiting-men; 1 key or store-keeper; 1 waiting-maid; 3 house-cleaners; 3 washer-women; 4 seamstresses.
> In addition, if there were any white children, each child had a nurse and each nurse her assistant boy or girl.[5]

Where the owner was non-resident and the overseer was in charge of the great house, his coloured mistress managed its affairs. Indeed, the words 'mistress' and 'housekeeper' became synonymous in Jamaican slave society. From all accounts, these coloured housekeepers were extremely efficient. The one on Lewis' estate was 'perpetually in the hospital, nurses the children, can bleed, and

[1] Evidence of Henry Coor, 1790–91.
[2] See Davidson's evidence, 1790–91.
[3] Beckford, *Situation of the Negroes . . .*, p. 13.
[4] Corbett, *op. cit.*
[5] Long, Vol. 2, p. 282.

mix up medicines, and (as I am assured) she is of more service to the sick than all the doctors'.[1]

Almost all the coloured slaves (i.e. slaves of mixed negro and white ancestry) on the plantation were recruited to the household staff. Many of the women, of course, were expected to perform both sexual, as well as domestic functions. On Orange Valley estate in 1824 there were fifteen brown females who were 'exempted from field labour'.[2]

Among the skilled slaves are to be included the boilermen, carpenters, smiths, coopers, masons and doctors and nurses. If the estate was very large and there were many of these people, there would be a head smith, a head boilerman, and the like. Since many of the skilled slaves – such as the boilermen and coopers – would be somewhat redundant out of crop, they were usually employed in assisting other tradesmen whose labour was less seasonal. Thus, on Friday, the 10th of January, 1823, we find the coopers on Green Park estate assisting the masons in building a wall in one of the pens, but by Saturday, 15th March, they were back to their normal duties, 'raising the hogsheads'.[3]

On very large estates there were usually four gangs each with its own driver and cooks. The great gang consisted of the strongest men and women among the slaves. Where there were four gangs, the distinction between the first and the second gang seemed to have been more for supervisory and administrative purposes than for any other. On Green Park estate, for example, both during and out of crop we find the great and second gangs employed in the very same tasks. The great gang, however, was usually much larger than the second gang – and they usually worked harder than any other. The third gang of the four-gang system (or the second gang of the three-gang system) consisted of slaves who were weakly or elderly or pregnant. The hogmeat gang consisted of young children between the ages of four or five and nine or ten. They were employed in minor tasks such as collecting food for the hogs, weeding, and the like.

The following set of data will best illustrate these vertical divisions among the slaves. On Orange River estate in 1823 there were:

[1] Lewis, *op. cit.*, p. 170.
[2] *The Jamaica Journal*, Vol. 1, No. 46.
[3] Green Park Estate Journal, MS. Jamaica Archives.

11 Carpenters	5 Drivers	Also:
7 Coopers	1st gang — 105	2 Doctors
5 Masons	2nd ,, — 47	1 Doctress
3 Blacksmiths	3rd ,, — 20	2 Midwives
25 Tradesmen	4th ,, — 15	22 Watchmen

Women having 6 children or more exempted from all labour	— 11
Invalids and old people not at work	— 33
Young children under 7 not employed	— 77
Nurses attending on these last 2 classes	— 18
Several brown females on property exempted from field labour	— 15

Total 421.[1]

Even more informative is the following extract from the Green Park estate journal, 1823:[2]

GREEN PARK: MONDAY 6 – FRIDAY 10 JANUARY, 1823

	M	T	W	T	F
Great Gang, drivers and cooks	90	75	82	87	83
Second Gang ,, ,, ,,	25	40	42	40	40
Third Gang ,, ,, ,,	20	20	28	29	30
Hogmeat Gang ,, ,, ,,	20	20	20	20	20
In the Hospital	27	29	29	29	29
Cartmen and Boys	2	2	2	2	2
Loaders	1	1	1	1	1
Mulemen	3	3	3	3	3
Lopper	1	1	1	1	2
Stock-keepers	14	14	14	14	14
Grass Cutters	14	17	18	18	25
Fishermen	2	2	1	1	1
Watchmen	27	30	30	30	30
Washerwomen	4	4	4	4	4
Pregnant	6	5	5	5	5
Laying in	3	4	4	4	4
Invalids	42	42	42	42	42
Young Children	88	89	89	89	89

[1] *The Jamaica Journal*, Vol. 1, No. 46.
[2] The Green Park Estate Journal, *op. cit.*

GREEN PARK—*contd*

	M	T	W	T	F
Indulged, having 6 children	4	4	4	4	4
Nursing	7	7	7	7	7
Variously employed	32	32	28	25	24
Taking Day	15	15	10	8	2
Hired out	2	2	2	2	2
Yaws	4	4	4	4	4
Great House Domestics	8	8	8	8	8
Overseers Domestics and Barracks	9	9	9	9	9
Carpenters and Cook	15	15	15	15	15
Masons and Cook	9	9	9	9	9
Blacksmiths and Cook	6	6	6	6	6

Several comments may be made on the above figures. First, they indicate a marked degree of interchangeability in the different occupations. If we take the gangs, it will be seen that on Tuesday the 7th, fifteen Negroes of the great gang had been recruited into the second gang; and on Wednesday the 4th, four of those variously employed and the five who were absent the day before were divided between the great gang and the second gang, two going to the second gang and seven to the great gang. One striking feature of the above figures is the large number of watchmen which would certainly lend support to the view that the slaves did not scruple to steal their master's stores or other property. Even more striking are the number of invalids which would indicate cruel and extremely severe labour. One is struck, too, by the fact that male slaves had a much wider range of occupations to choose from than females; apart from being domestics and field-hands, the latter could only be washerwomen, cooks, and nurses. According to Long, 'the place of a nurse is anxiously coveted by all of them, as it is usually productive of various emoluments'.[1]

Let us now examine the nature of status and authority among the various slave groups. We have already seen that the household slaves were directly under the coloured housekeeper or white mistress. Here what mattered most was skin colour. Lewis noted that the mulatto daughter of the coloured house-keeper had to be addressed as 'Miss Polly' by her darker skinned co-workers. It was

[1] E. Long, *op. cit.*, Vol. 2, p. 277.

unusual for any of these household slaves to be pure Negro. Age was also of some significance in this group. The old matriarchal nanny who had raised the white family or who was senior to all the other slaves in the house commanded respect from both whites and blacks. A Jamaican planter in his memoirs wrote how his nanny, 'an extraordinary favourite of his parents', had a great deal of power over his mind which 'partook . . . of something supernatural . . . a kind of mysterious terror'.[1]

Among the tradesmen each occupation had its own headman. Usually there were several apprentices who were under the complete control of their teachers. While few field Negroes aspired to the rank of the household, almost all of them would have preferred being tradesmen. Lewis tells us how much the slaves desired these jobs; if they were unable to acquire such skills themselves they avidly sought them for their children. The boilerman was in many respects the most valued slave on the estate. On his skill depended the quality of the sugar produced and one false move on his part could ruin an entire field of cane. Naturally, he had considerable independence and few overseers dared to antagonize him as he had it so much in his power to exact vengeance.

Among the mass of field slaves the highest post was that of driver, and since 'their worth [was] estimated by the strength of their bodies and the talent and disposition to perform their master's work' it was not unusual for 'the greatest villain' to occupy this post.[2] The attitude of the driver is well summed up in an incident reported by Mahon. On Crawle estate where the slaves were driven very hard, the driver was one day subjected to the indignity of being flogged by the overseer for not forcing enough work out of the other slaves.

After it was over he said, 'Never mind, I don't blame Busha (overseer) for this; but I will know what to do – I'm not going to take lick for all the gang in this way, and I dont care what I do – I will cut and chop away right and left'. He went to the field and took ample revenge on the poor slaves, flogging them all round till night.[3]

---

[1] The Rev. J. Riland, *Memoirs of a West Indian Planter*, pp. 3–4.
[2] Cooper, *Facts Illustrative of the Condition of the Negro Slaves in Jamaica*, (1824), p. 14.
[3] Mahon, *op. cit.* p. 48.

As one would imagine, these drivers often abused their authority. They had their own favourites, especially among the women; and if they bore a grudge against any of the slaves they could easily take it out on them in the field under the pretence of urging them on to work. This was made much easier by the fact that on most estates it was not necessary for a white person to supervise the lashing of a slave by a driver, something which led to great abuse even during the period of amelioration.[1] The driver's power was such that he could order another slave to work his provision ground for him. Kelly tells us that when he was a book-keeper, 'another part of my business was to see that the driver did not clandestinely send a Negro or two to work his provision grounds'.[2] And he had sufficient influence among the whites to plead on behalf of a slave who was ordered to be punished.[3] The various drivers of the different gangs and the tradesmen together formed a kind of élite among the slaves. Their superior status was recognized by the whites in such acts as giving them a much larger supply of provisions;[4] by generally exempting them from punishment, except in unusual circumstances; and Lewis tells us that when an absentee owner visited his estate it was customary to give these headmen each a special gift. Their authority was so strong among the slaves that they often formed themselves into courts and settled issues arising among the generality of field slaves, even to the extent of imposing fines and other penalties on them.[5] At the head of this élite and, as such, of the entire slave population, was a headman, sometimes called the head driver or the chief governor. Roughley wrote that 'the most important personage in the slave population of an estate is the Head Driver'.[6] De La Beche said much the same, informing us further that his main functions were to attend and direct the labours of the first gang; to receive from the overseer at the end of the day the orders for the quota of work the following day and to communicate them to the different classes of Negroes.[7] The chief-governor was greatly respected by the slaves. Lewis tells us how, on one of his estates, after demoting the headman for lying to the rank of a field

[1] See The *Jamaica Magazine*, Vol. I, No. 5, 1812.
[2] James Kelly, *op. cit.*, p. 19.
[3] For a detailed account of the driving system, see Cooper, *op. cit.*, pp. 47–60.
[4] De La Beche, H. T., *op. cit* (1825), p. 8.
[5] See Chapter 8 below.   [6] Quoted in Cooper, *op. cit.*, p. 49.
[7] *H. T. De La Beche, op. cit.*, p. 6, also Barclay, *op. cit.*, p. 317.

hand, a large number of slaves, including the new headman, came to plead on his behalf, 'for that all the Negroes said that it would be too sad a thing for them to see a man who had held the highest place among them, degraded quite to be a common field Negro'.[1]

One important aspect of these divisions among the slaves was the correlation of colour and status. We have already pointed out that most of the house servants were coloured slaves and that among them the darker paid deference to the lighter shaded. So it was too that most of the tradesmen of the estates were coloured. On the estate where Marly worked, there was a carpenter's, a mason's, a cooper's and a smith's gang, each with its own headman and nearly all coloured. They dressed much better than the field Negroes and were rarely punished. 'They considered themselves as a superior race to the blacks' always referring contemptuously to the latter's colour whenever the two groups had a quarrel. Significantly, the universal retort of the blacks was that 'you brown man hab no country . . . only de neger and buckra hab country', indicating the mixed ancestry of the coloured and their lack of an original home-land.[2] Thus we find colour operating at all levels of Jamaican slave society. From the point of view of the society as a whole, we find the free coloured group in a middle caste position between the white and slave group. Within the slave group itself, we find the less menial tasks being performed by coloured slaves. And among these coloured slaves we can detect a gradation in which deference was paid by the darker shaded to the lighter shaded, or those in greater proximity to the whites. Yet, we should be careful not to draw un-warranted conclusions about the attitude of the negro slave to the colour spectrum which confronted him. The data in no way suggests that Negro slaves internalized the colour ideals of the coloured group. If anything they seemed to have completely rejected it, were biased toward their own racial type, and felt little sense of racial inferiority in the face of the discriminatory behaviour towards them on the part of both the white and coloured group. Colour then – and this point cannot be over-stressed – was only of psychological significance to the coloured group and while it operated objectively to the Negroes' disadvantage, it, nonetheless, tended to remain subjectively meaningless to them.

[1] Lewis, *op. cit.*, p. 373.
[2] *Marly, or the life of a Planter in Jamaica*, pp. 94–95.

We may conclude this section by referring to our introductory remarks. It is clear that the slaves, as a group, were completely impotent in defining the criteria for the socio-economic status and divisions within their group. High or low status among them was merely a reflection of the attitudes and estimation of the masters. Of course, some of the initiative and qualities necessary for his own success must have come from the slave himself; but such qualities were largely ascribed – directly or indirectly – in terms of his value and proximity to the master.

SECTION 3
ANNUAL AND DAILY CYCLE OF WORK

(i) *The Annual Cycle* The cycle of production began, on the sugar estates, with the planting season and ended with the crop or harvest. The actual dates in the year when this period began and ended varied from one estate to the next. Some began as early as July,[1] others in August.[2] On all estates the annual cycle began with the ploughing and planting of the new canes. This was the period the slaves detested most since the work was tedious and hard. One crucial factor determining the amount of work to be done was the state of the soil. On most of the 'dry-weather' estates where the soil was fertile the sucrose content of the cane plant remained sufficiently high for the ratoons to be allowed to grow again, thus avoiding the necessity to replant. On the 'planting' estates, however, not more than two crops could be expected from each planting of canes, and, as such, the labour of the slaves was increased. But on even the most fertile estates, some amount of planting and holing was required – a particular field may have been exhausted or new ground was being broken. The holing was done by the two strongest gangs assisted by the white supervisors and tradesmen who carried the lines which ensured that the holes were dug in a straight line. First, the roots of the old ratoons were extracted, then a hole about two and a half feet square and six inches deep was dug for each new plant. The slaves worked two together, a weak person matched with a strong one.[3] Each slave was expected to open at least one hundred cane holes a day and failure to do so was punished by

[1] Marsden, *op. cit.*, p. 39.   [2] Marly, *op. cit.*, Ch. 10, also p. 46.
[3] Marly, *op. cit.*, p. 165.

whipping.[1] The work was so laborious and exhausting, however, that self-interest alone prompted most overseers to seek assistance for their slaves by hiring a jobbing gang.

The jobbing gang slaves were the most wretched and overworked of the Negro population. These gangs were usually owned by small-scale proprietors or sometimes by adventurers seeking a quick fortune.[2] Often they were communally owned, the owner of the largest batch usually being the supervisor of the gang for which task he was paid a commission by the other owners. Jobbing gangs were not only hired to dig holes, but also to make and repair roads, clear forests, and in general, to do the most arduous work on the estates and elsewhere.[3] They had no permanent homes and slept wherever night overcame them, in sugar mills, on the roadside, or in the huts of friendly estate slaves. It is easy to understand why the life expectancy of such a gang was estimated at seven years.[4]

After the planting of the canes, most estates also planted guinea-corn which was necessary for feeding the poultry, hogs, mules and dogs. In Vere parish and in other areas where the slaves did not have provision grounds, another crop of corn was planted during the early months of the calendar year, most of which was handed out to the slaves. After the planting of the first crop of corn the Negroes were primarily engaged in weeding the higher canes, each being given a row of canes per day. Around this time, too, the lime-stone, necessary for the crystallization of the cane juice, was collected and prepared. Other tasks, such as transporting the sugar of the last crop to the wharves; building and repairing roads, walls and the like, are also performed.

The Christmas holidays came about this time as a well-needed break. After the holidays, tasks such as weeding, repairing, manuring and the like were continued. Later on the coopers began cutting staves for their hogsheads and as March approached more and more preparations were made for the new crop.

During crop-time – which lasted on average about five months – it was necessary that the various operations of the estate were synchronized and ran smoothly. The length of time worked by the slaves increased greatly during this period, according to Stevens,

---

[1] De La Beche, *op. cit.*, p. 6.
[2] G. Mathison, *Notices Respecting Jamaica*, 1805–10.
[3] Cooper, *op. cit.*, p. 61.   [4] Evidence of Capt. Giles, 1790–91.

on average about 3 hrs 40 minutes more per day for each Negro.
At this period a system of shift-work was introduced. Estates which
were short-staffed – a little more than a half – formed all the Negroes
into two spells, one beginning at twelve noon, the other at midnight.
The boilers and other Negroes who formed the spell about the works
went to the field to cut the canes after lunch (i.e. about 1.30 p.m.)
and continued to do so until it became too dark, about 6.30 to 7
p.m. They finished off by carrying cane-tops or grass to the cattle
pens and then rested for about four to four and a half hours. At
twelve midnight they relieved the spell in the boiling house and the
rest of the works which had relieved them the previous noon. The
relieved spell then rested until about 4.30–5 a.m. when they returned
to the field where they worked until twelve noon at which time they
went for lunch and then returned to the works at 1.30 p.m.; and
so the cycle of work continued. Estates which had sufficient Negroes,
however, formed three spells thus making the task less gruelling.[1]
An apparent paradox of the crop season was that despite the greater
labour they had to perform, the slaves appeared least unhappy at
that time in their work. Almost every chronicler, including the most
anti-slavery, attested the fact, Edwards and others attributing it to
'the free and unrestrained use which they are allowed to make of
the ripe canes, the cane liquor and syrup'.[2] In addition, the opportunities for stealing sugar for the 'calabash market' and canes for
their hogs was much greater. De La Beche estimated the average
loss from the eating and pilfering of the Negroes during the crop at
10 per cent of the entire produce.

(ii) *The Daily Cycle out of Crop* The slaves' day began somewhere between 4 a.m. and daybreak by the head-driver ringing a
bell, or cracking his whip or by the blowing of a conch-shell.
Several 'before-day-jobs' had to be performed before actually going
to the field. These included carrying mould to cattle pens, cutting
up the dung, making mortar, carrying white lime to the works, or
doing various odd jobs in preparation for the tradesmen.[3] After
these jobs were through they went to the fields with their hoes or
bills and with their provisions for breakfast. A roll-call was made

---

[1] See Evidence of William Fitzmaurice, 1790–91.
[2] Edwards, *op. cit.*, Vol. 2, p. 160; also pp. 259–60; see also Marly, p. 44.
[3] Fitzmaurice, *op. cit.*

by the overseer and those late without a good excuse were whipped. They then worked until about ten o'clock when the driver gave the signal for breakfast which lasted for about half an hour. Another shell was blown and they returned to work. Between twelve noon and 12.30 the signal was given for lunch which usually lasted for two hours. Few of the slaves bothered to eat at this period, having had a large breakfast. Instead they either went to their kitchen gardens, or to attend to their pigs or poultry, or if they were within reach, to their provision grounds to do some extra work on them. Parents at this time sent their children to collect various plants for hog-meat. A half-hour before lunch break was up the signal was again given. Work then continued until sunset, or anywhere between 6.30 and 7 p.m. After leaving the fields they had certain extra tasks to perform, such as trashing the cattle pens, or carrying home grass for the mules and horses. Barclay claimed that this extra work ceased around the end of the eighteenth century.[1] A roll was finally called by one of the book-keepers after which they were discharged, reaching their huts anywhere between 7 and 8 p.m.

Stevens, on the basis of the evidence of pro-slavery witnesses and writers only, calculated the average number of hours worked per day by the slaves during the period of amelioration as follows:

a. Time and labour out of crop, as limited by the Colonial Acts and admitted to be the usage, from 5 a.m. till 7 p.m.; deducting two and a half hours for breakfast and dinner — 11 hrs. 30 mins.

b. Half of the two hours interval at noon employed in work on the Negro gardens or provision grounds, etc. including walks to and from field — 1 hr.

c. Mornings and evenings active employment before and after field work for master or themselves, including going and retiring from the huts, estimated together at three hours but taken at — 2 hrs. 30 mins.

d. Annual average of extra nocturnal work in crop-time — 1 hr. 40 mins.

[1] Barclay, *op. cit.*, pp. 311–12.

Thus the slaves worked an average sixteen-and-a-half hours per day throughout the year and during the five months of crop, eighteen hours per day.[1]

[1] Stevens, *op. cit.*, Vol. 2, Ch. 4.

CHAPTER III

The Treatment of the Slaves in Law and Custom

INTRODUCTION

IF WE are to have a thorough knowledge of any system of slavery it is essential that we understand the nature and functions of its slave code. For not only do these laws give a written statement of the official treatment and status of the slaves; but an analysis of their development, or lack of development, suggests the lines along which the attitudes and policies of the lawmakers or masters have changed.

In contrast to Latin America and North America, Jamaican slave society was loosely integrated; so much so, that one hesitates to call it a society since all that it amounted to was an ill-organized system of exploitation. In our chapter on the white society we have shown that not only were the non-legal institutions ineffective, but that they came very close to being non-existent. There was therefore no collectively held system of values, no religion, no educational system to reinforce the laws. Even more significant was the nature of the political system. Jamaica was the plantocratic society *par excellence*. The men who ruled the country and made its laws were themselves the planters who were the masters of the slaves. One can hardly be surprised, then, at the severity of the slave laws. Even where the laws, toward the end of the period of slavery, attempted to restrain the power of the master in some respects, the extent to which they could be made effective was partly limited by the extremely fragmentary nature of the society. Like most plantocracies, Jamaica is best seen more as a collection of autonomous plantations, each a self-contained community with its internal mechanisms of power, than as a total social system.

It is perhaps for this reason that the slave laws of Jamaica were not only severe and ineffective but incompetent and inadequately drawn up. The planters may have recognized the hypocrisy and waste of time entailed in the construction of a slave code. Perhaps they were simply incapable of resolving the serious legal problems that a slave code presented within the framework of the Anglo-Saxon legal tradition to which they had firmly committed themselves. Whatever the reason, the fact remains that for almost three-quarters of the period of slavery Jamaica did not possess a proper slave-code. All that existed between 1655 and 1788 was a series of *ad hoc* laws, most of which were prompted by sheer necessity, and were largely confused, vague, in parts, even contradictory.

After 1782, there were numerous attempts at codifying or 'consolidating' the laws relating to slaves. This, however, was a direct response to the abolition movement in England and the growing British interest in the condition of the slaves. Smith's implication that the laws after 1782 were mainly a kind of 'window dressing to mislead public opinion at home',[1] was to some extent true although the matter was more complex than this and it certainly is not sufficient grounds for neglecting these later laws. But it was true that both the abolitionists and the pro-slavery propagandists paid too much attention to the laws of the colonies in their campaign against each other.

The student interested in the legal history of slavery in Jamaica is therefore faced with the following problem: during the period when there was the minimum of external interference and when the laws may have been a reasonable guide to the actual treatment of the slaves there was no competent slave code, and those laws that did exist often tended to be out of date; while, on the other hand, when the slave codes were elaborately drawn up and regularly reviewed their use as pro-slavery propaganda makes it risky to rely too much on them as codification of the real situation.

This is all the more reason for examining these laws within their social and economic framework. Our analysis of the slave laws then, will be undertaken as one part of our account of the actual condition and status of the slaves.

[1] R. W. Smith, The Legal Status of the Jamaican Slaves Before the Anti-Slavery Movement', in *The Journal of Negro History*, Vol. 30.

SECTION I
THE LEGAL BASIS OF SLAVERY

Slavery has been legally defined as 'the status or condition of persons over whom any or all of the powers attaching to the right of ownership are exercised'.[1] What immediately becomes apparent in any consideration of this legal status is the peculiarly dual nature of the slave. On the one hand he was the property of another and was regarded as a disposable chattel. But it was impossible to deny that he was also a human being and the law had to be cognisant of this fact in some way.[2]

This was a dilemma inherent in the very nature of slavery. In Jamaica there was an additional dilemma which the planters never attempted to solve. It is the fact that slavery never had any positive legal basis; it was purely a matter of custom. As Stevens puts it:

> They found a condition of man called slavery, already established by custom, in their own and neighbouring islands; and being all slave-masters in right of that custom, before they became legislators, did not trouble themselves with enquiries into the legitimacy or extent of the private authority which they already in fact possessed.[3]

American legislators, when faced with this problem, boldly asserted that slavery was based on civil law, as for example, in the case of Belt v. Baldy – Supreme Court of Pennsylvania, 1786, – when an anti-slavery society in Philadelphia was defeated in its attempt to test the legality of slavery.[4]

But America was an independent country. It was different with Jamaica which remained an English colony until 1962. The planters faithfully copied every article of English law in their own hastily enacted legislations, and where peculiar local conditions demanded new laws, the declared intention of the Jamaicans was to pass laws 'not repugnant to the laws of England'.[5] Indeed, almost every body

---

[1] Anti-Slavery Convention of the League of Nations, 1926, Quoted in G. M. McInnes, *England and Slavery*, p. 13.

[2] The same was true of the United States, as indeed, of all slave systems. See K. Stampp, *The Peculiar Institution*, p. 189.

[3] Stevens, *The State Called Slavery in the B.W.I.*, Vol. I, p. 18.

[4] B. Hollander, *Slavery in America: its Legal History* p. 15.

[5] Lord Vaughn to the Earle of Carlysle, Nov. 1680; C.O. 138/3.

of acts was accompanied by a law which affirmed the existence of all the laws and statutes of England in Jamaica, 'except where attended by their own acts or by acts of Parliament expressly binding them and all customs to the contrary are void; and this without any exception to their slaves'.[1]

Such a position assumed that the laws of England permitted slavery. The few planters who troubled themselves with the problem justified their assumption on the grounds that the early laws were based on the slave code of Barbados which, it was claimed, were based on the English laws of villeinage.[2] This was the same line of argument partly used by Council in the famous case of James Sommersett which was brought to the English Courts in 1771. At the end of the hearing Lord Mansfield delivered his famous verdict:

> The state of slavery is of such a nature, that it is incapable of being introduced in any reasons, moral or political, but only by positive law, which preserves its force long after the reasons, occasion, and time itself from whence it was created, is erased from memory. It is so odious, that nothing can be suffered to support it, but positive law . . . I cannot say this case is allowed or approved by the law of England . . .[3]

Thus, at the zenith of Jamaican slavery, the ultimate source of its own laws declared slavery to be illegal. If the laws of Jamaica were to be consistent, slavery should also have been made illegal in the island. To the planters this was purely a technicality hardly worth worrying over. No law positively sanctioned slavery in Jamaica. If it was illegal in England, it could be claimed that it was not legal in Jamaica. But neither was it illegal.

SECTION 2
THE DEVELOPMENT OF THE SLAVE LAWS

We may distinguish four periods in the development of the slave laws of Jamaica: the first between 1662 and 1696; the second between 1696 and 1780; the third between 1780 and 1817; and the fourth between 1817 and the emancipation of the slaves in 1834.

---

[1] Stevens, *op. cit.*, Vol. 1, p. 20.
[2] See E. Long, *op. cit.*, Vol. 2, Bk. 3, pp. 493–96.
[3] Hollander, *op. cit.*, p. 4.

A. 1662–1696 This period is characterized by uncertainty and a great deal of brutality. The society as a whole was taking some time to settle down. This was reflected to some extent in general confusion as to the actual status of the slave.

The uncertainty towards the slaves was largely due to the relatively large number of indentured servants in the island at that time. These white servants were treated almost as barbarously as the slaves, perhaps even worse since their servitude was known to be temporary. In an act of 1681 'for Regulating Servants' we find, from observing the handwritten manuscript, that while in the text the term 'servant' is used, in the column summaries the word 'slave' is applied to the white servants.[1] Even more significant is the 52nd instruction to Sir Thomas Lynch before taking up his governorship of the island which directed that:

> You shall endeavour to get a law passed for the restraining of any inhuman severity which by ill masters or overseers may be used toward their Christian Servants *or other* Slaves.[2]

However, by at most a decade after the occupation, a distinction had been clearly drawn between white servants and Negro slaves. And by 1696 the term Negro was invariably identified with slave.

In general, the law during this period sought in no way to restrain the powers of the master. Where it was specific, it commanded the master to be severe. On more than one occasion the metropolitan power had to intervene. In a letter to Lynch in 1682, for example, the Committee for Trade and Plantations disallowed an act which imposed an incredibly small fine for killing a Negro, stating that it 'might encourage the wilfull shedding of blood'.[3]

As can be imagined, abuses in this period were excessive, partly because there was not yet a dominant creole slave society and the ethnic contrast between master and slave was as great as it could possibly be. The preamble to an act of 1673 entitled, 'An Act for the Better Ordering and Government of Slaves', describes the Negroes as '. . . being a heathenish, brutish . . . and dangerous kind of people'.[4] At the same time, it must be remembered that this was

[1] Acts of Jamaica, 1681, C.O. 139/4.
[2] Instr. to Sir. Thos. Lynch, C.O. 138/4.
[3] Committee. of Trade and Plantations to Lynch, C.O. 138/4.
[4] Acts of Jamaica, C.O. 139/3.

the period of small settlers when the owner actually supervised his slaves and might be expected, from pure self-interest, to care for them more than in the eighteenth century when absenteeism was prevalent.

B. 1696–1780   This period covers the rise of Jamaica to large-scale mono-crop farming, eventual prosperity, and the beginnings of economic decline. During this time the relationship between master and slave was to be regulated more by custom than by laws.

After the Act of 1696 several others were passed relating to slaves and Negroes (free Negroes being generally regarded by the laws as possessing the same status as slaves). For example, there were several laws passed attempting to prevent hawking and peddling by slaves; several also sought to regulate the practice of masters permitting their slaves to hire themselves out. Most of these laws soon became obsolete. They were largely the immediate response to a situation which threatened to grow out of hand and no sooner had it been brought under control than the laws fell into disuse.

Indeed, throughout this period, apart from the Act of 1696, only three acts were passed which were of any lasting significance for the status and treatment of the slaves. The first was in 1717, an act 'for the more effectual Punishment of Crime by Slaves',[1] which dealt mainly with the problem of masters protecting their valuable slaves, who had committed crimes, from prosecution. The second was an act passed in 1751 '. . . to Explain part of an Act for the better order and Government of Slaves and for inflicting further other Punishment on persons Killing Negroes or Slaves'.[2] This act declared in its preamble that the act of 1696, 'not having been found sufficient to deter Persons from committing such wicked and inhumane Practices', had to be altered, especially since the section dealing with the punishment of whites for such crimes was 'doubtful constructed'. Finally, in 1779, an act '. . . to explain and amend . . .' the act of 1696 was passed[3] mainly for the purpose of correcting certain 'improper practices' in the trial and execution of slaves.

Perhaps the best comment on the laws of this period comes from a contemporary, Corbett, who was well qualified to judge them:

There were a great many good Laws for the government of

[1] C.O. 139/8.   [2] C.O. 139/17.   [3] C.O. 139/36.

slaves made upon the first Settlement of the Island, but which are seldom or never executed; – the first Planters minded their own Business, saw themselves the inconveniences that naturally spring from Servitude, as they arose, and adapted their Laws to redress them. – There are some good laws still wanting but they clashing with the Planter's immediate Interest, which is all most of them mind at present, the Assembly have not been induced to enact them; in which, however, I must own they are not so much to be blamed; for what signifies making new Laws until the old ones are obeyed ?[1]

C. 1780–1817 This is the period marked by the beginnings and growing intensity of the abolition movement in England. In 1788 the Privy Council initiated a detailed enquiry into the slave trade, which made an extensive probe into the actual condition of the slaves in the colonies, particularly Jamaica.[2] Between 1790 and 1791 another set of enquiries was made by Parliament.[3] Numerous official enquiries followed after these, culminating in that of 1832.[4]

There are several reasons why the laws of this period were not purely tools of propaganda as so many of the abolitionists suggested. In the first place, it must be remembered that the movement to emancipate the slaves fell into two fairly distinct phases: that beginning with the 1770s and ending with the abolition of the slave trade in 1808; and that between 1808 and total emancipation in 1838. Most people, (including a great many of the abolitionists and almost all the planters) during the first phase, saw the abolition of the slave trade as the main bone of contention and only a very small number regarded the complete emancipation of the slaves as anything but the most remote of objectives. Thus when it became clear to the planters that the abolition of the slave trade was inevitable, a fair amount of effort was made to improve the condition of the slaves for the very selfish reason that soon their source of supply would be cut off and the renewal of the slave population would have to depend completely on improved conditions of mortality and reproduction.[5] It was during this period that we find the spate of books

---

[1] Corbett, *Essay Concerning Slavery*, p. 21.
[2] See B.T. 6: 9–11.
[3] Select Committee. on Slave Trade, 1790–91.
[4] Select Committee. of Lords, 1832.
[5] See Chapter on Population of Slaves.

and pamphlets written by planters and others explaining the art of good plantership and the best way of caring for slaves.

Secondly, it must be noted that by 1788 the relationship between master and slave, while not codified, had become clearly defined in custom. The absolute legal power of the master still remained and it was not uncommon for him to abuse it. But, generally, the slave had managed to extract certain customary rights which were more often than not respected by his masters. This respect the slaves could, and at times, even demand by virtue of the fact that they could ruin an estate or have an overseer dismissed should they choose to. Williams was perhaps correct when he wrote:

> The Negroes generally seem to know their rights well and to be actuated by a most lively *esprit de corps* whenever anyone is illegally punished or oppressed.[1]

Thus the laws of this period became largely a codification of what was already prevalent in custom.

Let us now take a brief look at their development. The first sign of a new policy came in 1780 when a short act was passed 'repealing and modifying' all former acts relating to the slaves.[2] By November of the next year the planters apparently decided that there was really very little to modify in the old laws and that a clean sweep was necessary. An act was therefore passed, repealing all former acts and clauses of acts relating to slaves, the Legislators feeling obliged to admit that they had all 'become very much confused, and in many parts contradictory and uncertain'.[3]

The first of the 'Melioration Acts', as they came to be called, was passed in January 1782.[4] If its intention was to improve upon the act of 1696 it was largely a failure, since it was nothing more than this earlier act with the modifications and further clauses that had been added since. If anything, it worsened the condition of the slave since custom had long improved on several of the clauses included. The act did not receive the Royal Assent and lapsed after three years. In 1787 another, and much better attempt, was made at creating a new code.[5] Among other things, severer penalties were imposed on masters wantonly killing their slaves; a list of the increases and decreases of slaves on all estates was ordered to be

---

[1] C. R. Williams, *Tour Through Jamaica*, 1823. [2] Acts of Jamaica, C.O. 139/37c. [3] C.O. 139/37c. [4] *Ibid.* [5] C.O. 139/43.

kept; and an attempt was made to improve the conditions of the slave courts and remove from the masters some of their powers of punishing crimes committed by their slaves.

The laws were revised in 1788, when the main changes were the inclusion of a clause encouraging the religious instruction of the slaves; the codification of the customary number of holidays allotted annually to the slaves; a clause specifying the amount of time to be given the slaves for meals; and another restricting the power of the slave courts in their punishment of convicted slaves.[1] There was another review of the laws in 1792 and improvements were further made in the clauses relating to the provisions for slaves, cruel punishment, the movement of slaves without tickets, and a mitigation of the punishment of slaves who had escaped from the workhouse. Additional clauses encouraged masters to improve the conditions of fertility among their slaves, further restrained their illegal assemblies, and redefined the meaning of 'running away' and 'rebellion'.[2]

In 1800 the first of what the Jamaican Assembly called 'The Consolidated Slave Laws' was passed. By this time the struggle over the abolition of the slave trade had reached its peak and there can be little doubt that these laws were partly meant to be an instrument in the conflict. For whatever they were worth, the clauses were generally far more humane than those of previous acts. Several of the clauses of this act were repealed between 1804 and 1805 and there was a change in the amount to be paid by the crown to masters whose slaves had been imprisoned or executed.

These laws were reviewed in November 1807[3] and in December 1809[4] but apart from a few minor changes they remained basically the same as those of 1800.

D. 1817–1834 We have earlier suggested that during the period 1780–1817 the laws did to some extent reflect a genuine improvement in the general condition of the slaves. The same cannot be said about the period between 1817 and 1834. The second phase in the abolition movement was now well under way and by the 1820s it was becoming increasingly clear that the planters were fighting a losing battle. All incentive for treating the slaves humanely

---

[1] C.O. 139/44.   [2] C.O. 139/47.   [3] C.O. 139/54.   [4] C.O. 139/56.

was now gone and the general attitude among the masters was to exact mercilessly as much labour from the slaves as possible before emancipation.

It was this new spirit of severity which partly accounted for the large number of slave rebellions throughout the 1820s, culminating in the great slaughter of 1832. From the enquiries made after the 1832 rebellion we learn that many planters, 'in their petulance and tyranny, would often taunt the slaves under them concerning their expected freedom'.[1] And there were many cases similar to that of William Hall (reported in the books of the Montego Bay court house), a slave who claimed that 'he often heard the Negroes complain that the overseers, while flogging them, would say, "You are going to be free, but we'll take it out of you"'.[2] This attitude reached its zenith during the apprenticeship period when the certainty of emancipation and the short time at their disposal led to unparalleled barbarities on the part of the masters.[3]

The ameliorative tendency continued in the laws. An Act of 1826 protected the person of the female slave against rape and in 1831 slave evidence was conditionally accepted against whites. But the British Government remained unimpressed by these gestures and the Royal Assent was refused to all the Acts of the 1820s. Finally, in 1833 it passed the famous Act for the emancipation of the Negro slaves.

SECTION 3

THE NATURE OF THE LAWS IN THEIR RELATION TO THE
ACTUAL CONDITION OF THE SLAVES

Having examined the legal basis of slavery and the development of the laws as a whole we must now take a closer look at the substance of these laws and the extent to which they influenced and were related to the actual condition of the slaves. Our examination will be made in terms of five basic categories: the slave in relation to his master; the slave in relation to other freemen; the slave in relation to the society as a whole; the slave in relation to the judiciary; and the laws as they related to the manumission of the slave. These

[1] Henry Bleby, *Death Struggles of Slavery*, Ch. 12.
[2] *Ibid.*
[3] For a moving account of such barbarities, told by a slave, see: *A Narrative of Events since the First of August 1834* by James Williams.

categories will be discussed in the light of the different periods described above.

(a) *The Slave in relation to his master*

The power of the master was made absolute by virtue of the fact that the slave was his legal property. Clause four of the act of 1674 enacted that:

> All Negroes lawfully bought as bondslaves shall here continue to be so and further be held and judged and taken to be goods and chattels and ought to come to the hands of Executors . . . as other assetts do, their Christianity or any Law, Custom or Usage in England or elsewhere to the contrary notwithstanding.

Quite apart from the fact that the slave thereby became the absolute possession of his master, there were other implications of this basic principle of slavery.

First, it meant that, legally, the slave could own no property; secondly, that he was liable to be sold at any time by his master; and thirdly, that he was liable to be levied upon at any time to settle debts owed by his master. The first of these implications was purely a technicality. Few masters were callous enough to rob the slave of what little he had acquired from the fruits of his labour during his spare hours. An act of 1826 eventually gave the slave legal right to his property although it was still possible for the master to take action in the Supreme Court, if he so desired, to contest the slave's right to the ownership of any property over the value of £20.[1] While it was customary for the slave to own property, there were several laws passed after 1696 which specified certain kinds of goods which it would be illegal for him to own. These include, at various times, horses, mules, mares, gelding, cattle, fresh meat and fire-arms. But, apart from fire-arms and horses, these restrictions were largely neglected.

The second implication was more serious, especially during the seventeenth and first quarter of the eighteenth centuries, when indebted masters would indiscriminately sell their slaves to others. 'Negroes' wrote Backford:

> 'are very sensibly attached to properties; they reverence a

[1] Acts of Jamaica, C.O. 139/65.

master who claims from inheritance; and frequently despond when (removed to other hands) they become the chattels of unwilling possession'.[1]

By the time Backford wrote, however, it was rare for Negroes to be sold individually. Often the entire estate with its Negroes were sold together. When it became necessary that some of the slaves had to be sold separately custom dictated that the slave was consulted as to whether he wished to be bought by the prospective buyer. An extract reprinted in the *Jamaica Journal* states that:

. . . The only transfers which take place are of domestic or tradesmen Negroes, and no man would buy a slave who did not previously agree to live with him. He would be little better than a madman who did so, as the slave would to a certainty run away; for while the purchaser requires a good character with the Negro, the latter is equally alive to obtain a knowledge of the habits and disposition of the person who may be inclined to purchase him.[2]

The third basic implication of the status of the slave as property was perhaps the most severe. Long, who was fanatically pro-slavery, had to admit that:

Making Negroes liable to be seized for bond and simple contract debts and hurried from one part of the island to another, constitutes the chief oppression under which they labour; renders their servitude more bitter and intolerable; and produces a very great annual loss to the public, by the mortality which it produces.[3]

Edwards, another pro-slavery writer, comes to the same conclusion, mentioning the forced separation from mates and children which this entailed.[4] Edwards further adds that cases of this sort occur 'every day, and under the present system, will continue to occur . . .'[5] And it was he who, in June 1797, introduced a bill in the House of Commons repealing the section of the Act of 1696 relating to this practice. In 1809, however, the Jamaican Assembly declared that

---

[1] Beckford, *Situation of the Negroes in Jamaica*, (1788), pp. 52–53.
[2] Extract from Hakewell's 'Slaves in Ja.' in the *Jamaica Journal*, Vol. 2, No. 8.
[3] E. Long, *History of Jamaica*, Vol. 2, Bk. 3, p. 499.
[4] B. Edwards, *The History . . . of . . . the W.I.*, Bk. 4, P. 183.
[5] *Ibid.*, p. 184.

the repeal had been too much abused and the clause was retro-
actively reinstated.[1]

It is significant that all the penal clauses of the Act of 1696 related
to offences committed by the slave outside the limits of the plantation (except in such extreme cases as the murder of one slave by another). The only clause which could be construed as a restraint
on the absolute power of the master in the act of 1696 was that which
made it a felony for wantonly killing a slave and which deemed it
murder in the case of a second offence. This law was made ineffective, however, by the fact that slave evidence could not be accepted
against white persons. The law was slightly changed in 1751 after
a master had barbarously butchered his slave. Long could only recall
one instance of a white man being convicted on this law, and 'being
his first offence, he was burnt in the hand'.[2] Most of the anti-slavery
witnesses in the enquiry of 1790 knew of cases of slaves murdered
by their masters. Dr Jackson, in Jamaica between 1774 and 1778,
mentions the case of a slave being flogged to death and the response
of the neighbouring whites who 'chiefly dwelt upon the loss that the
proprietor sustained'.[3] And Henry Coor knew of an overseer who
had killed three slaves, but since he was considered a 'valuable
overseer' was allowed to go 'privately away'.[4]

But these were committed anti-slavery witnesses and may have
been quoting isolated instances. If we are to generalize about the
extent to which masters abused their powers in the different periods
we may say, first, that until about the middle of the second quarter
of the eighteenth century brutality to the slaves was the norm.
Sloane, who never questioned the idea of slavery and whose evidence
is therefore reliable with regard to punishment, wrote that the usual
punishment for rebellion was:

> Burning them by nailing them down on the ground with
> crooked sticks on every limb and then applying the Fire by
> degrees from the feet and hands, burning them gradually up to
> the head, whereby their pains are extravagant . . .

> For crimes of lesser nature Gelding, or chopping off half of
> the foot with an Ax . . . For running away they put Iron Rings of
> great weight on their Ankles, or Pottocks about their Necks,
> which are Iron Rings with two long Necks rivetted to them, or a

[1] Acts of Jamaica, C.O. 139/56.   [2] Long, *op. cit.*, Vol. 2, Bk. 3, p. 493.
[3] Select Committee on Slave Trade, 1790–91.   [4] *Ibid.*

Spur in the Mouth . . . For Negligence, they are usually whipt by the overseer with Lance-wood Switches, till they be bloody, and several of the Switches broken, being first tied up by the hands in the Mill-Houses . . . After they are whip'd till they are Raw, some put on their Skins Pepper and Salt to make them smart; at other times their Masters will drop melted Wax on their skins and use several exquisite tortures . . .[1]

When Leslie published his account in 1739 the barbarities seemed to have been just as excessive. Slaves were still burned to death for striking a white man and 'others they starve to death with a loaf hanging before their Mouths . . .' Like Sloane, Leslie claimed that 'such severities may in some shape be excused'.[2]

In his first account of Jamaica, Stewart wrote that the earlier brutalities of the masters had passed and that 'self-love' and 'humanity' had led to an improvement in their treatment.[3] However, his later judgment, 'that the treatment of the slaves depends in a great measure upon the character and temper of his master and manager'[4] seems more correct.

While the power of the master went largely unchallenged almost all the slave laws made provision for the minimum clothing, food and shelter which the master should provide for his slave. The act of 1696 stated that jackets and petticoats were to be supplied to the females once every year and jackets and drawers to the men; to ensure proper food supplies an acre of ground for every five slaves should be cultivated.

Custom differed widely from the law in these areas. The clothes given the slaves annually became their working garb and it was expected that they acquire clothes to their tastes from their own resources. When the provision ground system was developed during the eighteenth century the clause relating to masters providing one acre of cultivated land for every five slaves fell into disuse. Some of the laws after 1780 continued to demand one acre to every ten Negroes 'over and above the Negro grounds, which land shall be kept in a Planter like condition'.[5] But as Mathison commented,

[1] Sir Hans Sloane, *Natural History of Jamaica*, Introduction.
[2] Charles Leslie *A New and Exact Account of Jamaica*, 1739, p. 94.
[3] Stewart, *Account of Jamaica*, 1808, pp. 223–24.
[4] Stewart, *A View of the Past and Present State of . . . Ja.* (1823), p. 222.
[5] Acts of Jamiaca, C.O. 139/43.

this law was largely a 'precaution against famine', and was 'universally disregarded'.[1]

The law varied over the different periods as to the amount of time to be allowed the slaves to care for their provision grounds. The act of 1696 did not oblige the master to give his slaves any free days, not even Sundays. The act of 1792, however, stipulated that the slaves should be given one day in every fortnight (in addition to Sundays) except during crop time when other arrangements had to be made.[2] Apparently the planters more than compensated for this extra free day during the crop so that in 1816 there was a proviso 'that the number of days so allowed . . . shall be at least twenty-six in the year'.[3] The act of 1826 finally curtailed Sunday labour during crop and enacted that mills should cease to operate between Saturdays at 7 p.m. and Mondays at 5 a.m.[4]

One other area of the master-slave relationship where the laws intervened was in the imposition of various restrictions on the movement of the slave out of the confines of the plantation. The Act of 1696 required owners of slaves not to allow them to leave their property without a ticket as a precaution against rebellious conspiracies. But this clause was only observed during or immediately after a rebellion. Corbett attributes this to the thoughtlessness and lack of foresight on the part of the planters. He quotes as an example the conspiracy in St. John's parish when 'the Civil and Military were alert and no Negroes allowed to pass without a Ticket . . . but in a Month's time, or less, the Masters and many Overseers were weary of signing their names'.[5] By the end of the eighteenth century it was rare for a slave to travel with a ticket or 'talkee-talkee' as the slaves called it.[6]

(b) *The Slave in relation to other Freemen*

The activities of the slaves were not always restricted to the direct supervision of their master. This was obvious in the case of the town Negroes, especially that group which hired themselves out and returned a portion of their earnings to their masters. But there

---

[1] G. Mathison, *Notices Re Ja.*, p. 32.
[2] C.O. 139/47.   [3] C.O. 139/62.   [4] C.O. 139/65.
[5] Corbett, *Essay Concerning Slavery*.
[6] *The Importance of Jamaica to Great Britain Considered . . . In a Letter to a Gentleman*. Printed for A. Dodd.

were many occasions on which the estate Negro had to leave the plantation, – visiting friends, performing duties for his master, such as going to the towns to get supplies, or carrying estate produce to the wharves. There was also the case of the jobbing gangs who were hired out to other masters to perform specific tasks.

On all such occasions the slave came in contact with freemen who did not have the same self-interest in him as his own master. In his relationship with such people he was exposed to all the potential brutalities and exploitation of the slave-system, for, as Stevens pointed out, it was characteristic of West Indian slavery that the slave could 'have no civil rights, for he has no civil character, no personality'.[1]

The legal implications of this were that the slave could neither sue nor be sued. Action on his behalf could only be taken by his master, or by the crown. But the former was limited to situations where he could prove that the utility of his slave had been impaired; and the latter was made almost totally ineffective by the fact that slave evidence was unacceptable against whites. Slave evidence against non-white freemen was acceptable, but it was possible for influential, free, non-white persons to have an act passed on their behalf forbidding the use of slave evidence against them.[2]

The overtly racial tone of the slave laws was most marked in the clauses pertaining to the assault on white persons by slaves. In the act of 1664 it was enacted that 'if any slave . . . shall offer any blow to any *Christian* for the first offence he or she shall be whipped, and for the second, in addition to being whipped his nose split and a part of his face burnt'.[3] In the act of 1674 there was a slight but significant change in the reading of this clause which now states that the slave shall be punished in the above manner should he 'offer any violence to any *white Christian*'.[4] By 1677 Christianity was discarded as a criterion for distinguishing masters from slaves. The penalty would be imposed on any slave found guilty of 'striking or the like any *white* person'.[5] In 1696 the penalty for striking a white person was death or any other punishment at the discretion of the judges, provided the act was not committed in the defence of

[1] Stevens, *op. cit.*, Vol. I, p. 117.
[2] The first of such acts were passed between 1707 and 1708 on behalf of John Williams and M. Bartholomew. See C.O. 139/8.
[3] Acts of Jamaica, C.O. 139/1.   [4] *Ibid.*   [5] C.O. 139/5.

his master's property or at his command. Self-defence was not considered sufficient reason for a slave striking a white man. After 1788 the judges were given more flexibility in the sentences they imposed although it still remained possible for a slave to be sentenced to death for striking a white man. The slaves themselves never bothered to seek redress from the courts knowing what a waste of time and energy that would entail. As Henry Coor stated in his evidence '. . . it was generally thought among the Negroes that they could have no redress but from their masters or attorneys'.[1] Thus the Negro was, as Stevens remarked, not only a slave to his master, but 'in some respects a slave to every white man in the community'.[2]

(c) *The participation of the slave in the institutions of the society as a whole*

We have already suggested that Jamaican slave society was extremely fragmentary in nature. At the same time the system was not one of anarchy and the masters, however tenuously, did maintain some links with the values and institutions of their parent society. The example of the masters would alone suffice to deter the slaves from assimilating the remnants of British culture which confronted them. But, as if to make certain that they did not, the slave laws of the island persistently proscribed any action which sought to acculturate the slaves. We may consider these legal proscriptions, and the extent to which they were successful, in the light of six heads: religion, marriage, education, independent economic roles, the judiciary and manumission.

(i) *Religion, Marriage, Education and Economy*   These four heads are discussed in much greater detail later and will therefore be mentioned in passing at the moment. An act of 1674 asserted that slaves, though 'goods and chattels' are nonetheless, 'reasonable creatures and capable of being taught the principles of our religion'.[3] The act of 1696 also encouraged baptism. But it was clear that such enactments were purely matters of conscience, and no one really took them seriously. During the nineteenth century various laws were passed prohibiting the conversion of slaves by clergymen other

---

[1] Select Committee. on Slave Trade, 1790–91.
[2] Stevens, *op. cit.*, Vol. I, p. 224.   [3] C.O. 139/3.

than those of the established church.[1] Since marriage was out of the question not only to the slaves, but to the majority of the white population, it is not surprising that the slave laws had almost nothing of significance to say concerning the institution. The same holds for education concerning which a few enactments were made during the nineteenth century prohibiting missionaries to teach slaves either to read or write as it was considered dangerous. By the end of the period of slavery a few slaves were able to read, but they were numerically insignificant. At various times during the eighteenth century laws were enacted with a view to restraining hawkers, especially those who went to the countryside, bought up the available provisions, then sold them in the towns at great profit 'by which means the prices of provisions of all kinds are greatly advanced'.[2] But it was in the domestic economy of the island that the slaves participated most in the total life of the society as we shall see in a later chapter.

(ii) *The Judiciary*   From as early as the seventeenth century there were specially created courts to try slaves for crimes which the master was not deemed qualified to judge. Theoretically, these courts also existed for hearing complaints by slaves against their masters, but since no precaution was taken against the master exacting revenge after such complaints were heard, and since it was almost impossible for the slave to indict his master because his evidence was not accepted in court against white persons, it was very rare during the seventeenth and eighteenth centuries for slave courts to sit on such complaints.

The procedure of the slave courts was laid down in the slave act of 1674. Slaves committing burglaries or other serious crimes were to be brought to a J.P. who should then send them immediately to jail. Later, at a time and date fixed by the J.P. the slaves were to be tried by five persons consisting of three freeholders, the J.P. first consulted and another appointed by him. 'All small . . . misdeamenour', however, 'shall be heard and determined by the master of the Slaves . . .'[3] It was also in 1674 that the first law was passed authorizing the Governor in Council to declare martial law in the

[1] See Slave Acts of 1802: C.O. 139/51; and of 1807: C.O. 139/54.
[2] Acts of Jamaica (Printed) C.O. 139/8.
[3] C.O. 139/1.

event of a rebellion or threat of rebellion by the slaves. Martial law continued to be used throughout and after slavery with much brutality and it was not until 1865, after the Governor Eyre controversy that the legal basis of martial law within the context of British law was successfully contested.[1]

It was not until 1800 that any significant changes were made in the nature of the slave courts. For crimes involving the penalty of death, transportation or life sentence, the court was now to consist of three J.P.s and a panel of eighteen jurors, not including the master or any supervisor of the slave. It was also enacted that the quarter sessions courts in the various precincts might form themselves into slave courts after they had completed their normal business. In such cases nine jurors were to be called from the panel of the quarter sessions court. Six days' notice should be given to the master of the slave on trial to prepare his defence. In December 1821 an act was passed which stated that no sentence of death should be executed without the warrant of the Governor except in cases of rebellion.

Some element of conflict existed between the financial interests of the master and the proper functioning of the judiciary. Quite often a master would resist all attempts made by the constables to arrest a valuable slave. It was mainly to resolve this conflict that the act 'for the more effectual punishing of Crimes by Slaves' was passed in 1717. This act allowed the courts to pay, out of the funds for suppressing rebel slaves, a maximum of £40 for any slave who was executed or transported. But the law clearly created more problems than it solved. In the first place, there were many slaves who were worth far more than £40 to their masters, particularly if they were skilled. Crimes committed by these slaves would often go undetected and it was not uncommon for slaves whose services could be more easily dispensed with to be substituted for the more valuable ones who had committed the crime. Even more pernicious was the practice, though not common, of masters falsely accusing weak or old slaves of capital crimes so as to be awarded the legal compensation for them.[2]*

[1] See B. Semmel, *The Governor Eyre Controversy*, 1963.
[2] Evidence of Capt. Thomas Lloyd, Select Committee on Slave Trade, 1790–91.
 * His evidence is substantiated by the report of a committee set up by the House of Assembly to inspect the implementation of the Act of 1717. See *Journals of the House of Assembly, Jamaica*, Vol. 3, p. 493.

The attempts of masters to interfere with the activities of the slave courts were apparently so common that in 1772 an act had to be passed to prevent the 'improper practice of soliciting Justices and Freeholders to sit upon Trial or Tryals of Slaves'.[1] A clause was also included in this act, extending the length of time between the conviction and execution of slaves found guilty of rebellion because 'such haste may be of evil consequence by preventing discoveries tending to the safety of the community'. But it appears that during the seventeenth and eighteenth centuries slave courts were generally little more than farces. Beckford, a pro-slavery writer, wrote in 1788:

> I know of nothing in the West Indies so shocking to humanity and so disgusting to individuals as the savage and indecent manner in which the trial of slaves is conducted.[2]

That same year (1788) a resident in the island wrote, after a visit to the Kingston Assize court, of his astonishment at the mockery of justice which the court appeared to be, concluding that:

> What astounded me beyond measure was that the Judges became evidence without being sworn and the Jury, although sworn to decide according to evidence, in every instance gave a verdict without hearing a witness, upon oath, upon the subject of their decision.[3]

Conditions may have improved during the first two decades of the nineteenth century. Lewis, a fairly reliable pro-slavery writer, after visiting a slave court commented that it was conducted 'with all possible justice and propriety'.[4]

By the 1820s, however, the slave courts, especially in cases of slaves charged with rebellious conspiracy, were nothing more than a travesty. The *Jamaica Journal*, a pro-slavery newspaper, wrote damningly of the practice of forcing slaves to become prosecution witnesses, of torturing suspects so as to get confessions of guilt from them, and of bribing Crown witnesses with the promise of manumission.[5]

---

[1] Acts of Jamaica, C.O. 139/36.
[2] Beckford, *Situation of the Negroes in Jamaica*, (1788) p. 92.
[3] Letter to the *Jamaica Gazette*, Vol. 6, No. 89, Nov. 1. 1788.
[4] M. G. Lewis, *op. cit.*, p. 179.
[5] The *Jamaica Journal*, Vol. 1, No. 42.

(vi) *Manumission:* Tannenbaum has rightly pointed out that it was in the attitude of the planters and the enactments of their laws with respect to the manumission of their slaves that we find the greatest difference between Anglo-Saxon and Iberian slavery.[1] In Latin America the laws, the church and the Masters all encouraged the slaves to buy their freedom; in America and the West Indies every obstacle was put in the way of manumission. Until the last two or three decades of slavery the free coloured group was socially and numerically insignificant.[*]

In the first few years after the occupation there was a favourable attitude toward Negro freemen. In 1660 D'Oyley was instructed to:

> Give such encouragements as security you may to such Negroes, natives and others, as shall submit to live peaceably under his majesty's obedience and in the due submission to the government of the island.[2]

But as more slaves came into the island this policy rapidly changed. Negroes were identified with slaves and the law assumed as much, since the burden of proving that he was free lay on the Negro freeman. Any free Negro who could not supply adequate proof of his status was arrested by the constables and sold by auction.

An act of 1774 imposed what amounted to a penalty on the master who freed his slave, since it obliged him to make provision for the manumitted slave by paying an annuity of £5 to the churchwardens. There was some mitigation of the manumission laws during the nineteenth century. For example, it was made easier for masters to manumit their slaves by will without the fear that his beneficiaries would nullify his action. The number of slaves manumitted annually showed a gradual increase, the average for the last two decades of slavery being 649.[3]

The slave could be freed in one of three ways. First, he could buy his freedom. This method was strongly disliked by almost all the masters, their main objection being, as one planter pointed out, that it was the most skilled and valuable of the slaves who would be

---

[1] F. Tannenbaum, *Slave & Citizen*, pp. 53–57.

[*] See S. Dunker, *The Free Coloured And Their Fight For Civil Rights in Jamaica 1800–30*, Unpublished M.A. Thesis, University of London, 1960. Ch. 1.

[2] Instructions (No. 11) to Col. D'Oyley, 1660, Appendix, Journals of House of Assembly, Ja. Vol. 1.

[3] Evidence of William Burge, Select Com. of House of Lords, 1832.

'most likely to avail themselves of this right'.[1] Secondly, the slaves could be manumitted by their master for loyal service or for some particular act of courage. This was usually done through a will and apparently in the majority of cases the slave was prevented from acquiring his freedom by the refusal of the beneficiaries to guarantee the necessary £5 annuity. This was avoided by the act of 1816 which obliged beneficiaries to pay the annual sum. Thirdly, the slave could be freed by an act of the Assembly for loyalty (which usually meant the betrayal of his fellow conspirators) or for acting as Crown witness against rebellious slaves, or for noteworthy acts of courage. Such cases of manumission were rare in the seventeenth and eighteenth centuries, but with the spate of slave conspiracies in the nineteenth century they became more common, a total of 3,981 slaves being freed between 1817 and 1829.[2]

The Jamaican slave was, rightly, quite cynical about the whole idea of manumission. It was easy for him to see that the free Negroes about him possessed little more than a beggar's freedom. If he was prosperous enough to be able to buy his freedom it was more than likely that he had fairly high status among the slaves on his plantation and was well treated by his master as most valued slaves were. As Barclay pointed out:

> . . . Freedom, joined with poverty and labour, is a thing they even ridicule; and I have more than once witnessed how much an independent, wealthy slave can look down on a poor freeman of his own colour.[3]

Baille told the committee that when he offered several of his slaves permission to purchase their freedom '. . . they laughed in my face, and an old man said, "We know better, massa, than take freedom" '.[4]

This much of what the planters and pro-slavery propagandists said of the slaves' attitude to manumission was correct. Where they were completely misleading, however, was in their assertion that, because he often refused the opportunity to be manumitted, he did not desire emancipation.

The reservations which the slaves had about manumission were

---

[1] Anon. Letter to *Jamaica Journal*, Vol. 2, No. 8.
[2] BPP 1833 (539) Slave Registrations, Jamaica.
[3] Barclay, *A Practical View* . . . 1827, p. 241; also pp. 239–290.
[4] Select Com. . . . House of Lords, 1832.

a reflection of the pathetic socio-economic position of the free Negroes. We have already hinted at their poor economic condition; many of them being dependent on estate slaves for their subsistence. Socially, they were held in as much contempt as the slave. Like the slave their evidence was not acceptable against white persons throughout the seventeenth and eighteenth centuries. It was possible, however, for an enactment to be made which exempted the freeman from slave evidence, or other Negroes. Thus, in the very act of elevating the free Negro, the laws of the island condemned his race. This was somewhat different from the Latin American pattern, according to which the freed slave was allowed to participate as a citizen in the institutions of the society. In Jamaica the Negro race had become identified with slavery and this was the basic assumption of all its laws. A vicious circle had been created in which, as Stevens well expressed it, 'the slave is more hated and despised because he is a Negro; and the more repulsive in his person because he is a slave'.[1]

CONCLUSION

In the light of the above examination we may now ask ourselves the questions, how oppressive was slavery in Jamaica? How ill-treated were the slaves? What degree of personal freedom were they allowed? The laws, we have seen, gave the master absolute power over his slave. Until about the middle of the eighteenth century this power was greatly abused; after this there was some mitigation in the treatment of the slave (although the extent varied with the personality of the master) culminating in the period of the first phase of the abolition movement; then, with the growing certainty of emancipation, a return to the excessive brutality of the pre-mid-eighteenth century period took place.

Slavery can be seen as one polar type of a system of total power, and like the victims of all such systems the slaves knew 'that . . . in the final analysis, their fate would be determined by the will of those who wield total power'.[2] It was partly out of an instinctive recognition of this fact that throughout the seventeenth and eighteenth centuries the slaves neither sought the support of agents in

[1] Stevens, *op. cit.*, Vol. I, p. 38.
[2] Karl A. Wittfogel, *Oriental Despotism*, p. 108.

the system other than their masters, nor sought to be free in a system in which the wielders of total power were against the principle of manumission.

At one extreme of all systems of total power we may place classical oriental despotism, in which power was highly centralized, both the state and society were well developed, and an efficient bureaucracy functioned.[1] At the other extreme there was plantocratic slavery of the type that existed in Jamaica where power was completely diffused, where state and society were very poorly developed and where a bureaucracy hardly functioned, and when it did, was extremely inefficient. In the latter case we expect the power of the master to be potentially more total and personal since it is so much more direct.

Yet, the very factors which increased the potential tyranny of the Jamaican slave system, paradoxically, led to a mitigation of the situation of its victims. For example, the numerical insignificance of the whites led to a fear régime in which there were periodic outbreaks of brutality; but it also meant that there was much that the slaves could do that went undetected. Absenteeism led to irresponsible and cruel overseers supervising the slaves; but their laziness led to a relaxation of tyranny outside the work situation, and their incompetence to a situation where they were often outwitted by their slaves.

In short, there was a wide area in which the slaves' activities were economically and socially irrelevant to the masters. It is with this area of the slaves' activities that we shall be primarily concerned in the later chapters.

[1] See *ibid.*

CHAPTER IV

An Analysis of the Slave Population of Jamaica

AN ANALYSIS of the slave population of Jamaica is vital for several reasons. First, a knowledge of the number of slaves on the island is essential if we are to assess the extent and significance of the slave system and, no less important, to appreciate the ratio between the white masters and their Negro slaves. Only then can we understand the frequency of slave rebellions, the almost continuous fear and tension on the part of the white community; and, to some extent, their barbarity to the slaves, this being to a large extent a function of their own relative numerical insignificance.

Secondly, in analysing the failure of the slave population to reproduce itself – because of the high rate of mortality and the low rate of reproduction – we see clearly the extent of the severity of the system and at the same time gain some insight into the attitudes towards mating and reproduction on the part of both masters and slaves. In so doing the ground will be prepared for our more detailed discussion of the slave family later on.

The material to be discussed will be considered under three headings: (a) the actual number of slaves at different periods, with remarks relating to the 'artificial' growth and the rate of natural decline of the population; (b) an analysis of the various causes of mortality among the slaves, and (c) a consideration of the problems of reproduction and the attitudes toward pregnancy and child-bearing on the part of both masters and slaves.

A. Population Growth and Rates of Natural Decline

Tables 1 and 2 which give the various estimates and compilations of the population between 1658 and 1829 differs from Pitman[1]

[1] Pitman, *The Development of the B.W.I.*, Appendix 2.

and Roberts[1] mainly in the fact that we have filled in a few estimates (the additional sources being given in each case) which we consider to be no more inaccurate than those included by the above writers for the period between 1658 and 1787. We have also extended the compilation of the period before 1800 to 1795.

TABLE I: SLAVE POPULATION OF JAMAICA, 1658–1795

Year	No. of Slaves	Year	No. of Slaves
1658	1,400	1734	86,546
1662	552[1]	1740	99,239
1664	8,000[2]	1745	112,428
1673	9,504	1762	146,805
1675	9,000 (over 12)[3]	1768	166,914
1693	40,000[4]	1778	205,261
1703	45,000	1787	217,584[6]
1715	60,000[5]	1789	250,000[7]
1730	74,525	1795	291,000[8]

Sources of Table I:
[1] Journals of the House of Assembly, Vol. I. Appendix.
[2] Anon, *The Colonization of Jamaica.*
[3] Cranefield, 'Observation, etc.' C.O. 138/2.
[4] Representation of the Merchants of Ja. to the Board of Trade, C.O. 137/4.
[5] C.S.P. Colonial, 1715, No. 358.
[6] *The Jamaica Almanack*, 1787.
[7] Minutes of the Joint Committee of the Assembly and Council of Jamaica, 1789.
[8] *The Jamaica Almanack*, 1795.
Otherwise, see Pitman, *The Development of the B.W.I.*, pp. 373–74.

A brief glance at these tables reveals that the slave population increased rapidly during the period between 1662 and 1807, especially after 1700, only beginning to decline in 1809, two years after the abolition of the slave trade.

The increase in the slave population before 1809 was due, of course, entirely to the slave trade which we shall partly examine in the next chapter. From the figures relating to the import and re-export of slaves we can calculate the number of slaves remaining on

[1] G. W. Roberts, *The Population of Jamaica*, p. 36, (1957).

the island each year,[1] and on this basis, the remarkable natural decrease of the slave population can easily be shown.

TABLE 2: SLAVE POPULATION OF JAMAICA, 1800–1829

Year	No. of Slaves	Year	No. of Slaves
1800	300,939	1811	326,830
1801	307,094	1812	319,912
1802	307,199	1813	317,424
1803	308,668	1814	315,385
1804	308,542	1815	313,814
1805	308,775	1816	314,038
1806	312,341	1817	345,252
1807	319,351	1820	342,382
1808	323,827	1823	336,253
1809	323,714	1826	331,119
1810	313,683	1829	322,421
		1834	311,070[1]

See Martin, *Hist. of the Br. Colonies*, V. 2, pp. 188–89. Also the *Jamaica Journal*, Vol. 2, No. 25.

[1] See, Slave Compensation Claims, BPP XLVIII, (215) Note: Figures before 1817 (when Registration was enacted) were based largely on the Tax Rolls which were invariably underestimated since only masters with over 6 slaves were liable for taxation. See Edwards, *op. cit.*, Vol. I, p. 922. The uncertainty of the figures between 1817 and 1823 may have been due to duplication and general lack of familiarity with the registration system. See Evidence of W. Burge, BPP, 1831–32.

One point to be noted in table 3 is that the unusually high rate of natural decrease and the corresponding low rate of increase of the slave population between 1722 and 1730 is the consequence of the inclusion in Robert's figures of the estimate of 80,000 slaves for 1722 which is likely to be very markedly in error.

We may compare the rates in Table 3 with those of Table 4, which includes the years 1817 through 1829, and, coming within the period of registration, are far more accurate.

[1] See Appendix I.

TABLE 3: ESTIMATE OF POPULATION GROWTH, NET
IMPORTATION, AND RATES OF NATURAL
INCREASE OF SLAVES

Year	Slave Population	Net Importation of slaves	Annual rate of increase (%)	Estimated rate of natural decrease
1658	1,400	—	—	—
1673	9,504	—	—	—
1703	45,000	—	—	—
1722	80,000	55,536	—	—
1730	74,525	32,379	0·7	3·7
1734	86,546	19,754	—	—
1739	99,239	20,341	2·8	1·5
1746	112,428	36,510	1·8	2·8
1754	130,000	43,295	1·8	2·3
1762	146,464	54,908	1·5	3·0
1768	166,914	41,472	2·2	2·0
1778	205,261	54,951	2·1	2·1
1787	217,584	73,754	0·6	2·9

Source: Roberts, *The Population of Jamaica*, p. 36, except for the year 1787 where we have included a higher estimate and the remaining figures changed accordingly.

It is clear from these figures that the mortality rate was significantly lower in the nineteenth century than in the eighteenth. The annual mortality rate between 1823 and 1826, for example, was approximately 1·75 per cent. This is somewhat extraordinary, especially in view of the fact that after abolition, the predominantly adult African population undoubtedly gave an artificial stimulus to the mortality rate since they increased the older sector of the population without having any influence on the reproduction of the total slave population. Two explanations may be offered for this apparent discrepancy. The first is the fact that the creole slaves,

TABLE 4: INCREASE, DECREASE AND TOTAL POPULATION
OF SLAVES 1817–1829

Year	Males	Females	Total	Increase by Birth		Decrease by Death	
				M	F	M	F
1817	173,319	172,381	346,150	—	—	—	—
1820	170,466	171,916	342,382	12,201	12,145	13,425	11,681
1823	166,595	169,658	336,253	11,685	11,564	14,030	12,321
1826	162,726	168,393	331,119	11,604	11,422	13,520	11,650
1829	158,254	164,167	322,421	10,986	10,742	13,435	11,702

Source: BPP, 1833 (539) *Slave Registrations, Jamaica*

who outnumbered the Africans during the nineteenth century,[1]
may well have experienced a significant fall in their mortality rate
due to the amelioration of the system, which more than counter-
acted the impact of the older African-born sector. The second is
that the discrepancy may simply indicate, as Roberts suggests 'the
unreliability of early estimates of the slave population'.[2]

B. The Causes of Mortality During Slavery

The causes mainly responsible for the excessive mortality rate of
the slave population may be treated under the following heads:
seasoning, mortality of children 0–4 years of age; epidemic diseases;
hard labour and general ill-treatment.

(i) *Seasoning*   During the period of seasoning (i.e. the adjustment
of the African to his slave status on the plantation) which lasted
from between one and three years, between one quarter and one
third of the Africans died.[3] If an epidemic broke out, which happened frequently, 'at least a half could be expected to die'.[4] Thus,

[1] Select Committee. on Slavery, BPP, XX 1831–32, Q7937.
[2] Roberts, *op. cit.*, p. 40.
[3] *Practical rules for the management . . . of Negro Slaves*, etc. by a Professional
Planter, p. 44; Evidence of J. Wedderburn, Select Committee. on . . . the
Slave Trade, 1790–91.
[4] J. Wedderburn, *op. cit.*

on Worthy Park estate, between March 1792 and late 1793, of the 181 Africans bought, one quarter died, the majority of deaths being due to dysentery and the yaws.[1] Long, however, blames the dropsy for most of the deaths during seasoning, asserting that one third of them die during the first three years from this disease.[2]

A fact of some significance regarding the mortality of newly arrived Africans was that far more women tended to survive than men. This difference in the mortality rate between the sexes began from the middle passage where the ratio could be as great as 2 to 1.[3] Apart from recovering their spirits earlier, the women's chances of survival were improved by their more spacious accommodation in the hull of the ships, by the fact that they were not chained, and also by the fact that since they were sexually exploited by the seamen, these latter probably ensured the better treatment of whatever woman or women had taken their fancy.[*]

During seasoning, we are told by an overseer, who resided in the island between 1776 and 1786, that 'three men die to one women', part of the explanation being the great sexual demand for women among the male slaves.[4]

Four factors were largely responsible for the heavy mortality among the newly arrived Africans. First, there were the diseases which they caught on the middle passage. The appalling health conditions on the average slave ship are too well known to be further documented here.[5] Smallpox, fevers of all kinds, inflammations, venereal diseases, guinea worms, dropsy, and above all, yaws and dietary diseases, especially dysentery, were some of the most common. And we need hardly add that the debilitated state of most of the slaves and their complete lack of will to live made the possibility of infection and death from these diseases all the more possible.

In addition, the pernicious practice of the captains of slave ships

---

[1] See M. Gaunt, *Where the Twain Meet*, pp. 133–149; U. B. Phillips, 'A Jamaican Slave Plantation', *Amer. Hist. Review*, 1914.

[2] E. Long, *op. cit.*, Vol. 2, p. 435.

[3] Evidence of Wilson, Select Committee. on Slave Trade, 1790–91.

[*] It has been suggested that among many West African and Congo tribes at the turn of the 20th Century females outnumbered males by as much as 120 to 100. But the assertion has not yet been substantiated. See, L. W. Malcolm, "Sex Ratio in African Peoples", *American Anthr.*, Vol. 26, No. 4.

[4] Evidence of W. Fitzmaurice, 1790–91.

[5] For a full account of such conditions see the Abstract of Evidence on the Trade 1790–91; and Manix and Cowley, *Black Cargoes*.

whereby they concealed these diseases by rubbing the slaves over with substances which, according to Long, included gunpowder, lime juice and iron rust, often made early detection and effective treatment impossible.[1]

The second factor accounting for the unusually high mortality was no doubt the climate, although the contemporary accounts were fond of exaggerating its responsibility. Although Jamaica is tropical, it appears that the cool night breezes, especially in the mountains, and the chilly morning dew, often led to fevers among the newly arrived slaves which, in their debilitated condition, they were often incapable of withstanding. And particularly was this so during the last three months of the year.[2]

Thirdly, too much labour too soon was perhaps the main cause of death among the newly arrived. This was the opinion of the planter who wrote that '. . . to press for sudden and unremitted exertion is to kill them, which many unfortunately do every year'.[3]

Severity and too little attention is the fourth factor responsible for the high mortality rate during seasoning. New Negroes were continuously dejected and the mildest punishment or rebuke induced them to run away. This was often physically dangerous as the country was unknown and the African unwittingly sought out the most unhealthy creeks and gulleys in which to hide himself. The result was over-exposure, starvation, and fevers which too often proved fatal. Speaking of the lack of attention to new Negroes the 'professional planter' wrote:

> They arrive on the plantation . . . some clothing is assigned . . . they are fed from the pot, or perhaps dispersed among seasoned Negroes, and put to work; if sick the doctor is sent for and medicines are prescribed, which are seldom taken, for a new Negro is not very tractable; he languishes for some time, then dies, and his death is ascribed to the climate, which has been but little to blame.[4]

And to make matters worse, the new Negroes were quite often ill-treated by the older slaves who were elected to supervise them.[5]

Finally, changes of diet also had their effect on the new Negroes

[1] See also Evidence of Henry Coor, 1790–91, *op. cit.*
[2] *Practical Rules, op. cit.,* p. 50.   [3] *Ibid.,* p. 52.   [4] *Ibid.,* p. 53.
[5] E. Long, Bk. 3, p. 435.

both with respect to the quality and quantity of food given and the different times of eating from those to which the African had grown accustomed in his old society. Thus dietary troubles, especially dysentery, were common among the new slaves.

(ii) *Mortality in Age-group 0–4 years* Mortality within this age-group was excessive throughout the entire period of slavery. On Worthy Park estate during the five years between 1787 and 1792 there were 345 births. Of these 186 died by the end of the period. Thus on this estate, which seemed to have had at least normal management by Jamaican standards, there was a mortality rate of over 50 per cent in this age-group.[1]

M. G. Lewis, who visited his estate in 1817, expressed concern over the mortality of his infant slaves throughout his journals despite the fact that he employed all the usual (but very inefficient) techniques of preventing it. He mentions the case of a 'tender mother' who 'had borne ten children, and yet has now but one alive';[2] of another who had given birth to seven although only one lived to puberty; of Nicholas who had fathered children though none survived; and of his 'wife' who had borne fifteen, 'twelve whole children and three half ones' (i.e. miscarriages) yet only two survived; 'and the instances of those who have had four, five, six children, without succeeding in bringing up one, in spite of the utmost attention and indulgence, are very numerous'.[3]

Tetanus was a primary cause of death among infants. According to the 'professional planter' a quarter of all babies died of this disease within a fortnight of birth.[4] Among the diseases credited for the death of children on Worthy Park estate were 'Locked Jaw' (tetanus), 'Fever and Sore Throat' and 'Cold and Sore Throat'.[5] And from Long we learn that they die also from 'worms' and 'lack of warmth'.

It seems certain that the major source of all these diseases was the general unhealthiness of the conditions that children were exposed to and the attitudes and practices of the Negro mid-wives or 'grandees'. These grandees tended to regard the first nine days

[1] U. Phillips, *op. cit.*
[2] M. G. Lewis, *Journal of a West Indian Proprietor*, p. 97.
[3] *Ibid.*, p. 97.
[4] Practical Rules, *op. cit.*, p. 139.
[5] Mary Gaunt, *op. cit.*, p. 141.

of the child's life with a fatalistic kind of resignation. Lewis, for example, wrote that 'the midwife told me the other day, "Oh Massa, till nine days over, me no hope for them",' referring to the tetanus. And there was also a practice of confining infants to the same clothes without change for the first nine days.[1]

Even more pernicious were the herbs and folk medicines of the grandees. In a letter to the editors of the Jamaica Journal a planter refers to the 'oils and other pernicious drugs' given to newly-born infants by the old mid-wives. We are told that the navels of babies were soaked too much in moisture to induce inflammation and several other practices unfavourable to the survival of the infant are noted. Insufficient time was given the mother to care for her child; there was a lack of suitable clothing and nourishment, and he recommends that children should be allowed 'at least one good meal every day'; he condemns the rather primitive view regarding up-bringing and stated that 'to expose them to the inclemency of the weather with a view to render them hardy, is a foolish practice, and ought long ago to have been exploded'; finally he suggested that the age at which children started to work, between four and five years, was too early.[2]

(iii) *Diseases*   We have already discussed diseases under the above two headings. Among the slave population taken as a whole the most fatal complaints were yaws, fevers, fluxes, smallpox, dropsy, worms, tetanus, dirt-eating and various maladies peculiar to women such as obstruction of the menstrual flow. Apart from the yaws and fevers most of these different diseases were weighted toward particular groups, or were more prevalent than others at certain times. Thus, dirt-eating was more common among Africans from the slave coast and was indulged in mainly by women and children;[3] and diarrhoea and 'fluxes' came mainly during the rainy months or after droughts or hurricanes when the Negroes, from want, were tempted to eat the unripe yams and corn.

The treatment of the more serious of these disases was often quite primitive. Slaves suffering from the yaws, for example, were

----

[1] Gilbert Mathison, *Notices Respecting Jamaica*, 1805–10.
[2] Letter written Nov. 1813; published in *Jamaica Magazine*, Jan. 1, 1814.
[3] For an interesting account of dirt-eating, see Long's statements appended to the Privy Council Enquiries, 1788 in, B.T. 6: 10.

confined either at the seaside or in a filthy mountain cabin where, 'a cold, damp, smoky hut for his habitation; snakes and lizards his companions, crude viscid food, and bad water his only support; and shunned as a leper; . . . he usually sink from the land of the living'.[1]

During 1791 on Hyde Park estate, fourteen of the two-hundred slaves died, six of them being males and eight females. One of the men died of 'inflammation of the lungs', another died of 'a stroke of palsie', a third of a 'flux', a fourth of 'being bloated' and another of 'pleurisy'. One woman died of an 'inflammation of the lungs', another by drowning, a third of 'obstructions in the stomach and dirt-eating' and the death of the other is unknown. The other four, who were children, died of 'worm fever', dropsy, dirt-eating and tetanus.[2] And on Maryland estate in 1817 sixteen slaves died of whom nine were males and seven females. Causes of death were 'of old age', child-birth (two cases), 'convulsions', 'of dropsy', 'of an hereditary venereal', from fire while isolated in the 'yaws' house (two cases occurring a day after each other) consumption, flux and the yaws.

(iv) *Ill-treatment, Malnutrition, etc.*   There can be little doubt that too much labour, cruel punishments, starvation and general malnutrition were greatly responsible for the high mortality rate of the slaves.[3] Sometimes these factors operated immediately as in the not uncommon cases of masters beating their slaves to death; or in periods of severe droughts, as in the 1790s when thousands of slaves died of starvation and malnutrition.

Corbett also emphasises scarcity of food in his account of population decline during the first half of the eighteenth century:

Tis certain besides, that out of the Rage to push on their estates as their term is, many buy more Negroes than they have taken care to get Provisions for; some of the poor creatures pine away and are starved, others that have some spirits go a stealing and are shot as they are caught in Provision Grounds; others are whipt, or even hanged for going into the woods, into which

---

[1] Benjamin Moseley, *A Treatise on Sugar*, (1799), p. 169.
[2] *The Kingston Journal*, No. 85, 1788.
[3] Mathison, *op. cit.*, p. 34.

Hunger and Necissity itself drives them to try to get Food to keep Life and Soul together.[1]

One important indication of the severe effects of ill-treatment lies in the large number of invalid slaves to be found on almost every estate in the island. Of the 355 slaves on Worthy Park Estate in 1792, thirty-three were either invalids or superannuated while thirteen were in hospital.[2] And from the Rose Hall Estate list for 1832[3] we find that, of the fifty-one male slaves, ten were described as 'weakly' apart from other complaints; while of the sixty women, thirteen were 'weakly', two had whitlow and two had only one leg. Eight of the men described as 'weakly' were over fifty years of age, yet they were still working, most of them being watchmen, an occupation which, contrary to popular opinion of the time, was extremely hazardous since it exposed these slaves to the cold night air and chill. Eleven of the 'weakly' women were fifty years of age and over, yet they were still working, nine of them being grass-cutters, a very strenuous task. Another 'weakly' woman of forty-nine was also in the fields, so was Pathenia, a woman of thirty-four; so too, were the two whitlow women. Rose, one of the women with only one leg, was only twenty-three and in hospital. The other girl with the single leg was even younger, being seventeen, and was charged with attending the stock.

C. The Pattern of Reproduction

Far more emphasis was placed on the failure of reproduction by contemporary writers, especially those who were pro-slavery, in explaining the failure of the slave population to reproduce itself. The reason, of course, was that most of these writers, being themselves planters, were anxious to discount the importance of mortality on the estates and to blame the fecundity of the Negroes for the decline. Even anti-slavery writers sometimes tended to have this bias, although the immorality of the slave system rather than the female slave was blamed for the supposed low fertility rate.

We cannot completely separate the problem of reproduction from that of mortality for, as Roberts rightly points out, 'the failure

[1] Corbett, *Essay Concerning Slavery*, p. 38.
[2] Phillips, *op. cit.*
[3] *In old St. James.* Compiled by J. Shore and edited by J. Stewart, pp. 140–151.

of reproduction as a means of assuring population growth among the slave was to a large extent rooted in the prevailing levels of mortality', a fact made evident by the large number of 'diseases that ravaged the island during slavery'.[1]

The most important factor in any consideration of reproduction during slavery is an analysis of the attitudes toward pregnancy and child-rearing on the part of both masters and slaves. We shall begin with:

(i) *Attitudes of the Masters* The attitude of the slave owners and its expression in their actual treatment of pregnant women and children is best considered separately in respect of three periods. First, there is the period of early slavery between 1655 and the beginning of the eighteenth century. During this period the majority of estates belonged to small landowners with relatively little capital. The average owner had very few slaves and these he took great care of since they constituted the bulk of his capital (land was then cheap and the method of producing sugar simple). He therefore had a vested interest not only in preserving his slaves, but in increasing their numbers by reproduction. This he attempted to do mainly by buying an equal number of males and females.[2] With the emergence of large-scale, mono-crop production in the eighteenth century, however, and the subsequent departure of the small-holder, attempts at natural reproduction of the slave population were largely abandoned. Dr Harrison, who lived in Jamaica between 1755 and 1765, claimed that there was no 'encouragement given to bring up families; the general opinion being, that it was better to purchase new Negroes, than to rear Negro children'.[3] Henry Coor, who was a millwright in Jamaica for fifteen years, between 1759 and 1774, confirms Dr Harrison's evidence and further stated that it was thought 'a misfortune to have pregnant women, or even young slaves', the general view being that it was more economical to buy an adult slave than to rear one from birth.[4]

[1] Roberts, *op. cit.*, p. 225.
[2] Blome, *A Description of the Island of Jamaica*, (1678), p. 37. H. Sloane, *op. cit.*, Introduction.
[3] See also *Practical Rules*, etc., p. 131.
[4] Evidence of Henry Coor, 1790–91. The cost of rearing a slave to age fourteen was estimated, in 1831, at £112; in Trinidad it was £165; in Barbados, £109; in Antigua, £122. See *The West Indian Reporter*, No. XLI, March, 1831.

With the inception of the abolition movement, however, and the enquiry into the West Indian slave system, the Jamaican planters responded by ameliorating the slave laws and by adopting a new policy towards reproduction. In this last period, attempts were made not only on the crude level of the early period of simply equating the sexes (perhaps partly by this time the increasing creole population had begun to balance out the sexes) but of improving the conditions of pregnant women and of birth and generally paying more attention to the rearing of children. It was during this period that most of the numerous books, pamphlets, and articles dealing with the slave population were written, all either attempting to explain the causes of depopulation or offering advice on the best means of rearing slave children.

In some cases the attempts met with success, but in the majority of instances the unfavourable practices were too entrenched to be eradicated. Thus, despite all his laudable effort at increasing the slaves on his estate, Monk Lewis met with little success although the Negro women of child-bearing age co-operated as best they could.

(ii) *Attitudes and Practices of the Female Slaves* The attitudes of the owners were reflected in those of their slaves. It would appear from the available material that a considerable number of slave women disliked the idea of having children. As a planter himself describes her situation, 'upheld by no consolation animated by no hope, her nine months torment issue in the production of a being doomed, like herself, to the rigours of eternal servitude, and aggravating, by its claims on material support, the weight of her own evils'.[1] Dr Jackson, in his evidence, said much the same, adding that he often heard Negroes 'wish their own children dead, or that they had not bourne them, rather than be obliged to witness their daily punishment'.[2]

And this was no vain wish, as the case of Sabina Park who was tried at the Half Way Tree slave court for the murder of her three month old child demonstrates. Sabina's complaint, according to the Crown witness, was that 'she had worked enough for buckra (master) already and that she would not be plagued to raise the child . . . to work for white people'.[3] Few slaves, of course, would

[1] *Practical Rules*, etc., p. 135.   [2] Select Committee on Slave Trade, 1790–91.
[3] The *Jamaica Journal*, Vol. 1, No. 42.

go to this length, and the woman in question may well have been slightly mad; but there can be little doubt that her extreme attitude reflected a great deal of what a significant number of the slave women felt.

There was another important reason for the female slaves taking the attitude they did. Throughout the eighteenth century they were greatly outnumbered by the men. According to Long, 'Of the slaves shipped from the coast, not a sixth part are women', and on the estates he places the ratio at five to one.[1] It was estimated that in 1789 there was an excess of 30,000 males over females.[2] John Wedderburn estimated the male/female ratio at five to three;[3] but Hibbert was perhaps more accurate when he stated that while the ratio of imported Negroes was five males to three females, on the estates (due, no doubt to the differential male/female mortality) the ratio was four to three.[4] All these figures except that of Long, related to the later part of the eighteenth century when the growth of the creole population had begun to even out the sex ratio. Thus, by 1817, when the creoles constituted 63 per cent of the total slave population, the total female population was 49·9 per cent of the whole.[5]

One other factor must be considered. It is the fact that this ratio was made more acute by the polygamous mating patterns of the more prosperous of the slaves, mainly the head Negroes. According to Edwards, 'It is reckoned in Jamaica on a moderate computation, that not less than 10,000 of such as are called Head Negroes . . . possess from two to four wives'.[6]

Thus, of the 110,000 females in the island in 1789[7] an average of 30,000 would have been monopolised by only 10,000 men, leaving the remaining 130,000 men with only 80,000 females. In other words, assuming that the women remained virtuous, at any given moment at least 50,000 men would be without a mate or potential mate.

[1] E. Long, *op. cit.*, Vol. 2, Bk. 3, pp. 435–36.
[2] Brian Edwards, *op. cit.*, Bk. 4, p. 175.
[3] Select Committee. . . . on Slave Trade, 1790–91.
[4] *Ibid.*
[5] Select Committee. on Slavery, BPP XX, 1831–32, (721) Q7937.
[6] Edwards, *op. cit.*, Vol. 2, Bk. 4.
[7] The Minutes of the Joint Committee. of the Assembly and Council of Jamaica, Dec. 31, 1789.

The slave women, of course, did not remain virtuous. Under such temptations, with their bodies in such great demand and the economic rewards no doubt bountiful, it is impossible to conceive how they could have done so. Furthermore, there were no social sanctions, no notion of chastity or any ideal of marital status to restrain them. The masters themselves, who were the ultimate source of all power and authority in the society, were completely corrupt and competed with the male slaves for their bodies. The inevitable consequence of the unusually high demand for their sexual services, then, was extreme promiscuity.[1]

Promiscuity itself, of course, does not necessarily impair fertility as so many of the planters thought; but there is reason to believe that venereal diseases were common among the women and this no doubt reduced fecundity. Even more important, however, was the fact that abortion was widely practiced. A planter claimed that 'they endeavour to obtain miscarriage either by such violence as they know to be generally effectual, or by some of the simples of the country, which are possessed of forcible powers'.[2] Williamson,[3] Long,[4] and a host of other observers also commented on the frequency of abortions.

Perhaps a distinction should be made between the African and creole Negro slaves with respect to their attitudes towards child-rearing. In the first place, it was invariably the creole Negro who was most in physical demand. She was less unsophisticated than her African-born counterpart and physically more aesthetically pleasing to the white masters. It was asserted that the creole woman felt that child-bearing 'diminished their charms for the white men'.[5] Again, if we compare the accounts of two planters, those of De La Beche and Monk Lewis, we find that on De La Beche's estate, where 197 of the 297 slaves were creoles, abortion was rife especially among 'the young women'.[6] On the other hand, on Lewis' estate, which had a very large African population there is no mention of the

---

[1] B. Edwards, *op. cit.*, Bk. 4, p. 176. E. Long, *op. cit.*, Vol. 2, Bk. 3, p. 436. Corbett, *op. cit.*, p. 34.

[2] *Practical Rules, op. cit.*, p. 134.

[3] Williamson, *Medical and Miscl. Obs. on the W.I.*, 1817.

[4] Long, *op. cit.*, Vol. 2, Bk. 3, p. 436.

[5] Evidence of Dr. Jackson, Select Committee. on the Slave Trade, 1790–91.

[6] De La Beche, *Notes on the Present Condition of the Negroes in Jamaica*, 1825 p. 18.

practice of abortion. Lewis was particularly interested in reproducing his slaves and it is very unlikely that such a practice would have missed his observant eye.

It seems reasonable to conclude then, that the indifference to child-rearing noted by the contemporary writers was restricted largely to the young, attractive creole slaves. The habit of child-bearing was too strongly rooted in the African woman for even the slave system to destroy it. As the creole population grew, however, the attitudes noted above became more prevalent. Thus, by the time planters changed their own attitudes towards the reproduction of slaves near the end of the eighteenth century the attitudes and practices of the creole women, who had then begun to dominate the population of child-bearing age, had become well entrenched. No wonder then, that the planters failed so miserably.

We may next enquire, just how fertile were the slave women? First, we may ask at what age were the African women brought over to Jamaica? Edwards tells us that while male slaves of thirty-five years of age were readily acceptable on the West Coast of Africa, between twenty-two and twenty-three was the usual highest age of females.[1] Generally, it seems that the age of most of the women brought into the islands varied between fifteen and twenty-five. In short, the women brought over came within the period when they were ripe for child-bearing.

Secondly, it must be enquired whether the nature of work on the estates impaired child-bearing. Here there is decided evidence that it did. The heavy labour of the women was no doubt responsible for the frequency of gynaecological complaints among them. One of the most common of these complaints was that described as 'menstrual obstructions'. A planter explains the symptoms:

> ... the Negro is heavy and listless, complains of pains in the limbs, with a paleness of the countenance, with indisposition to labour, and in general, with all these symptoms which are found in *mal d'estomach*.[2]

This obstruction he attributes to 'their negligence, their exposure to rain out of doors and to the wind within, at the crucial period'.[3]

It seems clear that this complaint was simply one type of amenorrhea

[1] Edwards, *op. cit.*, Vol. 2, Bk. 4, p. 139.
[2] Practical Rules, *op. cit.*, p. 325.   [3] *Ibid.*

which may be due to 'disturbance in the endocrinal glandular system, severe malnutrition, or injury to the ovary'.[1] That malnutrition was very possible there can be no doubt as we shall show in our discussion of the slave's diet. And injury to the reproductive organs was always possible from the excessive beatings often inflicted on the women.

Long tells us too that in addition to amenorrhea the women often suffered from excessive flow at the time of their period. This is also another gynaecological complaint, menorrhagia, that may influence fertility. It seems that these menstrual problems were so severe as to stimulate what appears to be an early menopause in quite a few of the women, for a planter tells us that, some women had apparently grown so used to the condition (i.e. the absence of their period in relatively early life) that they continued to work as vigorously as ever without their 'customary evacuations'.[2]

Several other factors no doubt played their part in reducing fertility. There were venereal diseases; there was the fact, too, of excessively long periods of weaning lasting, on average, up to three years; and it is possible that the crude drugs used to induce abortions would very likely damage the reproductive organs and create sterility.

The earliest statistical evidence we have relating to fertility is to be found among the C. E. Long papers in the British Museum and they relate to a sample of only 263 slaves during the mid-18th century. Pitman has tabulated these figures as follows:[3]

TABLE 7:   FERTILITY AMONG A SAMPLE OF 77 CHILDBEARING
           SLAVES

Year	Births	Boys	Girls	Deaths
1766	5	3	2	6
1767	6	3	3	8
1768	7	3	4	7
	18	9	9	21

[1] H. C. Hesseltine, Md., *Encyclopaedia Americana*, Vol. 18, p. 638.
[2] Practical Rules, *op. cit.*, p. 325.
[3] F. W. Pitman, 'Slavery in the B.W.I. .... in the 18th Century', *Journal of Negro History*, VII 639–40.

There were 123 male slaves in the sample and 140 females (unusual at the time) 77 of whom were of child-bearing age. Seventy-seven women therefore produced an average of only six births per year. It should be noted, however that only the live births are given in the above figures. Thus, of the 345 births occurring during the period covered by the Worthy Park Estate books, seventy-five were still-births. By this time, however, things had improved slightly (the new laws ensured that women who had borne more than six children should be relieved of work). There were eighty women of child-bearing age and these had given birth to an average of nine children per year, over a five year period, which, on a crude rate, was close to twenty-three per thousand.[1]

What is interesting about these figures, however, is the fact that, 'the child-bearing records of the women past middle age ran higher than those of the younger ones to a somewhat surprising degree',[2] Phillips attempts an explanation, along the lines that 'perhaps conditions on Worthy Park had been more favourable at an earlier period, when the owner and his family *may possibly* have been present'.[3] A more plausible explanation, however, is that in the earlier period of the estate there would have been more women of African origin with a far more favourable attitude to child-bearing than at the period of the records (1787–1792) when the creole women of child-bearing age would have become dominant.

Thus, during most of the eighteenth century when there were large numbers of African slaves and most of the women of child-bearing age were willing to bear children, the owners strongly discouraged the breeding of children. While there were large numbers of pregnancies, therefore, neglect, unhygienic conditions, and ill-treatment of pregnant women[4] led to many miscarriages and an excessively high death rate among children between 0 and 4 years of age. On the other hand, during the last two decades of the eighteenth century and in the early nineteenth century up to the

---

[1] Mary Gaunt, *op. cit.*, 147.

[2] Phillips, U., *op. cit.*

[3] *Ibid.*

[4] There was, for example, the pernicious practice of punishing pregnant women by burying them in a hole in the ground up to their waist and then beating them on their back; and Moreton tells us that pregnant women 'work till before a few days of delivery'. See the Evidence of Lieut. Baker Davison and of Dr. Jackson, to the Select Committee, 1790–91.

beginning of apprenticeship (by which time the certainty of abolition led to the most severe forms of ill-treatment), when an attempt was made to ameliorate the treatment of the slaves and to improve the conditions of reproduction, the slave women of child-bearing age, now largely creoles, were hardened in their anti-breeding attitudes with the result that most of the schemes for increasing the population by greater reproduction failed.

CHAPTER V

The Tribal Origins of the Jamaican Slaves

THE SLAVES of the New World almost all came from an area of the western section of the African continent stretching for more than five thousand miles from the region of the Senegal down to Cape Negro, several hundred miles south of Benguela. In this area were to be found hundreds of tribes with greatly varied customs and beliefs. If we are to understand the social values and behaviour of the Jamaican slave it is important that we examine his tribal origins. Such an examination will assist us in understanding both the nature of the adjustment which the African slave made to the culture of his master and the new social and cultural patterns that emerged as the result of this adjustment among the creole slaves. It is the object of this chapter to make such an examination.

The chapter will be divided into two parts. Part one will examine the supply side of the trade, the first section dealing with the various areas of trading on the coast and the second with an assessment of the nature and extent of British trading in the separate areas. Part two will examine the demand side of the slave trade considered from the particular point of view of Jamaica.

PART I

THE SOURCES OF THE SLAVE POPULATION

SECTION I
THE TRADING AREAS OF WEST AFRICA

There were six main areas of trading on the west coast of Africa: Senegambia; Sierra Leone and the Windward Coast; the Gold

Coast; the Slave Coast; the Bight of Benin and the region of the Niger and Cross deltas; and south-western Africa from the Cameroons down to Cape Negro. Each of these areas will be examined with a view to ascertaining (a) the main tribal groups and their relations with each other; (b) European contact with the area and the particular mode of trading for slaves; (c) estimates of the proportion of slaves exported; the distance inland from which these slaves came; and the tribes of the different areas which were especially subject to enslavement.

(i) *Senegambia* Four main tribes occupy the region south of the Senegal and on either side of the Gambia. They are the Mandingos (or Mandinka speaking peoples), the Fulas (also known as the Poula, Pholey, Fulbie, Fulani), the Jallofs (also known during the seventeenth and eighteenth centuries as Jaloffs, Wallofs and Walloff), and the Jolas, also known as Feloops and Floops. The dominant tribe in the area were the Mandingos who, because of their superior political and social systems were able to act as agents for the Europeans in the area, waging wars with the weaker tribes and selling their prisoners into slavery.

The Portuguese arrived in the area about the middle of the fifteenth century but the quality of these early traders was very poor.[1] The Netherlands was the first to challenge the monopoly of the Portuguese in the area and by 1637 had captured a large section of the latter's forts. It was not until 1620, when the Guinea Company was formed, that any serious British venture was made in the area. The company was a failure, but it is significant that when one of the captains was offered slaves for sale he politely refused, stating that, 'we are a people, who did not deale in any such commodities, neither did wee buy or sell one another, or any that had our own shapes'.[2] British interest in the area waned after this, but when, in 1651, they renewed their activities the attitude toward the purchasing of slaves had completely changed, for by this time plantations in Barbados and elsewhere were being opened up by British settlers who needed negroes to work on them. The Company of Royal Adventurers was founded in 1661, but as Davies pointed out, 'The whole venture was more reminiscent of an aristocratic

---

[1] J. D. Fage, *Introduction to the History of West Africa*, p. 53.
[2] Richard Jobson, *The Golden Trade*, (1623) Charles Kingsley edition, p. 112

treasure-hunt than of an organized business; indeed, its principal objective was the search for gold'.[1] Both this company, and its successor – the Gambia Company – failed, but matters changed for the better with the founding of the Royal African Company. With the subsequent withdrawal of the Dutch from the scene after the collapse of the Dutch West India Company, and the consolidation of the French after their capture of Goree, the area became an arena of sustained rivalry between the latter and the English.

Mungo Park has left us the most detailed account of the origins and manner of obtaining slaves in the area. First, he asserts that there were two basic types of slaves; those born into slavery and belonging to the household of their masters and who could not easily be sold; and those captured in war or bought into slavery[2]. And yet, Park claimed, the majority of slaves sold to the whites were already slaves, for three reasons. First was the fact that only a third of the entire population of the area was free and therefore the great majority of those taken in war would naturally belong to the slave group. Secondly, in the tribal wars, the free people were better armed, formed the bulk of the cavalry and were in a much better position to escape capture if routed by the enemy. Third, in the event of a free man being taken prisoner there was a good chance that his friends and relations would try to rescue him by offering two slaves in exchange. No slave could expect such an offer to be made on his behalf. In addition, the Slatees themselves preferred slaves from birth mainly because they were used to hard labour and were less likely to attempt an escape.

Of those who were born free and later became slaves, four main reasons were given. First, there were those captured in wars (Killi) or by raiding parties (Tegria). Secondly, in cases of famine, parents were often compelled to sell their children into slavery to prevent them from starving, and sometimes to prevent their own starvation. Thirdly, there were those sold into slavery to redeem their debts, this according to Park being the most common form of enslavement. Finally, freemen were enslaved for committing certain crimes, mainly murder, adultery and witchcraft.

From other evidence it would appear, however, that Park placed too much emphasis on the wars of the interior as the main source

[1] K. G. Davies, *The Royal African Company*, p. 41.
[2] Mungo Park, *Travels in the Interior of Africa*, Ch. 12.

of the slaves. The Swedish scientist, Wadstrom, who visited the coast in 1787 and 1788, contended that the principal means of obtaining slaves was by pillaging:

> The first is what they call General Pillage, which is executed by order of the King when slaving vessels are on the coast; the second by Robbery by individuals; and thirdly by stratagem, or Deceit, which is executed both by the kings and individuals.[1]

In a pamphlet he later wrote on the subject he tells us that the Mandingos, at the instigation of the French, often encouraged petty wars among the tribes of the interior, the prisoners of which were then taken and sold.[2] The French were the dominant power in this region during the eighteenth century and had such complete control over the petty principalities on or near the coast that they were often able to bribe or force the rulers to plunder their own villages.[3]

Compared with the other regions, this area produced relatively small numbers of slaves during the late seventeenth and eighteenth centuries. When Francis Moore traded there in the 1730s he found that 'the chief trade of this country' was 'Gold, Slaves, Elephant's Teeth, and Bees Wax'.[4] In addition, the Mandingo merchants bring down the river 'in some years slaves to the amount of 2000'.[5] According to Captain R. Healy, the number of slaves exported from the Gambia before 1770 was on average about 2,500 annually. In 1775, two thousand slaves were exported but the number fell off in each of the subsequent years and in 1788 'not above twelve or fifteen hundred are exported'.[6] A British Governor of the Senegal, Barnes, stated that the number exported annually from the area during the 1780s was between 1,400 and 1,500.[7] When Mungo Park toured the region at the beginning of the nineteenth century only 1,000 slaves were being exported annually.

---

[1] C. B. Wadstrom, 'Evidence Delivered before a Select Committee. of the House of Commons in the years 1790 and 1791'.

[2] C. B. Wadstrom *Observations on the Slave Trade*, 1789.

[3] *Ibid.*

[4] F. Moore, *Travels into the Inland Parts of Africa*, p. 40.

[5] *Ibid.*, p. 41.

[6] Evidence of Capt. Healy, Taken Before a Committee. of the Privy Council, B.T. 6: 10.

[7] Evidence of J. Barnes, B.T. 6:9.

The data on the distance inland from which the slaves came appear contradictory. Earlier accounts, such as Moore's, assert that the great majority came from areas far inland. Thomas Poplett, who frequented Goree and the Gambia between 1779 and 1783, stated that only one eighth came from the interior through 'the stealing of the Moors' while the remainder came from the country around the coast. A quarter of all the slaves, he further informs us, had been freemen who were enslaved for their crimes; another quarter were prisoners taken in war: and a half were born and bred in the country 'as stock to be sold to the whites'.[1] Poplett's view that most of the slaves came from the coastal belt during the 1770s and 1780s was substantiated by Wadstrom's evidence.[2] However, by the beginning of the nineteenth century it was claimed by Park that the majority of the slaves came from vast distances inland.

Summarizing, it would appear that during the early period of slaving many of the inland sources that used to feed the long established Arab trade route across the Sahara started sending their cargoes westwards to meet the new demand on the coast. During the eighteenth century, however, most of the slaves came from areas not far inland being mainly the prisoners taken in the wars deliberately incited by the slave traders or in pillaging parties. Finally, towards the end of the eighteenth century, as the coastal sources became exhausted, there was a return to the distant inland markets. More important is the fact that almost all the main tribes of the area seem to have been well represented although the weaker and smaller peoples would have contributed a greater proportion than the larger, more developed ones.

(ii) *Sierra Leone and the Windward Coast*   Snelgrave defined the Windward Coast as that part of West Africa stretching for two hundred leagues from the river Sherbro, round Cape Palmas to the River Ancober near Axim.[3] The area may be further divided into what was known as the Grain Coast, the Ivory Coast and the region on either side of the Sherbro and Sierra Leone Rivers. The entire region is occupied by three main linguistic groups. To the southwest

---

[1] Evidence of J. Barnes, B.T. 6:9.
[2] Evidence of Thomas Poplett, B.T.6:10.
[3] William Snelgrave, *A New and Exact Account of Some Parts of Guinea*, (1734), Introduction.

is a group of tribes speaking the Kru branch of the Kwa sub-family of African languages. These include the Bakwe, Bassa, Bete, Dida, Grebo, Kru, Sapo, Wobe, etc. To the northwest of this group, in the region of what is now Liberia and Sierra Leone, are tribes speaking the Atlantic sub-family of African languages.[1] These include the Sherbro Bullom, Temme, Goia, Kissi, etc. And there is a third group, designated by Murdock, the 'peripheral Mande', which includes the Dan, Gagu, Guru, Kono, Mende, Vai, Ngere, and Gbande. Although their languages differ greatly all these peoples have had considerable mutual contact with each other and there is a striking degree of cultural uniformity among them.[2]

There was relatively little slave trading in the areas of the Grain and Ivory Coasts during the late seventeenth and eighteenth centuries, the Europeans considering the Africans there particularly 'barbarous and uncivilized', perhaps because the natives wisely prevented them from coming ashore, going instead to the anchored ships in their canoes to trade.

In Sierra Leone, the African Company, apart from competition from illegal British traders, pirates and the French,[3] had to contend with the extremely independent local rulers who not only demanded 'cole' or duty, but obliged all Europeans to trade through a system of 'landlordship' whereby the Europeans hired a headman or 'respectable native' to act as agent for them in procuring slaves.[4]

Slaves were taken in much the same manner as in Senegambia, most of them being kidnapped by pillaging parties or captured in petty wars,[5] a great many of the latter being waged deliberately to obtain slaves.[6] The rulers of the area were also notorious for enslaving their subjects on fabricated charges, the most common of which was witchcraft, the accused being tried by an ordeal known as 'Red Water'.[7] According to Penny, who commanded a slave ship on the Guinea Coast between 1766 and 1784, about 2,500 slaves were

[1] G. P. Murdock, *Africa: Its Peoples and their Culture History*, pp. 222–29, 265–69.
   M. M'Culloch, *Peoples of the Sierra Leone Protectorate*.
[2] Murdock, M'Mulloch, *op. cit.*
[3] C. Fyfe, *Sierra Leone Inheritance*, pp. 63–5.
[4] J. Mathews, *A Voyage to the River Sierra Leone*, 1788, pp. 142–46.
[5] J. Newton, *The Journal of a Slave Trader*, 1750–54, p. 99.
[6] Evidence of John Simpson, 1790–91.
[7] *Journal of Zachary Macaulay*, No. 18, 1793; Nics Owens, *Journal of a Slave Dealer*, – (Owens lived in the Sherbro region during the 1750s).

exported annually from this area and of these two-thirds went to the British and a third to the French.[1] When Mathews traded in the area in 1785 he found that the total number of slaves exported 'amounts to about three thousand'.[2]

(iii) *The Gold Coast* Most of the peoples of the Gold Coast belong to the Twi speaking group of the Kwa sub-family of African languages. The largest linguistic sub-division in the area is the Akan. To the north of the Akan, in the hinterlands, are the less developed Guang peoples; and to their northeast are the speakers of the 'Togo remnant languages'. To their east are the Ewe speaking Ga and Adangme peoples.[3]

Until the middle of the eighteenth century, there was considerable movement and conflict among the various tribes of the Gold Coast. Indeed, on the basis of their oral tradition, it would seem that most of the major tribes now occupying the region did not arrive there long before the first Europeans.[4] When our period (i.e. between 1655 and 1807) opens, the Ga tribes who have been described by Field as 'remarkable fragments of tribes and families'[5] were nearing the end of a long and exhaustive war with the Akwamu, who in 1660 decisively defeated them. Twenty years later a large party of them migrated to Little Popo,[6] and the remainder only escaped total extermination from the slave raiding of their more powerful neighbours by forming a military confederacy.

Not long after their victory over the Ga, the Akwama were again at war, this time with the Akim and several other groups including the Dutch fort of Crovencoeur at Accra, the Agona, Akim, Obutu and several other tribes.[7] It was not until the beginning of the eighteenth century that the most powerful of all the Gold Coast kingdoms, Ashanti, began to make its bid for power among the larger coastal states. After their decisive defeat of Denkera in 1701, they were continuously at war until about the middle of the eighteenth century by which time they had become the largest and most

---

[1] Penny, Evidence of, 1788, B.T.6:9, f. 327.

[2] Mathews, *op. cit.*

[3] M. Manoukian, *Akan and Ga-Andangme Peoples of the Gold Coast*, pp. 1-10.

[4] Eva Meyoritz, *Akan Traditions of Origin.*

[5] J. S. Field, *Religion and Medicine Among the Ga*, p. 3.

[6] Ward, *A History of Ghana*, pp. 106-7

[7] *Ibid.*, p. 108.

powerful state in the area, having subdued numerous smaller kingdoms, including Bono, Gonja, Dagomba and the three Akim states.[1]

Another Akan tribe, the Fanti, also rose to prominence about the same time our period begins. They earned themselves the reputation for being the most unscrupulous and efficient traders on the coast. At times they played off the Europeans against each other, as in the Dutch-Kommenda wars;[2] at other times, one native tribe against another, often stealing prisoners from both sides while acting as auxiliaries.[3] Nor were the Fantis any less ruthless among themselves. A great number of their own people were sold into slavery for crimes they had committed and, as will be demonstrated presently, at one time the bulk of the coastal slaves came from among them.

Finally, there were the tribes of the interior who supplied the great majority of the slaves from the Gold Coast, being the last stage or reservoir of the elaborate shunting process beginning with the coastal traders, then moving to the middlemen of the midlands, and ending with them. The main tribes of this region were the Mamprusi, Dagomba, Nankanse, Talense, Isala, Lober and others of the very primitive Tengani regions.[4] These people were in a state of continuous turmoil during the length of our period, entire tribes being subdued by wandering bands of marauders.[5] Annual tributes of slaves were paid to the more powerful midland and coastal states by them. In 1700 alone a ransom of 2,000 slaves was imposed on the ruler of the Dagamba people by the Ashanti as the price for not supporting his rival for the stoolship.[6]

There were twenty-four European forts on the coast at the beginning of the eighteenth century. Of these, eight were English; twelve were Dutch; two belonged to the Brandenburgers; and two to the Danes. Cape Coast Castle belonging to the English, and Elimina, to the Dutch, were the headquarters of both of these

[1] W. W. Claridge, *A History of the Gold Coast and Ashanti*, Vol. 1, pp. 181–208.

[2] *Ibid.*, pp. 150–51

[3] Evidence of Dalzell, 1788, B.T.6:10, f. 148–49. E. Donnan, "Letters from Anambo", in her, *Documents Illustrative of the Slave Trade to America*, Vol. 2, pp. 526–528.

[4] R. S. Rattray, *Tribes of the Ashanti Hinterland*, Vols. 1 & 2.

[5] *Ibid* also, Eyre-Smith, *A Brief Review of the History ... of the Northern Territories of the Gold Coast.*

[6] E. F. Tamakloe, *A Brief History of the Dagamba People*, p. 33.

countries.[1] The manner of obtaining slaves was similar to that practiced in Senegambia and the Windward Coast but varied in emphasis from one period to the next. During the last half of the seventeenth century and the early eighteenth century the majority of the slaves came from the prisoners taken during the wars between the larger coastal peoples.[2] When peace was finally restored among the larger states about the middle of the eighteenth century increasingly large numbers of slaves came from the hinterland. Between 1763 and 1770 the proportion of slaves coming from the coastal tribes varied considerably although at times it could be as great as a half.[3] Jerome Weuves, who lived on the coast between 1778 and 1782 and was Governor of both Anambo and Cape Coast Castle, estimated that between 6,000 and 8,000 slaves were exported annually from the coast, and that 'the English have about two-thirds of this trade'.[4] He further estimated the number brought from the coastal tribes at a quarter of the whole, the remaining three-quarters coming from 'the interior countries'. Richard Miles, who was also at one time Governor of Cape Coast Castle, and whose knowledge of the area is confined to the period between 1765 and 1784 estimated the number of slaves annually exported by the English to be between seven and eight thousand. Miles, who knew the Fanti well and could speak their language, further informs us that of the total number of slaves exported 'one fourth or nearly . . . . are Fantees . . . who beyond a doubt are for Debts and Crimes of different descriptions . . .; the chief of their crimes are Debts, Thefts, Adultery and Witchcraft . . . the other three-quarters of the slaves are brought from the interior parts of the country to borders of Fantee or other Nations near the seaside'.[5] The method of obtaining slaves from the hinterland was often, to say the least, extremely wasteful. Claridge claims that:

> It has been computed that 20,000 were slaughtered in five such expeditions undertaken by the Bornus before three quarters of that number had been obtained as slaves, and that five

[1] Claridge, *op. cit.*, Vol. I., pp. 162–73.
[2] See Bosman, *A New and Accurate Description of the Coast of Guinea*, etc., 1705., pp. 70, 181–84.
[3] Dalzell, Evidence, 1788, B.T.6:10, f. 147.
[4] J. Weuves, Evidence, B.T.6:9, f. 473.
[5] Miles, Evidence, 1788, B.T.6:9, ff. 443–44.

twelfths of the captives of ten perished on the journey to the coast.[1]

(iv) *The Slave Coast* This area roughly approximates to what is now known as Dahomey. The Ewe speaking inhabitants of the area adhere to a highly homogenous culture[2] but not all the slaves that came from this part of the coast were of Ewe stock. Many of them were derived from the Yoruba speaking peoples of the Oyo and Benin empires and were known both on the coast and in the Americas as Nagos.

Like the Ashantis, the Dahomeans, about the turn of the eighteenth century, began to push towards the coast in an effort to eliminate the middlemen, in their case mainly the Ardras, Popos and Whydahs. Dahomey – which is the Fon dialectal group of the Ewes – was a military régime which lived almost entirely on war and pillage, profiting greatly from the prisoners captured in her wars. Ardra was first subdued; then Whydah and Popo (though not completely until near the end of the eighteenth century) and finally, in 1732, Jaquin.[3]

The great Oyo empire of the Yorubas was already beginning to collapse when our period begun. Like the Dahomeans they were in an almost continuous state of warfare which drained their resources and depopulated their countryside and eventually led to the collapse of the empire into civil war.[4] Most of the slaves sold by the Oyos were, like themselves, Yorubas. Until the end of the third quarter of the eighteenth century most of the slaves were sold on the Slave Coast but during the nineteenth century, as the Oyo and Benin kingdoms declined into civil wars vast numbers of them were sent down to the port of Lagos which grew rich on trading in them.[5]

Snelgrave, writing of the early eighteenth century, asserted that 'above 20,000 Negroes' were 'yearly exported from thence and the neighbouring places of the English, French, Dutch and Portuguese'.[6] Atkins, who visited Whydah about the same time as Snel-

---

[1] Claridge, *op. cit.*, Vol. I, p. 173.
[2] See M. J. Herskovits, *Dahomey*, 2 Vols.
[3] P. A. Talbot, *The Peoples of Southern Nigeria*, Vol. I. pp. 38–9; Snelgrave, *op. cit.*, pp. 6–20, 75–109. K. Madhu Panikkar, *The Serpent and the Crescent*, pp. 156–165.
[4] Panikkar, *op. cit.*
[5] Sir A. Burns, *History of Nigeria*, p. 36.
[6] Snelgrave, *op. cit.*, p. 4.

grave (1721) when it was at the height of its prosperity wrote that it was 'the greatest trading place on the Coast of Guinea, selling off as many slaves, I believe, as all the rest together'.[1] Dalzell, speaking of the period between 1763 and 1770, estimated that between ten and twelve thousand slaves were exported annually from this area. The French, by an early, foresighted support of the emerging Dahomean kingdom, had begun to dominate trading in the area from as early as the second decade of the eighteenth century and by the time Dalzell traded there, they were exporting approximately two-thirds of all the slaves which then amounted to between 10,000 and 12,000 annually. Of this number the English only exported between seven hundred and eight hundred and the Portuguese about 3,000 annually.[2]

(v) *Benin and the Area of the Niger and Cross Deltas* As early as 1510 Benin was trading exclusively in slaves with the Europeans.[3] By the end of the eighteenth century, however, it lay in almost complete waste due largely to internal strife.[4] and the English had already abandoned their trading post at Arebo.[5] It was not until after 1818, with the final collapse of the Benin and Oyo empires into civil wars, that vast numbers of slaves began once more to leave the area, now, however, going almost exclusively to the Brazilian and Portuguese traders.

Far more important for our period, however, are the regions of the Niger and Cross deltas. The main tribes of the area are the Ibos of the interior who are by far the most numerous, the Ibibios, the Edos and the aboriginal Ijos of the coastal area. In addition, there are numerous obscure tribal groups such as the Atisia, Ogoni, Epie and the like.[6]

The main slave-trading towns during our period were those of Kalabari (New Calabar) and Bonny, both of the Ijo tribal group and situated on the New Calabar and Bonny rivers respectively; and Old Calabar which was divided into three villages – Duke

---

[1] John Atkins, *Voyage to Guinea*, p. 168.
[2] Dalzell, B.T.6:10, f. 133.
[3] M. Crowder, *The Story of Nigeria*, p. 61.
[4] O. Dapper, *Description of Africa*, quoted in B. Davidson *Black Mother*, pp. 203–9.
[5] Bosman, *op. cit.*, pp. 430–31.
[6] G. I. Jones, *The Trading State of the Oil Rivers, etc.* p. 10.

Town, Creek Town and Old Town – and was peopled mainly by
the Efik tribe, a branch of the Ibibio peoples.

The great majority of the slaves from this area came from the
inland region and were brought down the rivers in large canoes in
which, according to Dapper, 'full sixty, nay, as many as eighty men,
can be carried'.[1] Trading was carried out through an elaborate
shunting process between the coast and about eighty miles inland,[2]
whereby the average slave was sold about six times before reaching
the European traders.[3] About three-quarter of the slaves sold at
Bonny were Ibos, an estimated 16,000 annually deported between
1800 and 1820.[4] Large numbers of slaves were also kidnapped
from tribes closer to the coast as the diary of Antera Duke, a
contemporary native trader, illustrates.[5]

At the beginning of the eighteenth century Barbot found that
'the Dutch have the greatest share in the trade; the English next;
and after them the Portuguese'.[6] Between 1776 and 1784, by which
time the area had become the largest exporter of slaves in Africa,
about 14,000 slaves were being exported annually from Bonny and
New Calabar.[7] By this time the English had become the dominant
trading nation there, exporting 11,000 of the slaves. The rest went
to the French who were the only other European traders at that time.
Basically the same pattern held for Old Calabar. In 1752 Liverpool
merchants alone bought 2,810 slaves; and in 1799 they took away
1,654. Between January 1785 and January 1788, slaves to the number of 7,511 or an average of 2,504 slaves per annum,[8] left the area.

(vi) *Southwestern Africa*   In this region we shall include the rest
of the West Coast of Africa down to Cape Negro. The number of
slaves from the Cameroon and Gaboon who found their way to
Jamaica and the rest of the West Indies were insignificant. Between
the avaricious Portuguese traders hungry for black labourers, and
the pious Jesuit missionaries, so desirous of black souls that they

---

[1] Dapper, *Description de l'Afrique*, (1686), French edition, pp. 315–316.
[2] Penny, *Evidence of . . . 1788*, B.T.6:9, f. 270.
[3] See the autobiography of Gustavus Vassa, an Ibo ex-slave, (1789), Ch. 2.
[4] J. Adams, quoted in Talbut, *op. cit.*
[5] D. Forde, ed., *Efik Traders of Old Calabar*.
[6] Barbot, *A Description of the Coasts of North and South Guinea*, (1732), p. 381.
[7] Penny, B.T.6:9, f. 277.
[8] 'The Diary of Antera Duke' in D. Forde, *op. cit.*

did not scruple to advocate 'preaching with the sword and rod of iron',[1] both the highly developed kingdom of the Congo[2] and the neighbouring country of Angola were reduced, by the time our period opens, to little more than warring groups of petty states totally and disastrously involved in the slave trade.

The English tended at first to neglect this area, concentrating on the Guinea coast. By the beginning of the last quarter of the seventeenth century, however, the abundance of cheap slaves in the area – and in particular Angola – began to attract large numbers of Britons, especially the private traders.[3] During the course of the eighteenth century, however, there was a rapid falling off of British trading in the area while the French and Portuguese consolidated their position. Penny, speaking of his experiences between 1776 and 1784, said that between 13,000 and 14,000 slaves were being exported from the Congo and Angola each year, the French exporting all but 8,400 of this number. And of this 8,400 only about 400 were taken by the English, mainly from Amberiss, the remaining 8000 by the Portuguese from the region between Loango St Paul and Fort Phillip.[4] It appears that by the last quarter of the eighteenth century the Dutch had emerged as a serious competitor to the French in the area.[5] During the last seventeen years or so of the British trade the near exhaustion of the Guinea supplies led to a resurgence of British interest in the area particularly the Congo, which then became the largest single source of slaves.

(vii) *Conclusions:* We have examined the nature of slave trading on the West Coast of Africa with particular reference to the latter half of the seventeenth and the eighteenth centuries. By 1640 the Dutch had completely destroyed the Portuguese monopoly and were themselves the main traders on the continent, their period of ascendancy lasting until 1640. The creation of the British monopoly trading companies and the inevitable political clash between the English and the Dutch, culminating in the wars of the 1650s – which, even

---

[1] C. R. Boxer, *Four Centuries of Portuguese Expansion 1415–1825*, p. 30.

[2] See Davidson, *Black Mother*, p. 126; *The African Past* pp. 191–94.

[3] J. Barbot and J. Casseneuve, *An Abstract of a Voyage to Congo River*, (1732) See extract in P. A. Walckenaer, Collection Des Relations de Voyages, p. 391–428.

[4] Penny, *Evidence*, 1788, B.T.6:9, f. 295–96.

[5] B. Edwards, *History of the W.I.*, Vol. 2, p. 61.

when officially ended in Europe, still continued in Africa – saw the beginning of the collapse of Dutch commercial and sea power. 'By about 1655', writes Newton, 'all the Negroes brought to Barbados, Jamaica and the Leeward Islands came in English ships'.[1]

After the beginning of the eighteenth century each European nation began to show a preference for particular areas along the coast, based partly on their financial commitments there, partly on their knowledge of the area, and partly on the extent to which they influenced the native population. Thus, the French, long before the middle of the eighteenth century, were the leading power in the Senegal, the Slave Coast, the Cameroons and parts of the Congo; the English were predominant in the Gambia, the Windward Coast, the Gold Coast and the region now known as Nigeria; the Dutch had a significant minority share of the Gold Coast, Nigerian and Congo trade; and the Portuguese, almost by default, continued to be the main European power in Angola and parts of the Congo.

With regard to the sources of the slaves and the distance inland from which they came, our examination has made it reasonably clear that the '1000 miles trek' theory, as Herskovits has already argued,[2] must be discarded. Apart from the two extremities of the trading areas of the west coast – the Senegal and Congo rivers – few of the slaves came from an area more than two or three hundred miles inland. In any case, what is important is not so much the distance from which they came geographically, but culturally. No doubt a considerable number of slaves sold on the Nigerian coast came from a great distance inland, but it is known that almost all these inland slaves came from one basic tribal stock, the Ibos, who despite their highly segmentary social structure and small area of political allegiance nonetheless speak basically the same language and adhere to what amounts to a remarkably uniform pattern of values and behaviour.[3]

---

[1] A. P. Newton, *The European Nations in the West Indies*, p. 282.
[2] M. J. Herskovits, *The Myth of the Negro Past*, Ch. 2.
[3] See D. Forde and G. I. Jones, *The Ibo and Ibibio-Speaking Peoples of South-Eastern Nigeria*, p. 9 and passim.

SECTION 2

THE GENERAL PATTERN OF BRITISH TRADING 1655–1807

It is now proposed to make a tentative assessment of the proportion and extent of British trading in the different areas of the West Coast of Africa during specified periods between 1655 and 1807. In so doing, we shall consider, in addition to the material already discussed, some new data and, where necessary, anticipate some of the material to be considered in Part 2.

There were, originally, two types of British slave traders; those who were employed by the various monopoly charter companies, and those who traded independently, or private traders. The first serious venture of the former were the Royal Adventurers which, as we have already remarked, was a failure. The only period in which it could have sent slaves to Jamaica was between 1660 and 1665 and most of its trading activities were restricted to the region of Senegambia and the Windward Coast.[1] The Royal African Company was a more serious affair. Founded in 1672, it maintained its monopoly with some success until about 1689. During the next decade the private traders broke its monopoly in fact, though it continued to hang on to it legally. Between 1698 and 1712 the 'ten per cent act' came in force permitting private slavers to trade as long as they paid the company a duty of 10 per cent to assist it in maintaining its forts. After 1712, however, the act became ineffective and the British slave trade, to all intents and purposes, became free.[2] In Jamaica, for example, between 1698 and 1708, private traders supplied 35,718 slaves compared with 6,854 by the Company,[3] while 1,804 were described as of 'unknown' source,[4] and after 1712 supplies by the company were insignificant.[5]

Our estimate of the relative size of British trading in the different areas of the coast will be made in the light of four periods: (a) 1655–1700, (b) 1700–1730, (c) 1730–1790, (d) 1790–1807.

(a) *1655–1700* This was largely the period of the monopoly

---

[1] Davies, *op. cit.*, pp. 41–4.   [2] *Ibid.*, p. 46.   [3] *Ibid.*

[4] Most of these slaves of 'unknown' source were supplied illegally by Dutch traders from Curacao and by ships fitted out from Jamaica. See, Abstract of Ships Departing from and arriving in Jamaica, 1685–1692, C.O. 142/13.

[5] Hamilton to Board of Trade, 8/3/1712; C.O. 137/10.

companies which centred their activities on Senegambia, the Windward Coast and the Gold Coast. Of the three the Gold Coast was by
far the most important and it can be said with some plausibility that
it was the single largest source of the Monopoly Companies' slaves
during this time. The private traders, since they were for part of
this period still illegal interlopers, would naturally have tended to
trade in areas less frequented by the ships of the monopoly companies. Of these areas Angola was the most important and large
numbers were also obtained from the Slave Coast and the Calabars.
As such, whatever bias the Companies may have had in favour of
Gold Coast slaves would have been balanced by private trading in
other areas. The data is too sparse to make any positive estimates
except, very tentatively, that the Gold Coast, Slave Coast and
Angola each supplied about a quarter of all the British slaves during
this period, the remainder coming from the other areas.

(b) *1700–1730*   This period marked the ascendancy of the Slave
Coast as the main area of trading for slaves, reaching its climax in
the early 1720s when it supplied as many slaves as all the rest of the
coast put together. The French had not yet asserted their dominance
and so the four main powers – Dutch, Portuguese, French and
English – would presumably have been supplied in approximately
equal numbers.

The Royal African Company, which had its headquarters on the
Gold Coast, was well placed to procure slaves from the Slave Coast
and it is well known that many of the slaves exported from their
forts in the former area were originally recruited from the latter.
Some idea of the relative importance of the different trading areas to
the Company may be derived from the following table:

TABLE I: EXPENDITURE ON GOODS FOR THE AFRICAN TRADE
BY THE ROYAL AFRICAN COMPANY, 1724.[1]

Gambia	£ 8,000	Whydah (Slave Coast)	£20,000
Sierra Leone	10,000	Bight of Benin,	
Windward Coast	7,000	Calabars & Gaboon	3,000
Gold Coast	36,000	Cabenda	14,000

[1] E. Donnon, *Documents Illustrative of the Slave Trade to America*, Vol. 2.
pp. 308–9.

These figures are likely to be slightly misleading since in some areas a substantial amount of the goods would have been traded for items other than slaves – for example, ivory and grain in Sierra Leone and the Windward Coast and some gold on the Gold Coast. But they do give some useful information on the relative amounts spent on slaves in the different areas by the Company. By this time, however, the company's trade was almost insignificant compared with the private traders. Our earlier discussion would certainly suggest that the favourite area of the private traders at this time was the Slave Coast. Taking both private and company traders together the following estimate may be suggested: the Slave Coast supplied about 33 per cent of all British slaves during this time; the Gold Coast about 25 per cent; the Niger and Cross deltas, which were now being increasingly exploited, about 15 per cent; and the remaining 27 per cent from the other areas, particularly the Windward Coast and Angola.

(c) *1730–1790* By the time this period opens the arrival of the Dahomeans on the Slave Coast had led to an almost complete collapse of its trading centres, and when it recovered the French had already monopolized the trade there. On the other hand, as this period progressed the British traders greatly increased their influence in the regions of the Niger and Cross deltas. Penny's figures, which we have quoted earlier, indicate that between 1765 and 1785 the Nigerian ports had become the largest source of British slaves; the Gold Coast was still the second largest supplier; the Windward Coast was third; the Slave Coast and Senegambia were supplying relatively small numbers; and Southwestern Africa was almost insignificant.

Edwards quotes a set of figures, claiming that their 'authenticity cannot be doubled', which specifies the number of slaves procured by British ships in the various areas of Africa in 1771. They are given in table 2.

These figures not only substantiate Penny's estimate that by far the largest single source of slaves at this time was the Niger and Cross deltas (Bight of Benin) but indicate that the numbers are even greater than he had suggested. There is also approximate agreement, in absolute terms, on the number of slaves exported from the Gold Coast. On the other hand, they strongly contradict the estimates of both Penny and Mathews with respect to the absolute and relative numbers supplied by the Windward Coast. The question is settled by the far more accurate figures given by the Liverpool Merchants to the Lords of the Privy Council in 1790.[1] The figures state first, that a total of 74,000 slaves were exported in 1789 from Africa.[2] Of these 38,000 were exported by the British; 20,000 by the French; 4,000 by the Dutch; 2,000 by the Danes; and 10,000 by the Portuguese. Secondly, of the 74,000 slaves, 700

TABLE 2: ACCOUNT OF SHIPS SAILING FOR AFRICA IN 1771 FROM BRITAIN[3]

Areas of Trade	No. of Ships		No. of Negroes
Senegambia	40	for	3,310
Windward Coast	56	,,	11,960
Gold Coast	29	,,	7,525
Bight of Benin	63	,,	23,301
Angola	4	,,	1,050
Total	192		47,146

came from the Gambia; 7,500 from the Windward Coast; 10,000 from the Gold Coast; 9,000 from the Slave Coast; 25,000 from Nigeria (of which 3,500 came from Lagos and Benin) and from Southwestern Africa, but particularly the Congo, 22,000.

The following conclusions may therefore be reached. First, with respect to the Niger and Cross deltas, between 1776 and 1784 the British slavers took 80 per cent of all the Negroes, amounting to 11,000 slaves. Assuming the same proportion in 1790, they were then exporting, on the basis of the figures of the Liverpool merchants, 22,000 slaves from the area, accounting for approximately 53 per cent of all the British slaves.

The second largest source of British slaves during this period

[1] Edwards, *op. cit.*, Bk. 4, pp. 67–8.
[2] Cf. Penny's estimate of 80,000 between 1765 and 1785, B.T.6:9.
[3] B. Edwards, *op. cit.*, Bk. 4, p. 65.

was the Gold Coast which, on the basis of Miles' figures, was supplying an annual average of between 7,000 and 8,000 Negroes between 1765 and 1784.[1] This constituted about 20 per cent of all the British slaves exported from Africa during this period.

The above conclusions relate more specifically to the second half of the period presently being considered. Assuming that there was an upward secular trend in the series of export figures of the slaves from Nigeria and Ghana between 1730 and 1790 and that there was no significant variation in the amplitude of fluctuations, the following conjectures may be made. Between 1730 and 1750 Nigeria exported an annual average of 33 per cent of the British slaves; Ghana an average of 33 per cent; the Windward Coast an average of 20 per cent; and the remainder distributed about evenly in the other areas. Between 1750 and 1770 Nigeria exported 40 per cent of British slaves; Ghana 30 per cent; the Windward Coast about 16 per cent and the remainder as above. Finally, between 1770 and 1790, Nigeria exported about 53 per cent of all British slaves; Ghana about 25 per cent; the Windward Coast about 10 per cent; and the remaining 12 per cent mainly from Southwestern Africa.

(d) *1790–1807* The most striking feature of this period was the rapid increase in the number of slaves exported by the British from Southwestern Africa, especially in the region of the Congo and Angola. These largely took the place of slaves from the Gold Coast, supplies from which were now reduced to a trickle. There was also a substantial overall increase in the number of slaves bought by the British, due largely to the anticipated Abolition Bill of 1807.

By this time the Liverpool merchants had all but monopolized the trade. In 1798 they sent out 149 ships to Africa compared with seventeen from London and five from Bristol; and in 1799 they fitted out 134 ships for the trade compared with the same number as in the previous year from London and Bristol.[2] The slaves procured by the Liverpool ships in these two years are summarized in table 3[3].

Before we close this section a word must be said concerning the tribal origins of the slaves sold in the different areas during the

[1] See the relevant pages in Section 1.
[2] Sir W. Young, *A West India Commonplace Book*, p. 8.
[3] E. Donnon, *op. cit.*, Vol. 2, pp. 642–9.

periods specified above; and also a few remarks concerning the death rate of different tribal stocks on the middle passage.

First, Ghana. Between 1655 and 1720 the majority of the slaves, perhaps as many as two-thirds, seem to have come from the prisoners taken in the wars between the Akan tribes of the coast but particularly from the weaker Ga and Andangme peoples. After 1720, however, at least two-thirds of the slaves came from among the Guang and other peoples of the hinterland while a quarter came

TABLE 3:   THE REGIONAL ORIGINS OF SLAVES BOUGHT BY
LIVERPOOL MERCHANTS IN 1798 AND 1799

Regional origins of	Year	
slaves	*1798*	*1799*
Windward Coast	3,278	3,418
Gambia	—	151
Gold Coast	3,587	4,277
Lagos	275	—
Whydah (Slave Coast)	296	420
Niger and Cross Deltas and		
Benin	20,586	19,745
Gaboon and Cameroons	1,292	613
Congo	—	697
Angola	23,303	13,798
Other areas	—	1,090

from among the Fanti tribe of the Akan peoples and the remainder from the other coastal tribes.

From the Slave Coast at least three-quarters of all the slaves came from among the Ewe speaking tribes which presently inhabit the state of Dahomey while the remaining quarter came from among the Yoruba speaking peoples of the upper sections of southwestern Nigeria. Until about the last quarter of the eighteenth century the slaves exported from Lagos and Benin were equally divided among the Ibos, Edos and Yorubas. After this, however, almost all the slaves exported from this area were Yorubas, or Nagoes, as they were then called.

Until about 1775 approximately 65 per cent of all the slaves exported from the region of the Niger and Cross deltas were Ibos; about 20 per cent were Ibibios; about 10 per cent were Chambas; and the rest came from among the other tribal groups of the area, particularly the Andoni.

Between 1775 and 1807 about 45 per cent of these slaves seem to have been Ibos; about 30 per cent Ibibios; about 20 per cent Chambas and the rest from the other tribes.[1] The vast complex of tribes in the areas contributing slaves to the European captains on Senegambia and the Windward Coast and the relatively great distance inland from which many of these slaves came make it a difficult, almost impossible, task to estimate the tribal origins of the slaves from this area. In the New World almost all the Kwa- and West Atlantic-speaking peoples in the areas bordering on the Windward Coast and Senegambia and most of those from the interior were described as 'Mundingos'. The qualitative data discussed in Section 1 would suggest that until about the last quarter of the eighteenth century roughly two-thirds of the slaves exported from Senegambia and the Windward Coast came from the interior while the other third came from among the tribes nearer the coast.

Both the historical and present data on the Congo and Angola are too sparse to allow us to attempt any estimate of the tribal origins of the slaves in these areas.

Finally, it should be noted that the estimates relating to the supply side of the slave trade will differ significantly from those derived from figures relating to the demand side of the trade, since a considerable number of slaves died on the middle passage between Africa and the Americas. The average mortality on the middle passage was calculated in 1789 at $12\frac{1}{2}$ per cent although there was considerable variation about this mean.[2] Just as significant is the fact that mortality on the passage varied with the different tribal stocks. According to Penny slaves from the Gold and Slave Coasts who were fed on Indian corn 'have in general little or no mortality'; those from the Windward Coast who were fed mainly on rice were 'next in degree most healthy'; while those from Nigeria, who were fed mainly on yams were 'subject to the greatest mortality.'[3]

[1] This estimate is based partly on data already discussed in Section 1; partly on material to be discussed later in Part 2.

[2] See bibliography of Official Publications, ii; p. 300 below. Mannix and Cowley, *Black Cargoes*, p. 123.

[3] Evidence of James Penny, 1788, B.T.6:9, f. 343.

PART 2

THE DEMAND FOR SLAVES IN JAMAICA

The data relating to Jamaica, which will be considered within the framework of the four periods specified above, are of four types. First, there is some statistical material relating to various aspects of the subject; secondly, there are the statements of contemporary historians and travellers; thirdly, there are certain historical incidents from which we may draw useful inferences bearing on the subject; and finally, there is the evidence derived from the workhouse advertisements of runaway slaves.

(a) *1655–1700* Although the charter companies dominated the overall pattern of British trading during this period, the Jamaican planters were strongly opposed to it, mainly on the grounds that it failed to satisfy their demand for slaves; its credit was too short; and its interest charges too high;[1] and, worst of all, that through the Assiento contract with Spain, it used Jamaica as a depot for re-exporting slaves and in so doing conveyed 'the choicest negroes to the Spaniards'.[2] We have already shown that between 1698 and 1708 the Company supplied 6,854 slaves to Jamaica compared with 38,718 by private traders. The fact that the private traders, at the most conservative estimate, supplied at least a half of all the slaves entering the island from Africa during this period is of significance since, as we have argued in Part 1, these traders tended to avoid the monopoly of the company by trading in different areas, more particularly, at Angola, the Slave Coast and the Calabars.

This period may be further sub-divided into two parts, that between 1655 and 1680 and the remaining twenty years. The most striking feature of the first part is that perhaps as much as a third of all the slaves imported into the island then came from the eastern Caribbean, particularly Barbados. An account taken in 1679 of all the slaves entering the island between 1671 and 1679 reveals that

[1] C.S.P. 1675, No. 673.
[2] C.S.P. 1689–92, No. 295; also R. Pares, *War and Trade in the West Indies*, p. 20.

three-quarters came from Africa and a quarter from the Eastern Caribbean.[1] The ratio was much higher during the first fifteen years of the English occupation since most of the slaves then in the island came in with their masters who had migrated from the Eastern Caribbean. It is therefore important to note that the Barbadian planters, unlike their Jamaican counterparts, tended to buy almost all their slaves from the Royal African Company, which, in turn, meant that the greatest single source of their slaves was the Gold Coast. There is evidence from Barbados to support this conclusion for in 1675, Jonathan Atkins, writing to London on a recent rebellion of the negroes in Barbados, claimed that it was due primarily to the Coromantins (or Gold Coast negroes) whom he described as 'a warlike and robust people' and stated that they constituted 'much the greater number of any one country.'[2] From all this it may be inferred that Gold Coast Negroes formed the largest single group of slaves in the island during the crucial first twenty years of its British occupation when the creole slave society was being laid down. The fact, too, that they were already seasoned slaves meant that they were more valuable, in the eyes of the whites, than the other slaves coming directly from Africa, and, as such, they may well have monopolized all the influential slave posts in the slave community.

With regard to the second part of this first period we have an extremely revealing abstract of all ships and cargoes arriving in the island between 29 September 1685 and 20 February 1692.[3] From this we gather that of the 11,281 slaves brought from Africa, 4,474 came from Angola, 3,124 came from the Slave Coast (mostly from Whydah), 307 from the Gambia, 871 from Old Calabar, 240 from 'Cape Devards' (presumably Cape Verde), 22 from 'Malagasco' (presumably Madagascar) and 2,275 from what was simply described as 'Guinea'. Since all the other regions on the West Coast except the Gold Coast and the Windward Coast were specified in the abstract (except in one instance where 'Accra' is mentioned) it seems almost certain that 'Guinea' referred to these two areas. Assuming that these six years and five months were representative of the pattern of trading during these last twenty years of the seventeenth century, it would seem that approximately 40 per cent of

[1] C.S.P. 1677–1680, No. 945.   [2] C.S.P. 1675–76, No. 690.
[3] C.O. 142/13.

the Jamaican slaves at that time came from Angola; about 30 per cent from the Slave Coast; about 20 per cent from the Gold and Windward Coasts; and the rest mainly from the Cross delta.

Sloane, the only writer during this period who offers us any useful information concerning the origins of the slaves, stated only that they came from different parts of Guinea; the few derived from Madagascar were 'not coveted' because of their high mortality rate. Already the planters had begun to develop a liking for particular tribal types, 'choosing their Negroes from whence they come and their look'.[1] Although great numbers of slaves were still being brought into the island from Angola at the time he visited the island they were not favoured since they 'run away from their Masters, and fancy on their deaths they are going home again which is no ludicrous Experiment, for on hard usage they kill themselves'.[2] Perhaps this was the reason why, by the beginning of the eighteenth century, there was a rapid decline of the number of slaves bought from Angola.

(b) *1700–1730* The Jamaican data offers little statistical evidence bearing on the subject at issue during this period. The only useful information that can be derived from the abstracts of goods and ships arriving in the island between March 1709 and the end of the present period is that almost all the slaves are described as coming from 'Guinea' (in a few cases the term 'Africa' is used) and since a distinction was made at the time between Guinea (which stretched in an arc from the Senegal down to the Cross river)[3] and the rest of the west coast of Africa it is not unreasonable to conclude that the number of slaves coming into the island from Angola during this period was insignificant.[4] Leslie, in his discussion of the religion of the slaves, referred to two African deities (which we shall identify in a later chapter as of Dahomean origin) in a manner which would suggest that he thought all the slaves believed in them. One explanation why Leslie, an otherwise careful observer, could have come to this erroneous conclusion is that the majority of his slave informants were of Dahomean origin, implying, possibly, a substantial number of them in the island at that time.[5]

---

[1] Sir Hans Sloane, *op. cit.*, Introduction.   [2] *Ibid.*
[3] See enclosed maps.   [4] C.O. 142/14–15.
[5] Leslie, *A New History*, p. 307.

(c) *1730–1790* The most important piece of statistical evidence relating to this period comes from an account published by Stephen Fuller on the slave trade in 1789.[1] This report contains the accounts of five brokerage firms with records relating to their trade in slaves. From the records of four of these firms operating at various periods between 1764 and 1788 Herskovits has made the following tabulation:

TABLE 4: THE REGIONAL ORIGINS OF SLAVES BOUGHT BY
4 JAMAICAN BROKERAGE FIRMS, 1764–1788[2]

Region	No. of Slaves Bought
Gambia	673
Windward Coast	2,669
Gold Coast	14,312
Slave Coast	3,912
Niger Delta (Benin, Bonny, Calabars)	10,305
Gaboon	155
Angola	1,984
Total	34,010

Assuming that these figures are in some way representative of the general pattern of slave-buying in the island during this period, it would seem that a little over 40 per cent of the slaves were derived from the Gold Coast; over 35 per cent from the Niger and Cross deltas; about 12 per cent from the Slave Coast; and the remaining 13 per cent mainly from the Windward Coast and Angola. This pattern differs somewhat from that which we earlier inferred applied to British slave trading as a whole. The difference is to be explained partly in terms of the relative mortality of Gold Coast and Nigerian slaves during the course of the middle passage, but, far more important, in terms of the 'perverse' preference of Jamaican

[1] S. Fuller, *Report on ... the Slave Trade,* 1789.
[2] Herskovits, *The Myth of the Negro Past,* p. 49.

planters for slaves from the Gold Coast, despite their major role in the slave revolts of the island.[1]

On the other hand, the Jamaican planters had an aversion to Nigerian Negroes, especially the Ibos who were considered to be 'the lowest and most wretched of all the nations of Africa', possessing a relatively marked tendency to suicide.[2] To some extent, the prejudices of the Jamaican planters seemed to have had some basis in fact as the following table of the average height of the creole and other tribal groups of slaves in the island demonstrates.[3]

TABLE 5: THE AVERAGE HEIGHTS OF CREOLE AND VARIOUS AFRICAN TRIBAL GROUPS OF JAMAICAN SLAVES

Country of Origin	Males	Females
Creoles	5' 3$\frac{4}{5}$"	5'
Coromantees (Gold Coast)	5' 5$\frac{2}{5}$"	5' 2$\frac{2}{5}$"
Congos	5' 4"	5'
Ibos	5' 4"	5' 0$\frac{3}{4}$"
Ibibios (Mocos)	5' 3$\frac{3}{5}$"	5' 0$\frac{1}{2}$"
Chambas	5' 4"	5' 1"
Mundingos	5' 3"	5' 0$\frac{3}{4}$"
Nagos (Yorubas)	5' 4$\frac{3}{5}$"	5' 1$\frac{1}{2}$"
Mungolas (from Benguela)	5' 3$\frac{3}{5}$"	5' 1$\frac{2}{5}$"

The preference of the Jamaican planters for Gold Coast Negroes, then, and their dislike from those for Nigeria led to the fact that despite the greater supply of the latter by British traders the former constituted the single largest stock during the major part of this period. The fact, too, that Gold Coast Negroes were rejected by

[1] See Ch. 8. Various writers referred to this 'great predilection' on the part of the planters. See, Edwards, *op. cit.*, Bk. 4, pp. 83–4; Beckford, *Situation of the Negroes in Jamaica*, (1788), p. 11.

[2] Edwards, *op. cit.*, pp. 88–9.

[3] The Table was computed from the advertisements by the work-houses of the island of runaway slaves in their possession. The computation was made from samples taken from a total list of approximately 3,150 slaves covering the years 1794, 1813 and 1814, advertised in the *Jamaica Royal Gazette*, Ref. C.O. 141/1; C.O. 141/2; C.O. 141/3; C.O. 141/4; 141/5.

Inspection & Sale of a Captive in Bangalang, Guinea, 1827
The slaver Theodore Canot observed that each captive was examined 'without regard to sex, from head to foot. A careful manipulation of the chief muscles, joints, arm-pits and groins was made to assure soundness. The mouth too was inspected. Eyes, voice, lungs, fingers and toes were not forgotten; so that . . . he might have been readily adopted as a good "life" by an insurance company.'

Branding in Africa before Embarkation, 1827
Canot wrote that: 'Two days before embarkation, the head of every male
and female slave is neatly shaved; and if the cargo belongs to several
owners, each man's brand is impressed on the body of his respective
negro. The operation is performed with pieces of silver wire, or small irons
fashioned into the merchant's initials, heated just hot enough to blister
without burning into the skin.'

Opposite: Plan & Section of Slave Ship, *Brookes*. Inset depicts
rebellion on a slave ship
The *Brookes* carried 609 slaves: 351 men, 127 women, 90 boys & 1 girl.
Between 1500 and 1866 approximately 12.52 million captives were
transported to the Americas, 26% of them children. A total of 1,017,109
went to Jamaica, incredibly, over 2.6 times the number taken to all of
North America. Average duration of the middle passage was 62 days
during which 12–13% died.

PLAN AND SECTIONS OF A SLAVE SHIP.

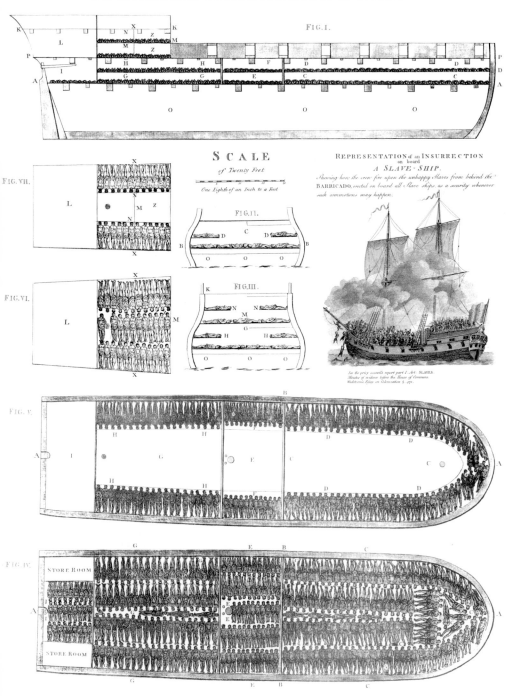

FIG. I.

FIG. VII.

SCALE
of Twenty Feet

One Eighth of an Inch to a Foot

FIG. II.

FIG. VI.

FIG. III.

REPRESENTATION of an INSURRECTION
on board
A SLAVE-SHIP.

Shewing how the crew fire upon the unhappy Slaves from behind the
BARRICADO, erected on board all Slave ships as a security whenever
such commotions may happen.

See the privy councils report part I. Art. SLAVES.
Minutes of evidence before the House of Commons.
Wadstroms Essay on Colonization §. 291.

FIG. V.

STORE ROOM

STORE ROOM

FIG. IV.

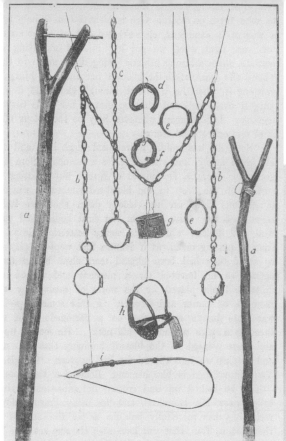

IMPLEMENTS USED BY SLAVE-TRADERS.

(By permission of the British and Foreign Anti-Slavery Society.)

a, a, The Yoke or Goree: *b, c,* Chains used to fasten slaves; *d,* Iron ring welded on to limb of a slave, which had to be severed by a chisel in order to be removed; *e, f,* Fetters; *g,* Iron Collar; *h,* Helmet used for gagging slaves, with pieces of iron to force tongue down; *i,* Corbash or whip made of rhinoceros hide.

Chains and Other Instruments Used by Slave Traders, 19th Century
Shown are wooden neck yokes (or Goree), chains, manacles, leg fetters, whip, helmet used for gagging slaves with pieces of iron to force tongue down.

An Iron Gibbet on which Rebellious Slaves Awaited a Slow and Painful Death
Designed for torture, killing and public display of corpses of executed slaves. The body was often suspended from a post. The victim was left to die of thirst and starvation. The gibbet shown here was relatively small and the bones found in it seemed to have been those of a woman.

Africans Liberated from Captured Slave Ship, *Zeldina,* **Fort Augusta, St Catherine, Jamaica 1857**
The 370 captives were survivors of 500 taken in Cabinda (Angola) 45 days earlier. They were naked, covered in dirt and vermin and half-starved. On board they had only 18 inches to turn on each of the two 30-feet-long decks and were brought up in platoons once daily for air. Fort Augusta is now a female prison.

INTERIOR OF A SUGAR-BOILING HOUSE.

The boiling house had what Adam Hochschild called a 'satanic ring'. This was among the most hazardous work on the plantation. Pressure to work fast increased the risk of scalding, or falling in.

Opposite, top: Slave Auction of Woman and Two Children
Paraphernalia for branding the slaves are in the foreground. Some 87% of trafficked Jamaican slaves were traded in Kingston.[1] This was probably an internal trade of local slaves likely to suffer separation from family and friends.

[1] T. Burnard & K. Morgan, 'The Dynamics of the Slave Market and Slave Purchasing Patterns in Jamaica', 1655–1788, WMQ, 58, No.1. p. 223.

Opposite, bottom: Field Gang of Men and Women, Digging Cane Holes for Planting
There were more women than men in what was the most onerous work on the plantation Pregnant women worked up to a few days before birth and returned to field within days of delivery. They worked from dawn to dusk with a short break for lunch. Most were malnourished and hungry.

Interior View of Jamaica House of Correction, 1834–1838
Illustration shows man on left being flogged; woman's hair being shorn; and those on treadmill also being whipped. These punishments were forbidden for women under the Apprenticeship laws, but persisted.

A West India Sportsman: 'Make haste with the Sangaree, Quashie, and tell Quaco to drive the birds up to me – I'm ready' (1807)
A satiric depiction of the parasitism of the slaveholders who descended to barbaric decadence within weeks of arriving in Jamaica Too torpid to walk or stand while hunting., they were better at killing people than birds.

Koo-Koo or Actor Boy
Among the many forms of resistance was the psychological which included Quashee play-acting discussed on pp. 174–181. Another was the saturnalia in which the enslaved pantomimed the Whites, who condescendingly tipped them, to the dark humour of the Blacks.

Drawn after Nature *on Stone by I. M. Belisario.*   Printed by A. Duperly.

BAND of the JAW–BONE JOHN–CANOE.

Kingston Jamaica — Aug 1837.

Band of Jaw-Bone John-Canoe
The artist, Belisario, drew attention to 'the tattered urchin' in front, 'many such half-attired ramblers being daily seen in the streets of Kingston'. Enslaved children were considered a burden by the planters and a tragedy in waiting by their mothers.

Slaves Talking Informally

A rare example of slaves conversing comes from Thistlewood's diary, Saturday 11th January 1766: 'Margaritta today in the Trash-house telling how a Buckrah (white man) wanted her to go in the bush with him near the Styx bridge, after mentioning how he spoke to her, began thus: "Me bin say, heh, no me go, bin say warrah" [what?]. One can only imagine the price she paid for resisting his advances.'

Carrying the Coffin

In Jamaica, the enslaved viewed 'death as a welcome relief from the calamities of life, and a passport to the never-to-be-forgotten scenes of their nativity'. The funeral was a raucous ritual celebrating the end of their living social death (discussed on pp. 195–198).

Old Cudjoe: Snatching Treachery from the Jaws of Heroism

After repeated defeats, the slaveholders signed a treaty in 1739 with Cudjoe, leader of the formerly enslaved Maroon rebels, giving them sovereignty within their domain on the island. This is the first victorious slave revolt in human history. Sadly, the Maroons agreed to aid the planters in all future revolts and return runaways for a bounty.

Spanish-Town, 1ˢᵗ February, 1781

RUN AWAY

from the Subscriber,
the following NEGROES, vis.

PRESTON, about four weeks ago; He is of a yellow complexion; his breast very remarkable, appearing full, like that of a young girl; stout made; has very crocked legs, with a sore on one; speaks English very well; is marked on both shoulders JH, diamond on top; supposed to be gone in the country, he being seen a few weeks ago in the old Harbour road.

SAM (a few days after) a Creole, of a black complexion, a most well made fellow, he went in search of PRESTON with a ticket, but through a mistake did not mention when he was to return. He is well known in the towns, formerly the property of Abraham Gabay, deceased; he has a large family, among whom he is supposed to he harboured.

Maria, about two weeks ago:- she is a short, stout wench, of a very yellow complexion, has her country marks on both sides of her face; marked on one or both shoulders JH, diamond on top, formerly the property of John Collard merchant in Kingston: supposed to be harboured about the Red Hills by a negro man named SHARPER, belonging to the estate of Abraham Gabey, deceased.

Whoever takes up either of the above Negroes, and will deliver them to the Subscriber, shall receive a reward of 10 s. for PRESTON or MARIA, and for SAM £2 15 s. – If any person will give information where any of the said Negroes is harboured, so that the offender or offenders be brought to justice, shall, on conviction, if a white person TWENTY POUNDS, if a free Mulatto or Negro, TEN POUNDS, by

JACOB HILL.

The Royal Gazette (Kingston),
Saturday February 10 to Saturday February 17, 1781.

Runaway Advertisements

Flight was a common form of resistance. Between 1718 and 1795 there were 740 ads for 4,150 runaways in surviving Jamaican newspapers,[1] but this was likely a small fraction of the total for this period. For example, between 1770 and 1776, Sally, raped 12 times by her slaveholder, Thistlewood, ran away 11 times, in spite of repeated brutal punishments. There were no ads.[2]

[1] Chambers, Douglas B., 'Jamaica Runaway Slaves: 18th Century'. 2013. https://ufdc.ufl.edu/AA00021144/00001.
[2] D. Hall. 1989. 'In Miserable Slavery: Thomas Thistlewood in Jamaica', pp. 198–201.

Roehampton Estate before Destruction by Revolutionaries
Located in St James Parish it was owned by John Baillie, an absentee who was paid 5,745 pounds in compensation for the emancipation of his 322 slaves, the equivalent of 574,500 pounds in today's value.

Destruction of Roehampton Estate, during the Baptist Slave War of 1831–1832
A scene from the island's largest slave revolt that took place over five weeks between 1831
and 1832. Involving over 30,000 slaves, it resulted in the destruction of 207 plantations and
other property valued conservatively at 1,154,589 pounds sterling in 1832, the equivalent of

115,458,900 pounds in today's value. Over 200 of the revolutionaries died in battle and 340 martyred, including 75 women.[1]

[1] Tom Zoellner. 2020. *Island on Fire: The Revolt that Ended Slavery in the British Empire*, pp. 176–177.

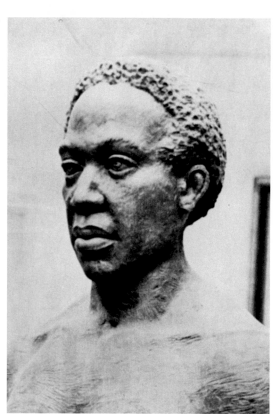

Bust of The Rt Excellent Samuel Sharpe, Jamaica National Hero (1801–1832)
Sharpe was a Baptist Deacon who put into practice the spiritual and social liberation principles of his faith, anticipating by over a century Latin American liberation theology.[1] Although they lost the battle, Sharpe and his fellow revolutionaries won the war because news of the uprising tilted the wavering British Parliament towards passing the 1833 Slavery Abolition Act, thereby freeing all of the enslaved in Jamaica and throughout the British Empire.

[1] 1. Tom Zoellner. 2020. *Island on Fire: The Revolt that Ended Slavery in the British Empire*, pp. 80–82; 207–208; 257–259; 278–279.

A Slave Family in Exaltation
A drawing of elated enslaved Africans after they heard that slavery would be legally abolished on 1 August 1834. The actual year turned out to be 1838, following the brutal period of apprenticeship.

most of the planters of the Eastern Caribbean (there was even a law in Barbados forbidding their entry into the island) meant that it was that much easier for the Jamaicans to procure these slaves.

(d) *1790–1807:* Whatever the Jamaicans may have thought of their Ibo slaves, however, there can be little doubt that starting from about the last quarter of the above period they had little choice but to buy them in increasingly large numbers, for by now the reserves of slaves in the interior of the Gold Coast were being rapidly exhausted. The following table summarizes the accounts of slaves sold by two firms of slave auctioneers in Jamaica between 1793 and 1799.[1]

TABLE 6:   AN ACCOUNT OF NEGROES SOLD BY ASPINALL AND HARDY; AND HARDY, PENNOCK AND BRITTAN, 1793–1799

Year	Gambia	Windward Coast	Gold Coast	Gaboon* Bonny, Calabars	Angola
1793	469	828	636	493	627
1794	—	—	—	432	1,259
1795	—	211	292	791	927
1796	—	—	468	339	—
1797	—	—	—	2,184	2,133
1798	—	—	—	1,576	433
1799	—	—	—	2,605	618
Total	469	1,039	1,396	8,420	5,997

The irregularity of the above figures cautions us against too much reliance on them but they certainly indicate a rapid falling off of slaves entering the island from Senegambia, the Windward Coast and the Gold Coast, and alternatively, a much greater proportion of Negroes from Nigeria. Even more striking is the return of large numbers of Angolan Negroes. The majority of slaves from

[1] From the Journals of the House of Assembly, Vol. 10, p. 436.
* Only 290 slaves came from Gaboon, all in the year 1799.

Southwestern Africa came at this time, however, not from Angola, but from the Congo and the kingdom of Benguela. Members of the latter group were known as 'Mungolas' or 'Munguelas' in Jamaica.[1]

Our argument is further substantiated by figures taken from the advertisements of runaways by the Jamaican work-houses between 1794 and 1813. These have been included in table 7.

There is no evidence to support the view that any particular tribe of Africans were more prone to run away than others (as Phillips argued)[2] and we can draw the obvious conclusion from these figures, namely that larger numbers in the work-houses reflected larger numbers in the island. Before such conclusions are drawn, however, one observation must be made. It is the fact that newly arrived Africans were far more prone to run away than those already seasoned or creole slaves. Thus, whatever group dominated the work-house list in the years 1794 and 1803 did so, not so much because there were many of this group already in the island, but more because larger numbers of them were arriving in those years. With this observation in mind, the essential features of this last period may be noted. First, there is the sudden increase of slaves from Southwestern Africa which now formed the single largest source of slaves although Southeastern Nigeria, as the second largest source, was contributing increasingly larger numbers. We observe too,

---

[1] It is not entirely certain who the slaves referred to as '*Mungolas*' were. The first explanation that comes to mind is that the term referred to the Bantu singular noun, '*A Mangola*', in which the suffix '*Mu*' attached to the root '*ngola*' would read '*Mungola*'. Among the Kimbundu cluster of tribes which inhabit west central Angola is a tribe known as the *Ngala*, but the people referred to by the Jamaicans may well have been the *Mbangalas* which is the name of a group of tribes of which the *Ngala* is one. The difficulty with this explanation, however, is that several of the runaways were also referred to as 'Angolans' which would suggest that they were considered to be different from the 'Mungolas.' This being the case, the neighbouring kingdom of Benguele (now the southern part of the Portuguese colony of Angola) whose countrymen would no doubt have described themselves to the whites as 'Munguelas' may have been the regional origin of these slaves. But there is an additional complication. Among the equatorial Bantu is a cluster of tribes known as the *Ngala* (now a part of the north western section of the Congo) and three of the six tribes comprising this group are known as *Mangala*, *Mongalia*, and *Ngola*. It is more than likely that the Jamaican whites confused these different groups. See, C. M. N. White, 'The Noun Prefixes of the West Central Zone of Bantu Languages' in *Journal of African Studies*, Vol. 3, No. 4, 1944; G. P. Murdoch, *op. cit.*

[2] Philips, *American Negro Slavery*, p. 44.

TABLE 7: REGIONAL AND TRIBAL ORIGINS OF SLAVES ADVERTISED BY THE JAMAICAN WORK-HOUSES 1794, 1803 AND 1813[1]

Country of Origin	1794	1803	1813
Creoles	266	488	(including 620
Congos	135 ⎫	185 ⎫	American- 169 ⎫
Mungolas (Benguela)	100 ⎬		born) 142 ⎬
Angolans	5 ⎭	259 ⎭	13 ⎭
Ibos	93 ⎫	284 ⎫	157 ⎫
Mocos (Ibibios)	85 ⎬		(Ibos & 86 ⎬
Chambas	39 ⎭	60 ⎭	Mocos) 30 ⎟
Coromantees (Gold Coast)	68	70	71 ⎭
Nagos (Yorubas)	50		(Nagos & 24
Papaws (Slave Coast)	20	57 ⎭	Papaws)
Mundingos: Senegambia & Windward Coast	79	101	75
Africans (Country unknown)	77		15
Scattering (almost all Africans)	55	30	28
Unclassified	3	187	31
Total:	1,075	1,721	1,461

that Yoruban slaves (the majority no doubt coming from Lagos and Benin) have also made a reappearance making up a substantial minority of the newcomers.

Another very informative piece of evidence relates to the total number of slaves from different parts of Africa advertised for sale by slave dealers in the island for the year 1794. From these advertisements we have constructed table 8.[2]

The table indicates that in 1794 (and from the other data it is clear that the trend continued during the rest of the period) a little

---

[1] The figures for the years 1794 and 1815 were computed from the *Royal Gazettes* of those years, in C.O. 141/1; 141/2; 141/3. Those for the year 1803 were computed by Phillips in his *American Negro Slavery* p. 44.

[2] From *The Royal Gazette*, Dec. 28, 1793–Dec. 20, 1794: C.O. 141/1.

TABLE 8: THE REGIONAL ORIGINS OF AFRICAN SLAVES
          SOLD IN JAMAICA IN 1794

Ibos	2,011	Gold Coast, Papaw & Whydah	995
Angola	420	Gold Coast & Windward Coast	220
Cape Mount	219	Gold Coast & Angola	50
Windward Coast	902	Gold Coast	1,132
Congo	7,642	Coromantees, Fantees, & Ashantees	1,648

Total: 15,239

over a half of all the slaves in the island came from the Congo; the
Ibos were also contributing a substantial section of the African
slaves and so too were the Negroes from the Gold Coast. A planter,
writing during this period, informs us that the 'Ebboes and Bbo-
bees' (Ibos and Ibibios) 'constitute the greater part' of the slaves
sold in the islands, and that 'very few' ever came from the Slave
Coast or Gaboon.[1]

GENERAL CONCLUSIONS

On the basis of all that has gone before we may now draw the
following conclusions. First, during the earlier half of the period
between 1655 and 1700 the largest single group of slaves came from
among the Akan and Ga-Andangme peoples of the coastal strip of
Ghana. Many of these slaves, coming from the eastern Caribbean,
were already seasoned and were well placed, both historically
and socially, to impose their own patterns of behaviour and
speech on the creole slave society which was then in its nuclear
stage. Forty per cent of the slaves entering the island during the
last quarter of the seventeenth century came from Angola, the
particular tribal provenance of which is uncertain since this was
one of the areas from which slaves came from a considerable distance
inland. About 30 per cent of these later arrivals came from among

[1] *Practical Rules for the Management & Medical Treatment of Negro Slaves
in the Sugar Colonies*, by a Professional Planter, 1811, pp. 37–8.

the Ewe speaking people of Dahomey, particularly from among the Fon. Although only 20 per cent came from among the coastal tribes of Ghana during the latter half of this period, these would doubtless have assisted in consolidating the Akan and Ga-Andangme bias which the young creole slave community would already have had.

During the period between 1700 and 1730 there was a rapid falling off of the number of slaves coming from Angola while the number from the Slave Coast greatly increased to the position of being, quite possibly, the largest single contributor. While the slaves from this area did not hold this position for long, they left their mark on the slave society that was eventually to emerge, as our subsequent analysis will demonstrate. The slaves from Ghana had also increased proportionately and may well have been the second largest section of the African slaves in the island. By this time, about a half of the slaves from this area were still coming from among the Akan, Ga and Andangme tribes, while the other half came from the tribes of the hinterland. The rest of the slaves came in about equal proportions, from Senegambia, the Windward Coast and the Niger and Cross deltas.

During the first half or so of the period between 1730 and 1790 there was a rapid falling off of slaves from the Slave Coast and a proportionate increase in those from Ghana and the Niger and Cross deltas. Between them they supplied about 70 per cent of the African slaves entering the island, those from Ghana contributing about 40 per cent and from the Niger and Cross deltas about 30 per cent. By this time no less than two-thirds of the slaves from Ghana came from among the more primitive Mole cluster of tribes in the interior such as the Dagomba, Tallensi, Mamprusi, Mossi, Wala and Nandeba. The great majority of the remaining one-third of the slaves (possibly as much as a quarter of all the slaves from Ghana) came from among the Fanti tribes of the Akan-speaking peoples. About three-quarters of all the slaves coming from the Niger and Cross deltas belonged to the Ibo tribe while the other quarter came from among the Chambas, Okrika, Andoni, Edoes and particularly the Ibibios. About 12 per cent of the other African slaves during the first half of this period came from the Slave Coast and the majority of the remainder from among the Kra-speaking peoples of the Windward Coast.

Much the same pattern applied during the second half of this period, except that increasingly large numbers of slaves were now coming from Nigeria, and slightly fewer from Ghana. By about the beginning of the last quarter of the eighteenth century they had changed places, Nigeria producing about 40 per cent of the slaves and Ghana about 30 per cent.

Finally, during the last seventeen years of the trade there was a striking reappearance of slaves from Southwestern Africa, particularly from the region of the Congo. In all, about 40 per cent of all the slaves entering the island during this period came from this area; about 30 per cent from the Niger and Cross deltas; about 20 per cent from the Gold Coast; another 5 per cent from the Windward Coast; and the remainder from the other areas of Africa.

CHAPTER VI

The Socialization and Personality Structure of the Slave

THERE were two types of adjustments to slavery. First, there was that of the African slave whose introduction to the system was sudden and traumatic; and there was that of the creole slave whose socialization was gradual and less painful. This chapter examines these two types of socialization into slavery and the subsequent personality traits that the system appears to have produced.

Both types of adjustments were closely related to each other. The basis of the creole slave society was originally laid down by the first group of Africans enslaved in the island. On the other hand, once the creole slave society was established it formed the main host society for the newly arrived African slaves. However, if we were to examine the slave society at any given time we would find a basic division between the community of the African and Creole slaves. The extent to which one group dominated the other varied from one period to the next. Before examining the processes of socialization, therefore, we shall trace briefly the development of the relationship between the two groups.

SECTION I
CREOLE AND AFRICAN SLAVES

Until near the end of the seventeenth century about a quarter of the slaves came from other West Indian islands, mainly Barbados, while the rest were brought directly from Africa. We cannot say what proportion of the slaves from the other islands was creole, but since Barbados succeeded more than any other island in breeding her own slaves and, since the planters who brought over their slaves with them were the very ones who were more likely to breed their own slaves, it is likely that a substantial minority of them were Barbadian creole. One may speculate that these slaves may have contributed to the speedy development of a creole slave community in Jamaica.

After 1800 the small creole minority in the island was swamped by the greatly increased inflow of African Negroes. The records relating to the late seventeenth and early eighteenth centuries make little reference to the creole minority.[1] By the 1760s, which is about the time Edward Long began writing his *History of Jamaica*[2] we are informed that the African slaves 'are chiefly awed into subjection by the superior multitude of Creole Blacks . . .'[3] In 1789 it was estimated that the Africans constituted 25 per cent of the total population[4] but the more accurate figures of 1817 showed them to be 37 per cent of the total,[5] an increase which may be partly accounted for by the large influx of Africans during the last decade of the slave trade. As early as the 1760s Long found that the creoles differed from the Africans 'not only in manners, but in beauty of shape, feature and complexion',[6] and to a friend of Edwards they 'exceed the Africans in intellect, strength and comeliness';[7] but these views are likely to be biased. More important was the fact that the creoles held the Africans 'in the utmost contempt styling them 'salt-water Negroes' and 'Guineybirds'.[8]

On Lewis' estate, where the Africans, mainly Ibos, formed a substantial minority, there was strong rivalry and dislike on the part of each group for the other. The Ibos exhibited marked tribal solidarity and were organized around elected leaders and after an incident in which the Africans were mortified by the mistaken zeal

[1] Leslie, speaking of the fear of the Africans for the military 'muster and exercise' of the Whites, adds, 'Tis true, the Creolian Negroes are not of this number; They all speak English and are so far from fearing a Muster, that they are very familiar with it, and can exercise extremely well'. *A New History of Jamaica*, p. 311.

[2] Long went to Jamaica in 1757 at the age of 23 and published his *History* in 1774; see Vol. 1 of the history of his family by R. M. Howard, entitled *The Longs of Jamaica and Hampton Lodge.*

[3] E. Long, *History of Jamaica*, Vol. 2, Bk. 3, p. 444.

[4] Report of the Select Committee of the Jamaican House of Assembly, 1789.

[5] BPP XX 1831–32. Select Committee. on Slavery (1721) Q7937.

[6] Long, *op. cit.*, Vol. 2, Bk. 3, p. 410.

[7] Bryan Edwards, *The History . . . of the Br. Colonies in the W.I.* Bk. 4, p. 185.

[8] Long, *op. cit.*, Vol. 2, Bk. 3, p. 410.

of one of the leaders, the creole head cook appealed to Lewis that 'Massa ought to sell all the Eboes, and buy Creoles instead'.[1]

At holidays and festivals both groups tended to have separate recreations. Differences may be discerned too, in their funeral practices, eating habits, dress[2] and the like. Yet, one should be careful not to over-emphasize this distinction for there were many areas of life in which both groups participated. The most important was their work situation where bodily strength and fitness mattered far more than place of birth. Again, the most feared and respected Negro on every estate (though not necessarily the most liked) was the obeahman who in the great majority of cases was African. Finally, it must be remembered that the African born slaves, even when they were in the minority, had considerable influence over the first and second generation creole slaves. Lewis wrote of the strong influence of an African women over her mulatto daughter who having 'imbibed strong African prejudices from her mother' refused to become a Christian.[3] Martin also informs us that 'the Negro population is ... formed into classes, according to the country they came from, or that which their progenitors belonged to'.[4]

SECTION 2

THE ADJUSTMENT OF THE AFRICAN SLAVE

Elkins has described the transformation of the African tribesman into a New World slave in terms of a series of shock experiences, namely – capture, journey to the coast, sale to the white captains, the middle passage and enslavement on the plantation.[5] Such categorization, while of some use, is too schematic, and neglects certain important factors. First, many slaves were captured in genuine warfare, as we indicated in Chapter Five, and as soldiers, one would hardly expect them to be shocked at being taken prisoners of war.

---

[1] M. G. Lewis, *Journal of a West Indian Proprietor*, 1816, p. 190.

[2] Lewis tells us that creole and African slaves competed with each other in their funeral festivities, see *ibid*, p. 335; Long and Lewis stated that Africans were very fond of cane field rats while the creoles had nothing to do with them, or so they said; Africans tended to be more scantily dressed.

[3] Lewis, *op. cit.*, p. 335.

[4] R. M. Martin, *op. cit.*, Vol. 4, pp. 95–6.

[5] Stanley Elkins, *Slavery*, pp. 98–103.

Secondly, many of the slaves came from the coast itself and were thus spared the horrors of the journey from the interior. And thirdly, it must be admitted that many of the slaves sold into slavery were guilty of genuine crimes for which they would otherwise have been executed. But these reservations aside, there can be little doubt that most African slaves had a terrifying experience, both in the nature of their capture, transportation and sale on the coast and in the West Indies. The Ibo slave, Equiano, has left us a vivid account of his capture and later experiences.[1]

He was captured when alone with his sister in his family compound; gagged, tied up and carried to the woods. When he cried out he was placed in a sack.[2] After many days of travel, he was sold. For the next three months he was resold several times. But he was generally well treated and understood the language and customs of his masters. Finally he was sold by a widow to some traders from the coast. This turned out to be his first real and lasting shock experience. 'The change I now experienced', he wrote, 'was as painful as it was sudden and unexpected', involving 'such instances of hardship and fatigue as I can never reflect on but with horror'.[3]

As he passed through strange countries on his way to the coast he was forcibly struck by the differing customs, but more, by the new, awe-inspiring natural sights. The sight of a large river for the first time filled him with astonishment as he had 'never before seen any water than a pond or a rivulet'. It was not until the end of seven

---

[1] *The Interesting Narrative of the Life of Olaudah Equiano or Gustavus Vassa, the African, Written by Himself.* (London, 1789). 2 Vols.

[2] There are a few other slave autobiographies, but none as vivid as Equiano's. A Fanti slave published an autobiography entitled, *The Narrative of the Enslavement of Ottobah Cugoano, a Native of Africa*, in 1787. Like Equiano, Cugoano was kidnapped when still a youth. The technique used in his case was slightly different, he being duped into going to the coast rather than being brutally pulled along. A short autobiography of a Jamaican slave is appended in Madden's 'Twelve Months Residence in the W.I.' and is entitled, *The History of Abon Beer Sadiki, known in Jamaica by the name of Edward Donlan.* Donlan claimed that he was from 'Timbuctoo' and could read and write Arabic. Describing the first stage of his enslavement, he wrote: 'As soon as I was made prisoner they stripped me, and tied me with a cord, and gave me a heavy load to carry . . .' In 1834 a Senegambian ex-slave published an autobiography entitled *Some Memoirs of the Life of Job, the Son of Solomon, the High Priest of Boonda in Africa.* It includes interesting material on capture and transportation to the coast.

[3] Equiano, *op. cit.*, Vol. I, pp. 65–6.

months after he was first kidnapped that Equiano finally reached the coast. The physical confrontation with the sea immediately filled him with sheer terror. No less terrifying was his experience of being forced aboard ship; and the strange sight of the white men who came to inspect him, juxtaposed with that of a large copper boiling on the ship, convinced him that the whites intended to eat him,[1] whereupon he fainted on the deck.[2] Taken to the hold of the ship, together with the rest of the black cargo, the atmosphere became 'absolutely pestilential':

> The closeness of the place, and the heat of the climate added to the number in the ship, which was so crowded that each had scarcely room to turn himself, almost suffocated us. This produced copious perspiration, a variety of loathsome smells, and brought on a sickness amongst the slaves, of which many died, thus falling victims to the improvident avarice, as I may call it, of their purchasers. This wretched situation was again aggravated by the gulling of the chains, now become insupportable, and the fifth of the necessary tubs[3] into which the children often fell and were almost suffocated. The shrieks of the women and the groans of the dying, reduced the whole to a scene of horror almost inconceivable.[4]

Like most of the other slaves, Equiano was overcome with extreme dejection and would have committed suicide had he the opportunity. Isaac Wilson, a surgeon on one of the slave ships, said that melancholy and dejection were 'one great cause' of death. Both Wilson and Falconbridge reported cases of outright insanity caused directly by the impact of the slave ship.[5]

Then followed the indescribable horrors of the middle passage. There is no need to repeat here the well known barbarities of this journey. One experience did take place on the middle passage which was of lasting importance, and paradoxically, of great subsequent

---

[1] Cugoano wrote, '... in the evening (we) came to a town, where I saw several white people, which made me afraid that they would eat me, according to our notion as children, in the inland parts of the country'.

[2] Equiano, *op. cit.*, pp. 70–71

[3] These 'tubs' were the lavatory of the holds.

[4] *Ibid.*, pp. 78–9.

[5] Minutes of Evidence 1790–91. The findings of this Committee support Equiano's descriptions in every detail.

comfort to the slave. It was the formation of the strong bonds of friendship between all the slaves on the slave ship. These friends became known in the West Indies as 'shipmates' and their love and affection for each other was proverbial. Stewart tells us that the term shipmate 'seems synonymous in their view with brother or sister',[1] and according to Kelly, 'Shipmate is the dearest word and bond of affectionate sympathy amongst the Africans . . . they look upon each other's children mutually as their own'.[2] It was customary for children to call their parents' shipmates 'uncle' or 'aunt'.[3] So strong were the bonds between shipmates that sexual intercourse between them, in the view of one observer, was considered incestuous.

After the horrors of the middle passage came the sale at the West Indian ports. The pernicious practice of sale by scramble continued in Jamaica until well into the 1780s. On one such scramble the ship was darkened beforehand by covering it over with sails; male slaves were exhibited on the main deck, females on the quarter deck. At the shot of a gun a large horde of waiting planters scrambled aboard and dashed madly for the slaves of their choice 'with the ferocity of brutes'. This created terror among the slaves, many of whom flung themselves overboard.[4]

Equiano wrote that during this time fears of being eaten were again revived among the slaves. When bought by means other than scramble, the experience of being bought in the island, coming after the horrors of the middle passage, was not particularly harsh. Indeed on such occasions most of the slaves 'express great eagerness to be sold',[5] no doubt so as to get the whole thing over with.

Finally came the long period of seasoning. The slave was taken to the estate, branded with a silver brand heated in spirits, and given a name.[6] What took place after this varied from one estate to the next. On most estates the official period of seasoning was three

[1] J. Stewart, *The Past and Present State of Jamaica*, p. 250.
[2] J. Kelly, *Voyage to Jamaica and Narrative of 17 years Residence in that island*. (1838), p. 45.
[3] M. G. Lewis, *op. cit.*, p. 350.
[4] W. Falconbridge, *op. cit.*
[5] Bryan Edwards, *op. cit.*, Bk. 4, p. 153.
[6] African slaves were often given names taken from popular literature or the Greek classics. On Rose Hall estate there were: Hannibal, Ulysees, Scipio, Hercules, Othello, Antony, Mark, etc.

years but in actual practice the period was usually restricted to a year. Beckford wrote that there were two basic forms of seasoning, that in which new Negroes were put under the supervision of elderly seasoned slaves from their own country; and that in which the master assumes primary responsibility for their safeguard, keeping a provision ground 'ready planted, full of provisions, and apportioned to them upon their arrival'.[1] The first type of seasoning often led to tyranny on the part of the supervising slaves, the latter forcing his ward to work his ground for him at the expense of the ward's ground, and this neglect was often responsible for leading the new Negro to steal in order to prevent himself from starving.[2] Edwards, however, paints a brighter picture of the relationship between the new Negroes and their wardens, claiming that old seasoned Africans usually avidly sought after newcomers from their homeland with whom they could revive memories of their youth and whom they sometimes adopted.[3] But this is quite likely a gross overstatement.

The disadvantage of the second type of seasoning, according to Beckford, was that it led to discontent and feelings of injustice among the new Negroes since they were forced to work on Sundays on the grounds prepared for them, not of their own free will, but under the supervision of a driver. Some masters got around this problem by simply allowing the new Negroes one year's provisions from the stores.

What of the personality of the Africans in these first few months on the island? Beckford has left us a penetrating account of them which strongly suggests all the symptoms of a broken trauma-ridden personality. They were cold, unfeeling and completely unpredictable, their general attitude being one of total indifference:

> It is amazing to see how little they interest themselves in the common occurrences of life; they do not foresee the want of

[1] Beckford, *The Situation of the Negroes in Ja.*, 1788, p. 27.

[2] H. Coor, Evidence of, 1790–91.

[3] B. Edwards, *op. cit.*, Bk. 4, pp. 155–56. This passage reads unconvincingly, like so many of Edwards' remarks concerning the slaves. Slave fathers had little control over their sons, and, as a rule, cared even less about them. They certainly would not have gone out of their way to seek suitable wives among the new Negroes for them. But there may have been some truth in the other remarks relating to the relationship between newly arrived slaves and their supervisors.

means, are careless of what may happen and thoughtless of what they have; in short, their characters for many years after their arrival can hardly be defined by the most perspicacious eye of those by whom they are governed, so that for what we know they may be happy when silent or dangerous when sullen.[1]

The Seasoned African Slave By the time the African's period of seasoning was over he was sure to find himself defined in a certain social position and drawn towards certain groups. During the early period, when the Africans formed the majority of the slaves, divisions between the different African tribes were as great as that between the Africans as a whole and the creoles. Leslie wrote that:

> The slaves are brought from several Places of Guiney, which are different from one another in Language, and consequently they cannot converse freely; or, if they could, they hate one another so mortally, that some of them would rather die by the Hands of the English, than join with other Africans in an attempt to shake off their yoke.[2]

These differences continued until the end of slavery, a nineteenth century observer noting that at the Christmas festivities the different tribal stocks 'formed into exclusive groups competing against each other in performing their national music'.[3] But the differences were now only expressed in amusements. The different African groups from a much earlier date had far more in common with each other, by virtue of being African, in their confrontation with the creole group. Later on in the celebrations Kelly informs us:

> These Africans took the sides and corners of the hall, whilst the Creoles occupied the centre and piazzas, and evidently considered themselves entitled to the best places, which the Africans cheerfully conceded to them, evincing the greatest deference to the superior civilization of the upstarts! The one class, forced into slavery, humbled and degraded had lost everything and found no solace but the miserable one of retrospection. The other, born in slavery, never had freedom to loose; yet did the Creole proudly assume a superiority over the African . . .[4]

[1] Beckford, *op. cit.*, 1788, p. 88.
[2] Leslie, *A New History of Jamaica*, pp. 310–11.
[3] J. Kelly, *op. cit.*, pp. 20–21.
[4] *Ibid.*

It is the common view that Gold Coast Negroes dominated the rest of the Africans, and indeed the entire slave community. There are, however, no grounds for this assertion. Certainly, it cannot be denied that a significant number of Gold Coast cultural elements have survived in Jamaica. According to Cassidy, Twi words make up a half of the two-hundred and fifty loan-words found in the Jamaican dialect.[1] The spider hero of the Akan speaking peoples, Anansesem, survives in the Jamaican spider hero, Anancy; and so on. We shall discuss these cultural problems in more detail as we come to them. For the moment, only a few salient points need to be made. Firstly, it is not justifiable to draw conclusions about the historical dominance of a group solely on the basis of the survival of its cultural elements; and secondly, the survival of cultural elements from the Gold Coast is in no way out of proportion to the number of slaves brought from that region. The importance of the historical priority of this group has been demonstrated in Chapter V. Unlike the viewpoint of the modern scholars, it would appear that large numbers of cultural survivals indicate social isolation rather than social dominance. The data suggest that Gold Coast Negroes managed to preserve more of their culture partly because they kept to themselves and were generally disliked by the other slaves. 'On many estates', Long wrote, 'they do not mix at all with the other slaves, but build their houses distinct from the rest; and, herding together, are left more at liberty to hold their dangerous cabals without interruption'.[2] The passage quoted above from Leslie is also of relevance here. He tells us that the different tribal groups hated one another. What is more significant is his statement that they would rather die than 'join with other Africans in an attempt to shake off their yoke'. Now until the time that Leslie wrote, every rebellion in the island was carried out by the Coromantee slaves and there seems little doubt that Leslie was here obviously referring to the hatred of the other African groups for the Coromantees.

Finally, it should have been obvious that slavery was no place for one enslaved group to dominate another. It was common for the weaker party in a dispute to declare: 'This no for we country; this for Buckra (whites) country; Buckra country everybody have right'.[3]

[1] Cassidy, *Jamaica Talk*, pp. 21; 397.
[2] Long, *op. cit.*, Vol. 2, p. 475.
[3] Evidence of John Wedderburn, 1790–91.

In any case, the whole problem of cultural domination of one African group by another is largely an overplayed issue when it is considered that almost all the Africans imported to Jamaica came from the same culture area,[1] where, as Daryl Forde observes, 'underlying the great regional or tribal differences . . . there is a very widespread substratum of basic ideas that persists in the rituals, myths and folk-tales of West African peoples'.[2]

SECTION 3

THE SOCIALIZATION OF THE CREOLE SLAVE

(a) *Birth and Infancy* In considering the birth and rearing of children three factors must be borne in mind. The first, already dealt with in a former chapter, is the ambivalence of creole women to child-bearing and the fact that for the greater part of the period of slavery children were usually considered a nuisance by most estate supervisors. As one planter, speaking of the attitude of the women, pointed out, 'many mothers who are fond of their children when once they have brought them into the world, would yet very gladly avoid having them'.[3] The second fact to be noted is that slave mothers came from both the African and creole groups. Thus we should expect that many of the rites and taboos relating to birth and early infancy in Africa would have been practiced by the African mothers. Thirdly, there was a marked difference between the treatment of the children of field and household slaves. The latter had much better care and were often brought up with the white children.

The most striking feature of the birth and early infancy of the creole slaves was the almost ritualized neglect, and attitude of resignation, toward the child during its first eight or nine days. The midwife (or grandee) on Lewis' estate told him, 'Oh massah, till nine days over me no hope for them'.[4] It was common practice to confine babies to the same clothes for their first nine days,[5] and it was also customary never to set it 'to the mother's breast till eight

---

[1] See M. J. Herskovits 'The Culture Areas of Africa', in *Africa*, Vol. 3, 1930 where 9 cultural areas are demarcated.

[2] Daryl Forde 'The Culture Map of West Africa', Ottenburg, *Culture and Societies of Africa*, p. 123.

[3] *Practical Rules, etc.*, p. 147.

[4] Lewis, *op. cit.*, pp. 97–8.

[5] G. Mathison, *Notices Respecting Jamaica*, 1805–10.

days be over,' a wet-nurse with a child of two to four months being used to feed the infant.[1] Since most of the babies who died were 'lost within so short a period as nine days after birth'[2] the first explanation that comes to mind for these quaint customs and attitudes toward the child during its first eight or nine days is the frequency of tetanus. But this scientific explanation is not sufficient in answering the question of the almost ritualized neglect during the first eight or nine days.

Throughout many West African peoples there is a ghost-child (or born-to-die) notion relating to newly born infants. Among the Akan every child, for the first eight days of its life, is seen as the possible embodiment of an evil spirit and is therefore neglected until the eighth day when it is taken out, bathed and receives a personal name.[3] If the child dies within the first eight days of birth this is taken as proof of the fact that it was a ghost, and it is deprived of a proper funeral. It is difficult to resist the conclusion that this is a case of cultural re-interpretation. Corresponding to the fear of the ghost-child during the first eight days in Africa, was the fear of tetanus in Jamaica. The old notion was therefore re-interpreted in terms of the new, more rational medical explanation.

We have discussed the length of time devoted to teething in another chapter. Here there was a clear conflict between the overseers who wished the period to be as short as possible, and the mothers, who, if permitted, would have prolonged it for years. The average period seems to have been between eighteen months and two years. Among the taboos of the mothers during breast-feeding was the fear that should the child belch while sucking, the mother's breast would swell dangerously.[4] When the child was about two months old it was taken out to the field,[5] strapped, African fashion, to the mother's back,[6] and there handed over to an old grandee. Under her care, they lay, in the view of one observer, 'in trays beneath an arbour made of boughs . . . like so many tadpoles'.[7]

---

[1] Evidence of Henry Coor, Select Committee. on Slave Trade, 1790–91.

[2] Beckford, *Situation of the Negroes in Jamaica*, p. 24.

[3] See G. Parrinder's discussion of W. African birth customs in his *West African Religion*; also Herskovits, *Dahomey*, Vol. I, pp. 261–62.

[4] M. G. Lewis, *op. cit.*, p. 349.

[5] Barclay, *A Practical View of the Present State of Slavery*, p. 318.

[6] Hans Sloane, *op. cit.*, Introduction.

[7] C. Williams, *Tour Through Jamaica*, pp. 13–14.

On some estates they were placed on sheepskin or other soft material.[1] The mothers of infants still at the breast usually had a shift system whereby they alternated every two hours or so with each other between assisting the grandee and working with the grass or little gang of old and weak slaves.[2] The infant slaves, apart from their mothers' milk, were fed on a pap called 'Parrada' by the slaves which was made of a mixture of bread, flour and sugar.

(b) *Childhood, Youth and Adulthood:* The young slaves were introduced to the rigours of plantation labour from an early age. On some of the more benignly governed estates such as De La Beche's they began working at the age of six when they joined what he called the 'small gang' which, in addition to gathering grass from the stable also carried green slips and vines to the hogs, under the supervision of an old woman.[3] On most estates, however, slaves began their working life between the age of four and five years. The 'Professional Planter', who was describing what he admitted to be the ideal condition, said they began working at the age of five, at which time the fruits of their labour was sufficient to defray the expense of their support.[4]

We have discussed in Chapter II the organization and functions of the different gangs. For the moment we are interested only in the movement of the slave from one gang to the next over the period of his life. A more precise picture is obtained by observing the situation on one estate, that of Rose Hall.[5] Among the males, we find that none of the five between the ages of seven months and three years were at work. One boy of four, however, was already in the hogmeat gang, and so was another of five years of age. Between the ages of six and thirteen we find the male slaves employed in various occupations. Two were cattle boys; three were in the overseer's house; one was already in the fields; one was 'with

[1] J. B. Moreton, *Manners and Customs in the West Indies*, 1793, p. 152.
[2] A. Barclay, *op. cit.*, p. 318.
[3] H. T. De La Beche, *The Present Condition of the Negroes in Jamaica*, 1825, p. 7. Sir Hans Sloane wrote that 'Their children call'd Piganninies or rather Pequenos ninos, go naked till they are fit to be put to clean the Paths, bring Fire-wood to the Kitchen, etc. when a Boy Overseer with his Wand or White Rod, is set over them as task Master . . .'
[4] *Practical Rules*, etc. *op. cit.*, pp. 149–150.
[5] *In Old St. James*, Compiled by J. Shore, ed. J. Stewart, pp. 140–151.

Mrs Palmer' and the remaining one was 'not at work', although described as 'able and healthy'. It is significant to note that this boy was a mulatto.

The situation was different with the girls. They too, started to work at the age of four, but they all remained in the Hogmeat Gang until the age of nine. Between the ages of twelve and nineteen their occupations varied. One girl of twelve was already in the field. So were two others aged nineteen. Of the other four girls in this age group two were attending stock, one was with Mrs Palmer, and the other was a domestic. The great majority of the women between the ages of nineteen and fifty-four were in the field. The proportion of women in the field was larger than that of the males. This was due partly to the fact that men had a wider range of occupations to choose from, and, at Rose Hall in particular, they were outnumbered by the women.

Apart from the privileged minority who were chosen for non-field occupations, the period of really hard, adult work began in the case of males after puberty; and in the case of females generally after adolescence. In the four gang system, as existed on Green Park, Radnor and other estates, they would go first to the second gang, and by the age of twenty-five (when a slave was considered to be at his fittest and most expensive) he would be recruited to the first or great gang which was the backbone of the labour force of every estate.

(c) *Elderly and Superannuated Slaves* By the age of forty-five, when most slaves would have passed their prime, the slave was demoted to the second gang and soon after to the third. On most estates, male slaves in their fifties and sixties were generally occupied as watchmen or tiers. Far from involving a reduction in the intensity of work, these new jobs were usually more 'arduous'. Watchmen had to sit up all night exposed to the chilly and unhealthy night air,[1] and the tiers, who collected and bound up the canes for carriage, often had to remain in the field all day without any interval of rest, especially during crop.[2]

The condition of the elderly female slaves was slightly better. Many of them were reduced to the third gang and on Rose Hall

[1] Stewart, *Past and Present State of Jamaica*, 1823, p. 231.
[2] W. Beckford, *The Situation of the Negroes in Jamaica*, pp. 46–7.

estate the majority were engaged in grass-cutting. But the more fortunate became nurses – some in the hothouse (hospital) and others as midwives in charge of the infants – or cooks attached to the different gangs. After the last decade of the eighteenth century many women benefited from the law which made any mother who had six children alive free of labour.

But many of the slaves who survived to old age may well have regretted their longevity. A few humane masters made provisions for them; but these were rare. 'If they had not relations or friends', an observer stated, 'they must have wanted everything'.[1] And those without relatives were confined to a corner of a cane field and given a weekly ration of plantains to ward off starvation,[2] or allowed to wander about aimlessly and 'left to take care of themselves as well they could'.[3] A few masters even turned them out of the estate and there was one barbarous owner during the eighteenth century who murdered all his weakly and old slaves by throwing them over a cliff. He became so notorious that a popular slave song was made about him, telling of a slave who while being carried to be slaughtered protested that he was not yet dead.[4] Fortunately for the slave, the well known African behaviour pattern of great respect for old age survived throughout slavery,[5] and most of these superannuated slaves had relatives or friends they could depend upon.[6]

---

[1] Evidence of Dr. Harrison, Select Committee. on Slave Trade, 1790–91.
[2] *Ibid.*
[3] Evidence of Mark Cook. Select Committee. on Slave Trade, 1790–91.
[4] Several versions of this song exist. The following is Lewis':
  Take him to the Gully! Take him to the Gully!
  But bringee back the frock and board.
  Oh! massa, massa! me no deadee yet!
  Take him to the Gulley! Take him to the Gulley!
  Carry him along!
[5] Bryan Edwards, *op. cit.*, Bk. 4, pp. 98–9.

[6] It should be noted that the three-gang system was just as common as the four-gang. Stewart wrote that in the former, the first gang consisted of the ablest Negroes between sixteen and twenty years. The second contained elderly and weakly adults and Negroes between age twelve and sixteen. The third gang contained children between the ages of six and twelve years.

SECTION 4

MATING PATTERNS, PARENT-CHILD RELATIONS, KINSHIP,
AND THE WHITE OUT-GROUP

So far we have been concerned mainly with the socialization of the
slave into his work situation. We must now consider some of the
more informal aspects of the slaves' development and the agents of
socialization primarily responsible for their formation. Our observations will relate mainly to the creole slaves. It should be remembered, however, that the African slaves had no other choice than
to fall into the patterns of behaviour they found on the island.

(a) *Sexual Behaviour and Mating Patterns* Slavery in Jamaica
led to the breakdown of all forms of social sanctions relating to
sexual behaviour, and with this, to the disintegration of the institution of marriage both in its African and European forms. According
to one missionary 'the sanctions of marriage were almost unknown'
and the institution was largely ridiculed by the slaves. 'Every estate
on the island – every Negro hut – was a common brothel; every
female a prostitute; and every man a libertine'.[1] This breakdown of
sexual mores and the institution of marriage among the Negroes
occurred all over the New World.[2] But in no other area was the
degree of sexual abandonment so great as in Jamaica. The reason
for this is to be found largely in the similar breakdown of such
mores among the dominant white group which we have examined
in detail in our chapter on the whites. The scarcity of white women
and the absence of moral sanctions led to a ruthless exploitation of
the female slave. Sometimes this exploitation was crude and direct,
being against the will of the woman, who would be 'compelled
under pain of corporal punishment to yield implicit obedience to the
will of the master'.[3] Another witness stated that 'if an overseer
sends for a girl for such purposes she is obliged to come, or else
flogged'.[4] Whitely was told by a book-keeper that he had had twelve

[1] J. M. Phillippo, *Jamaica, Its Past and Present State*, 1843, p. 218.
[2] See for the U.S., F. G. Frazier's *The Negro Family in America*; also Kar-
diner's *The Mark of Oppression*, for Brazil, G. Freyre's *The Masters and the
Slaves*.
[3] Cooper, *Facts Illustrative of the Condition of the Negro Slaves in Jamaica*,
pp. 13–14.
[4] Evidence of Cook, Select Committee on Slave Trade, 1790–91.

'Negro wives' in six months; and when he refused to participate in the custom of the country he was regarded 'with mingled contempt and suspicion'.[1] The male partner dared not complain if his 'wife' was called upon to satisfy the lust of the overseer, for if he did all he could expect was a flogging 'couched under the name of some other misdemeanour'.[2]

Quite apart from this exploitation by the whites, the sex-ratio of the slave population would inevitably have led to promiscuity. We have already discussed this problem in an earlier chapter. Purely biological reasons, therefore, prompted the female slave to promiscuity. The sex life of the creole Negroes began quite early; from one report they began to have sexual intercourse 'even at the age of nine, and with a multitude of men . . .'[3] Phillippo found that they had 'sacrificed all pretensions to virtue before they had attained their fourteenth year' and that 'hundreds were known to have become mothers before they had entered their teens'.[4] Another missionary also found that 'the men go astray as much as the women, and girls of fourteen are said to be common instruments of pleasure'.[5]

Where young girls resisted they were raped, many cases of which were reported by Mahon. Particularly gruesome was his account of the rape of an eleven year old girl by the attorney of Richmond estate.[6] But rape was often unnecessary since the slave women soon gave in to the overwhelming pressures and made the best of its rewards, for, 'not only did these connections exempt the poor female from the toils of field labour, but it gave her many enviable exemptions in other respects, and in her own eyes especially raised her to a fancied superiority among the other slaves'.[7] Yet, within this seeming chaos, one may discern some pattern of mating and sexual behaviour. This pattern fell into five basic types of associations: sex-work; unstable unions; stable unions; multiple associations; and monogamous associations which were sometimes made legal. Each will be discussed in turn and then their relationships analysed.

---

[1] H. Whiteley, *Three Months in Jamaica*, 1832.
[2] Evidence of H. Coor, *op. cit.*
[3] Report of Stephen Fuller (assisted by Messrs. Long and Chisholme) to the Committee of the Privy Council, 1788, in B.T.6:10, p. 23.
[4] Phillippo, *op. cit.*, p. 42.
[5] Cooper, *op. cit.*, p. 42.
[6] B. Mahon, *Jamaica Plantership*, pp. 69–71.
[7] B. Lucock, *Jamaica: Enslaved and Free*, p. 122.

(i) *Sex-work* Sex-work, in the strict sense of this term, was widespread. Long found the women, 'in general, common prostitutes' practicing frequent abortions 'in order that they may continue their trade without loss of time, or hindrance of business'.[1] Cooper attributed a great part of the natural decline of the slave population to the prevalence of sex-work among the young women. On the estates there were well known pimps who procured the sex-workers for strangers, usually whites, who wished their services. According to Cooper, these pimps were usually the estate mid-wives.[2] And an overseer tells us that 'when a white man is inclined to get a mongrel or black girl for a night the usual mode is to hire a boy or old woman to procure one'.[3] But often the mother, or mistress, of a sex-worker acted as her pimp. On the estates the mother of an attractive sex-worker could be a powerful figure:

> Those gypsies (i.e. the sex-workers mothers) have a wonderful ascendancy over men and have injured many, both powerful and subordinate; the poor slaves on a plantation are obliged to pay them as much adoration as the Portuguese the Hostess or Virgin Mary, for the government of the cowskin depends in a great measure on their smiles and frowns.[4]

Sex-work was most rife, however, in the towns. Here there were many white men having no authority over slave women – clerks, sailors, soldiers, artisans and the like – who were obliged to satisfy their sexual needs in this manner. Many of these town prostitutes were free coloured women, and the majority of enslaved domestics in the towns were expected to support themselves in this manner.[5] Leslie wrote of the 1720s that some of the town women 'go neat enough, but these are the Favourites of young Squires, who keep them for a certain use'.[6] It was common for the mistresses of slaves in the towns to live off the immoral earnings of their slave sex-workers many of whom they trained specifically for this purpose. Moreton informs us that 'Mongrel wenches from their youth are taught to be whores: you cannot affront one of them more than to

---

[1] E. Long, *op. cit.*, Vol. 2, p. 436.   [2] Cooper, *op. cit.* p. 42.
[3] Moreton, *op. cit.*, p. 132.   [4] *Ibid.*, p. 127.
[5] Evidence of Mark Cook, Select Committee. on Slave Trade, 1790–91.
[6] C. Leslie, *A New History of Jamaica*, p. 35.

give any hint of her being dull and unskilled in the magical art'.[1] Lewis mentions an old watchman on his estate who hired a coloured mistress from a brown man in the mountains at the rate of £30 per year. But this was a very unusual case, especially with respect to the woman being coloured. The latter were notorious for their contempt not only for black men, but men of their own colour.[2]

(ii) *Unstable Unions* This type of association was perhaps the most common, especially among the young adult slaves. According to one missionary:

> They were frequently at a loss to determine which was the proper husband or wife. For instance: a female wishes to become a member of society; but was the man with whom she was then living the first she had agreed with? No; she had lived with many others; and the first man with whom she was connected had many more women since he left her; and perhaps was living with one at that time by whom he had several children . . .[3]

Phillippo also mentions the 'frequent interruptions' to their alliances and gives an account of a quaint divorce ceremony in which the couple mutually divided a cotta (i.e. a head-pad made of plantain leaves) before separating.[4] But there is no evidence of this ceremony being widespread, and Edwards' remark that these unions were formed 'without ceremony and dissolved without romance' seems to have described the general pattern.

[1] Moreton, *op. cit.*, p. 129.

[2] Sexual intercourse between coloured women and their male counterparts was so rare that Long stated categorically that they were incapable of having children together. Bickell wrote in 1825 that 'such is the contempt with which the men of colour are treated . . . and such is the poverty of most of them that most of the brown women prefer being kept by a white man to being the wife of a man of her own colour and rank . . .' (*The W.I. as they are*, etc., p. 112–13.) This contempt for men darker then themselves was universal. Lewis wrote that, 'The difference of colour . . . is a fault which no mulatto will pardon; nor can the separation of castes in India be more rigidly observed than that of complexional shades among the Creoles. My black page Cubina, is married: I told him that I hoped he had married a pretty woman: why had he not married Mary Wiggins? He seemed quite shocked at the very idea, 'Oh massa, me black, Mary Wiggins sambo; that not allowed'. p. 79.

[3] Statement of Mr Bromwell; quoted in R. Watson's *A Defence of the Wesleyan Methodist Missions in the West Indies*, 1817.

[4] Phillippo, *op. cit.*, p. 219.

(iii) *Stable Unions and* (iv) *Multiple Associations:* These two cate-gories will be considered together since the former usually existed within the wider framework of the latter. Among the older and more prosperous male slaves (boilers, coopers, smiths, other skilled mechanics, headmen, and the like) a stable relationship with one woman was established, in conjunction with a series of loose rela-tionships with other 'wives' who were not only changed frequently, but were permitted to have other lovers. It was this combination of quasi-polygyny and quasi-polyandry which so shocked most of the contemporary observers. Long, who wrote before the abolition movement began, has left us the most penetrating account of these relationships:

> They are all married (in their way) to a husband, or wife, *pro tempore*, or have other family connexions, in almost every parish throughout the island; so that one of them, perhaps, has six or more husbands or wives in several different places; by this means they find support when their own lands fail them; and houses of call and refreshment whenever they are upon their travels . . . perhaps because of the whole number of wives or husbands, one only is the object of particular, steady attachment; the rest, although called wives, are only a sort of occasional con-cubines, or drudges, whose assistance the husband claims in the culture of his land, sale of his produce, and so on; rendering to them reciprocal acts of friendship, when they are in want . . .[1]

The economic aspects of these relationships, especially as they related to the cultivation of provision grounds, was obviously im-portant. Coor said much the same in 1790 although he does not emphasize the reciprocal nature of these contingent economic factors:

> It was not looked upon as anyways disadvantageous to an estate for the men to have a number of wives, from one, two, three or four, according as they had property to maintain them. What I mean by property is provisions on their little spots of ground . . .[2]

The pattern did not change markedly in the 19th century. In 1823

[1] E. Long, *op. cit.*, Vol. 2, p. 414.
[2] Evidence of Henry Coor, *op. cit.*

Reid observed that, 'The husband has commonly two or three wives, and the wives as many husbands which they mutually change for each other'.[1]

It is important to understand that while these quasi-polygynous relations of the males were synchronic, the countervailing quasi-polyandrous relations were generally diachronic or sequential. As Bromwell pointed out, 'Sometimes a man had several wives at the same time and the woman had many husbands *successively*, so that almost every child had a different father'.[2]

(v) *Stable Monogamous and Legal Marriages:* The attitude of the slave toward stable monogamous unions and (during the nineteenth century) legal marriage, tended to vary over the span of his life. Young slaves generally ridiculed the idea of stable unions of this kind. Despite his efforts, De La Beche 'could not prevail upon a single pair to marry' on his own estate.[3] Many women disliked marriage because it entailed extra work and felt it silly to be confined to one man.[4] The apparent contempt for marriage was greatest in the towns. Bickell recalls the case of a young mechanic who wished to get married but who 'had been much laughed and scoffed at by many in the town'. After the ceremony 'the rabble followed, shouting and jeering as if the newly married pair had committed some dreadful crime'.[5]

Paradoxically, one of the main reasons for the overt contempt shown to the slave who got married was the high status associated with legal marriage on the part of the slaves themselves, who 'regard the marriage tie with a reverence and respect approaching to superstition'.[6]

Because marriage was so rare in the island, and because it was practiced mainly by the wealthy proprietors, it inevitably became associated with the privileged, and one can well understand why the slave would jeer at one of his fellows partaking in this high

[1] *An Address to the Right Hon. Geo. Canning on the Present State of This Island and Other Matters, by Denis Reid*, 1823.

[2] Evidence of Mr Bromwell, quoted in Watson, *op. cit.*

[3] De La Beche, *op. cit.*, pp. 17–18.

[4] Cooper, *op. cit.*, p. 9.

[5] Bickell, *op. cit.*, p. 93.

[6] G. Jackson, *A Memoir of the Rev John Jenkins, Wesleyan Missionary in Jamaica* (1832), p. 120.

caste ceremony. Marriage, as we saw in Chapter 1, was 'out of the question' even for subordinate whites, and Walker observed that 'rank and privilege, which are strongly marked in every thing, seem to turn marriage into a distinction somewhat of the nature of nobility and to reserve it in general for the proprietors and leading men of the country'.[1] It was different, however, with the old couples. Even before the possibility of legal marriage in the nine-teenth century, it was common for the old Negroes to settle down in stable monogamous unions.[2]

In the nineteenth century, when the laws made it possible, such old couples sometimes got legally married, often under pressure from the missionaries; indeed 'the great amount of marriages appeared to be of this kind'.[3] In such cases, respect for the age of the couple and their proven affections, led to less scepticism and mockery from the younger slaves.

(vi) *A Developmental View* So far, for the sake of clarity, we have adopted a static approach in our discussion of the five types of mating patterns found among the slaves; seeing them as distinct entities without any ordered relation to each other. In fact, these different patterns are really not distinct categories, but phases in the development of the mating habits of the creole slaves over the entire span of their lives.[4]

We may summarize this cycle of mating in the following manner. In general, there existed a system of mating which was a combina-tion of a synchronic quasi-polygyny and a sequential quasi-polyan-dry. In the case of the female slaves, regular sexual activity began quite early in life with sporadic relations not far removed from sex-work.[5] Later, the plantation Negroes progressed to the phase of being either one of the temporary wives of an older and more prosperous male slave, or the lover of one or more younger males,

---

[1] J. Walker, *Letters on the West Indies*, pp. 165–66.
[2] Bryan Edwards, *op. cit.*, Vol. 2, p. 98.
[3] James Kelly, *op. cit.*, p. 45.
[4] Note that the social anthropologist, R. T. Smith, in his study of the Br. Guianese Negro family (see *The Negro Family in Br. Guiana*) and in his general discussion of the West Indian family (see for ex. 'The Family in the Caribbean') analyses the 'development cycle of the household' in three phases.
[5] With female slaves in the towns prostitution remained the dominant pattern for much of their lives.

or – more often – both. Next, she entered the phase in which she became the 'wife' of a young adult male in a series of exclusive but unstable unions. Finally, in middle or late middle age, now rapidly dwindling in attractiveness – since, naturally, women aged rapidly under the brutalising impact of slavery – more than likely burdened with children and in need of some security, she settled down to become what Long described as 'the object of particular steady attachment' of an elderly male slave. With old age, this phase developed into an ordinary monogamous union as the male partner gave up his quasi-polygynous activities, and was sometimes legalized. Many women experienced a fifth phase which may be described as matriarchial. Often, this matriarchal phase was brought about by the death of the 'husband'. But even where the final 'husband' was present his authority dwindled beside the influence of his 'wife' in their household. This was due to the fact that none of the children in their household would have been his own since his union with his last 'wife' began after her child-bearing period, and his own children would be living with their mothers (his former wives), often on another estate. The old woman, on the other hand, would command all the respect with which (as we shall show below) children treated their mother.

The pattern was simpler for males. Regular sexual activity began at a much later date.[1] Early sexual experiences were highly irregular and took place with much younger women then going through their sporadic phase. Later, these men generally became the lovers of the temporary wives of older men. Next, they became partners in unstable unions and, after this, established a stable relationship with one particular woman while being engaged to several temporary 'wives', the number of which depended on their economic position.[2]

[1] Thus the turnover of each generation of sexually available females would be much faster than that of sexually mature males, a factor which no doubt played an important part in redressing the imbalance of the sexes.

[2] While I am in no way suggesting a historical link, an analogy between the mating patterns of Jamaican slave society and the Lele of Kasai, studied by Mary Douglas, is very suggestive. While there was an equal ratio of males to females, the extreme monopolization of the young women by a small minority of old men, led to a situation bearing a remarkable resemblance to the Jamaican pattern. There was the same combination of polygyny and polyandry; extensive marital unfaithfulness on the part of wives who had lovers from among the young men; there were village wives not very different from the slave sex-workers; and women began their sexual lives at a much earlier age than men, thus reducing the imbalance. See Mary Douglas, *The Lele of Kasai*.

(b) *Household, Parent-Child Relations and Kinship:* So far we have considered the sexual and mating patterns of the creole slave. We must now examine how this pattern affected parental authority as well as the other authority-figures and relations who functioned in the socialization of the slave.

It is to be noted, first of all, that the nuclear family could hardly exist within the context of slavery. Such families were actively discouraged by the masters, and throughout the seventeenth and eighteenth centuries ran the risk of being brutally severed at any time by the creditors of their master. Furthermore, even where such families did develop, the male head could not assert his authority as a husband or as a father. His 'wife' was the property of another, and as Cooper pointed out, 'the concerns of the family must be to her matters of very inferior moment, compared with the work of her owner. He insists on all the prime of her strength being devoted to his business; it is only after the toils, the indecencies, the insults and miseries of a day spent in the gang that she can think of doing anything to promote the comfort of her household'.[1] Slavery abolished any real social distribution between males and females.[2] The woman was expected to work just as hard; she was as indecently exposed and was punished just as severely. In the eyes of the master she was equal to the man as long as her strength was the same as his. In addition to this, the system gave her many opportunities to exploit her sex to her own advantage. Since her sexual services were in great demand by both blacks and whites she often found herself in intimate association with the white masters. If she became the overseer's housekeeper she could wield great power not only in the domestic affairs of the household of the great house, but also in the general running of the estate. We have already seen how even mothers of attractive sex-workers could exert considerable influence.

The net result of all this was the complete demoralization of the Negro male. Incapable of asserting his authority either as husband or father, his sexual difference in no way recognized in his work situation by the all powerful outgroup, the object of whatever affection he may possess, beaten, abused and often raped before his very eyes, and with his female partner often in closer link with the

---

[1] Cooper, *op. cit.*, pp. 45–6.
[2] George Jackson, *A Memoir of the Rev John Jenkins, Wesleyan Missionary in Jamaica*, pp. 113–14.

source of all power in the society, it is no wonder that the male slave eventually came to lose all pretensions to masculine pride and to develop the irresponsible parental and sexual attitudes that are to be found even today. 'Patent submission to the lash and manly feelings' as an abolitionist observed, 'are incongruous'.[1]

The woman became, then, the dominant, often the sole factor in the rearing of the creole slave during the eighteenth and nineteenth centuries, although there is some evidence that during the seventeenth century, when the policy of buying an equal number of males and females was followed, parental authority may have been shared between father and mother. Husbands certainly seem to have had more authority over their wives then, being 'very much concerned if they prove adulterous'.[2]

Long also wrote of the strong affection of Negro mothers for their children

> In their care for their children some are remarkably exemplary . . . They exercise a kind of sovereignty over their children which never ceases during life; chastising them sometimes with such severity; and seeming to hold filial obedience in much higher estimation than conjugal fidelity.[3]

He was able to detect, however, a certain degree of ambivalence in the attitude and treatment by Negro mothers of their offspring. In a later passage he tells us that 'they in general love their children, though sometimes they treat them with a rigour bordering on 'cruelty'. We have already seen that many women considered having children a great burden, especially since few masters bothered to make any extra provisions for them.

This combination of extreme cruelty and great love and affection for children is to be found among Negro mothers in Jamaica even today.[4] Her cruelty to her children was partly the displacement of aggression and hatred for the driver and overseer; partly her own ignorant way of inculcating respect and loyalty in her children. It should not hide the fact of her strong maternal affection and love,

---

[1] *The Negro Slave in the Br. Colonies*, by an Abolitionist.
[2] Sir Hans Sloane, *op. cit.*, Introduction.
[3] Long, *op. cit.*, Vol. 2, p. 414.
[4] See M. Kerr, *Personality and Conflict in Jamaica*, p. 45; see also Judith Blake's *Family Structure in Jamaica*, pp. 58–62.

which struck many observers as 'astonishing'.[1] This love of children was also expressed in the willingness to adopt other slaves' children despite the burden of her own, many moving instances of which were mentioned by Lewis.[2]

Children were also seen by their parent as a form of security. In the first place, they were regarded by their mothers as their future supporters in old age. We have already referred to the wretched existence of those slaves who had no younger relations to provide for them. Secondly, the mother gained the labour of her child in working her provision ground and later, might even control the extra provision ground given to her children when they had attained adulthood. Thus slave mothers did everything to keep their children within their household and to discourage any attempt at forming permanent unions outside, one nineteenth century writer stating that to be the main reason for the lack of stable unions among the slaves, some mothers thus controlling their children 'sometimes to the age of forty years and even after'.[3] Such cases however were the exceptions rather than the rule.[4]*

The respect for the mother was extended to all elders and these no doubt played some part in the upbringing of the slave. Elders were always addressed with a prefix to their names as a mark of respect. Indeed, something of the kinship terminology of West African society survived among the Jamaican slaves.

Lewis noted that:

Among the Negroes it is almost tantamount to an affront to address by the name without affixing some term of relationship such as 'grannie' or 'uncle' or 'cousin'. My Cornwall boy, George,

[1] Beckford, *The Situation of the Negroes in Jamaica*, 1788, p. 24.
[2] Lewis, *op. cit.*, p. 176.
[3] Anon, 'Notes in the Defence of the . . . Colonies', in *Jamaica Journal*, Vol. 2, No. 8, 1824.
[4] The author overstates his argument to the point of contradicting himself. If it was true that young adult Negroes were dominated by their parents this would imply that families were universal and closely knit, the absence of which being exactly what he was trying to explain. His arguments make sense, however, if he was referring to female dominated household units. But it was only in a minority of such cases that mothers enclosed the provision grounds of their children since the master often intervened and re-allocated these grounds. See later chapter on provision grounds.

* This same pattern of what Edith Clarke has called the 'cycle of reciprocal dependence' still exists today, see her, *My Mother who Fathered Me*, p. 163.

told me one day that ' "Uncle Sully" wanted to speak to massa" '. 'Why, is Sully your uncle George ?' 'No massa; me only call him so for honour.'[1]

It was customary for persons of their parents' generation to be addressed with the prefix 'Ta' or 'Ma' (Father or Mother)[2] or in other cases, 'Uncle, Aunty, Tatta, Mama, Sister, Boda', even where no obvious blood relation existed.[3]*

(c) *The Influence of the White Group* Despite the strong bond between mother and child, in the long run other agents were of more importance in the slaves' upbringing than she was. This was due to the fact, already mentioned, that the amount of time she could devote to her children was very limited. Usually less than two years after they were weaned, children were placed under the command of a driveress in the grass gang and later moved to other gangs which were always separate from their parent. The driver became, then, the direct authority figure for the child. But it was

---

[1] Lewis, *op. cit.*, p. 258.

[2] Edwards, *op. cit.*, Vol. 2, p. 99.

[3] Moreton, *op. cit.*, p. 159.

* Radcliffe-Brown (in his introduction to *African Systems of Kinship and Marriage*) wrote that 'There is a widespread custom of privileged familiarity between grandparents and grandchildren' in Africa based on the 'structural principle. that 'one generation is replaced in course of time by the generation of their grand*parent*'. Further, that 'The replacement of grandparents by their grandchildren is in a way recognized in the widespread custom of giving a child the name of a grandparent'. Now this very custom was noted by Lewis who wrote: 'Nepture came this morning to request that the name of his son, Oscar, might be changed for that of Julius, which (it seems) had been that of his own father. The child, he said, had always been weakly and he was persuaded that ill-health proceeded from his deceased grandfather's being displeased because it had not been called after him' (Lewis, p. 349). Not only did the African custom of naming the grandchild after the grandparent survive, but also what Radcliffe-Brown described as 'another aspect of the same principle', namely, 'the merging of alternate generations' in which 'a man with his father's father, his son's sons and his "brother" in the classificatory sense form a social division over against his "fathers" and "sons", who constitute another division'. The terminological aspect of this principle survives even today among the Jamaican peasantry. The term 'granny' is used universally among them to designate the grandmother. Yet Cassidy has discovered that a ' "granny" is not the grandparent among the folk, but a grandchild'. He also tells us that 'This is true, at least, among the Accompong Maroons'. It is well known that the Maroons exhibit the greatest degree of African cultural survivals among Jamaican pe sant Communities.

not long before the child became aware of the fact that the driver's authority was derived from a higher source and that this higher source was the white group. He would have been told this by his mother. More important, he would constantly see the authority of the whites demonstrated in the frequent orders given by the white book-keepers or overseers to the drivers.

In the case of the children of domestic slaves – who always formed a significant minority of the slave children – the social superiority of the whites was demonstrated from an early age through their relationship with their white peer group. In our chapter on the creole whites we have seen that white children were allowed to mix freely with their black peers. Mahon has left us an account of what happened in these early peer group associations:

> The inbred arrogance of a white child brought up among black children is painfully pressed upon the observation of a person unaccustomed to such a land of tyranny as a slave colony always is. At even two years of age the black child cowers and shrinks before the white child, who at all times slaps and beats it at pleasure and takes away its toys without the smallest manifestation of opposition on the part of the piccaninni. I have frequently seen a white child crying, when the little slave, so utterly a slave from his birth, would say to the crying child, – 'Massa, knock me, don't cry; you my massa; me you nega'.[1]

In later life, the slave discriminated between the different orders of whites. Generally, if the owner was absentee, the attorney (who paid periodic visits to the estate) was seen as their owner and true master. Should the absentee owner visit the island, his authority was immediately recognized and all the apparent adoration due to him was given. Note for example, the tumultuous welcome given M. G. Lewis when he visited his estate for the first time. Of course, if the owner actually lived on the estate, the matter was made that much simpler.[2]

On one level, Long's assertion that 'they eye and respect their master as a father and are extremely vain in reflecting on the connexion

---

[1] Mahon, *op. cit.*, p. 293.

[2] It should be remembered that while the majority of owners lived on the island, because of the unequal distribution of slaves among whites, the majority of slaves were owned by masters who were absentee.

between them'[1] may have been generally true. Thus their own estimation *vis-à-vis* the slaves of other estates was largely a reflection of their master's status in the community. The slaves also appeared to emulate their masters and copied 'not only their dress but imitate their every action and expression'.[2] The status of the master was so important in the slaves' assessment of themselves and of each other that they considered it the greatest disgrace if their ownership was in doubt. Lewis mentions the case of the mulatto Mary Wiggins who threw herself at his feet with joy when it was finally established that she belonged to him, adding that 'to be told by the Negroes of another estate that they belong to no massa is one of the most contemptuous reproaches that can be cast upon them'.[3] One aspect of this veneration for the master was the almost childlike habit of the slaves of making quite fatuous complaints to him simply to be able to be near him and to address a few words to him.[4] Lewis also wrote that many of his slaves regarded him as their kin and addressed him as such:

> In particular, the women called me by every endearing name they could think of. 'My son! my love! my husband! my father! You no me massa, you my tata!' said one old woman . . . and when I came down the steps to depart, they crowded about me, kissing my feet and clasping my knees, so that it was with difficulty that I could get into the carriage.[5]

The word 'tata' meant father and was a common mode of expression for the master, especially among the slave children. Barclay wrote of masters who, on returning to their estates were greeted by 'the little Negro children . . . vociferating the endearing expression, "Tata come, Tata come" '.[6]

Not only was the master overtly loved and venerated, but his decree was considered infallible. Lewis was amazed at the manner in which the slaves accepted his judgment on disputes among them:

---

[1] Long, *op. cit.*, Vol. 2, p. 410.
[2] T. Jelly, *Remarks on the Condition of the Whites and Free Coloured Inhabitants of Jamaica*, p. 42.
[3] Lewis, *op. cit.*, pp. 68–9.
[4] Both Lewis and De La Beche noted this habit.
[5] Lewis, *op. cit.*, p. 240.
[6] Alexander Barclay, *op. cit.*, p. 212.

I must acknowledge, however, that the Negro principle that 'massa can do no wrong' was of some little assistance to me on this occasion. 'Oh! quite just, me good massa! what massa say quite just! me no say nothing more; me good massa!' Then they thanked me 'for Massa's goodness in giving them so long talk!' and went away to tell all the others how just massa had been in taking away what they wanted to keep, or not giving them what they asked for.[1]

While the overt attitudes of the slaves to their masters were clearly those of respect and adoration one must remain doubtful about the sincerity of their feelings. The masters themselves were not always fooled by their slaves. Lewis wrote of his jubilant welcome: '. . . whether the pleasure of the Negroes was sincere may be doubted; but certainly it was the loudest I ever witnessed'. Later he wrote that they were excellent flatterers 'and lay it on with a trowell'. Long also pointed out that they were great 'dissemblers', and McNeill warned his readers that 'he (the slave) has great art and may deceive you'.[2]

The relationship with the overseer was quite different from that with the master. He may have stimulated fear and terror, but never respect or co-operation. To the slaves he was an enemy never to be trusted, and to be foiled at every opportunity. We have shown in another chapter the barbarity of these whites and it is not surprising that there was constant conflict between them and the slaves they supervised. There was some flexibility in the overseer-slave relationship in that, while he was always covertly despised, the slaves were often prepared to be tractable if the overseer treated them with moderation, one of their favourite expressions being 'Good massa, good Negro'.[3]

This basic distinction in the attitude of the slaves to their masters and their overseers is to be noted in a slave song recorded by Moreton, one verse of which expresses the longing for the master as against the restrictions imposed on them by their overseer:

> *If me want for go in a Kingston,*
> *Me cant go there!*

1 Lewis, *op. cit.*, pp. 404–5
2 Hector McNeill, *Observations on . . . the Negroes in Ja.*, p. 29.
3 Kelly, *op. cit.*, p. 36.

Since massa go in a England,
Me cant go there ![1]

Unfortunately, it was under the overseer that the slave spent most of his working life. Thus all the psychological techniques which had to be employed in outwitting him and thwarting his every action, were constantly in use and eventually became 'a kind of second nature'.[2] It was primarily within the context of the overseer-slave relationship, then, that the peculiar personality traits of the slaves, noted by almost every one of the multitude of chroniclers, came about and functioned. To the nature of these personality traits we shall now turn our attention.

SECTION 5
AN ANALYSIS OF 'QUASHEE'

The various traits of the personality of the Negro slave fell into a general pattern that has been recognized all over the New World. Stanley Elkins has recently analysed what he termed the 'Sambo' personality.[3] His descriptions bear a remarkable resemblance to those which existed in Jamaica. The term used in Jamaica to designate this personality pattern was Quashee. This term came originally from the Twi day-name meaning 'Sunday'.[4] In addition to being a popular name for slaves, Long's own use of the term demonstrates that by the beginning of the second half of the eighteenth century at the latest it came to designate peculiarly Negro character traits. Writing at the beginning of the nineteenth century, Stewart, speaking of the illiteracy of the creole white women, remarked

---

[1] Moreton, *op. cit.*, p. 153.
[2] B. Lucock: *Jamaica, Enslaved and Free*, pp. 91–2.
[3] S. Elkins, *Slavary: A Problem in American Institutional and Intellectual Life*, 1959, Ch. 3, passim.
[4] Long gives these day-names, commonly used among the slaves, as follows:

Male	Female	Day
Cudjoe	Juba	Monday
Cubbenah	Beneba	Tuesday
Quaco	Cuba	Wednesday
Quao	Abba	Thursday
Cuffee	Phibba	Friday
Quamin	Mimba	Saturday
Quashee	Quasheba	Sunday (Long, Bk. 3, p. 427.)

that many of them exhibit much of the 'Quasheba' (the feminine of Quashee). Cassidy has pointed out that today 'Quashie simply means a peasant, but one also finds it glossed as "fool" '.[1] From my own experience as a Jamaican I have often heard the word used in the hyphenated manner 'quashie-fool'. It is clear, however, that during slavery the term related specifically to Negro personality traits.

Perhaps the best comment on quashee was made by Stewart, who wrote that: It is not an easy matter to trace with an unerring pencil the true character and disposition of the Negro, they are often so ambiguous and disguised.[2]

This evasive, indefinable, somewhat disguised and ambiguous quality was the most essential element of Quashee. Stewart also remarked: 'The Negroes are crafty, artful, plausible; not often grateful for small services; but, frequently deceitful and over-reaching.'[3]

The evasiveness of quashee manifested itself in various ways. It was evident, first, in what appeared to have been a compulsion to lie. Cooper speaks of his 'low cunning and contempt of truth'.[4] The editors of the *Jamaica Journal* who, though pro-slavery, were liberal minded within the context of Jamaican slave society, wrote:

> There is in the Negro character such an inherent sense of falsehood, and so ready a talent for the perversion of truth, that we fear even the dread of capital punishment would not effectually eradicate this favourite and habitual vice. We know of no mortal torture that would prevent or deter them from indulging this propensity; indeed, so strong is the predilection in some Negroes for the perversion of facts, that even where they expect reward for a 'plain unvarnished tale', they generally find more difficulty in relating the real truth, than in uttering a lie. Those who have had the longest and most frequent intercourse with Negroes are aware that theft and lying are amongst their most besetting sins: And that to discover the truth through means of

---

[1] F. G. Cassidy, *Jamaica Talk*, p. 157.
[2] Stewart, *Account of Jamaica*, 1808, p. 234.
[3] *Ibid*.
[4] Cooper, *op. cit.*, p. 14. According to Bickell, *op. cit.* p. 94: 'As soon as they are born they go away and speak lies.'

Negro evidence is one of the most hopeless tasks any manager can undertake. The most clever and intelligent Negro is usually the most deceitful and we have seen some with art enough to baffle the most expert lawyer that ever put question . . .[1]

Lewis, after detecting one of his slaves lying for no apparent reason, remarked that 'I am assured that unless a Negro has an interest in telling the truth, he always lies – in order to "keep his tongue in practice" '.[2] Even Madden, an anti-slavery writer and strong sympathizer of the slave had to admit that they were pathological liars.

The evasiveness of the slave was also expressed in his peculiar mode of arguing, the essence of which seemed to have been to stray from the point as far as possible. It was this quality which was partly referred to as 'congo saw'. It could be one of the most exasperating experiences that a white person might have with a slave and one strongly suspects that its primary purpose was deliberate annoyance. Edwards has a detailed account of this trait[3] and Lewis gives several amusing instances. McNeill acidly remarked that:

. . . a Negro, without much violence of metaphor, may be compared to a bad pump, the working of which exhausts your strength before you can produce a drop of water.[4]

Another frequently noted trait of Quashee was distrustfulness, allied to which was a strong grain of conservatism. 'They are so accustomed to be the subject of exaction', wrote Mathison, 'that every innovation, though intended for their benefit, gives rise to a suspicion that it is intended for their oppression'.[5]

Quashee was also extremely capricious, a quality noted by many writers. Beckford observed that:

Negroes are capricious, the recurrence of everyday life will evince. Give them a house ready built, they will not inhabit it – a ground ready cleared, they will not work it – if you study their convenience, their ease, and happiness, they will be discontented – they must have everything their own way; and would sooner

---

[1] *Jamaica Journal & Kingston Chronicle*, Vol. 2, No. 32.
[2] M. G. Lewis, *op. cit.*, p. 129.
[3] Edwards, *op. cit.*, Bk. 4, p. 100.
[4] McNeill, *op. cit.*, p. 15.
[5] Mathison, *op. cit.*, 101.

complain of a good overseer, than not covet an exchange by the risk of one who is bad.[1]

The laziness of quashee became proverbial and hardly needs any documentation here.[2] Quashee was, in addition, extremely childlike, a quality which Lady Nugent, among others, often remarked on.[3] Quashee was also, from all reports, gay, happy-go-lucky, frivolous and cheerful. To Stewart, 'He is patient, cheerful, and commonly submissive, capable at times of grateful attachments where uniformly well treated, and kind and affectionate toward his kindred and offsprings'.[4] And Sir John Keane found it 'a most extraordinary thing' that 'they are always singing, and seem excessively delighted'.[5] But Quashee's darker traits were stressed just as often. He was revengeful, harbouring grudges for a long time; when placed in positions of authority he was likely to be extremely cruel and tyrannical; he was 'possessed of passions not only strong but ungovernable . . . a temper extremely irascible; a disposition indolent, selfish and deceitful; fond of joyous sociality; riotous mirth and extravagant show'.[6]

In addition, the contemporary accounts almost all attribute an element of stupefaction to Quashee, and an almost complete lack of judgment. Quashee somehow managed to do everything wrongly. Repeated attempts at correction were doomed to failure. Lewis, despite his fondness for his slaves, wrote toward the end of his journal that, 'Somehow or other, they never can manage to do anything quite as it should be done. If they correct themselves in one respect today, they are sure of making a blunder in some other manner tomorrow'.[7] This stupidity was often quite consciously feigned, as Madden makes clear:

> It is a difficult thing to get a Negro to understand anything which he does not wish to hear; the more you try to explain a

[1] Beckford, *op. cit.*, 1788, p. 90.
[2] The classic exposition of the stereotyped view of Quashee's laziness was written several years after slavery by Thomas Carlyle in his *An Occasional Discourse on the Nigger Question*.
[3] *Lady Nugent's Journal*, ed. Cundall, see for ex. p. 288.
[4] Stewart, *op. cit.*, 1808, pp. 234–35.
[5] Evidence of Sir John Keane, House of Lords C'ttee on Slavery, 1832, p. 179.
[6] McNeill, *op. cit.*, p. 28.
[7] Lewis, *op. cit.*, p. 392.

matter that is disagreeable to him, the more incapable he appears of comprehension; or if he finds this plan ineffectual, he endeavours to render the matter ridiculous; and his talent at rendering ridicule sarcastic is really surprising.[1]

On the other hand, several penetrating observers did not fail to notice the acuteness of the slave in judging the character of those about him. Phillippo noted, for example, that, 'so far from being more deficient in acuteness and discrimination than other men, none can penetrate more deeply than the Negro into the character, or form an opinion of strangers with greater correctness and precision'.[2]

That Quashee existed there can be no doubt. The problem is to ascertain how real, how meaningful, this psychological complex was in the life of the slave. A full answer to this question would involve a digression into existential and role psychology which is outside the confines of this work.[3] We may, however, make a few tentative observations.

Quashee may be said to have existed on three levels. First, as a stereotyped conception held by the whites of their slaves; secondly, as a response on the part of the slave to this stereotype; and thirdly, as a psychological function of the real life situation of the slave. All three levels of Quashee's existence were closely related and mutually reinforced each other.

Let us begin with the third level. The real life situation of the slave, as we have shown, was one in which there was a complete breakdown of all major institutions – the family, marriage, religion, organized morality. This situation was made worse by the fact that the white group offered no alternate mores and institutions, but were just as disorganized socially as they were. There could be no kind of guiding principle, then, in the socialization of the slave, except that of evasion, which he learned from hard experience. The habitual laziness of the slave was also largely the function of his

---

[1] Madden, *op. cit.*, Vol. 2, pp. 155–56.

[2] J. M. Phillippo, *Jamaica: Its Past and Present State*, 1843, p. 204. Similarly it was often remarked by American slave owners that 'a Negro understands a white man better than the white man understands the Negro', Phillips, *American Negro Slavery*, p. 327.

[3] For an extremely suggestive analysis of similar personality complexes as Quashee, see R. D. Laing's discussion of 'The false-self system' in Chapter 6 of his book, *The Divided Self*. See also J. P. Sartre's analysis of 'bad faith' in his *Being and Nothingness*.

work situation. From early childhood he was stimulated to work, not by the expectations of reward, but entirely by the threat of punishment. Naturally, he grew to hate work and could only be industrious if forced to. The happy-go-lucky irresponsibility of the slave could also be explained in terms of his upbringing, especially with regard to males when we recall the demoralizing effect of slavery on them.

But the complexity of Quashee cannot be completely explained in situational terms. The explanation of the element of evasiveness and dissemblance, the pathological lying, must be sought elsewhere. To some extent this was to be found in the stereotype the whites had of Quashee.[1] This stereotype undoubtedly possessed what Prothro and Milikian have called a 'kernel of truth' about the real situation. But stereotypes, as the above writers pointed out, also reflect the 'characteristics of the individuals holding stereotype or the state of politico-economic relations between groups'.[2] The same principle holds for the plantocrats of Jamaican slave society. The outright brutality and unrestrained exploitation of the system made even the most hardened plantocrat desirous of a system of rationalization. Certain aspects – usually either those which were the worst, or the most easily patronized – of the personality traits of the slaves were therefore seized upon and elaborated into a generalized body of 'truths' about the Negro.

At this point, Merton's concept of the 'self-fulfilling-prophecy' becomes useful. As he wrote: 'The systematic condemnation of the outgrouper continues largely irrespective of what he does; more; through a freakish exercise of capricious judicial logic, the victim is punished for the crime'.[3] Since masters had absolute control over their slaves, it was not difficult for them to create the conditions that would actualize the stereotypes they had of these slaves.

The self-fulfilling-prophecy, however, has a further dimension which Merton failed to point out. It is the fact that the subordinate

[1] 'Stereotyping may be defined as the tendency to attribute generalized and simplified characteristics to groups of people in the form of verbal labels and to act towards the members of these groups in terms of these labels'. – from, W. E. Vinacke; 'Stereotyping Among National-Racial Groups in Hawaii: a Study in Ethnocentricism', in *The Journal of Social Psychology*, Vol. 30, 1949.

[2] Prothro & Milikian, 'Studies in Stereotype: Familiarity and the Kernel of Truth', in *The Journal of Social Psychology*, Vol. 41, 1955.

[3] R. K. Merton, *Social Theory and Social Structure*, p. 186.

group, in addition to being forced into situations which fulfil the stereotype of the superordinate group, also responds directly to these stereotypes by either appearing to, or actually internalizing them. The slave, in fact, played upon the master's stereotype for his own ends. Playing the stereotype had three broad functions.

First, with his acute sensitivity, the slave easily saw that although the master might consciously protest at his stupidity or frivolity or whatever Quashee trait he was playing up, he was nonetheless, inwardly pleased by the slave offering further proof of his rationalizations. From the slaves' point of view, this was a direct appeal to, and exploitation of, the inevitable see-what-I-mean mentality of their masters.[1]

Secondly, by playing the stereotype, the slave both disguised his true feelings (which it was his cardinal principle never to reveal since no one, least of all the master, could be trusted)[2] and had the psychological satisfaction of duping the master. The well known Jamaican Negro proverb, 'Play fool to catch wise', well sums up this form of stereotype playing.[3]

Thirdly, if the slaves strongly resented an overseer or book-keeper and wanted to get rid of him, in the majority of cases they could achieve their objective by simply being the perfect Quashee – stupid, bungling, exasperating and completely inefficient. Long has left us a penetrating account of the overseer-slave relationship which illustrates all three types of stereotype playing:

. . . Their principal address is shown in finding out their

---

[1] The American psychologist, Allport, identified this kind of behaviour as 'clowning'. He wrote: 'And if the master wants to be amused, the slave sometimes obligingly plays the clown . . . Richard Wright in *Black Boy* describes the coloured elevator man who wins his way by exaggerating his Negro accent, and affecting the traits ascribed to his racial group: begging, laziness, and tall tales. His passengers give him coins and make him a pet.' Allport also speaks of 'protective clowning', a perfect example of which was the "spook" personality among Negro soldiers, of whom he writes: 'A spook can't be hurt; he can't be downed; he doesn't talk back, but he can't be coerced. He will come right through doors and walls whatever you do; he has a sassy if silent invulnerability.' from G. W. Allport, *The Nature of Prejudice*, p. 144.

[2] There is the problem, however, of deciding exactly what the true feelings of the slave were. This goes to the heart of the problem of deciding where the difference lies between *conscious* role playing and *natural* role playing. See Elkins' discussion in *Slavery*, p. 131–33.

[3] See also Anderson & Cundall's *Jamaica Negro Proverbs*, in particular, Nos. 263–68; 536; and 544.

master's temper, and playing upon it so artfully as to bend it with most convenience to their own purposes. They are not less studious in sifting their master's representative, the overseer; if he is not too cunning for them, which they soon discover after one or two experiments, they will easily find means to overreach him on every occasion, and make his indolence, his weakness, or sottishness, a sure prognostic of some comfortable term of idleness to them; but if they find him too intelligent, wary and active, they leave no expedient untried, by thwarting his plans, misunderstanding his orders, and reiterating complaints against him, to ferret him out of his post; if this will not succeed, they perplex and worry him, especially if he is of an impatient, fretful turn, till he grows heartily sick of his charge, and voluntarily resigns it. An overseer therefore, like a prime minister, must always expect to meet with a faction, ready to oppose his administration, right or wrong; unless he will give the reins out of his hands, and suffer the mob to have things their own way; which if he complies with, they will extol him to his face, condemn him in their hearts, and very soon bring his government to disgrace.[1]

---

[1] Long, *op. cit.*, Bk. 4, p. 405.

CHAPTER VII

Social Institutions of the Slaves

1. WITCHCRAFT, SORCERY AND RELIGION

IN THIS and the following chapter we shall examine the supernatural beliefs and practices of the slaves in conjunction with their
other main forms of behaviour. This will entail an analysis of their
internal economy; their recreational patterns; and their internal
forms of social control. We shall begin with their supernatural
views and practices.

PART I

SUPERNATURAL BELIEFS AND PRACTICES OF AFRICAN ORIGIN

This aspect of the slaves' lives may be considered under two heads.
First, the survivals of African supernatural behaviour as they were
reshaped during slavery; and secondly, the impact of Christianity
on the slaves. The latter was of no real significance until the last
three or four decades of slavery and will be considered last. The
former, which we shall presently consider, was neither approved
of nor fully understood by the whites, and this includes those on
whose writings we must depend for data.

In one respect, however, our position is far better than that of
contemporary observers in that we are now able to draw upon a
wealth of anthropological material on Africa. This material clarifies
much that must have appeared utterly confusing in this aspect of
the slaves' lives as seen through the eyes of the contemporary
chroniclers. Our present knowledge of African tribal life makes it
possible for us to re-read the descriptions of the chroniclers and
extract from their statements implications of which they themselves
were not aware. Where the chroniclers are too vague, or silent, we
have the assistance of modern sociological researches into the life

of the descendants of the slaves, the findings of which are significant with regard to the light they throw on the past.

Let us begin then, with a few observations on the African background of the slaves as it relates to this aspect of their lives. There
is a remarkable uniformity in the supernatural beliefs of all West
African Negroes. We have already noted Daryll Forde's and Herskovits' concurrence on this fact. Other writers may be cited.
Geoffrey Parrinder has made a careful examination of the literature
on West African religions and has demonstrated the uniformity in
these beliefs all over the Guinea coast.[1] This is even more true of
witchcraft and sorcery beliefs. Here there is a continuous process
of external influence due to the strong belief that the magical
practices of a neighbouring or distant tribe are always more powerful
than one's own.[2]

Further a clear distinction was often drawn between the different
categories of the supernatural. This may seem an obvious point
but its importance will be demonstrated later. Field has given us
what is perhaps the clearest account of these categories in relation
to West Africa. The primary distinctions are those between religion,
medicine, and witchcraft. The main features of West African
religion are the beliefs in a supreme being too remote to be active
in the ordinary affairs of man; the worship of a pantheon of gods
which are usually non-human spirits associated with natural forces;
ancestor worship; and the belief in and use of charms and fetishes.
Revolving around these various areas of beliefs are large numbers
of cults.

Medicine in West Africa means anything which possesses a
'power' or 'breath of life' and 'is the abode of a spiritual being or
won'.[3] A *won* is morally neutral and can be employed for either evil
or good, 'as long as the proper ceremonies are performed'.[4] On
this basis, the Ga, like other West African peoples,[5] make a distinc-

---

[1] Geoffrey Parrinder, D.D., *West African Religions.*

[2] M. J. Field, *Religion and Medicines of the Ga People.* She tells us that most
Ga medicine practises come from their neighbours, especially the Dahomeans.
She also quotes Tylor's remark that, 'every tribe believes its barbaric neighbours
to be more deeply steeped in darkly wonderful magic than it is itself'. See pp.
124–25.

[3] *Ibid.*   [4] *Ibid.*

[5] Thus, among the Dahomeans, one 'cardinal tenet in the theory of the gbo'
'is that good and bad magic are merely reflections of two aspects of the same
principle'. M. J. Herskovits, *Dahomey*, Vol. 2, p. 285.

tion between the good medicine-man (*wontfe*) who uses a combination of good medicine and ordinary herbs for good purposes only; and the bad medicine-man (*wontfulo*) who is 'exclusively engaged in killing and harming and is employed by people who wish to hurt others'.[1]

Witchcraft, on the other hand, has nothing to do with either bad medicine-men, or the tangible embodiment of their medicines. Witchcraft is defined by Field as: 'a bad medicine directed destructively against other people, but its distinctive feature is that there is no palpable apparatus connected with it, no rites, ceremonies, incantations, or invocations that the witch has to perform.'[2]* The precise nature and function of witchcraft and witchcraft-beliefs has attracted a considerable amount of anthropological interest and speculation.[3] From the various points of view advanced on the subject we may select the structural framework – the main proponents of which are Nadel and Wilson – as being most useful for our purposes. According to Nadel:

> Witchcraft beliefs enable a society to go on functioning in a given manner, fraught with conflicts and contradictions which the society is helpless to resolve; the witchcraft beliefs thus absolve the society from a task apparently too difficult for it, namely, some radical readjustment.[4]

Monica Wilson emphasizes the moral and psychological functions of such beliefs in her study of the Nyakyusa, writing that witchcraft 'is perhaps the main sanction for moral behaviour within the village'.[5] People who are moody, solitary, irascible and generally not

---

[1] M. J. Field, *op. cit.*, p. 128. Note that there is not only a remarkable uniformity in the witchcraft beliefs of the West African tribes, but in the entire African continent south of the Sahara. Cf. for example, Field's study of the Ga with E. W. Smith's study of witchcraft among the Ila of Northern Rhodesia in his 'Inguikizi': *Africa*, Vol. 8, No. 4.

[2] Field, *op. cit.*, p. 135.

[3] For a summary of the literature (theoretical) on the subject see, introduction to Middleton and Winter, *Witchcraft and Sorcery in East Africa*.

[4] S. F. Nadel, 'Witchcraft in Four African Societies' in *The American Anthropologist*, 1952.

[5] Monica Wilson: *Good Company: A Study of Nyakusa Age Villages*, p. 108.

* Evans-Pritchard (in *Africa*, 1935) distinguishes between witchcraft and sorcery; but this dichotomy is far too simple as it blurs the important distinction between good medicine-men and bad medicine-men, common to most West African tribes. The bad medicine-man may be identified with Evans-Pritchard's 'sorcerer'.

'good company', who are proud and unsociable, tend to be those who are accused of witchcraft. Witchcraft victims are also people whose conspicuous happiness or success arouses envy. The Nyakyusa recognize that the type of person accused of witchcraft is usually himself a 'victim' of the society, feeling isolated, unwanted and inadequate.[1] Very common among African peoples too, is the belief that illness is caused by a witch eating the *Kla* (to use the Akan term meaning life-blood) of another.[2]

In the light of the above observations, let us now examine the material relating to the subject during slavery in Jamaica. To begin with, it must be noted that the clearly defined categories of supernatural practices which one finds in Africa were not to be found in Jamaica, where elements of ancestor worship, of the various divinities and of the cult of the dead, were all incoherently combined in the supernatural beliefs of the slaves.

The two words used by writers on Jamaica to describe these beliefs were *obeah*[3] and *myalism*. Obeah or Obi was sometimes used in the generic sense to designate all forms of supernatural beliefs and practices among the slaves, including myalism. This is the sense in which it is used both by Long[4] and in the Fuller report,[5] But generally a distinction was drawn between *obeah* proper and *myalism* in which the latter was seen as the opposite of the former.

There has been some controversy regarding the etymology of these words.[6] Williams and later Cassidy suggest the Twi word *bayi*, meaning witchcraft.[7] However, the closely related Twi word *obeye* (which in pronunciation is far closer to the Jamaican word)

[1] *Ibid.*, pp. 91–108.

[2] See H. Debruner, *Witchcraft in Ghana*, p. 14; and pp. 76–80.

[3] According to the Fuller Report: 'The term Obeah, Obiah, Obea ... we conceive to be the adjective and Obe or Obi the noun substantive,' in, *Report of Stephen Fuller with Assistance of Messrs. Long and Chisholme*, 1788, P.R.O. MS. B.T.6:10, p. 171.

[4] E. Long, *History of Jamaica*, Bk. 4, p. 416.

[5] Fuller, *op. cit.*, p. 172.

[6] Long erroneously derived the word *obiah* from the Hebrew *ob*. Herskovits wrote that in a conversation with Westerman the latter suggested the origin of the practice in the worship of the Bia river on the Gold Coast. (Herskovits, *On the Provenience of New World Negroes, Social Forces*, Vol. 12, No. 2, Dec. 1933) Sir Harry Johnson suggests a corruption of the Efik or Ibo word for Doctor, which may have been the source of the Oxford English Dictionary: *The Negro in the New World*, 1910.

[7] J. J. Williams, *Voodoos and Obeahs*, pp. 120–121; Cassidy, *Jamaica Talk*, p. 241.

seems more convincing, especially in view of the fact that *obeye* has far greater currency among West African peoples. Ga medicine-men, for example, use *obeye* to describe the *won*-like entity within witches.[1] The fact that the word *obeah* is derived from West African witchcraft and not sorcery should also be borne in mind.

The origins of the word *myalism* is not known. An anonymous writer has informed us, however, that one of the principal compo-nents of the drugs used in the myal dance is extracted from a plant known as the myal weed[2] but he does not explain how the weed got its name, and it may well be that the weed was named after the dance.

Let us now examine the nature of the difference between obeah and myalism. Long, who first wrote of these practices, described the obeah-men as conjurers and magicians.[3] Myalism, on the other hand, which appeared later, was from the beginning 'a kind of society' or cult, centred on a special dance. Initiates were supposedly invulnerable to white men, and the leader of the cult had the power to restore life.[4] A report in 1788 stated that myal-men were those who '. . . by means of narcotic potion made with the juice of an Herb, said to be the branched Calalue, a species of Solonium, which occasions a trance, a profound sleep of certain duration, endeavour to convince the deluded spectators of the power to reincarnate dead bodies'.[5] Madden also distinguishes clearly between the two types of practices, obeah being a kind of incantation, and myalism 'the administering of medicated potions'.[6] Phillippo has left us much useful information on the subject. 'Obeism', he informs us, is 'a species of witchcraft employed to revenge injuries or a protection against theft'. It also involves the use of fetishes as well as the 'art' of causing 'the death of victims by pretending to catch their shadows, or holding them spell-bound, as within a magic circle'.[7] This element of shadow-catching was extremely important in obeah practices. The followin agccount of it was given by a witness in a trial that took place during the early nineteenth century:

[1] M. J. Field, *op. cit.*, p. 137.
[2] *The West Indies: Comprising a Detail of Facts in Opposition to Theory*, 1832, by a Proprietor and Attorney.
[3] E. Long, *op. cit.*, Bk. 4, p. 416.
[4] *Ibid.* p. 417.   [5] Fuller, *op. cit.*, p. 172.
[6] Madden, *A Twelve Months Residence in the West Indies*, 1835, Vol. 2, p. 97.
[7] H. M. Phillippo, *Jamaica: Its Past and Present State*, 1843, p. 247.

'Do you know the prisoner to be an Obeah man?' 'Ess, massa, shadow-catcher true'. 'What do you mean by shadow-catcher?' 'Him heb coffin, (a little coffin produced) – him set fo catch dem shadow'. 'What shadow do you mean?' 'When him set obeah for somebody him catch dem shadow, and dem go dead.'[1]

And at the beginning of the twentieth century Martha Beckwith also defined obeah as the practice of exploiting one's 'power over the shadow world'.[2]

From two detailed accounts[3] we learn that the myal dance was meant largely to exhibit the magical powers of the cult leader, usually called 'Doctor'. The chosen initiate was placed within a circle formed by the Doctor and his assistants. The Doctor then sprinkled him with several powders, gave him a drink of various herbs, then blew upon and danced around him frantically. He was then whirled rapidly around until he fell into a deathlike trance. The Doctor then departed, with loud shrieks, to the woods from which he returned a few hours later with different kinds of herbs, the juice from part of which was squeezed into the mouth of the entranced initiate and the remainder rubbed on his eyes and finger-tips. At the same time pieces of glass-bottle, snakes, reptiles and other particles were produced under the guise of coming from beneath the skin of the initiate. This was accompanied by a chant, to which the assistants, holding hands, danced in a circle around both Doctor and initiate, stamping their feet in time with the rhythm of the chant. When, some time later, the initiate dramatically recovered, a miraculous resurrection was proclaimed.[4]

Four years after the complete abolition of slavery a remarkable outbreak of myalism took place in the Island. Banbury has left us a description of the situation in 1842:

> They went by the name of Myal people; they were also called angel men. They declared that the world was come to an end; Christ was coming, and God had sent them to pull all the Obeahs, and catch all the shadows that were spell-bound at the cotton

[1] *Ibid.*, pp. 247–48.
[2] Martha Beckwith, *Black Roadways: A study of Jamaican Folk Life.* p. 104.
[3] Lewis, *op. cit.*, p. 355, Phillipps, *op. cit.* pp. 248–249.
[4] Phillippo, *op. cit.*, pp. 248–49.

trees. In preparation for these events they affected to be very
strict in their conduct . . . Persons who were known to be notorious were excluded from their society . . . They accompanied
their operations with violent animal excitement . . . Sometimes
one would bolt out of the ring and run into the bush and then
the others would go after him declaring that the spirit had taken
him away.[1]

On the basis of the above material we may make the following
contrast between obeah and myalism. Obeah was essentially a type
of sorcery which largely involved harming others at the request of
clients, by the use of charms, poisons, and shadow catching. It was
an individual practice, performed by a professional who was paid
by his clients. It is not difficult to see that obeah approximates
closely to what we earlier defined as bad medicine in the West
African sense and it undoubtedly had its origins largely in these
African practices. On the other hand, certain elements of witchcraft are also discernible in obeah. The origin of the word itself
hints strongly at this fact. The extent to which witchcraft, strictly
defined, was covered by the term 'obeah' will be more closely examined when we come to discuss the functions of these practices.
Myalism, on the other hand, was obviously a form of anti-witchcraft and anti-sorcery. The proponents of myalism were just as
aware of the techniques and 'wons' of the obeah-men but used
them for good rather than evil. It was no doubt largely for this
reason that many observers confused it with obeah.[2] The most
important difference from obeah, however, was the fact that it was
not an individual practice between practitioner and client, but was
organized more as a kind of cult with a unique dance ritual. To a
large extent myalism may be said to approximate closely to standard
West African good medicine.[3] There are certain important elements
in it, however, which seem to be of religious origin. The dance
ritual of 'death' and 'resurrection', for instance, bears some resem-

[1] R. T. Banbury, *Jamaica Superstition, or the Obeah Book*, pp. 19–22.
[2] Rampini wrote for example that the Myal-man '. . . is to the former (obeah-man) what the antidote is to poison . . . but it must be confessed that, both in its operation and results, the cure is often worse than the disease. In truth, the boundary line between the two classes of professors is sometimes but a shadowy one'. C. Rampini, *Letters from Jamaica*, 1873, p. 142.
[3] Note that myal-men were also herbalists – See below.

blance to the 'Resurrection' rite of the Mawu-Lisa ceremonies performed on initiates as the first test for entry into the Sky-cult of Dahomey.[1] Throughout West Africa, and particularly among the Ga, there were certain good-medicine-men who specialized in immunizing people from witchcraft and in curing people who had been made witches. Clearly, this function was also performed by the myal-men especially during the spate of anti-obeah activities after slavery.

Of especial interest is the concept of the shadow, by capturing and impaling which, as we have seen, the obeah-men harmed their victims; and by releasing which the myal-man cured their adherents. Now among the Ga people, the essential aspect of the human personality was the *Susuma*. The same word *Susuma* was also used for shadow among these people. Closely related to the susuma or shadow is the *Kla* concept which designates the life-blood of a person; when the Kla leaves the individual, he dies. We are told further, that a bad medicine-man, for a fee, will call upon a victim's Kla or susuma (the words are often used synonymously) and 'either tie it up with a string or gaze at it in a bowl of water and, on seeing it, stab it through the heart'.[2] Almost exactly the same practice is found among Jamaican obeah-men; and the opposite art of releasing these tied up shadows, among the myal-men.[3]

Who were these obeah-men? First, they were, with few exceptions, Africans,[4] and those from 'The Papaw or Popo country' (Dahomey) seem to have been particularly prone to the art'.[5] What is very significant is the fact that they 'were generally old, misshapen or deformed Negroes of African origin', especially those skilled in poisonous and medicinal herbs.[6] Both sexes were known to be obeah practitioners although men were more common. According to Moseley, obean-women tended to 'dispose of the passions', and 'they sell foul winds for inconstant mariners; dreams and phantasies for jelousy; vexation and pains in the heart, for

---

[1] M. J. Herskovits, *Dahomey*, Vol. 2, p. 121.

[2] M. J. Field, *op. cit.*, p. 93.

[3] More detailed information on these practices in Jamaica are to be found, for the post-slavery period, in Martha Beckwith, *op. cit.*, and in J. J. Williams, *Psychic Phenomena in Jamaica*.

[4] Fuller, *op. cit.*, pp. 171–82.

[5] *Ibid.*

[6] Madden, *op. cit.*, Vol. 2, p. 106.

perfidious love, etc.'[1] We gain some idea of the number of obeah-
men in the island from an estimate made by an obeah-man on trial
in 1824 who stated that there were one hundred and fifty of his
kind at large in the island.[2]

The ingredients used as fetishes and charms by the obeah-men
were of all sorts. An act of 1760 declared a Negro guilty of obeah
if he was found with 'blood, feathers, Parrots Beaks, Dog's Teeth,
Alligator's Teeth, Broken bottles, Grave dirt, Rum, Egg Shells . . .'[3]
Madden described an obeah ceremony, performed by a coloured
woman to break up her former lover's betrothal to a white lady,
in which, '. . . the initiated person's vesture is dispensed with;
there was an iron pot in the centre of the room, round which the
dancing was going on, and in it was a cock's head, serpent's eggs,
blood and grave dirt'.[4] He further informs us that 'there is nothing
held in so much estimation for obeah rites as a perfectly white
cock'. The snake or snake's head and tooth were highly valued.[5]
One obeah-man in Spanish Town was known to have kept two
large snakes under his bed, and it was generally believed that the
saliva of the snake, in licking the bare skin, was a good charm.[6]
The wands carried by the obeah-man in many cases had a carved
serpent twisted round them and according to Beckford Davis, the
Negroes were 'in great dread' of these sticks.[7]

The Functions of Obeah and Myalism: Obeah and myalism performed
both individual and social functions within the context of the slave
society. We shall begin with the individual functions. First, obeah
was used in preventing, detecting and punishing crimes among
the slaves. It was quite common to employ the planting of fetishes
on provision grounds to protect them from thieves.[8] Several ordeals

[1] B. Moseley, *A Treatise on Sugar*, p. 173. Typical of the obeah-man was
Three-Fingered-Jack, the outcast and bandit, of the 1780s described by Moseley,
pp. 173–80.

[2] The *Jamaica Journal*, Vol. 1, No. 45.

[3] Acts of Jamiaca, C.O. 139/21.

[4] Madden, *op. cit.*, Vol. 2, p. 98.

[5] James Grainger, *The Sugar Cane, a Poem.* Bk. 4, p. 148.

[6] *The West Indies: Comprising a Detail of Facts . . .*, 1832.

[7] Evidence of Beckford Smith to the Royal Commission on Jamaica, 1866.

[8] Among the fetishes mentioned by De La Beche were, wood-ants nest;
grave dirt; bunches of feathers; small coffins with black and white cloth filled
with grave dirt. De La Beche, *Note on the Present Condition of the Negroes in
Jamaica*, 1825, p. 30.

were used for detecting crimes, one of which involved assembling at a grave and swallowing bits of grave dirt, the guilty party's belly being expected to swell and burst should he take it.[1] Most of these ordeals later came to be employed by ordinary slaves not necessarily versed in obeah.[2]

Obeah was also employed in punishing supposed crimes, which usually meant the injury of the suspected person; at other times the revenge motive was replaced by pure malice. On most of these occasions the obeah-man resorted to plain poisoning although it appears that the client was not always aware of the deadly nature of the drugs given to him to place in the victim's food. Lewis remarked that 'their worst faults appear to be this prejudice respecting obeah, and the facility with which they are frequently induced to poison to the right and to the left'.[3]

Obeah in its myal form served certain important medicinal functions during slavery. Phillippo claimed that the practice of medicine among myal-men after the emancipation was a result of their experience gained in attending the sick in the hospitals during slavery.[4] But it is clear that he was somewhat confused here. More than likely, the myal-men were employed in the estate hospitals because of their knowledge of herbs which they took with them from Africa, having acquired it there during their training as good-medicine-men.[5] In 1866, Beckford Smith, asked if obeah-men possessed the art of curing, replied, 'No, it is another class that do that, called 'Myal-men'; they profess to undo the work of the obeah men'.[6] It was well known that most slaves would only allow themselves to be treated by black doctors,[7] one of Lewis' slaves, Bessie, telling him flatly that 'the white doctor could do her no good'.[8]

---

[1] C. Leslie, *A New History of Jamaica*, p. 308.

[2] Madden mentions two such ordeals, the first, a book ordeal in which Bible and Key were employed; the second a broom ordeal involving the use of ashes, water and a broom wicker: Madden, *op. cit.*, Vol. 2, pp. 100–101. But both ordeals seem to have been more European than African in origin.

[3] Lewis, *op. cit.*, p. 145.

[4] Phillippo, *op. cit.*, p. 263.

[5] Thus it is interesting to note that most chief myal-men were called 'doctors', as previous quotations demonstrate.

[6] Evidence of Beckford Smith, *op. cit.*, 1866.

[7] Madden, *op. cit.*, Vol. 2, pp. 144–45. These doctors jealously guarded their medical secrets from the whites. See, *The Importance of Jamaica to Gt. Britain Considered*, p. 20.

[8] Lewis, *op. cit.*, pp. 147–49.

Thirdly, obeah functioned largely in the numerous rebellions of the slaves. This was particularly the case with the obeah-men from the Gold Coast, one of whom took a leading part in the serious uprising of 1760. In the plotting of these rebellions the obeah-man was essential in administering oaths of secrecy, and, in cases, distributing fetishes which were supposed to immunize the insurgents from the arms of the whites.[1]

We come now to what may be described as the structural functions of obeah. It is at this point that our earlier discussion on the anthropological theory of witchcraft becomes relevant. At the same time, our task is now to identify those elements in obeah which suggest the existence of genuine witchcraft beliefs. Such an identification can only come about by the mutual combination of deductive and inductive reasoning on the subject. That is, one may draw a few tentative conclusions on the basis of the available facts, which are very few; then supplement these, through certain inferences from anthropological theory, by conclusions concerning the functional possibilities of certain witchcraft beliefs in Jamaican slave society on the basis of our knowledge of its structure and of the known ancestry and biases of its inhabitants.

First let us look at some of the facts which seem indicative of witchcraft. In 1775, a Jamaican planter, on returning to his estate from England, found 'a great many of his Negroes dead and a half of those remaining debilitated, bloated and in a very deplorable condition',[2] a state of affairs which seemed to have been a straightforward case of epidemic among the slaves, a not uncommon occurrence in the island at that time.[3] The slaves, however, accused an old Dahomean women of causing the deaths – totalling one hundred over a period of fifteen years – through her witchcraft, and on finding what appeared to be obeah ingredients in her house, she was transported to Cuba and her belongings burnt. The slaves, according to their master, revived immediately after she left.[4] Now the view that one old woman could, through her obeah, cause the death of one hundred slaves was obviously sheer nonsense. Clearly

[1] See Chapter ix below on Slave Rebellions.
[2] Appendix A, *The Fuller Report*, 1788, B.T. 6: 10.
[3] Note that this was the period of the American War of Independence when the withdrawal of supplies from the continent (cod-fish, flour, etc.) in conjunction with bad weather, led to malnutrition and disease among the slaves.
[4] Appendix A, The Fuller Report, 1788, *op. cit.*

this is a case of *post hoc* witchcraft accusation along the well known African pattern, which is known to be particularly evident during periods of epidemics.[1] That a presumably literate white planter could actually believe this accusation of the Negroes only demonstrates the extent to which the slaves were able to talk their master into their own point of view. Fuller, *et al*, even went further, claiming that in view of 'the multitude of occasions which may provoke the Negroes to exercise the powers of Obi against each other . . . we cannot but attribute a very considerable portion of the annual mortality among the Negroes of Jamaica to this fascinating mischief'.

While we reject the explanation of obeah as being the cause of the deaths of the hundred slaves mentioned above, we accept the fact of the accusation as being of sociological significance. By a process of deduction, we may now draw certain conclusions about the functions of these accusations on the basis of modern witchcraft theory.

Few systems could have been more 'fraught with conflicts and contradictions' (to use Nadel's expression) than slavery in Jamaica. Such conflicts, tensions and anxieties would naturally come to a head during an epidemic, and it was vital that a scapegoat be found on whom to give vent and outlet to these tensions. Such a scapegoat was the old woman accused of killing the hundred slaves. What is even more significant is the fact that most of the slaves accused of obeah were themselves the 'victims' of the system, in the sense in which Monica Wilson spoke of these 'victims' among the Nyakyusa. We have earlier seen that people accused of obeah were in the great majority of cases poor, abused, uncared for, often sick with yaws, and isolated from the other slaves. They were also usually old people and Africans. In short, they themselves embodied the slave system at its worst and most severe. To the young, they represented the fear of growing old under a system which had no use for old people; to the healthy, they represented the fear of falling ill, especially with the yaws which was the most dreaded and horrible disease among the slaves;[2] to the gregarious and not very

[1] See S. F. Nadel, 'Witchcraft and Anti-Witchcraft in Nupe Society', *Africa*, Vol. 8, No. 4, p. 432.

[2] B. Moseley, *op. cit.*, tells us that most slaves suffering from yaws were put in quarantine and with 'a cold, damp, smoky hut for his habitation; snakes and lizards his companions, crude, viscid food, and bad water, his only support; and shunned as a leper; – he usually sunk from the land of the living'. He further

insecure, they represented the threat that hung constantly over them; and to the creoles they represented the despised African group, their 'primitiveness' and the assumed bad name they gave all the slaves to the whites.

As is the case in Africa, since the people accused of obeah were themselves the 'victims' of the system and therefore usually maladjusted persons, we find that the accused invariably pleaded guilty to the preposterous charges made against them. There was the case, for example, of an old slave who incriminated himself by admitting that, by magical means he had repeatedly caused the illness of a young child simply by smoking a certain herb. His explanation, which sounded remarkably like those of self-confessed witches in Africa, was that he had simply seen the child 'and could not resist the instigation of the devil to obeah it'.[1]

But in addition to those who were obviously 'victims' of the system, obeah accusations were also made against people who either threatened to be too successful or were the source of much anxiety, maintaining in this way, what Marwick had called 'the virility' of the social structure by allowing a 'periodic redistribution of structural forms'.[2] The following is a case in point: At the head of the Ibo faction on Lewis' estate was one Edward, an industrious slave of whom Lewis was rather fond. Edward and his close childhood friend, Pickle, had become estranged when they found themselves rivals for the hand of a certain dark maiden. Pickle proved the successful suitor and the two men became friends once again after Edward had 'married' the sister of Pickle's 'wife'. Several years later, however, after an incident involving a theft at his house and partly at the instigation of another slave, (who bore a grudge against Edward) Pickle, who had suddenly fallen critically ill, got out of bed, and 'attended by the whole body of drivers', went to his master and not only accused Edward of the theft, but of having obeahed him. On cross-examination by Lewis, Pickle's only foundation for his charge was that Edward still bore him a grudge 'for the loss of his mistress . . . that they never would live happily together, and

---

[1] Madden, *op. cit.*, Vol. 2, pp. 93–5.
[2] M. G. Marwick, 'The Social Context of Cewa Witch Beliefs', *Africa*, Vol. XXII, Nos. 2 and 3.

tells us that many of their visitors are obeah-men and that they themselves tended to become obeah-men. See pp. 169–71.

they never lived happily and well together'.[1] We may speculate that the obeah-accusation against Edward served two basic functions. First, Pickle's accusation was an obvious case of psychological projection. Consumed with feelings of guilt, for having wronged a best friend, which he had been unable to suppress, Pickle had projected his own guilt-feelings on Edward and had lived in constant dread of the retaliation he felt he deserved. The accusation was clearly the final outlet of his own fears and anxieties. It is interesting to note that after Lewis settled the whole matter the two men became the best of friends again.

Secondly, it is significant that when Pickle made his accusations he was 'attended by the whole body of drivers'. These were the very poeple who would stand most to gain by ruining Edward's reputation, thus leading to his demotion from his position of headman. Quite apart from the material gains however, the accusation seemed to have served the structural function of releasing group tension and demolishing someone who threatened to be too successful. It was no accident that Edward was, in addition to being headman, also head of the Ibo slaves. This must certainly have enraged the creole group, and as we observed elsewhere, tension between the two groups was very strong on this estate.

The Burial of the Dead; Spirit Beliefs; and Ancestor Worship
(a) *The Burial of the Dead:* To the African tribesman, death and burial were perhaps the most important phase in a man's life cycle. On the funeral depended not only the prestige of those kin of the deceased surviving him, but the safe journey and status of the deceased in his new abode of the spirit world. It is not surprising then, that the funerary rites of the West African slaves in Jamaica survived more than most other cultural elements.

The material on the subject is comparatively rich. Sloane wrote during the seventeenth century of the slaves' belief in a return to Africa after death, 'imagining they shall change their condition by that means, from servile to free, and so for this reason often cut their own throats'. He also noted the practice of throwing 'rum and victuals' into the graves of the deceased 'to serve them in the other world'.[2]

[1] M. G. Lewis, *op. cit.*, pp. 133–39.
[2] Sir Hans Sloane, *op. cit.*, Introduction.

Leslie, writing of the early eighteenth century, also noted this belief in a return to Africa after death, claiming that 'they look on death as a blessing . . . are quite transported to think their slavery is near an end, and that they shall revisit their . . . old Friends and Acquaintances'.[1] A planter writing about the same time also makes the same observation, adding that to prevent suicide as a result of this belief 'they are often hanged up' by the planters to demonstrate to the living that the dead remained in Jamaica.[2] Leslie has also left us one of the most detailed accounts of the burial customs of the slaves and is the first to mention the survival of the well known West African custom of 'carrying the corpse':[3]

When a Negro is about to expire, his Fellow-slaves kiss him, wish him a good Journey, and send their hearty recommendations to their Relations in Guiney . . . When one is carried out to his Grave, he is attended with a vast Multitude, who conduct his Corpse in something of a ludicrous manner. They sing all the way, and they who bear it on their Shoulders, make a Feint of stopping at every Door they pass, pretending that if the deceased Person had received any Injury the Corpse moves towards that House, and that they cant avoid letting it fall to the Ground, when before the Door. When they come to the Grave, which is generally made in some Savannah or Plain, they lay down the Coffin, or whatever the Body happens to be wrapt up in: and if he be one whose circumstances could allow it, or if he be generally beloved, the Negroes sacrifice a Hog, in honour of him; which they contribute to the expenses of among themselves. The manner of the sacrifice is this: The nearest Relation kills it, the entrails are buried, the four Quarters are divided, and a kind of Soup made, which is brought in a calabash or Gourd, and, after waving it Three times, it is set down; then the Body is put in the Ground; all the while they are covering it with Earth, the Attendants scream out in a terrible manner, which is not the Effect of Grief, but of

[1] Leslie, *op. cit.*, pp. 307–10.
[2] Anon. *The Importance of Jamaica to Gr. Britain Considered*, p. 19. (London; printed for A. Dodd).
[3] There is a striking uniformity in the death customs of West African tribes. See also Ako Ddjei, 'Mortuary Usages of the Ga People of the Gold Coast', *Africa* Vol. 45, p. 84; also J. A. Moore, 'A Preliminary Examination of the Death Concepts of the Ibo', *American Anth.*, Vol. 44, No. 4, pt. 1.

Joy; they beat on their wooden Drums, and the women with their Rattles make a hideous Noise: After the grave is filled up, they place the Soup which they had prepared at the Head, and a bottle of rum at the Feet. In the meantime cool Drink (which is made of the Lignum Vitae Bark or whatever else they can afford) is distributed amongst those who are present; one half of the Hog is burned while they are drinking, and the other is left to any Person who pleases to take it; they return to Town, or to the Plantation, singing after their manner, and so the Ceremony ends.[1]

Long also claimed that 'every funeral is a kind of festival' and described the practice of 'carrying the corpse'. He mentions also the rite, after burial, of scratching up some earth and, with their backs turned to the grave, throwing it behind them between their legs so as to prevent the deceased following them home. Further:

When the deceased is a married woman, the husband lets his beard remain unshaved, and appears rather negligent in his attire, for the space of a month; at the expiration of which, a fowl is dressed at his house, with some messes of good broth, and he proceeds, accompanied by his friends, to the grave. Then he begins a song, purporting that the deceased is now in the enjoyment of complete felicity; and that they are assembled to rejoice at her state of bliss, and perform the last offices of duty and friendship. They then lay a considerable heap of dirt over the grave, which is called covering it; and the meeting concludes with eating their collation, drinking, dancing and vociferation. After this ceremony is over the widow or widower, is at liberty to take another spouse immediately; and the term of mourning is at an end.[2]

Edwards was at pains to deny the notion that the slaves looked foward to their return to Africa after death. But this may have been partly because the creole slaves far outnumbered the Africans by the time he wrote and partly due to his own biased view that the slaves generally enjoyed their lot.[3] But there can be little doubt

---

[1] Leslie, *op. cit.*, pp. 307–10.
[2] Long, *op. cit.*, Bk. 4, pp. 421–22.
[3] B. Edwards, *op. cit.*, Vol. 2, p. 104.

regarding the strength of the belief among the African slaves that they would return to Guiney after death.[1] This belief was clearly the retention and slight re-interpretation of the common African belief that on death one rejoins one's ancestors. Indeed, the very notion of 'returning home' after death was held by many of the tribes in Africa from which the slaves came. Among the Ibos, for example, when a man dies he is said to 'have gone home' or 'gone to the land of the spirits'.[2]

In his account of the funeral rites of the slaves, Phillippo also mentions the practice of partial burial followed later by a more elaborate ceremony. Modern researchers on the Jamaican folk indicate the strong African influence still existing in their funerary rites.[3] In particular, there is the ninth-night ceremony which bears striking resemblance to the post-burial ceremonies of West African peoples.[4] It is impossible to locate the particular areas in West Africa from which the different rites described came. The practice of 'carrying the corpse' is well known among the Akan, Ga-Adangme and Voltaic peoples of Ghana as well as in other areas of West Africa; the rite of partial burial may have been of either Fon or Ibo extraction; some of the mourning rites bear a striking resemblance to the after-burial rites of the Ibo peoples. But it is more fruitful to regard the rites described in Jamaica as syncretisms of what existed all over West Africa. In the light of the known uniformity of these rites in this area of Africa such syncretisms would certainly be not unlikely.

Ancestor worship No other area of the cultural life of the African slaves brought over to Jamaica was more shattered than their religious institutions. Nonetheless, both from the historical material and from modern sociological research on the religious life of the Jamaican folk one can extract fragments of African religious ritual. It is significant that all such religious survivals are related only to the ancestor-worship aspect of West African culture. We under-

---

[1] See Stewart, *A View of the Past and Present State of . . . Jamaica*, 1823, pp. 280–81. See also the evidence of Capt. Thomas Wilson and Capt. Hall to the Select Committee on the Slave Trade, 1790–91.

[2] S. T. Basden, *Niger Ibos*, p. 282.

[3] See for example, Martha Beckwith, *Black Roadways* ...; J. J. Williams, *Psychic Phenomena in Jamaica*.

[4] G. E. Simpson, 'The Ninth-Night Ceremony in Jamaica', in *Journal of American Folklore*, 1957.

stand why this is so when we note that in West African religions the most important elements are invariably concerned with ancestor worship.[1]

Two cults of definite African origin have been unearthed by twentieth century writers. First, there is the *Cumina* which has been found to be an ancestral cult the main object of which is possession by the ancestral spirits through drumming and dancing.[2] The first mention of cumina in the literature is to be found in Zora Hurston's *Voodoo Gods*, in which she tells us that 'Koo-min-ah' means 'The Power'. She described a cumina ceremony in which a 'house' or tomb was built for the 'duppy' (ghost) of a man eighteen months after his death. It was explained to her that if the tomb was closed before this time the 'duppy' would have been unable to get in and would have become a wandering spirit.[3] During the ceremony of building the 'house' and enclosing the 'duppy' there was feasting on a special dish known in Jamaica as 'jerk-pork' and, more significant, the sacrifice of a goat. The goat was sacrificed during dancing and drumming and its blood was drunk by the participants. The dancing then became more intense and elaborate and continued until daybreak.[4]

There is no doubt as to the African origins of this cult. There is one clue, however, in the period of slavery which strongly suggests its actual tribal origin. In his *New History of Jamaica* published in 1730, Leslie wrote:

> Their Notions of Religion are very inconsistent and vary according to the different Countries they come from: But they have a kind of occasional Conformity, and join without Distinction

[1] Field writes that, while in theory the gods are more powerful than the ancestors among the Ga, in practice it is usually the other way around. Further: 'I do not think any wulomo is half so much afraid of his gods as a man is of his ancestors or an official of his dead predecessors. No system of "functional relationships" ever held together a body of customs half so firmly as this one idea – the idea of the ever-present watchful dead and their power to smite or bless the living'. (Field, *op. cit.*, p. 197).

Among the Ashanti the warrior ancestors were of far more significance than say, the agricultural gods and the 'stool' played a greater part in religious ceremonies than the shrines. See Rattray, *Religion and Art in Ashanti*; and Parrinder, *op. cit.*

[2] See Cassidy, *Jamaica Talk*, pp. 235–240.

[3] For an account of this belief in West Africa, see Ako Ddjei, *op. cit.*

[4] Zora Hurston, *Voodoo Gods*, pp. 56–60.

in their solemn Sacrifices and Gambols. They generally believe there are two Gods, a good and a bad one; the first they call *Naskew* in the Papaw Language, and the other *Timnew*; the good God they tell you, lives in the Clouds, is very kind, and favours Men; 'twas he that taught their Fathers to till the Ground, and to hunt for their subsistence. The evil God sends storms, Earthquakes, and all kind of Mischief. They love the one dearly and fear the other as much.

There is much in this passage that is confusing, as one would expect. However, the two 'gods' mentioned can now be identified. The word *Naskew* comes from the Dahomeah *Nesuxwe* and the word *Timnew* also from the Dahomeah word Tovodu.[1] The Tovodu, according to Herskovits, means the 'deified dead of the sib'. These Tovodu occupy a place in the hierarchy of the spirit world immediately below the spirit of the dead rulers and other important people (tohwiyo) and their associates. Herskovits also tells us that, '. . . the newly-dead sib-member is not entitled to his full place in this company until the proper ceremonies, carried out by those of his sib who survive him, deify him and bring him into the class of "sib gods", the tovodu'.[2] Strictly speaking, the *nesuxwe* ancestral rituals 'are those for the princely dead'. But since almost every one in Dahomey is in some way related to the royal sib, the nesuxwe ceremonies are celebrated by all but a few of the people. The ordinary use of these two terms therefore, is as follows:

> Just as when, in speaking of the ancestors, the word *Tovodo* was applied to them, so in speaking of the ancestral dances, the term *nesuxwe* was heard.[3]

Herskovits has given us a detailed account of one of the more representative of 'these dramas of the dead brought back to the world of the living by their descendants'.[4] The ceremony he describes bears such a remarkable resemblance to the modern cumina cult ceremonies as to leave us in little doubt as to the link between the two. In the Jamaica *cumina* ceremony there was an orchestra of four drummers and four 'rackling men'. So too in Dahomey there

[1] See Herskovits, *Dahomey*, Vol. I, Ch. 12.
[2] *Ibid.*, p. 195.
[3] *Ibid.*, p. 211.
[4] *Ibid.*, p. 213.

was an orchestra consisting of 'drums. gongs and rattles'. Corresponding to the Jamaican cult's 'house' was the 'ancestral house' of the Dahomey nesuxwe cultists. And most significant, as in the case of the Cumina in Jamaica, one finds the sacrifice of a goat by the *tovoduno* or chief priest of the ancestral cult, the sacrifice being performed for the returned ancestors. Finally one finds in Dahomey the same intense dancing leading to possession by the spirit of an ancestor. While the Dahomey cult ceremony was longer and more elaborate than the Jamaican cumina cult, the basic similarities can leave us in no doubt that the latter was derived from the former.

The significance of the identification we have just made cannot be overstressed. For in addition to establishing the origins of the *cumina* cult in Jamaica, there are several important implications of this link. In the first place, it is clear that *cumina* existed in Jamaica from at least as early as 1730, the date of Leslie's book. The fact that for the next two hundred and eight years (Hurston's account was published in 1938) nothing is heard of the cult means either that throughout the period of slavery and for the century afterwards these rites were held in great secrecy by the slaves and their descendants, or that the chroniclers did not pay sufficient attention to them and perhaps meant to include them in their rather vague references to the post-funeral ceremonies of the Negroes.[1] Secondly, if we assume that Leslie was not completely confounded by his slave informants, the passage from his work quoted above could certainly be taken as one of the most striking pieces of evidence we have on the process of acculturation and adjustment among the slaves. We have just identified Naskew and Timnew and shown how the rites associated with them have survived in Jamaica to this day. If we go back to the passage by Leslie quoted above,[2] however, we see immediately that the attributes given to them were quite wrong. 'The good God' mentioned by Leslie, 'who lives in the Clouds; is very kind, and favours men . . . that taught their Fathers to till the ground, and to hunt for their subsistence' is no other than *Mawu* the female head of the Dahomey sky pantheon.[3] On the other hand, 'The evil God' who 'sends storms, Earthquakes, and all kind of mischief' and who is feared very much, is immediately recognized as *Xevioso*,

---

[1] There is also the possibility that the ritual died out and was later restored.
[2] See pp. 199–200.
[3] Herskovits, *op. cit.*, Vol. 2, Ch. 16, passim.

the head of the Thunder pantheon, 'the little brother'[1] of the head of the Earth pantheon, who punishes with his 'axe' or thunderbolts, 'who renders supreme justice . . . sends heat and . . . sends rain . . . kills men and . . . destroys houses, trees and fields',[2] and is associated with lightning, thunder and storms.[3] Now it is noticeable that these two gods come closest to the Christian parallel of God and the Devil. Is it not possible that this is an early adjustment on the part of the Dahomean slaves in Jamaica to the vaguely conceived christianity of the whites ?[4]

The second cult recently discovered by modern sociologists, indicating undoubted African ancestry, is that of the 'convince' or 'Bongo' cult found in the eastern part of the island and which apparently came from among the Maroons of the Blue Mountains. According to Hogg, this is also 'an ancestral cult of sorts' although it is based on 'association' rather than kinship. Hogg tells us also that, 'It rests on the assumption that men and spirits exist within a single, unified structure, interact with one another, and influence each other's behaviour'.[5] The cult closely resembles the *Cumina* in its ceremonies which consists of drumming and intense dancing and certain ritual performances which reach their climax in the possession of the dancer by one of the spirits of the ancestors. Hogg makes no attempt at identifying the particular area in West Africa from which this cult is derived but simply claims that its origin is African.[6]

Spirit Beliefs The belief in the existence of spirits goes hand in hand with the existence of ancestral cults. It is interesting to note, however, that the belief in ghosts and in the existence of ancestral spirits is far more widespread in Jamaica today than is the ceremonial worship of ancestors. The common word in Jamaica for any form of ghost or spirit is 'duppy'. But this was not always the case.

---

[1] *Ibid.*, Vol. 2, p. 136.

[2] *Ibid.*, p. 150.

[3] *Ibid.*, pp. 166–67.

[4] It is well known that the descendants of Dahomey slaves both in Haiti and Brazil reinterpreted the pantheon of Roman Catholic slaves within the context of their own pantheon of gods. See Herskovits, *Life in a Haitian Valley*.

[5] D. Hogg, 'The Convince Cult in Jamaica', in *Papers in Caribbean Anthropology*, compiled by S. W. Mintz: Yale Univ. Pub. 1960.

[6] *Ibid.*; passim.

Writing of the 1920s, Williams tells us that a distinction was made between a duppy and a shadow. We have already explained the concept of the shadow. *Duppy* on the other hand were 'selfish, malicious and vindictive' spirits that haunt the neighbourhood where they used to live, while alive. It was commonly believed that they could only be seen by 'foyeyed'[1] or four-eyed people, that is, people having special sight for ghosts.[2]

Writing during the 1920's, Beckwith tells us that, 'Duppies live in the roots of cottonwood trees and bamboo thickets and feed upon bamboo root, "fig" leaves and the gourd-like fruit of a vine called duppy-pumpkin'.[3]

Even more interesting, however, were the remarks of two of her informants:

> The philosophy of the ghost sometimes depends upon the belief that every man is accompanied by two duppies, a good and a bad, or a 'trickify one', as Wilfred says . . . Sometimes this same tricky spirit will worry a man in a nightmare. At death it is this tricky spirit which remains behind at the grave . . . There seems to be an idea that this tricky spirit is to be identified with the shadow. . . . 'It's not the soul' (that makes the duppy) said old Hannah, caretaker at Butler's, 'for the soul goes to heaven, and its not the body, for we know that goes away into the earth, but its the shadow'.[4]

There are only two references to *duppy* in the literature on slavery. The first comes from Long who writes that, 'They firmly believe in the apparition of spectres. Those of deceased friends are duppies; others, of more hostile and tremendous aspect, like our raw-head-and-bloody-bones, are called bugaboos'.[5] Lewis deals with the subject more extensively. He claims that the 'character and qualities' of *duppy* vary from one part of the island to another, and he adds:

> At first, I thought that the term Duppy meant neither more

---

[1] Note that among the Chambia of Northern Nigeria a person who is gifted with the ability to see ghosts is also said to be 'four-eyed'. See Meek's account of the tribe in his, *Tribes of Northern Nigeria*.

[2] J. J. Williams, *Psychic Phenomena in Jamaica*, pp. 156, 158, 160.

[3] M. Beckwith, *Black Roadways*, p. 89.

[4] *Ibid.*, pp. 97–8.

[5] Long, *op. cit.*, Bk. 4, p. 416.

nor less than a ghost; but sometimes he is spoken of as 'the Duppy', as if there were but one, and then he seems to answer to the Devil. Sometimes he is a kind of malicious spirit who haunts burying grounds . . . and delights in playing tricks to those who may pass this way. On other occasions, he seems to be a supernatural attendant on the practitioners of Obeah, in the shape of some animal, as familiar imps are supposed to belong to our English witches . . .[1]

We may summarize by saying that the term *duppy* both during and after slavery was used in two senses. First, in a generic sense to refer to all kinds of spirits, but more particularly to wandering ghosts. And secondly, that it was used in a more specific sense, especially during slavery and the rest of the nineteenth century, to mean a malicious, vindictive, imp-like spirit which haunts forests and burying grounds. The word is clearly African and a full understanding of its origins would help to clear up the uncertainty of its more popular use during slavery.

Both Williams[2] and Cassidy[3] have etymologized quite inplausibly on the subject. A closer observation of the West African material strongly suggests that the word *duppy* comes from the Adangme word *adope* meaning one of the 'senior ghosts' or fairies. Unfortunately, no serious study has yet been done on the Adangme tribe. The only reference in the literature on West Africa to the *adope* comes from a passage by Field in which she writes:

The people of Osudoku, on the Shai Plain, descended partly from immigrants and partly from the people whom the immigrants found there, have two organized cults connected with the veneration of these beings which are known to them as akotia, *adope*, abodo and shulu. They are said to be of two kinds, black and 'red' (mulatto coloured): the former are friendly and kind and they are

[1] M. G. Lewis, *op. cit.*, pp. 290–91.

[2] J. J. Williams, *op. cit.*, (1934). This writer, who is so obsessed with the idea that almost every cultural trait in Jamaica of African origin came from Ashanti (largely because it was one of the few seriously studied areas in Africa at the time when he wrote) suggests, quite absurdly, the Akan word, *dupon*, which means the large part of the root of certain trees: he also – and Cassidy after him – suggests the Bube word 'Dupe'. This appears at first a more plausible etymology, but since the Bube hardly contributed any of the Africans that were enslaved in the West Indies, it does not seem at all likely.

[3] F. G. Cassidy, *Jamaica Talk*, p. 247.

worshipped as deities, having a priest, women mediums to practice spirit-possession, a little temple, and annual sacrifices, songs and dances exactly as have the other deities of the district. The 'red' dwarfs, believed malicious, are propitiated annually with food and other rites outside the town, a barrier being across the path to prevent their entering.[1]

If this etymology is correct, then it seems that the term duppy was probably first used during slavery to mean the malicious, imp-like spirits that haunt woods and burying grounds, and only later took on the more general meaning of ghosts and all forms of spirits.

We may deal briefly with the remaining aspects of the supernatural beliefs of the Jamaican Negro which seem to be of obvious African origins. First, there is some vague survival of a water spirit. The first reference to this spirit comes from a tale collected by Leslie in which the *Mamma Luna* detected the person who stole her pot by the river, went down to it and drowned her.[2] Later in the nineteenth century Banbury referred to the *rubba missis* which is 'believed to inhabit every fountainhead of an inexhaustible stream of water in Jamaica'. He claims also that the sources of such streams were worshipped and that sacrifices were offered to them.[3] Later, Beck-with gives us further information on this water spirit which would certainly indicate one of its functions during slavery when we consider the prevalence of the skin disease known as yaws. She wrote that for the *rubba muma* (River mama), '. . . dances are performed and sacrifices of a white goat, a black cock, and silver money are made to the water-being called Mamadjo who cures disease, especially that West Indian form of leprosy called "Yaws" '.[4]

There is one other possible indication of the survival of some form of animism among the slaves and that is the worship of the cotton tree. In 1832 Knibb told a Parliamentary Committee that he had not 'heard of any act of superstitious reverence to trees for the last four years: they used to worship the cotton tree but I have not heard of that for some time'.[5] By the 1920s, as Beckwith ob-

[1] M. J. Field, *Search for Security: an Ethno-psychiatric Study of Rural Ghana*, p. 44.
[2] Lewis, *op. cit.*, pp. 253–59.
[3] T. Banbury, *Jamaica Superstitions, or the Obeah Book*, 1894, pp. 24–35.
[4] Beckwith, *op. cit.*, (1929), pp. 101–102.
[5] Evidence Upon Oath, Committee of the House of Lords, 1832, p. 768.

served, the cottonwood tree was more venerated and feared because it was felt to be the habitation of ghosts than because of any belief in its intrinsic spiritual qualities.[1]

Another superstitious belief of African origin which was first mentioned only after the abolition of slavery, is that of Old Hige (or old Hag). According to Banbury this is a witch that delights in sucking human blood, especially that of infants during their first nine days. He tells us that it was common practice among the Negroes 'of keeping up the ninth night after the birth of an infant. This night is thought the most critical, as on it the old hag uses her utmost endeavour to get at the babe'.[2] No doubt there was some connection between this practice and the 'ghost-child' belief during the first eight days which we mentioned in the previous chapter, for Banbury also tells us that 'The locked jaw was always believed an invariable sign of the suck of an old hag'. It is not unreasonable to derive the belief in 'old hige' from the well-known African witch-craft belief. The kra-eating, cannibalistic feasts of these witches and their other attributes bear a close resemblance to the 'old hige' attributes of Jamaica.[3]

Among the Negro folk in Jamaica today the belief in a unique form of poltergeist is still quite prevalent. Hardly a year passes without an evening newspaper reporting the most extravagantly human behaviour of stone pellets thrown by unseen hands and at least one trained European sociologist has been left convinced of the reality of these happenings.[4] The belief in poltergeist is almost certainly of African origin, and, as such, must have been known to the slaves. The belief may well have been derived from the *Ga asamanukpa* or Senior Ghosts who are '. . . definitely associated in Ga tradition with polished stone weapons and with stone missiles. The holed stone discs . . . are used, according to Ga lore, as missiles by the asamanukpa, who are also said to dance on flat-topped stone

[1] Beckwith, *op. cit.*, p. 145. Herskovits, in his review of Beckwith's book in *The Journal of American Folklore*, Vol. 43, 1930 strongly criticizes this statement. But I am afraid I found his remarks both confusing and pedantic. I can verify this statement on the basis of my own experiences growing up in the country parts of Jamaica.

[2] Banbury, *op. cit.*, pp. 24–35.

[3] Note that this belief was also common among American slaves. See John Hawkins, 'An Old Mammas Folklore', in *Journal of American Folklore*, Vol. 9, 1896.

[4] Williams, *op. cit.*, see especially pp. 1–22.

outcrops'.[1] Finally, there are the very common folk beliefs in the 'rolling calf', a terrifying calf-ghost which runs around in the night with a chain dangling from it; and the three-foot horse, another animal ghost of much terror. These beliefs may have come from any of the common West African beliefs in imps or forest monsters such as the sasabonsam[2] of the Akan peoples.

PART 2: CHRISTIANITY AND THE SLAVES

Until the end of the eighteenth century one of the most striking features of Jamaican society was that almost the entire slave population remained ignorant of the religion of their masters. Near the end of this period, however, the abolition movement and the religious revival in England led to some efforts being made on the part of the established church to amend their dismal record as well as the beginning of the conversion of the slaves by nonconformist sects. We shall trace the impact of each denomination without regard to their chronological order, then make some concluding remarks on the general response which this sudden interest in their religious welfare stimulated among the slaves.

The Established Church The hopeless inefficiency and corruption, of the established clergy has been demonstrated in another chapter. The masters being as irreligious as they were, it is not to be wondered that they were never bothered by the complete neglect with which the clergy treated their slaves. The few who gave the problem any thought tended, like Long, to rationalize their position by arguing that the slaves were incapable of understanding the complexities of christian worship. But even if the masters were willing to convert their slaves the attitude of the established church made this impossible. In 1774 to have a slave baptised cost the master £1-3s.-9d,[3] and by the end of the century over £3.

Under pressure exerted both by the abolitionists and by the success of the nonconformist sects in the early nineteenth century, an act was passed in 1816 appointing curates to assist the rectors in propagating the gospel among the slaves. They were paid £300 per annum, and:

[1] M. J. Field, *The Search for Security*, p. 44.
[2] See for example, Rattray's *Religion and Art in Ashanti*.
[3] Long, *op. cit.*, Vol. 2, p. 429.

The several parishes were required to provide 'proper places besides the church, where divine service might be performed on Sundays and holidays, by the rector or curate'; and the baptismal fee for a slave, which had in some cases been unreasonably exacted was now limited to two shillings and sixpence.[1]

In 1818 the salary of the curates was increased to £500. Quite a few 'respectable clergymen' were induced to come out to Jamaica as a result. But these activities on the part of the established church had little effect and in many ways were largely farcical.

In the first place, many proprietors, while they supported the bill for the religious instruction of their slaves – no doubt appreciating its propaganda value – refused to allow their slaves the necessary time for such instruction. Cooper, a minister sent out by an absentee owner to instruct his slaves, found that despite the approval of the master and the fact that he actually lived on the estate, the slaves were so hard worked that they had little time to hear him.[2]

Secondly, there seemed to have been general cynicism on the part of the curates towards their duties. A slave owner wrote in 1826 of the almost total cynicism and failure of the Established Church in converting the slaves. It was customary simply to assemble from fifty to one hundred slaves, ask them their names and then baptise them *en masse*, the rector receiving two shillings and sixpence for each slave.[3]

Not only was the established church incompetent and cynical but also extremely intolerant of other denominations. Being the religion of the masters it strongly supported the status quo and violently opposed the nonconformists on the grounds that their preaching constituted a threat to the slave system. This intolerance on the part of the white supporters of the church reached its climax after the slave rebellion of 1832 when the infamous Colonial Church Union was formed which, while not officially supported by the church, was recognized as having been master-minded by one of the best known clergymen of the island – the Reverend G. W. Bridges. The *Cornwall Courier*, which was the extremist pro-slavery newspaper of the island, became the mouth-piece of the Union and declared that its objectives were:

[1] G. W. Bridges, *The Annals of Jamaica*, Vol. 1, p. 555.
[2] Cooper, *op. cit.*, pp. 2–8.   [3] De La Beche, *op. cit.*, p. 27.

. . . To rid the 'island of those vermin, – those pests, – who coming in the garb of religion, endeavour to pull down her institutions, to level property in the dust and amid the carnage that must inevitably follow in the conservation of their diabolical schemes, secure to themselves wealth and power. To drive these miscreants away . . . are the objects of the Colonial Union . . .'[1]

The Union, supported largely by the more militant lower class whites, committed the most atrocious acts of violence against the missionaries and their slave supporters, including burning their chapels, tarring and feathering the missionaries and abusing their wives.

The Moravians These were the first non-conformist missionaries to arrive in the island. In 1754 two absentee planters who had been converted to their faith sent out a couple of missionaries to their estate in Cornwall. Coming before the start of the anti-slavery movement, they did not arouse the suspicion of the planters and their work was, at first, mildly encouraging. Their activities prompted several planters on neighbouring estates to employ Moravian missionaries in instructing their slaves.[2] The first conflict of the Moravians with the established order came in 1763 when they pleaded exemption from militia duties, a plea which was considered treasonable by many planters in the light of the unrest among the slaves at the time. The Moravians managed to settle their problems with the Assembly and continued to have the tacit support of the more prominent of the white group even during the hostile period of the early 19th century. The price which the Moravians paid for this tacit acceptance, however, was poor response on the part of the slaves. In 1804, after fifty years of activity, they could only show 938 converts as the fruits of their labour. Bridges' assessment of them, that they were respectable, harmless and generally ineffective, was doubtless correct.[3]

The Methodists While starting much later than the Moravians, this sect was eventually to prove far more successful in their impact

[1] Bleby, *The Death Struggles of Slavery*, p. 222.

[2] See W. F. Pitman, 'Slavery in the B.W.I. Plantations in the 18th Century', in *The Journal of Negro History*, Vol. XI, pp. 584–650.

[3] Bridges, *op. cit.*, Vol. I, p. 548.

on the non-white population. Their mission was started by Dr Coke in 1789. When he first arrived he attracted considerable congregations, many of them whites, and was only interrupted occasionally by a few white drunks. He returned to the island in 1791, preached widely and established a chapel. By this time opposition against him had grown, especially after a permanent missionary had been appointed for the island. In 1792, another chapel was built in Kingston, but in that year, when Coke made his third visit, he found that the opposition his mission experienced in the island far exceeded that in the rest of the West Indies taken as a whole.[1] Nonetheless, the number of converts grew rapidly. By the end of 1792 there were 234; in 1803 the number in Kingston alone was 530, of whom 14 were whites, 98 browns and 418 blacks. Most of these were free Negroes. As their numbers grew, so did the white opposition and they soon became the centre of white animosity. The host of a visitor to the island in the early 1820s contrasted his attitude to the Moravians whom he considered 'peaceable, moral, industrious, painstaking' with that of his opinion of the Methodists who were described as 'cunning, intriguing, fanatical, hypocritical canting knaves, cajoling the poor Negroes of all their little savings . . . under the pretense of saving them from the devil and everlasting damnation'.[2]

The Baptists This was the most successful of all the sects in converting the slaves. One of the main reasons for this success was the fact that it was introduced to the slaves by Negro preachers. The first such preacher was George Liele, an American ex-slave who came to the island in 1784. Liele grew up in Virginia and Georgia and was won over to the Baptist faith of his master two years before the American War of Independence, and, on his preaching abilities being recognized by the white parsons, he was made a 'probationer'. Some years before his master's death Liele was given his freedom. When the Empire Loyalists evacuated the country Liele was obliged to go to Jamaica with one Colonel Kirkland to whom he was indebted. Eventually he paid off his debts, in the meantime earning a good name for himself in the service of the household of the Governor of the island. He began preaching in a small private house in

[1] T. Coke, *History of the West Indies*, 1808, Vol. 2.
[2] C. Williams, *Tour Through Jamaica*, 1826, p. 37.

Kingston 'to a good smart congregation', adding that he formed the church with 'four brethren from America'.[1] His preaching 'took good effect with the poorer sort, especially the slaves'.[2] As one would expect, Liele suffered considerable persecution but his perseverance and good name among many of the whites won out. In 1780 he wrote that 'they seldom interrupt us now'. By that year they had 15,000 followers 'in different parts of the country' many of them won over from 'Mr Wesley's people'. He wrote also 'I have deacons and elders a few; and teachers of small congregations in the town and country where convenience suits them to come together, and I am pastor'.[3] He even, with the assistance of 'thirteen school-masters', founded a school for instructing the children of Negroes. Liele eventually bought himself a little farm and a team of horses and waggons for haulage and in 1790 wrote that he had become 'too entangled in affairs of the world to go on' in 'supporting the cause', and asked for assistance from the Baptist Society of England.

Another figure of equal importance among the early Baptists was Brother Moses Baker, also a Negro American who was baptized by Liele in 1787, and under the encouragement of his Quaker master, began preaching the next year in St. James parish.[4] Soon he had converted the slaves on twenty neighbouring estates and a letter to the Baptist society in London stated that Brother Baker claimed to have had 14,000 'justified believers', 3,000 'followers' and 'many under conviction of sin'. Unhappily, the letter concluded that he 'has undergone a great deal of persecution and severe trials for the preaching of the gospel, but our Lord has delivered him safe out of all'.[5] The Baptist missionary society sent out its first missionary in 1813, John Rowe, to help Baker and Liele in their work and later many more were to come.

It was not long, however, before a rift took place in the Baptist church of Jamaica. The more orthodox sectarians who took over the work started by Baker and Liele, soon found that many of the 'class leaders' they had trained broke off and formed their own

[1] Letter of Rev J. Cook of Funaw, South Carolina, dated Sept. 15, 1790, in, *The Journal of Negro History*, Vol. I, pp. 70–73.
[2] *Ibid.*
[3] *Ibid.*
[4] W. J. Gardner, *The History of Jamaica*, p. 344.
[5] T. N. Swigle to Dr Rippon, Oct. 1802, in, *The Journal of Negro History*, Vol. I.

independent churches at the same time re-interpreting and African-
izing the Baptist creed to suit their own tastes. As happened in
America:

> . . . The Negro insisted upon making a choice. That choice
> was determined by the demands of his perceptual consciousness
> for the exercise of which he found plenty of room in current
> Methodist and Baptist beliefs and practices. And as he chose
> those particular types of Christianity best suited to his needs so
> he proceded to choose the elements which were to make up for
> him his particular type of Methodist and Baptist Religion.[1]

So it was in Jamaica that many of the slaves from America and
several of those who had broken away from the orthodox Baptists
began to formulate their own native baptist creed. Here, in fact,
were the roots of Revivalism and Pocomania which remain today
the main religious sects of the Jamaican Negro.[2] A report of the
established church stated in 1828 that 'they demonstrated themselves Baptists; although the Ministers in town disclaim all connexion whatever with them, or even any knowledge of them' and
from the description of the effects of their nightly meetings it
seems that the report was speaking of early forms of spirit possession
among the Negroes.[3]

The response of the slaves to this sudden upsurge of christian
proselyting among them varied in many respects. Many of the
older slaves, and particularly the Africans, remained aloof or
accepted the new faith with some degree of cynicism. Typical of
the apathetic was Daniel, the faithful old house slave of John Riland
of whom the latter wrote:

> Daniel also died; and grieved I am to confess that he went to
> his grave, not indeed a depraved and ostensibly unreligious

[1] P. F. Laubenstein, 'Racial Values in Aframerican Music', in, *The Musical
Quarterly*, Vol. 16, 1930.

[2] Martha Beckwith in her *Black Roadways*, claimed that Revivalism was
derived from a combination of this early native Baptism and myalism (see
above) during the period between 1838 and 1860, largely as a counter to obeah;
while Pocomania grew out of a syncretism of Revivalism and obeah.

Philip Curtin in his *Two Jamaicas*, supports this view in so far as it relates
to the origins of revivalism in the period with which he is specially concerned,
i.e. Jamaican society between 1830 and 1865.

[3] Report of the Diocese of Jamaica, 1828.

character but in a state of indifference. He never professed himself a Christian, and did not directly oppose religion in others. He was naturally kind-hearted and cheerful, but he took no interest in what he read and heard. There was an apathy about him and an acquiescence in the truth of what we told him; but beyond this he seemed never to advance.[1]

Lewis quotes several instances of this indifference on the part of the older slaves.[2] In particular, there were the cases of two women who, while they allowed their children to be christened, themselves refused to have anything to do with the ceremony.

Some of these older slaves accepted christianity simply because they felt it was an effective antidote to obeah.[3] Others saw it as 'a kind of talisman which is to render the most culpable action innocent'.[4] But perhaps the most common cause for baptism among this group was simply to be able to get rid of the absurd names by which they were originally known. In such cases names either of the owner or of some respectable white person was chosen. As a planter pointed out:

> Most . . . desire the baptismal rite merely to gratify their vanity by possessing themselves of a fine, high sounding name, or that of some respectable gentleman in the neighbourhood, which is a patent of nobility and confer dignity and honour in exact proportion to the wealth and consequence of the unconscious god-parent . . .[5]

Among those of the non-white population who developed a genuine interest in christianity, religion became inseparably linked with social status and political action. In the first place, there were the Methodists. This sect rapidly became the stronghold of the free coloured and Negro group. To them Methodism struck the right balance between piety and propriety. On the one hand, it lacked the unattainability of Anglicanism which was identified with the status quo against which they were engaged in asserting their civil rights. And on the other, it was more respectable than

---

[1] John Riland, *The Memoirs of a West Indian Planter*, p. 148.
[2] Lewis, *op. cit.*, pp. 229–31; 343–45.
[3] Stewart, *op. cit.*, 1823, p. 278.
[4] *The Jamaica Journal*, 1824, Vol. I, No. 48.
[5] *Ibid.*, Vol. I, No. 45.

the Baptist sect with its mass Negro support. This was one of the main reasons for the hostility of the whites to the Methodists.[1]

Among the Negro slaves the Baptist sect had great social significance. First, the leader-system whereby influential slaves became class leaders and were given charge of instructing a number of other slaves, 'underwent' as Curtin points out, 'some strange transformations':

> The class-leaders became something more than simply the teachers of the new converts. They were the real spiritual guides, taking a position equivalent to leadership of a myal cult group, and their power over the classes was authoritarian to the point of tyranny. They could refuse baptism to an applicant or expel rebels from the church – an important power that could be extended beyond simply religious matters.[2]

Even more important was the fact that the slave saw the Baptist missionaries as his allies against the planters in their fight for freedom. While the missionaries strongly denied ever expressing any abolition sentiments to the slaves it is difficult to see how they could have avoided giving them this impression. What is certain is that it was the class leaders of the Baptist sect who played a prominent part in the famous rebellion of 1832.[3] To the slaves this rebellion was known as 'the Baptist war'.

When we consider, therefore, the social functions of the nonconformist sects during slavery and the superficiality of the religious impact of the orthodox creed of these sects, it is not to be wondered that by the middle of the nineteenth century, less than twenty years after the abolition of slavery, there was a rapid falling off of membership in these churches. As early as 1839 Chandler had written that, 'I cannot keep my own mind from the fear that the work of religion hitherto is but superficial, as it respects the great mass of the people'.[4] Curtin shows that there was an increase in membership of all denominations until 1845 but that after this, membership began to decline until in the 1850s there was a complete collapse.

There were three main reasons for this decline. In the first place,

---

[1] P. Duncan, *A Narrative of the Wesleyan Mission to Jamaica*, 1849, p. 159.
[2] P. Curtin, *Two Jamaicas*, p. 33.
[3] See Chapter below on Slave Rebellions in Jamaica.
[4] John Chandler, *The Journal of . . . 1839*.

as a contemporary writer pointed out, the devotion and enthusiasm of the slaves during and immediately after emancipation were largely the expression of the slaves' 'zest for freedom and a token of gratitude to the preachers'. And 'as the epoch of emancipation retires into the past, the missionaries, though equally faithful, are not equally influential'.[1] Secondly, it will be noted that the decline of church membership correlated with the upsurge of myalism among the Negro population which we have dealt with earlier on in this chapter. At the same time the native Baptist sects were growing rapidly. In 1862 a climax was reached when the entire population was hit by a great wave of religious fervour. At first, this religious upheaval was gladly received by the orthodox nonconformists and even by the Anglican clergy. But suddenly the whole movement 'turned African'. Myalism and native baptism converged and in doing so shattered the high hopes of the orthodox christians while laying the foundations for modern Jamaican revivalism.[2]

[1] Rev D. King, *The State of Prospects of Jamaica*, 1850, p. 100.
[2] See Beckwith, *op. cit.*,; Curtin, *op. cit.*; Gardner, *History of Jamaica*, pp. 458–471; see also, Williams, *Psychic Phenomena in Jamaica*.

CHAPTER VIII

Social Institutions of the Slaves

2. ECONOMY, RECREATION AND CONTROL

IN THIS chapter we continue our discussion of the institutionalized patterns of behaviour among the slaves. The three areas of behaviour which will be examined are the domestic economy of the slaves; their internal forms of social control and their patterns of recreation.

SECTION I
THE ECONOMIC LIFE OF THE SLAVES

One of the anomalies of Jamaican slave society was the fact that by about the middle of the eighteenth century the entire population of free people became dependent on the slaves not only to provide the labour that was the life-blood of the economic system, but almost all their vegetable and cash crop. In the case of freemen not directly connected with the sugar estates, it was the slave who provided their sugar also. How the slaves managed to produce these goods, and the manner in which they were marketed, form the subject of the first section of this chapter.

The most important element of this domestic economic system was the provision ground of the slaves. There were, however, five other forms and sources of property owned by the slaves playing a significant part in the system. These were: the poultry, cattle and other small stock owned by them; goods stolen from the estate and elsewhere; the provisions given annually by the master to the slaves; handicrafts; and the relatively few cases of slaves being the property of other slaves. We shall consider each in turn.

(i) *The Provision Grounds:* Jamaica was the first of the West Indian islands to utilize the provision-ground system as the main source of supplying the slaves with their subsistence and it was the island in which the system was most highly developed. At first the masters had to provide the food for their slaves by supervising the cultivation of special areas of their plantations in provisions. In 1678, the first of many acts was passed requiring masters 'to have . . . one acre of ground well planted in provision for every five Negroes and so proportionately for a greater or lesser number under the penalty of £10 for every acre wanting'.[1]

The same requirement was made in the Act of 1696, although, significantly the penalty for each acre wanting was now only forty shillings. This would suggest that already the slaves had begun to rely on their own resources for their nourishment, for we find that toward the end of the eighteenth century when the provision ground system was well developed, only one acre was required for every ten slaves; but by then the law itself had become merely a formality.[2]

During the seventeenth century the slaves had Saturday afternoons, Sundays, and the Christmas and Easter holidays to cultivate their grounds on which they grew potatoes, yams, plantain and the like.[3] By the 1720s the system had developed to the stage where the majority of slaves could provide for themselves and many of the more industrious had already begun to sell their excess produce at the Sunday markets using the cash thus procured to buy otherwise unobtainable provisions such as salt-beef, salt-fish, pork and the like.[4] But conditions were by no means uniform throughout the island and there were still enough loop-holes in the system to lead many slaves to beg and steal for their daily sustenance. Often they could be seen at lunch time 'scraping the Dunghills at every Gentleman's Door for Bones, which, if they are so happy to find, they break extremely small, boil them, and eat the Broth'.[5] Corbett, who knew the island well, and who wrote of the period between the late 1730s and 1740s, also suggested that the provision ground system had not yet succeeded in satisfying the basic needs of the slaves, '. . . some of the poor Creatures', he wrote, 'pine away and are starved, others that have somewhat more spirits, go a stealing

[1] Acts of Jamiaca, C.O. 139/5.
[2] See Chapter on Legal Status of Slaves.
[3] Sir Hans Sloane, *op. cit.*, Introduction.
[4] C. Leslie, *A New History of Jamaica*, p. 306.   [5] *Ibid.*

and are shot as they are caught in Provision Grounds; others are whipt or even hang'd for going into the Woods, into which Hunger and Necessity itself drives them to try to get Food to keep Life and Soul together'.[1] But this state of affairs seems to have been more the result of the rapacity of the planters who were then at the peak of their expansionist drive, buying more slaves than they had land to support, than of the failure of the provision ground system which, however, had yet to develop fully.

By the late 1750s Jamaica's golden period of prosperity had begun. The basic socio-economic pattern of the island had been finally laid down. By the 1760s, the provision ground system seemed to have matured with the society of which it had become an integral part and with which, as Mintz and Hall remarked, 'it would have been profitless and dangerous to interfere'.[2] Long observed during this period that the slaves already had 'the greater part of the small silver circulating among them'.[3]

Having traced the development of the provision ground system to the point of its maturity, let us now examine the nature and extent of its operations. On mountain estates the grounds were located in the backlands. On the plains or lowlands, where most of the large sugar estates were situated, 'provision grounds are kept quite distinct and are at a distance among the mountains'.[4] This distance could be as much as ten miles[5] but was usually less. On several estates situated on extensive plain-lands the provision ground system was dispensed with and a section of the plantation planted in corn which was distributed weekly to the slaves. This was particularly the case in the parish of Vere where the corn ration was partly used for rearing poultry and other small stock.[6]

Vere, however, was the striking exception to the general pattern. The amount of land allotted to each slave in the other parishes varied. A writer 'in Defence of the British Colonies' claimed that it

---

[1] Corbett, *Essay Concerning Slavery*, p. 38.

[2] Mintz and Hall, 'The Origins of the Internal Marketing System in Jamaica': *Papers in Caribbean Anthropology*, Yale, 1960.

[3] E. Long, *op. cit.*, Vol. 2, p. 411.

[4] M. G. Lewis, *op. cit.*, p. 81.

[5] The Rev Cooper, *Facts Illustrative of the Condition of the Slaves . . .*, p. 5.

[6] Evidence of W. Taylor, Parliamentary Committee on Slavery, House of Lords, 1832, p. 622.

averaged two acres per Negro, costing the master about £20 per lot.[1] A pro-slavery writer in a letter to the *Jamaica Journal* asserted that on Orange Valley estate in 1823 a total of 1,200 acres were divided between 421 slaves, an average slightly under three acres per Negro.[2] But these cases seemed not to have been typical. Stewart, a reliable pro-slavery writer, estimated the amount of land per Negro at half an acre. This estimate is supported by the figures given by Lord Seaford who was strongly pro-slavery. On the three properties which he owned there were 864 slaves owning approximately 589 acres of provision ground, or about ·67 acres per Negro.[3]

In addition to these provision grounds in the hills, called *polincos*, the slaves also planted on the small plots of land behind their huts. These they designated their 'kitchen gardens' and in them they grew 'plantains, ochras, and other vegetables ... also ... cocoa-nuts and calabash trees',[4] in addition to oranges, shaddochs, peppers and abba 'or palm trees'.[5] On the provision grounds almost every variety of tropical foods was grown.

Edwards claimed that the negroes very imprudently tended to 'trust more to' plantain groves, corn and other vegetables that were liable to be destroyed by storms than to roots such as yams and potatoes. But while it was true that storms and droughts did cause great suffering and mortality among the slave population near the end of the nineteenth century the real reason for such disasters was not the over-reliance of the slaves on plantains, but economic, political and climatic factors beyond their control.[6] Almost all the other contemporary writers stated that the slaves diversified their crops, the three staple foods being yams, plantains and cocos. In addition there were pumpkins, bananas, achee, 'catalue' or calalue and many others. Indeed, we are told that the slaves tended to keep

[1] Anon. 'Notes in Defence of the Colonies', *Jamaica Journal*, Vol. 1, No. 52.
[2] The *Jamaica Journal*, 1824, Vol. 1, No. 46.
[3] Evidence of the Lord Seaford, Parliamentary Committee, House of Lords, 1832.
[4] Barclay, *A Practical View of Slavery* ..., (1827), pp. 313–14.
[5] M. G. Lewis, *op. cit.*, p. 108.
[6] Edwards was perhaps referring to the series of droughts and storms that hit Jamaica between 1780 and 1788. This, plus the scarcity of provisions from the recently independent U.S. led to large-scale starvation and ill-health among the slaves in which, according to one estimate, 16,000 slaves died. See 'Defence of the Br. Colonies', Anon.; also, B. Edwards, *op. cit.*, Vol. 1, pp. 234–35 and 305–6; Vol. 2, pp. 161–62.

yams and cocos for their own use and sold the plantains at the Sunday markets.[1]

The amount of time the slave had to work his ground varied not only over the period of slavery, but, at any given time, from one estate to the next. During the seventeenth century, the slaves generally had Sundays and Saturday afternoons.[2] In the early eighteenth century, as the large landowners took over the estates, the slaves were pushed much harder and it is doubtful whether Saturday afternoons were given any longer.[3] With the beginning of the nineteenth century alternate Saturdays, out of crop, were legally given but there is reason to believe that the owners more than made up for this during the crop. If the provision grounds were not very far away some slaves attended them during the two hour break at lunch; and a few of the very industrious even went to them at nights.

Regarding their method of cultivation, the usual practice, according to Beckford, was to plant most of their provisions on the hillside which 'they commonly prefer' while cultivating the plantains 'upon the flat', but he also wrote that 'some will pursue a contrary method'.[4] The practice of clearing the ground to be planted by fire seemed to have been prevalent for in 1807 the 'Consolidated Slave Laws' contained a new clause which punished slaves who cleared their grounds in this manner. The act declared that the practice was a hazard to neighbouring estates and overseers who knowingly permitted their slaves to indulge in this habit were also to be fined.[5] This may have been the survival of the common West African technique.[6]

Most of the labour on these grounds was performed with the co-operation of close friends or relatives. Mothers worked with their infants on their backs while older children carried baskets and performed other odd jobs.[7] As we suggested in an earlier chapter, mothers tried to keep control of their adult children especially when males, as long as possible, so as to have the benefit of their labour

---

[1] Evidence of Mr Barry, Parliamentary Committee on Slavery, House of Lords, 1832.

[2] See Sloane, *op. cit.*

[3] Leslie, for example, mentions only Sundays.

[4] Beckford, *Account*, Vol. 2, p. 151.

[5] Acts of Jamaica, C.O. 139/54.

[6] See Ottenburg, *Cultures and Societies of Africa*, p. 23.

[7] Beckford, *Account*, Vol. 2, pp. 155–56.

and the extra ground allotted to them. But it is doubtful whether they were generally successful. It was customary for couples living together to unite their efforts and grounds.[1]*

(ii) *Poultry, Cattle and Small Stock* Until near the end of the eighteenth century, the laws of the island disapproved of slaves rearing cattle of any kind. From the fequency with which the laws were re-enacted, however, it seems clear that even during the earlier part of the eighteenth century they failed to be effective. Certainly, by the beginning of the nineteenth century, it was taken for granted that slaves could own cows and the island depended almost entirely on them for its poultry and a sizeable proportion of its live-stock. Each night the chickens were gathered and hung up in baskets to keep them from the rats while the fowls roosted in the trees about their huts.[2] It was claimed that the slaves allowed their pigs to roam at nights so as to feed on the master's property and that they were called home before daybreak by a special whistle or some other concealed signal.[3] Most of the cows were held in common ownership, one sometimes being owned by as many as four slaves.[4] These cows were generally allowed free pasturage on the master's property, Lewis estimating the annual cost of such pasturage to the master at £12. The master, however, expected to be sold the cows at a rate somewhat below the current market price, usually amounting to between £10 and £15 for a three-year-old beast. The 864 slaves on the three estates of Lord Seaford had between them 131 cows, 26 steers, 53 heifers, 41 bull-calves and 40 cow-calves, in addition to 522 hogs and 1,728 heads of poultry.[5]

[1] Bickell, *The West Indies as they Are, or a Real Picture of Slavery.*
[2] A. Barclay, *op. cit.*, p. 515.
[3] Anon, 'Notes in Defence . . .', *Jamaica Journal*, Vol. 2, No. 1.
[4] Williams, *A Tour Through . . . Jamaica in 1823*, p. 61.
[5] Evidence of Lord Seaford, *op. cit.*
* In West Africa, among the tribes of Northern Nigeria, and the Ibos, Mossi, Chamba, Ibbibio, the Ewes of the interior, Twi and the Temme of Sierra Leone, there is a general sharing of agricultural activities between the sexes, the men performing the more difficult tasks of clearing the bush before first-planting; among the Yoruba and the Fon of Dahomey men perform almost all the agricultural tasks except collecting the harvest; among the Efik and several other tribes of Southern Nigeria, the tribes of the Togo coast and the Kru, almost all agricultural work except clearing new ground, is performed by slaves (especially in the past) and women. See, H. Baumann, 'The Division of Work According to Sex in African Hoe Culture', *Africa*, Vol. 1, No. 3.

(iii) *Stolen Goods* As a rule, the slaves rarely missed an opportunity to steal from the stores of the plantation or other sources
belonging to the whites. It appears that they genuinely felt no sense
of wrong in such forms of theft; or that there was any incon-
sistency in, at the same time, abhorring any form of theft among
themselves. Many writers, both pro- and anti-slavery, made mention
of this double standard on the part of the slaves. Stewart wrote
that they were 'strangely addicted to theft', and added:

> ... To pilfer from their masters they consider as no crime,
> though to rob a fellow-slave is accounted heinous; when a slave
> makes free with his master's property, he thus ingeniously argues
> – 'What I take from my master, being for my use, who am his
> slave, or property, he loses nothing by its transfer.'[1]

On the estate where Marly worked, theft from the master was
condoned by the entire slave population, and when one woman
was caught red-handed stealing a calabash of sugar and called a
thief, 'She exclaimed indignantly that "him no tief from Massa,
him take from Massa" '.[2] But it was not only from the estates that
the slaves pilfered. In 1825 a slave was brought to court charged by
the captain of a ship with stealing coffee and sugar from the ship's
shallops which were carrying goods from Port Henderson and
Passage Fort.[3] What was astonishing was the fact that the society
tacitly supported this wide scale stealing by the slaves, as we shall
see when we come to discuss marketing.

(iv) *Provisions* At least once every year, the master was bound by
law to give a minimum of clothing and salted meat and fish to his
slaves. By the latter half of the eighteenth century most masters
gave allowances of salted meat and fish, called simply 'salt' by the
Negroes, twice a year and clothing and other articles every Christmas. The clothing given was usually oznaburg, a very coarse kind
of linen, baize and checks, and occasionally blankets and woollens.
Other articles such as hats, knives, needles, iron pots and the like,
were given when needed. The more prosperous slaves had little to
do with the oznaburg and often sold it at the markets. Others only

---

[1] Stewart, *The Past and Present State*, p. 249. See also Marsden, *op. cit.*, p. 43.
[2] *Marly, or the Life of a Planter in Jamaica*, 1828, pp. 40–42.
[3] *The Kingston Chronicle*, Sat. July 9th, 1825.

used it for working in. Many headmen, as a mark of recognition to their superior position among the slaves, were given extra provisions. De La Beche, a moderately pro-slavery writer, claimed that he made a distinction between four classes of slaves when distributing their annual supplies of clothes: the first class was the head driver who received twenty yards of oznaburg, eight yards of blue baize; the second, were the heads of the various groups who received sixteen yards of oznaburg and eight yards of blue baize; the third were the women who received eleven yards of oznaburg, 4 yards of blue baize and five long ells; the fourth class were the children who receive each six yards of oznaburg and three yards of blue baize.[1]

For all excess or undesired provisions, the slaves found a ready market on Sundays. The impression should not be had however, that the slaves were well provided for by their masters. Quite the contrary. Even as strongly pro-slavery a writer as Edwards, writing at the end of the nineteenth century had to admit that 'of clothing, the allowance of the master is not always so liberal as might be wished, but much more so of late years than formerly'.[2] The slaves, however, often preferred to satisfy their own tastes when they could and so there was much circulation and exchange of the provision goods at the Sunday markets.

(v) *Artisans* As one would expect, the African slaves carried over with them whatever skills they may have possessed in their homeland. The most prominent of such skills were basketry and straw-plaiting. Bed-mats, bark-ropes, wicker-chairs, and baskets, earthen jars, pans and other such articles were often produced.[3] Some slaves also made a rough kind of shoe called *sampatter* from leather or rawhide or from discarded saddle straps which were used when walking over rough ground or making walls.[4] Included in this group would also be the makers of John-Canoe and other masks which were seen on festive occasions. These men were hired by others, more prosperous to prepare and play the John Canoe for them and later share the takings.[5]

[1] De La Beche, *op. cit.*, p. 11.
[2] B. Edwards, *op. cit.*, Vol. 2, p. 165.   [3] *Ibid.*, p. 162.
[4] The *Jamaica Journal*, Vol. 1, No. 49, 1824.
[5] See for example, Lewis, *op. cit.*, pp. 75–6.

(vi) *Slaves Belonging to Slaves* A few valuable slaves, who were the favourites of their masters, were permitted to own, and sometimes even given slaves by their own masters. The practice was illegal but usually given a blind eye. Such slaves were held in utter contempt by the other slaves, were 'the poorest of the poor, trampled on by all and pitied by none'.[1] Often the slave-owners of such slaves could have obtained their freedom should they have been so inclined, but, for economic reasons, preferred to remain technically enslaved to their white masters.[2]

The Marketing of Slave Goods

The origins of the slave-dominated Sunday markets that became an integral part of the domestic economy of the island by the latter half of the eighteenth century, are somewhat obscure. The first market established for the white community dates back to 1662,[3] and there is some plausibility in Mintz and Hall's speculation that such markets provided the first opportunity for the slaves to exchange their goods.[4] Hawking and peddling is known to have been practiced by the slaves as early as 1662 for, enclosed in the first manuscript volume of the laws of the island is a reference to the mischief done by 'wandering Servants, and Slaves on Sundays, Saturdays in the afternoon and other days when the said Servants and Slaves do not work'. The mischief, it was stated, was that at such times goods stolen from the master were sold.[5] An act of 1678 implies that Negroes had already began to use the market established for the white community for it enacted penalties against Negroes who were in the habit of stealing timber from the boats docked at the wharves as well as canes from the estates and selling them at the different markets in the island.[6]

While the domination of the internal market by the Negroes was to take some time, hawking and peddling seemed to have expanded rapidly throughout the seventeenth and early eighteenth century judging from the frequency with which attempts were made by the

[1] Cooper, *op. cit.*, pp. 54–5.
[2] Evidence of Mr Sharp, House of Lords Committee on Slavery, 1832.
[3] Mintz and Hall, 'The Origins of the Internal Marketing System in Jamaica', *Papers in Caribbean Anthropology*, p. 13.
[4] *Ibid.*, p. 14.
[5] Acts of Jamaica, C.O. 139/1.
[6] Acts of Jamaica, C.O. 139/5.

Assembly to regulate this method of marketing. The most severe and revealing of these laws was passed in 1735. Hawking of goods, wares and merchandise of all kinds was forbidden to Negroes, Mulattoes or Indians mainly because this 'practice tend to the manifest prejudice of Trade and to the great discouragement of housekeepers'. Fish, fruits, milk, poultry, 'and other small stock', were officially allowed, 'provided the Persons have a ticket from the Master and Owner of Such Goods', which would suggest that these hawkers were not, as yet, entirely independent.

Very revealing, however, was the restraint on Negroes attempting to 'engross' the market, the official reasons for the proscription being:

> For the better preventing of Hawkers and Forestallers of the Market as go a considerable way out of the respective Towns in this island to meet such persons as bring in Plantation-provisions, and other Stock, and do buy up, and engross the same; by which Means the prices of provisions of all kinds are greatly advanced.[1]

This would suggest that from as early as the 1730s there was a fair degree of complexity and sophistication in the Negroes' activities in the internal marketing system of the island. Whether it was due to legislative enactment or not, by the latter half of the eighteenth century this engrossing of the internal market by shrewd middlemen seemed to have declined. By this time the trip to the markets every Sunday by the slaves had become not just a purely economic venture, but one with many important social overtones.

By the 1760s the slave-dominated marketing system was well developed. That in Kingston was the largest although there the majority of sellers seemed to have been white settlers, some of whom, like the grass-planters, could earn 'upwards of £1,500 per annum'.[2] Vegetables and fruits from Europe and America were to be had there, in addition to tropical foods, beef and salt from the neighbouring countryside and even parishes as far away as St Ann's.

By the last years of the eighteenth century even the Kingston market seemed to have been dominated by the Negroes, at least in numbers,[3] 10,000 of them being estimated to have attended it every

---

[1] *Acts of the Assembly of Jamaica*, 1681–1737, (Printed).

[2] E. Long, Vol. 2, p. 106.

[3] Although the volume of trade may still have been dominated by the minority of free settlers from surrounding districts. See evidence of Admiral Flemming, anti-slavery witness, 1832, pp. 590–91.

Sunday morning.[1] Negro markets were established not only in the towns but any part of the rural areas where there was a potential demand, such as ports, villages, cross-roads and the residences of large and wealthy families.[2] But it was the town markets which strongly attracted the slaves, many of them travelling as many as twenty-five miles in order to sell their produce there.[3] The attraction of the large town markets was largely social, Baille recalling that while on their way he 'often met Negroes and offered to purchase their articles, but they preferred going to the market'.[4]

Most Negroes carried their load – which weighed between thirty and fifty lbs.[5] – on their heads; but a few of the more prosperous had asses to assist them.[6] Some of the better-off slaves who did not own asses paid less successful Negroes to carry their provisions to market. On Hope estate in 1818 the average cost for such services was two shillings and sixpence.[7]

The prices at which these provisions were sold varied, sometimes substantially, in different parts of the island. Kingston and Spanish Town prices were roughly the same although the Kingston market was more efficiently run and supplies were more regular.[8] There was however, a much wider margin between the prices in Kingston and those on the north side of the island. The *Jamaica Magazine* gave the following differences in the prices of basic foods:

	Kingston	North-side
Ground Provisions: Yams, cocos, etc.		
per cwt:	10s – 13/4	10s – 12/6
Plantains, per cwt.	11/8 – 12/6	5s – 6/8
Indian Corn, per bus.	7/6 – 0	10s – 12/6
Guinea Corn, per bus.	10s – 0	unconfirmed
Beef per lb.	1/3 – 0	1/3 – 0
Pork, per lb.	1/3 – 0	10d – 0

[1] Edwards, *op. cit.*, Vol. 2, p. 162, footnote g.
[2] Evidence of Mr Baille, 1832, p. 114; evidence of Sir John Keane, 1832, p. 165, House of Lords Committee on Slavery.
[3] Evidence of Mr Baille, *op. cit.*, p. 120.
[4] *Ibid.*
[5] Evidence of Mr Barry, 1832, *op. cit.*, p. 425.
[6] *Ibid*; and Mr Morgan, p. 708.
[7] The *Jamaica Journal*, Nov., 1818.
[8] Long, *op. cit.*, Vol. 2, p. 105.

	Kingston	*North-side*
Mutton, per lb.	2/6 – 0	1/3 – 1/8
Goat, per lb.	1/8 – 0	1/– – 1/3
A hen	3/4 – 5/–	3/4 – 0
A turkey	13/4 – 15/–	13/4 – 15/–[1]

In 1825 De La Beche gave a list of commodities sold by Halse Hall slaves.[2] We shall quote this list in full, not so much to show the prices but to illustrate the great variety of goods sold at these Sunday markets:

A good fat farrow	1 – 1½ doubloon
A middling sized farrow	8 – 10 $
A small pig	1½ – 2 $
A suckling pig	1 $
A good milch goat	9 – 10 $
A fat goat, for killing	6 – 8 $
A kid	2 $
A couple of pigeons	4 bits (2/6d)
A couple of fat capons	10 $
A couple of fat pullets	5s – 1 $
A common breeding hen	4 bits
A common cock	½ $
A large bunch of bananas	¼ $
A middling sized bunch of bananas	1/3
A large bunch of plantains	½ $
A middling sized bunch of plantains	4 bits
Six large sweet potatoes	5d
A large root of sweet cassada	5d
3 pints of great corn (maize)	5d
1 qt sugar beans	1 bit (10d)
1 qt of peas	10d
1 pineapple	10d
2 coco-nuts	5d
A large water-melon	10d
A large pumpkin	10d – 2 bits.
12 mangoes	5d
12 large oranges	5d

[1] The *Jamaica Magazine*, Vol. 1, Oct. 1812.
[2] De La Beche, *op. cit.*, appendix.

18 naseberries	5d
A large shaddock	5d
6 sweet sops	5d
1 qt cashew nuts	5d
4 large avacado pears	5d
5 good cocos	5d
1 qt ochros	5d
2 cassada cakes	5d
A large yam	2 bits
3 small yams	10d
Twisted tobacco, per yard	5d

In addition to the above articles, wrote De la Beche, there were also articles from allowances given on the estates such as iron pots, herrings, corn, rum, etc.[1]

Despite this near exhaustive list, there was one important item which De La Beche failed to mention: sugar. The market for stolen sugar sold by the slaves was referred to as 'calabash estate' or 'calabash market'.[2] There is no reason to believe that this 'calabash market' existed separately from the ordinary Sunday market of the slaves. This was the main source of sugar for whites in the towns as well as free non-whites and non-praedial slaves. The sugar was both stolen and sold in calabashes, the price varying with the size of the gourd.[3]

Estimates vary greatly concerning the amount which the slaves earned from their weekly sales. Between 1758 and 1774 average weekly earnings was estimated at about four bits or two shillings and sixpence.[4] Between 1774 and 1790 it was stated that an industrious couple could earn between 1s 10½d and 2s 6d.[5] In 1824 a pro-slavery writer estimated their annual earnings at £3 5 0, or a little over one shilling per week.[6] Another pro-slavery writer asserted in 1832 that each slave earned between ten shillings and eleven shillings per week, but this was clearly a preposterous overstate-

---

[1] De La Beche *op cit.*, appendix

[2] Correspondence between George Hibbert and the Rev T. Cooper, 1824, from the *Jamaica Royal Gazette.*

[3] *Marly*, op. cit., pp. 43–4.

[4] Evidence of Henry Coor, Select Committee on Slave Trade, 1790–91.

[5] Evidence of Henry Coor, *ibid.*

[6] 'Notes in Defence', *Jamaica Journal*, Vol. 2, No. 1.

ment.[1] One can only say that the amount the slaves earned weekly was determined by his own strength and industriousness, and by the location and state of the market. There seems, however, to have been a general consensus among the many chroniclers writing on the subject, that the slave earned just enough to enable him to buy his salt for the week, i.e. salt, fish and beef, and on a few occasions, some pieces of cloth and a few trinkets. Very few slaves managed to save anything, despite the sensational accounts usually given by strong pro-slavery writers of old women dying and leaving great sums of money to their relatives, or even more dramatically, faithful old slaves offering great sums of money to help out their financially insecure masters.[2]

Finally, what exactly were these Sunday markets like? From two excellent first hand accounts[3] we learn that from early dawn the road was coloured with long lines of slaves, most of them with baskets on their heads cushioned by a *cotta* made of coiled-up, dried plantain leaves, while a few of the more prosperous were riding mules or leading asses. The market itself was all noise and bustle and wild, extravagant gestures which seemed always on the verge of, but never quite, exploding into violence. In the midst of this seeming chaos a few, too exhausted after their long walk, lay on the ground, dust-covered and fast asleep. Amidst the throng there were always a large number of coloured and black belles, mainly from the town, all dressed to kill 'having apparently no object but to display their persons and their tawdry dresses' and affecting total disdain to those about them, despite the fact that a few of them were always to be seen limping along in their newly acquired and still alien pairs of shoes. Brothers, sisters, temporary 'wives' and 'husbands', aged friends and week-end lovers are all intently looking for each other. When they meet, especially the old women with their 'chints pelisses and closely bound handkerchiefs', the gossip 'which refinement has not taught them yet to dignify with the more appropriate

---

[1] Evidence of Sir L. Halsted, House of Lords C'ttee on Slavery, 1832.

[2] *The Royal Gazette* of Aug. 1825, for example, tells of an old slave woman dying and leaving £400 for her relatives; and a contributor to the *Jamaica Journal* claimed that on Aug. 2, 1820 an old women gave the attorney of an estate in Trelawney £150 which she asked him to pass on to her master in England as a gift.

[3] G. Mathison, *Notices Respecting Jamaica*, 1805–10, pp. 2–3; and T. Foulks, *Eighteen Months in Jamaica*, 1833, p. 48.

name of scandal', begins at once. 'Chantoba will tell Cooba how Quaw teifed her fattest hog: how Mumba's John left his old wife Venus to attach himself to Pussy; while the younger ladies in closely knotted clusters, some laughing, some with serio-comic countenances, relate how Jupiter lub Jelina for tru'; or how Soger Buckra handsome for too much. As the day advances these conversations yield to the more important bustle of traffic'.[1]

SECTION 2:
INTERNAL PATTERNS OF CONTROL

While the masters on the estate always existed as a kind of *deus ex machina* in relation to the slave community, there were certain social and individual agents of control within this community. With regard to social pressures, perhaps the strongest was that of ostracism. If a slave had committed a grievous crime in the eyes of the other slaves – for example, *obeah* – he would immediately arouse the suspicion of all the other slaves and his company would be shunned.[2] A second powerful means of social control was derision. This is a well known form of what Radcliffe-Brown has designated as diffused primary sanctions.[3] Often it was directed against the whites both in song and mimicry, but no less often against members of the slave group. We shall discuss the operation of such sanctions in the next section.

But the slave community also had its own forms of 'secondary' sanctions. On every estate there were several headmen who exercised considerable influence in the slave community. Some of these men appointed themselves judges and conducted courts which tried slaves who had committed some breach of accepted behaviour. The courts usually consisted of three judges who, having taken their seats, began the session by consuming a great quantity of rum provided by both plaintiff and defendant. When sufficiently inebriated they sat and listened patiently, sometimes for hours on end, to the arguments put forward by both parties. At length, the hearing was closed and the judges gave their verdict, which often

---

[1] Theodore Foulks, *op. cit.*, p. 48. Note that by the time Foulks was writing the Sunday markets had been made illegal and these markets were now largely held on Saturday.

[2] See the section on Obeah in Chapter 7.

[3] Radcliffe-Brown, *Structure and Function in Primitive Society*, pp. 205–11.

involved the imposition of excessive fines. Apparently these sentences were often very partial and influenced to a great extent by
bribery.[1]

There were also amateur lawyers who pleaded on behalf of their
fellow slaves not only at these courts but also to the whites. Often he
settled disputes among the slaves before they reached their own, or
the masters' courts. He was usually shrewd and loquacious and had a
great deal of *congo-saw* and *sweet-mouth* and knew how to flatter
and play upon the vanity of the whites. But 'among his own people'
as one penetrating observer noted, 'the obsequious slave becomes
the consequential man, impatient of all temporary restrictions on
his liberty, and morbidly alive to every wrong, real or imaginary,
that seizes on his attention'.[2]

These Negro lawyers apparently played an important part in
destroying the apathy of the slaves to the idea of emancipation and
may well have incited many of the conspiracies and unrest among
the slave population during the nineteenth century. During the
apprenticeship period, for example, (i.e. 1834–1838) one of them
was charged with 'putting the Negroes in a state of insubordination
. . . (and) of asking quibbling questions of a Mr Lloyd, the magi-
strate who had been sent to explain the new laws to them'.[3] He
also wrote of another 'amateur lawyer' who advised one of the slaves
seeking a divorce from his wife who had left him for a white man.

SECTION 3:
THE RECREATIONAL PATTERNS OF THE SLAVES

(a) *Development* To break the routine of their harsh daily existence
the slaves participated in various forms of recreation whenever they
had the opportunity. These activities were sometimes sporadic and
restricted purely to the slave group; at other times, particularly
in the last decades of slavery, the holidays were seasonal and the
entire population participated.

In the early period of slavery recreation was largely sporadic,
taking place on week nights or week ends when they 'dance and sing'.
As early as the end of the seventeenth century one may detect forms

---

[1] Stewart, *op. cit.*, 1823, pp. 262–3.
[2] Madden, *A Twelve Months Residence* . . ., Vol. 2, pp. 149–50.
[3] *Ibid.*

of the merry-andrew type dances resembling the John Canoe which was to be of great significance later. Sloane wrote that:

> They have likewise in their dances Rattles ty'd to their Legs and Wrists and in their hands with which they make a noise, keeping time with one who makes a sound answering it on the mouth of an empty Gourd or Jar with his Hand. Their Dances consist in great activity and strength of Body and keeping time, if it can be. They very often tie Cows Tails to their Rumps and add such other things to their bodies in several places, as gives them a very extraordinary appearance.[1]

Leslie wrote of the 1720s that Sunday afternoons were their main times for recreation and that wrestling was the most popular sport among them, in addition, of course, to the usual vigorous dancing.[2]

It was not until the last half of the eighteenth century that the seasonal holidays began to acquire the form of national festivals. These seasonal festivals rapidly developed at the end of the eighteenth century and the beginning of the nineteenth, reaching their climax about the time Lewis visited the island. The decline began about the 1820s and by the time Bellisario published his account (1837) the John Canoe and many of the elaborate ceremonies of the late eighteenth century were both unpopular and discredited.[3] This decline was partly a reflection of the rapid collapse of the slave system: it was due partly to the disapproval of the non-conformist missionaries who were then very influential among the slaves; partly to their association with slavery and the consequent stigma which they acquired for the slave anticipating freedom.

(b) *Non-Seasonal Recreations* Sometimes these took place only on Sunday nights; at other times they would begin on Saturday night, break off early Sunday morning, and start again late Sunday afternoon.[4] Occasionally dances were held during week nights. What were known as 'Grandy Balls' were held occasionally by the 'better sort' of slaves and were visited only by those who could afford to pay for the food and musicians made available.

[1] Sloane, *op. cit.*, Introduction.   [2] Leslie, *A New History*, p. 310.
[3] There was a revival of the John Canoe in the late 19th and early twentieth century. See Beckwith, *Christmas Mummings in Jamaica*, 1925.
[4] De La Beche, *op. cit.*, p. 41.

These ordinary diversions were usually described as 'plays', a word which was used in Jamaica, as it still is in Africa, to mean dancing.[1] But sometimes plays, in the normal sense of the word, were acted by the Negroes, especially at Christmas. For many slaves and free Negroes these ordinary diversions were paying propositions to which invitations were issued in the neighbouring plantations and an entry fee charged.[2]

Long has described these dances or 'plays' as he saw them in the 1760s:

Their tunes for dancing are usually brisk, and have an agreeable compound of the Vivace and Larghetto, gay and grave, pursued alternatively. They seem also well-adapted to keep their dancers in just time and regular movements. The female dancer is all languishing and easy in her motions; the man, all action, fire, and gesture; his whole person is variously turned and writhed every moment, and his limbs agitated with such lively exertions, as serve to display before his partner the vigour and elasticity of his muscles. The lady keeps her face towards him, and puts on a modest demure look, which she counterfeits with great difficulty, in her paces she exhibits a wonderful address, particularly in the motion of her hips, and steady position of the upper part of her person: the right execution of this wriggle, keeping exact time with the music, is esteemed among them a particular excellence; and on this account they begin to practice it so early in life, that few are without it in their ordinary walking. As the dance proceeds the musician introduces now and then a pause or rest, or dwells on two or three pianissimo notes; then strikes out again on a sudden into a more spirited ear, and propriety of attitude; all which has a very pleasing effect.[3]*

Marsden gives much the same description of these dances.[4] But Moreton, Stewart, Phillippo and others describe another kind of

---

[1] See Herskovits review of Beckwith's *Black Roadways*, in the *Journal of American Folklore*, 1924.

[2] De La Beche, *op. cit.*, p. 40. As much as 5s were charged as fare to these 'plays'.

[3] Long, *op. cit.*, Vol. 2, p. 424.

[4] Marsden, *op. cit.*, pp. 33–4.

* Cf. Evans-Pritchard's 'The Dance' in *Africa*, Vol. 1, No. 4.

dance where they 'form a ring round a male and a female dancer, who perform to the music and drums and the songs of the other females of the party, one alternately going over the song, while her companions repeat in chorus . . . When two dancers have fatigued themselves, another couple enter the ring and thus the amusement continues'.[1] This seems the best moment to discuss the musical instruments used to accompany these dances.* The most popular of these instruments were the membranophones of which there were several kinds. The *gombay* (goombah) Long described as:

> A hollow block of wood, covered with sheepskin stripped of its hair. The musician holds a little stick of, about six inches in length, sharpened at one end like the blade of a knife, in each hand. With one hand he rakes it over a notched piece of wood fixed across the instrument, the whole length, and across with the other alternately using, both with a brisk motion; whilst a second performer beats with all his might on the sheep-skin, or tabor.[2]

Other types of drums were mentioned, including an ebo drum, which seemed to have been relatively large. African percussion-beams and concussion-sticks went under the general name of *cotta* in Jamaica and were made from old chairs and pieces of board.[3] There were several varieties of chordophones and Sloane was no doubt referring to different types of idiochord and heterochord zithers brought over by the African slaves when he wrote that:

> They have several sorts of instruments . . . made of small Gourds, fitted with Necks, strung with horse hairs, or the peeled stalks of climbing Plants or Withs. These instuments are sometimes made of hollowed Timber covered with Parchment or other skin wetted, having for its Neck the Strings ty'd or shorter, so as to alter their sounds.[4] Leslie was the first to speak of the 'Banjil'[5] an instrument which Long, not very long after described as a 'marry-wang'.[6] The

---

[1] Stewart, *Past and Present State*, pp. 269–70.

[2] Long, *op. cit.*, Vol. 2, pp. 423–4.   [3] C. Williams, *op. cit.* p. 26.

[4] Sir Hans Sloane, *op. cit.*, Introduction.

[5] Cassidy claims that this is the first mention of the word in the English language. See *Jamaican Talk*, p. 264.

[6] Leslie, *A New History*, p. 310, Long, *op. cit.*, Vol. 2, p. 423.

* For an exhaustive account of African musical instruments, see E. M. Von Hornbostel, 'The Ethnography of African Sound Instruments', *Africa*, Vol. 6, Nos. 2 and 3.

Banjo was quite probably a later development, partly under European influence, of the tanged lute which Sloane described. Wind instruments included the flute, one variety of which was known as the 'Caramantee-flute' which was about a yard long and was 'made from the porous branches of the trumpet-tree'.[1] Its notes were plaintive and had a haunting, beautiful air of melancholy.[2] Beckford describes another instrument, the 'bender', as:

> An instrument upon which the Whydaw Negroes . . . in particular excel. It is made of a bent stick, the ends of which are restrained in this direction by a slip of dried grass; the upper part of which is gently compressed between the lips, and to which the breath gives a soft and pleasing vibration; and the other end is graduated by a slender stick and beats upon the nerve, if I may so express it, and confines the natural acuteness of the sound, and thus together produce a trembling, a querulous and a delightful harmony.[3]

This was very likely a variety of the African musical bow.[*] Marsden, writing about the same time as Beckford, described much the same instrument, asserting that 'they used formerly to have no other'.[4] Finally, there was a variety of percussion idiophones, rattles and clappers. The most common of these was the jaw-bone of a horse; others included 'the Rookaw, which is Two Sticks jagged; and a Jenkgoving, which is a way of clapping their Hands on the Mouth of Two Jars'.[5] A nineteenth century writer tells us that during ordinary 'plays' they were accompanied by a 'kind of rattles, being small calibashes filled with the seed of a plant called by the Negroes Indian Shot'.[6]

One of the first signs of the decline in the recreational patterns of slavery was the shift from the instruments described above to more European-type instruments and music. In 1825 De La Beche spoke of the 'old school' and the 'new school' among the Negroes, stating that the former still clung to the 'goombay and African

[1] Beckford, *Account*, Vol. I, p. 217.
[2] *Ibid.*, pp. 217–18.
[3] *Ibid.*, p. 216.
[4] Marsden, *op. cit.*, 1788, p. 34.
[5] Leslie, *A New History*, p. 310.
[6] Stewart, *Account of Jamaica*, (1808), p. 261.
[*] See Von Hornbostel, *op. cit.*, p. 309.

dances', but that the latter much preferred the fiddles, reels and other music and dances of the whites. A year later Barclay wrote that African dances were being replaced by Scottish ones and the Gumbay by the fiddle. This tendency, had of course, been long prevalent among the mulatto slaves and the free people of colour.

(c) *Seasonal Festivals and Recreations*   There were, generally, four annual holidays during the latter half of slavery: Christmas, Easter or 'Picaninny Christmas', Crop-over or harvest home, and the yam festival. In the first three both freemen and slaves participated, in the last, only the Negroes. The most important of these holidays was Christmas. On most estates only three days were given – Christmas-day, Boxing-day and New Year's day. During the amelioration period, however, many more benign masters such as Lewis, gave four days, including the day after Boxing-day.

The most striking feature of the Christmas festivities, as indeed of all the other seasonal holidays, was the remarkable change that overcame the Negroes in their dress, their manner, and, most significant, their relationship with their masters which assumed the character of a kind of ritual license. Stewart wrote of this change that:

> On these occasions the slaves appear an altered race of beings. They show themselves off to the greatest advantage, by fine clothes and a profusion of trinckets; they affect a more polished behaviour and mode of speech; they address the whites with greater familiarity; they come into their masters' houses and drink with them; the distance between them appear to be annihilated for the moment, like the familiar footing on which the Roman slaves were with their masters at the feast of the Saturnalia. Pleasure throws a temporary oblivion over their cares and toils; they seem a people without the consciousness of inferiority or suffering.[1]

As if to emphasize the temporary metamorphosis of their status, there was a ritual changing of names on these occasions and the slaves all assumed what were termed their 'gala day names' which, significantly, were often those of the most prominent whites of the island: 'One is General Campbell, another is Admiral Rowley, and

[1] Stewart, *Past and Present State*, pp. 270-1.

a third is Colonel Russel, a fourth Mr Scarlett, a fifth Governor Conran, and so forth; and by these names they are generally addressed at their festive meetings'.[1]

The Christmas celebrations began early on Christmas morning when a chorus of Negroes came up to the great house and serenaded the masters with the singing of songs like 'Good morning to your night cap, and health to master and mistress'.[2] After this they all went to their grounds to get provisions for the next two or three days.[3]

On the first day it was customary only for the head Negroes and the more prominent female slaves to pay a ceremonial visit to the whites, dressed in their very best clothes and exhibiting their most valuable trinkets '... coral and coconelian necklaces, bracelets, etc...'[4]

Sometimes, however, the possession of the great house began on Christmas evening, after the bulk of the slaves had returned from their provision grounds and had dressed themselves. They then assembled on the lawn before the great house with:

... gombays, bonjaws and an ebo drum made of hollow tree, with a piece of sheepskin stretched over it. Some of the women carried small calabashes with pebbles in them, stuck on short sticks, which they rattled in time to the songs, or rather, howls of the musicians. They divided themselves into parties to dance, some before the gombays, in a ring, to perform a bolero or a sort of love-dance, as it is called, where the gentlemen occasionally wiped the perspiration off the shining faces of their black beauties, who, in turn, performed the same service to the minstrel. Others performed a sort of pyrrhic before the ebo drummer, beginning gently and gradually quickening their motions until they seemed agitated by the furies. They were all dressed in their best; some of the men in long tailed coats, one of the gombayers in old regimentals; the women in muslins and cambrics, with coloured handkerchiefs tastefully disposed round their heads, and earrings, necklaces and bracelets of all sorts in profusion. The entertainment was kept up until 9 or 10 o'clock in the evening, and during

[1] *Report of the Secret Committee at Close of Session on Late Disturbances, Jamaica,* 1824, Footnote to p. 74.
[2] Williams, *Tour through Jamaica,* p. 21.   [3] *Ibid.*
[4] J. Kelly, *Ja. in 1831 ... a Narrative of 17 years Residence,* p. 20.

that time they were regaled with punch and santa in abundance; they came occasionally and asked for porter and wine. Indeed, *a perfect equality seemed to reign among all parties;* many came and shook hands with their master and mistress, nor did the young ladies refuse this salutation any more than the gentlemen. The merriment became rather boisterous as the punch operated and *the slaves sang satirical phillippics against their master*, communicating a little free advice now and then; but they never lost sight of decorum, and at last retired, apparently quite satisfied with their saturnalia, to dance the rest of the night at their own habitations.[1]

On Boxing day the celebrations began a little after breakfast. New costumes were worn and the main attraction on this day was the John Canoe dance which will later be examined in greater detail. In addition to the John Canoe there was the usual dancing and merry-making.

On these occasions marked social distinctions between the slaves were observed. In an earlier chapter we mentioned the distinction between the Creole and African groups. Within these groups, however, further distinctions were made. First, there were the tribal divisions within the African group. On each estate each tribal group formed a party appointing its own King or Queen who wore 'a mask of the most hideous appearance and attired from head to foot in gaudy, harlequin-like apparel'.[2] The Creole slaves not only kept to themselves, but imitated the whites in their recreation, and, what is more, also had marked distinctions within their own group based largely on colour. Stewart wrote that:

> The creole Negroes affect much to copy the manners, language, etc. of the whites, those who have it in their power, have at times, their convivial parties; when they will endeavour to mimic their masters in their drinking, their songs, and their toasts; and it is curious to see with what an awkward minuteness they aim at such imitations. The author recollects having given an entertainment to a party of Negroes, who had resided together, and been in habits of intimacy for twenty years or more. After a variety of curious toasts, and some attempt to entertain each other with European songs, one who conceived himself more knowing

[1] C. Williams, op. cit., pp. 21–3.
[2] Phillippo, *op. cit.*, p. 242.

and accomplished than the rest, stood up and very gravely drank, 'Here's to our better acquaintance, gentlemen!'[1]

Beckford also noted how closer observation of the festival assemblies revealed 'a very striking discrimination' in both 'colour and features'.[2]

Sometimes the celebrations were continued the day after Boxing day, if it was free, but by then most slaves were usually too exhausted to continue and used the day instead for recovery and rest, or sometimes in making preparations for the New Year's day. On this day, which to the majority of slaves was the most festive, celebrations were centred on the towns. Long processions of slaves dressed mainly in white, their favourite colour, were to be seen walking two abreast from the plantations to the nearest main town.[3]

The John Canoe may have been indispensable on New Year's day, but there can be little doubt that during the nineteenth century the centre of attraction was the procession of Blue and Red Set-girls. This extravagant mummery was almost completely Jamaican in origin and commenced in the 1780s when an admiral of the Blue succeeded an admiral of the Red at the Kingston Station. Both of them gave balls for the local coloured beauties which subsequently led to a division in Kingston between the Reds, symbolic of the English and their supporters, and the Blues or Scots and their followers. From these early balls the festival of the Set-Girls developed and rapidly spread throughout the island.[4] The main figure among the set-girls was the 'queen' although she was sometimes accompanied by a 'king'.[5] She was dressed, like the rest of her set, in lavish and expensive costume, the making and design of which was held in great secrecy. The Queen had complete authority over her Set which she exercised with mock severity, carrying a cow-skin whip to symbolize her power.[6] In this manner the set-girls paraded the town from 10 or 11 o'clock until night during which time they were invited into the houses of the more prosperous whites to sing

---

[1] Stewart, *Account of Jamaica*, 1808, p. 266.
[2] Beckford, *Account of Jamaica*, 1709, Vol. I, pp. 391–2.
[3] M. G. Lewis, *op. cit.*, pp. 51–2.
[4] *Ibid.*, p. 53.
[5] *Ibid.*, p. 55.
[6] I. M. Belisario, *Sketches of Character ... of the Negro ... in Jamaica* (1837), No. 1.

and dance.[1] Apart from the set-girls, there were other personages in this procession, including mascots such as a woman dressed up in absurd fashion as 'Britannia'[2] (a demonstration of contempt by the 'Scots' of the Red or 'English' set-girls), and Jack-in-the-Green, covered in coco-nut leaves.[3] The order of procession varied. Lewis gave the following:

> First marched Britannia; then came a band of music; then the flag; then the Blue King and Queen – the Queen splendidly dressed in white and silver (in scorn of the opposite party, her train was borne by a little girl in red); his Majesty wore a full British Admiral's uniform, with a white satin sash, a huge cocked hat with a gilt paper crown upon top of it. These were immediately followed by 'Nelson's car' being a kind of canoe decorated with blue and silver drapery and with 'Trafalgar' written on the front of it; and the procession was closed by a long train of Blue grandees (the women dressed in uniforms of white with robes of blue muslin) all Princes, Dukes and Dutchesses, every mother's child of them.[4]

Bellisario describes a more complicated order of procession, including a commodore, adjutants bearing flags and the like. More important, he tells us that in one part of the island the slaves satirized through impersonation and mimicry, several prominent members of the white community, including the governor.[5] Songs were to be heard all during the procession. The following are two examples. First:

> There is a regiment of the 64th, we expect from home,
> From London to Scotland away they must go,
> There was one among them, that I really love well,
> With his bonny Scotch plaid, and his bayonet so shining,
> Now pray my noble King, if you really love me well,
> Disband us from slavery, and set us at large.
> *Chorus*: La la la, la la la.

---

[1] I. M. Belisario, *op. cit.* No. 1. Phillippo (pp. 243–4) condemns the turn these processions took when night fell, suggesting that the set-girls then became little more than common sex-workers and were expected to share their earnings with their mistress or whoever assisted in financing the costumes.

[2] Lewis, *op. cit.*, p. 54.   [3] Belisario, *op. cit.*,

[4] Lewis, *op. cit.*, p. 55.   [5] Belisario, *op. cit.*

Lewis heard many times the old Scottish air, 'Logie of Buchan' and another in praise of Wellington, as follows:

> *Come, rise up our gentry,*
> *And hear about Waterloo;*
> *Ladies, take your spy-glass,*
> *And attend to what we do;*
> *For one and one makes two,*
> *But one alone must be.*
> *Then singee, singee Waterloo,*
> *None so brave as he !*[1]

Belisario informs us that there was also a procession of housekeepers or the coloured mistresses of the whites; but this was a relatively staid affair. In addition to the processions, plays were usually performed by the Negroes. Several weeks before Christmas a Negro who could read was hired to teach them extracts from published European plays. *Richard the Third* was one of their favourite plays. A master wrote that on Easter Monday his estate was visited by a party from a neighbouring plantation:

> consisting of musicians and a couple of personages fantastically dressed to represent Kings or warriors; one of them wore a white mask on his face, and part of the representation had evidently some reference to the play of Richard III; for the man in the white mask exlaimed, 'A horse, a horse, my kingdom for a horse!' The piece, however, terminated by Richard killing his antagonist, and then figuring in a sword dance with him.[2]

Lewis witnessed a performance of the quarrel between Douglas and Glenalvon and the fourth act of 'The Fair Penitent' and another observer informs us that 'Pizarro was also one of their

---

[1] Lewis, *op. cit.*, pp. 56–7. The Scottish influence on these recreations was very marked. Marly recalled that the most popular song, when he observed the procession, were the following lines from the 'Woodpecker':

> *I knew by de moke dat so gracefully cull'd*
> *Abode de green ems dat a cottey was hee;*
> *And I said if dere's peace to be foun in dis world,*
> *A ha't is umble mit ope for it hee.*
> *Ebry leap was at est, and I ha'd not a soun,*
> *But de Wood pecka tappin de ollow beet tee.*
> > *Ebry leap, etc.*

Marly, *op. cit.*, p. 293.

[2] De La Beche, *op. cit.*, p. 42.

stock pieces'. Whatever the play however, it always ended 'in a combat-till-death scene between the two main characters; as soon as one dies the music strikes up and everyone joins in the victory dance.[1]

Easter, or 'picanniny Christmas', was much the same as Christmas except that there were no set-girls and celebrations were on a much less lavish scale. The crop-over celebrations usually came towards the end of August but since each estate had its own annual cycle there were different celebrations by the various estates, the Negroes in the neighbourhood taking the opportunity to attend as many of them as they could. Marly has left us the most detailed account of these recreations: 'As soon as the crop was over, the Negroes assembled in and around the boiling house, dancing and roaring for joy to the sound of the gumba'.[2] Later that same day, the celebrations were interrupted as provisions from the stores were given out by the overseer, mainly salt-fish, sugar, santa (a kind of drink) and rum. Later in the day, the overseer was visited by whites from the neighbourhood and they had a feast among themselves. Then, at early evening, a messenger was sent to call the fiddlers from the Negro village. This was the signal for the rest of the slaves who all ran to the great house, having previously regaled themselves for the occasion. 'When the fiddlers struck up the whites left the table, and on choosing their stable partners, the reels commenced'.[3] This inter-racial dancing continued until supper time when the whites retired to the dining room, leaving the hall to the slaves. 'After supper, however, the whites resumed their place in the room when country dances commenced, in which the Negro girls performed their parts extremely well'.[4] The ball then continued till early next day.

Finally, there was the yam festival. Lewis wrote that there was a general harvest of the yams each year by the Negroes but made no mention of the accompanying festivities, perhaps assuming that they were no different from the usual 'plays'. In fact, there is only one reference in the literature to the existence of this festival. In 1824, fourteen slaves from two adjoining estates were brought to trial on a charge of rebellious conspiracy. From the minutes of this

[1] Belisario, *op. cit.*, No. 2, (1838)
[2] *Marly, or the Life of a Planter in Jamaica*, p. 46.
[3] *Ibid.*, p. 47.   [4] *Ibid.*, p. 48.

trial[1] it is learned that the conspiracy was supposed to have taken place during the celebration of a yam festival. One witness stated that September was the 'time of yams'. Another, the overseer of Spring Garden estate, said:

> It has been customary for the Negroes to have a merry making at yams time – on one estate at one time, and on another at another, in common. The driver, or some of the Negroes in whom I can confide, asks my leave, and I give leave and hold that person responsible. If one asks it, there is a general play all night.[2]

One of the slaves, Richard Mowat, said that 'at yams time they generally have a dance'. And Betsy Bartibo, a free woman in close contact with the slaves, said that: 'All the Unity Hall people eat yams together, same time all over the estate. They had a dance at night, at Cunningham's house ... The Guinea Negroes played goombah too, and danced ...'[3] What is of much interest in these statements was the important role which they suggested the John Canoe played during the yam festival, one witness claiming that they were 'generally the worst characters'.[4] Before we attempt to suggest the possible implication of this link between the yam festival and the John Canoe, let us move on to a more detailed examination of this dance.

Long was the first to use the term 'John Connu'. He wrote:

> In the towns during Christmas holidays, they have several tall robust fellows dressed up in grotesque habits, and a pair of ox-horns on their head sprouting from the top of a horrid sort of vizor or mask, about which the mouth is rendered very terrific with large boar-tusks. The masquerader, carrying a wooden sword in his hand, is followed by a numerous crowd of drunken women, who dance at every door, bellowing out John Connu! with great vehemence ... In 1769, several new masks appeared; the Ebos, the Papaws, etc. having their respective Connus, male and female, who were dressed in a very laughable style.[5]

---

[1] *Report on the Trial of Fourteen Negroes on a Charge of Rebellious Conspiracy. Montego Bay, Jan. 28, 1824.* For the full account of this trial, see C.O. 137/157 which contains both the MSS and a printed copy of all 'Judicial Proceedings relative to the Trial and Punishment, of Rebels, or Alleged Rebels, in ... Jamaica since the 1st Jan. 1823, with the premoils, Informations, the Minutes of Evidence, and the final fate of the Prisoners.'
[2] *Ibid.*   [3] *Ibid.*   [4] *Ibid.*   [5] Long, *op. cit.*, Vol. 2, pp. 424–5.

While 'the whole of the John-Canoe fraternity always wears a mask'[1] the rest of their costume varied from one period to the next, as well as from one African tribe to the other. A later development was the House-John-Canoe, which Lewis described:

> The John-Canoe is a merry andrew dressed in a striped doublet and bearing upon his head a kind of paste-board house-boat, filled with puppets, representing some sailors, others soldiers, others again slaves at work on a plantation etc.[2]

Williams described a variant of this form as 'a man dressed up in a mask with a grey beard and long flowing hair, who carried the model of a house on his head. This house is called the Jonkanoo, and the bearer of it is generally chosen for his superior activity in dancing'.[3]

This dance is clearly of 'true African extraction' as a few contemporaries observed,[4] but the origin of its name is doubtful.*

From what areas of African culture, then, did the John-Canoe come? In West Africa there is the highly developed institution of the secret society. Among its basic functions is that of taking a central part in the seasonal festivals and recreations of the tribes to which they belong.[5] This is particularly the case in the rites associated with the yam harvest – taking place usually between September and October – when the gods and ancestral spirits are invoked.[6] Some secret societies such as the Wunde of Sierra Leone, appear 'to function today mainly as a dancing society'.[7] Often the secret societies hired professional bands of entertainers on important festival occasions, as for example, during the Homowo festival of the Ga.

Now we are suggesting that John-Canoe and several of the accompanying entertainments mentioned above (barring always of, course, the set-girls) were the product of a syncretism of the fragmented elements of the various recreational patterns of West African secret societies and their hired bands of entertainers.

---

[1] Belisario, *op. cit.*, No. 1.   [2] Lewis, *op. cit.*, p. 51.
[3] C. Williams, *op. cit.*, 1826, p. 25.
[4] See C. Williams, *op. cit.*, p. 26; Marly, *op. cit.*, p. 294.
[5] Butt-Thompson, *West African Secret Societies*, pp. 86–91.
[6] Parrinder, *West African Religions*, p. 120.
[7] McCulloch, *Peoples of Sierra Leone Protectorate*, p. 37.

* For a thorough discussion of the etymology of this word see F. G. Cassidy, *Jamaica Talk*, pp. 256–62.

Further, there were three clusters of recreations in West Africa which seem to have contributed more than any other to the recreational patterns of the slaves. These were: the yam festival activities of the Mmo secret society of the Ibo peoples; the recreational activities of the Eguugun secret society of the Yorubas; and the Homowo harvest festival of the Ga peoples. Let us take a closer look at each of these. The Mmo are 'ancestral spirits personated by maskers who appear in public at seasonal periods, at festivals, and at celebrations of final funeral rites'.[1] Some Mmo have certain specific functions of social control; others specialize in amusements; and others do both.

The primary annual festival of the Eguugun commemorates the ancestral ghosts of the Yoruba when sacrifices are made to them and their assistance requested in agricultural activities of the tribe. It is 'a masquerade performed by male members of the Eguugun cult in order to make visible the ancestral spirits and to command their power'.[2] The ancestors are represented by some twenty to thirty members of the Eguugun society who, in their magnificent costumes, patrol the streets for a week, to the great excitement of the onlookers.[3]

The Homowo festival of the Ga involves elaborate yam feasts and drinking and dancing in lament and remembrance of the dead. The feast is followed by a well organized procession in which novices of the society, wearing masks, take the lead. The hired band of entertainers follow the recently promoted members in the procession:

> These, headed by the barbaric noise of amateur musicians, move slowly amid the whistle and shouts and cheer of the hoarse, admiring crowds. Buffoons with weapons of bladder or cow-tail clear the way for the dancers in their motley, shaking rattles. There follow mimics and tumblers, contortionists and merry-andrews who gyrate about the road and lead an ever increasing crowd of riotous youth from the villages, who sing and clap and try to help on the fun by attempts to copy the agile antics of the professionals. Some of these latter have reputations that cause

[1] C. K. Meek, *Law and Authority in a Nigerian Tribe*, pp. 66, 69–70.
[2] P. Morton-Williams, 'Yoruba Responses to the Fear of Death'. *Africa*, Vol. XXX, No. 1.
[3] G. Parrinder, *op. cit.*, p. 123.

their services to be very expensive ... *The improvised masks seen in this section are often native caricatures of local European Officials.*[1]

It is difficult to read the above passage without being impressed by the similarity between the rites they described and those which we have earlier dealt with in relation to Jamaica. First, there is John-Canoe. We have shown earlier that while this dance functioned in all the festivities of the slaves it played a central part in their yam festivals. We may suggest, then, that the John-Canoe was originally derived either from one of the dances of West African secret societies, or from the main dance of the band of hired entertainers, or, more likely, from both these sources. Any of the African slaves who used to perform a dance with masks at any of the festivals in his homeland would utilize his skills at the festive occasions in Jamaica since there were then no longer any taboos or restrictions attached to the times and places where the mask could be worn or the accompanying dances performed.* Cassidy's etymology for John-Canoe – the Ewe word meaning sorcerer-man or witch-doctor[2] – strengthens our case when it is noted that witch-doctors were often the head of secret societies and themselves performed the main ritual dances involved.

Secondly, we may suggest that recreational patterns of the slaves such as the plays they performed and individual personages such as 'koo-koo' or 'actor-boy'[3] were partly derived from such African counterparts as those members of the Eguugun secret society who 'go first to the chief's house and then perform plays there and other places in the town'.[4] This clearly resembles what took place in Jamaica where the 'chief's house' was replaced by the house of wealthy merchants and planters.

Finally, the 'mimics and tumblers, contortionists and merry-

---

* For discussion on African masks and their functions in dance and ritual as well as their psychological significance see: L. Underwood, *Masks of West Africa*; also; L. Segy, *African Sculpture Speaks*, pp. 52–6; 82–5. Segy points out that masks are used by ancestor, initiation, magical and other cults, in war, play, and nearly always in prescribed ritual dance. To the African the mask is 'inseparable from movement, whether used in public or in rituals of a secret society. It is worn in a dance where gesture, rhythm, and singing hold significance and excitement for participants and spectators'. p. 84.

[1] Butt-Thompson, *op. cit.* pp. 94–95.
[2] Cassidy, *op. cit.*, p. 259.　　[3] See Belisario, *op. cit.*, No. 2.
[4] Parrinder, *op. cit.*, p. 123.

andrews' and others of the hired band of entertainers of Yoruba whose 'improvised masks . . . are often caricatures of local European officials' have a direct parallel in the band of musicians, entertainers and mimics who followed the John-Canoe procession and who on many occasions mimicked the local whites in Jamaica.

So far we have considered the nature of the main forms of the recreational activities of the slaves and have also suggested the possible African origins of some of them. We must now consider the problem of the social functions which these activities performed for the total structure of the slave society. From this point of view, perhaps the most striking feature of the seasonal festivals is the familiarity exhibited in the relation between masters and slaves. This temporary privileged familiarity, we suggest, constitutes one aspect of what Max Gluckman has called 'the license of ritual'.[1] To be sure, the ritual license manifested in Jamaican slave society did not attain the high level of functional integration which has been detected among many primitive peoples in which there was a complete reversal of roles indicative, on the one hand, of 'a protest against the established order', yet, on the other, 'intended to preserve and even to strengthen' this order.[2] Our analysis suggests that the Jamaican situation was an approximation to the ideal type of the 'rites of reversal'.

We may see these seasonal festivities, then, as performing an essential cathartic function within the structure of the slave society. This they did in two ways. First, they offered well needed relief from the tedium and severity of slavery and from the constant onslaught on the self-dignity and pride of the slaves. On these days they could discard the filthy oznaburg clothes and dress themselves in fine cloth and trinkets; they could drink and dance and make merry to their heart's content; and, most of all, they could re-assert in some small way their own ravished self-dignity simply by virtue of their temporary familiarity and equality with the whites. Nor were the whites entirely unaware of these functions. As one of them pointed out, 'The Negroes must have their annual display of fine clothes and suitable ornaments, if they should go in filth and raggedness all the rest of the year'.[3]

[1] M. Gluckman, *Custom and Conflict in Africa*, ('The License in Ritual'), pp. 109–36.
[2] *Ibid.* [3] Stewart, *Past and Present State*, p. 274.

Secondly, these recreations offered well needed outlets for pent up aggressions and hostilities. It is inevitable that under a system of total domination and exploitation the exploited should in some way hate their exploiters. But the slave system offered few outlets for such feelings. One of the few exceptions were their recreations. The aggression of the slaves found expression in their dancing, the violence and intensity of which was so great that death sometimes ensued. More subtle was the organized competition against each other, as for example the rival sets of girls, which safely displaced tensions against the white group in the direction of the rival set of slaves. So intense was the rivalry between these opposing parties that fights often broke out between their supporters.[1] Some of the aggression toward the master was directed against him, but in a permitted and disguised form. Thus, the mimicry and caricaturing of the whites and the satire of the songs sung on these occasions.

One objection which may be made to the functional viewpoint is the fact that in America, where one found the same stock of African slaves as in Jamaica, similar recreational patterns were not detected or nothing like as well-developed.[2] The answer to this objection goes right to the heart of the difference between the two systems of slavery. As we have repeatedly emphasized before, in America there was a white host society which was not only culturally cohesive, but, in most areas, numerically superior to the slave population. Against this background the American slave has, in some way, the usual institutional channels – not excluding recreation – through which he could find an outlet for the extreme frustrations of his status. There was, for example, his religion which developed relatively early on the basis of the nonconformist religion of his masters. The Jamaican slave, on the other hand, did not even have the institution of religion to come to his assistance for the greater part of the period of slavery. Thus the seasonal recreations became the only channel, for the release of aggressions, which approximated the status of an institution. Its relatively high development then, was itself a consequence of the non-functioning of other institutions within the fragmented and artificial social system of slavery.*

---

[1] See Belisario, *op. cit.*, No. 1.

[2] For an account of recreation during slavery in the U.S.A. see, Phillips, *American Negro Slavery*, p. 314.

* A striking functional similarity is to be found in the role of the gingaun

(d) *Folk-lore and Folk Songs:* The folk-hero of the Jamaican slaves, as of their present descendants, was Anancy, the spider-man. There is hardly any reference among contemporary writers on slavery to these folk-tales but their prevalence even today and their obvious African origins point to the fact that they must have existed during slavery. Lewis mentioned that the slaves had 'nancy tales' but he quite misunderstood the meaning of the word and the nature of the folk-hero, thinking it to refer to a girl. Some indication of the prevalence of the tales during slavery is derived from the statement of a slave who, in defending himself by promising to be a good Negro and giving up his amusements, said that he would cease to 'tell oder neger nancy stories all day long.[1]

Anancy falls into the well known folk-type of the trickster hero tales. Beckwith has given us the following portrait of him as depicted in the stories she collected:

Anancy is a little bald-headed man with a falsetto voice and a cringing manner in the presence of his superiors, who lives by his wits and treats outrageously anyone upon whom he has the chance to impose his superior cunning. He is a famous fiddler and something of a magician. In some stories he has the form of a man, in others that of a Spider, and in still others his transformation into a Spider, at the moment of supreme danger is pointed to as the explanation of spiders and their habits at the present day. He has a wife and family of children who share his exploits, notably a quick-witted son who eventually outdoes his father. The name Tachoman, said to distinguish another form of spider from the true Anancy, is supposed sometimes to be his

---

[1] Madden, *op. cit.*, Vol. 2, p. 153.

---

ritual festival among the Mossi-Dagomba tribes of the hinterland of Ghana. As in Jamaican slave society, there is a high degree of tension and lack of social cohesion 'both within and between the major communities which constitute Tale society', and the main structural function of the annual festival is to 'insulate each group from the other while at the same time uniting them in common responsibility for the welfare of the country'. Dance and festival ritual, it is further suggested, is the media selected for expressing social equilibrium in an otherwise tense and almost chaotic social order, because 'they have a compulsive power which pragmatic institutions oriented to the demands of the objective world could never have'. See M. Fortes, 'Ritual Festivals and Social Cohesion in the Hinterland of the Gold Coast', *The American Anthropologist*, Vol. 38.

wife or to be the quickwitted son, but more often to be a neigh-
bour, his accomplice in strategy and butt of his knaveries.[1]

From other collections we learn that he is also voracious, selfish
and lazy, though strong and efficient when it suits him. His cruelty
and treachery excites no remorse, and 'his only redeeming point is a
sort of hail-fellow-well-met-ness which appeals so much to his
associates that they are ready almost, if not quite, to condone his
offences'.[2]

The African origin of the Jamaican spider hero is no doubt the
Ananse of the Akan peoples who have a similar spider trickster hero.
Tacoomah, mentioned above, is derived from the Akan *ntikuma*
who is the son of the Akan folk-hero.[3] Much has been made of this
etymology by writers who wished to substantiate the untenable
argument that the Coromanti Negroes culturally dominated the rest
of the slave population. In explaining the reasons for the survival
of the Akan folk-hero rather than, say, the tortoise of the Yorubas
or the hare of the Ibos, we may throw further light on this whole
problem of African cultural survivals.

First, the spider tales survived for simple historical reasons. It
was carried over by the Akan whom, we have already seen, were the
main body of slaves first arriving on the island. As such, the spider
tales established a kind of historical priority over other West African
folk-heroes.[4]

Secondly, it seems reasonable to assert that the spider-hero of
the Akan stood a better chance of survival than any other in West
Africa because the spider figured more prominently in the folk-lore
and cosmology of these peoples than any other creature. It is known
as a folk-hero in tribes as far apart as the Temme and the Duala
and it is also the central figure of the Krachi.[5] It plays a prominent
part in the secondary funerary rites of the Chambra and is identified
with the rain-god, Chi, among the Beron of the Bauchi plateau. It
has even been suggested that 'the role played by the spider in Hausa

---

[1] M. Beckwith, *Black Roadways*; see also her *Jamaica Anancy Stories*, p. 219.
[2] W. Jekyll, *Jamaica Song and Story*, pp. 1–2, 4–5.
[3] See Williams, *Psychic Phenomena in Jamaica*, pp. 23–49; also Cassidy, *op. cit.*, pp. 275–6.
[4] A general linguistic priority was likewise established, see, Cassidy, *op. cit.*, pp. 17–21, 394, 397.
[5] P. Radin and J. J. Sweeney, *African Folktales and Sculpture*, pp. 28–30.

and other Negro folk-lore is due to an earlier association of the Spider with Ancestral ghosts'.[1]

Thirdly, the spider may have survived in Jamaica because the other animals which were also trickster-heroes in Africa were not to be found, or were rare, in Jamaica. This is true of the hare as well as the tortoise. The spider, on the other hand, is indigenous to Jamaica. This argument cannot be taken too far since many animals not found in Jamaica – Brer Lion, Brer Tiger and Brer Monkey – figure nonetheless, in the stories. Yet, the point is not to be neglected, especially when we find plots recorded by Jekyll which, as Werner pointed out in his introduction to the book, are usually associated with the tortoise in Africa, but which were retold in Jamaica with more familiar animal characters.[2]

Fourthly, the spider-hero tales survived largely because they were functionally adaptable to New World slave society. It should be noted that the spider-hero belongs to one family of African folk-tales, the animal trickster-hero, itself only a sub-family of the animal tales which, in turn, are still only 'one of several cycles of Negro tales'.[3] Now it is remarkable that despite this wealth of aboriginal folk material to choose from, the slaves both in Jamaica and the Americas selected the animal-trickster tale.

It seems plausible that the trickster-hero type tale survived, not by accident, but because it was socially and psychologically best suited to the condition of the Negro in the New World. Many students of the subject have drawn hasty and unwarranted conclusions concerning the psychological functions of these tales for the slaves. But as Herskovits remarked:

> Such tales, in their New World setting, have been spoken of as technique developed by Negroes to compensate for their impotence as slaves. Yet the presence of these tales in Africa itself forces us to regard this as at best only a partial explanation and to conclude that we are faced with an adaption and re-inforcement

---

[1] C. K. Meek, *Tribal Studies in Northern Nigeria.* The lore surrounding these religious attributes of the spider, while bearing a close relation to folk-lore proper, must be seen nonetheless, as sacred tales or myths, to be distinguished from the secular tales.

[2] Jekyll, *op. cit.*, pp. xxiv–xxv.

[3] M. J. Herskovits, 'Negro Folklore', in Ottenberg, *op. cit.*, pp. 443–57.

of African ways of thought rather than something devised to fit the new situation in which these people found themselves.[1]

Indeed, we may suggest that no aspect of West African culture was more suited to, and, as such, more easily adapted to New World slave society than the animal-trickster-hero folk tales. Let us take a closer look at the social and psychological functions of such tales in their African setting.

In West Africa story-telling is invariably a period of great license during which people are allowed to impersonate and ridicule other people and objects which ordinarily they are forbidden to do. Among the Ashanti, for example, the occasion was used for venting grievances against such things as 'the cheating and tricks of Priests, the rascality of a chief – things about which everyone knew, but concerning which one might not ordinarily speak in public'.[2] The teller protected himself by declaring the tale to be fictitious and by using the traditional folk characters instead of the real ones. Eventually, 'such a mild exposé in the guise of a story came to be related *qua* story' and so the stock of tales was built up.[3]

There is one Jamaican folk-tale which strikingly illustrates the way in which the functions and mode of construction of African story-telling were adapted to the island. Elsewhere, we noted how, during the eighteenth century the slaves made a song about a cruel master who attained notoriety for his practice of murdering his old and weak slaves by throwing them down a gulley.[4] During the nineteenth century this song became incorporated into a folk-tale, later collected by Jekyll, called *Dry Bone*.[5] In this tale Dry-Bone represented the weak old slave, Brer Anancy the cruel master and Rabbit and Guineypig, whites who generally felt encumbered by the possession of weak and useless slaves.

The identification of Anancy with the cruel master strongly suggests that the slaves did not always relate to their folk-hero simply

[1] M. J. Herskovits, 'Negro Folklore' in Ottenberg, op. cit p. 540.
[2] Rattray, *Akan-Ashanti Folktales*, p. xl. There were other forms of institutionalized outlets for grievances against one's superiors. Chiefs could be insulted at their enstoolment. There was also *bo akutia* or 'vituperation by proxy'. *Ibid.* p. xli.
[3] *Ibid.*
[4] Lewis, *op. cit.*, p. 322. See footnote 4, p. 158 above.
[5] W. Jekyll, *Jamaica Song and Story*, pp. 48–50.

on the basis of a direct identification. The relationship, instead, could be far more complex. Now from the portrait of Anancy's character given earlier, it is immediately recognized that his character traits form a kind of caricature of the Quashee traits which we have described in an earlier chapter. Anancy, then, was to some extent an object upon which the slaves displaced a great deal of their self-contempt and self-hate. Representing as he did every aspect of the personality of the slave which was undesirable, Anancy performed two basic psychological functions. First, by objectifying all the unpleasant features of Quashee, Anancy made it possible for the slave to reprimand and censor the undesirable part of himself without a sense of self-persecution. Secondly, having censored this part of himself, the slave could then find it possible to laugh at it and even learn to live with and accept it. Witness the fact that Anancy, despite all his despicable personal and social traits, always manages, in the end, to win the forgiveness and acceptance of the other characters in the tale. But by identifying Anancy with the brutal white overseer (as in the tale of Dry-Bone) the process was taken a step further. The self-hate, having been displaced on Anancy, was now deflected on the white master; a kind of dramatic irony of the subconscious. Of course, we should not neglect the simpler and more obvious explanation of a direct identification with Anancy, the small animal of great cunning and intelligence who unscrupulously outwits his more powerful neighbours.

Folk-songs Like the folk-tales, the folk-songs of the Negro slaves were easily adapted to the conditions of slavery. Although the melody of the songs was to change much in Jamaica,[1] the construction, form, and rhythm remained basically African throughout slavery, and to a lesser extent, to this day. Generally speaking, perhaps the most fundamental aspect of African song was its tendency to 'musicalize life'.[2] So it was in Jamaica that the songs of the slaves related to almost every aspect of their lives, however harsh and brutal.

The African sought refuge in his song from the very earliest moments of enslavement. The surgeon of a slave ship said that he

[1] See Appendix A and B of Jekyll, *op. cit.*, where this problem is discussed.
[2] Lubenstein, 'Racial Values in Aframerican Music', *Musical Quarterly*, Vol. 16, 1930.

often heard the Negroes singing and on asking an interpreter at Bonny what they were saying, he was told that 'they were lamenting the loss of their country and friends'.[1] When forced to sing by the Captain of one ship, the words of their song were 'Madda! Madda! Yiera! Yiera! Beinini! Madda! Anfera!', meaning that they were all sick and would soon die.[2] Another crew member said that 'they also sung songs expressive of their fears of being beat, of their want of victuals, particularly the want of their native food, and of their never returning to their own country'.

Jekyll distinguished three types of songs: Digging songs, dancing songs, and ring songs.[3] These categories no doubt held just as well during slavery although the ring songs show marked European influences by the time Jekyll made his collection. Digging songs are the work songs of the Jamaican Negro. Long remarked at the spontaneity of their songs and the alternation between solo and refrain in the singing of them. He found most of the tunes flat and melancholy and the words largely satirical, usually 'at the expense of the overseer'.[4] Edwards made the same observations but also noted that the melodies differed with the various tribes, those of the Ibos being 'soft and languishing', and the Gold Coast slaves' 'heroic and martial'.[5]

A recurring theme in most of these songs is the barbarity of the whites or some reference to their status as slaves. This is in marked contrast to the American slave songs where 'there are surprisingly few references to the servitude of the blacks in their folk-songs, which can be traced to ante-bellum days'.[6] Indeed, Fisher, from his study of the slave songs of the American Negro came to the view 'through the medium of songs, that the slaves were dutiful, obedient, and well adjusted to their lot'.[7]

The following are some examples of the slave theme in the songs of the slaves.

---

[1] Evidence of Falconbridge, Select Committee on Slave Trade, 1790–91.
[2] Evidence of James Town, Select Committee on Slave Trade, 1790–91.
[3] Jekyll, *op. cit.*, pp. 157–8.
[4] Long, *op. cit.*, Vol. 2, p. 423.
[5] Edwards, *op. cit.*, Vol. 2, p. 103.
[6] Krehbiel, *Afro-American Folksongs*, p. 13.
[7] M. M. Fisher, *Negro Slave Songs in the United States*, p. IX.

Song A

Tink dere is a God in a top,
No use me ill, Obisha. (i.e. overseer)
Me no horse, me no mare, me no mule,
No use me ill, obisha.[1]

Song B

If me want for go in a Ebo,
Me cant go there!
Since them tief me from a Guinea,
Me cant go there!

If me want for go in a Congo,
Me cant go there!
Since them tief me from my tatta,
Me cant go there!

If me want for go in a Kingston,
Me cant go there!
Since massa go in a England,
Me cant go there![2]

Lewis says of the slave songs that 'they seem, as far as I can make out, to relate entirely to their own private situation, and to have nothing to do with the Negro state in general'.[3] But Lewis' own evidence flatly contradicts him. He tells us, for example, of the way in which the slaves sung all night about the dismissal of an overseer they detested.[4] Perhaps Lewis failed to recognize some of the oblique references to their status in the songs he himself recorded. Immediately after the remark quoted above, he records a song entitled 'We very well off', sung by the Negroes in praise of his kindness to them; yet the second of the two verses went as follows:

Hey-ho-day! neger now quite eerie (hearty)
For once me see massa – hey-ho-day!

[1] Moreton, *Manners and Customs*, p. 153.
[2] *Ibid.*
[3] Lewis, *op. cit.*, p. 233.
[4] Marly informs us that, on the dismissal of the overseer by the Attorney the Negroes sung all afternoon the following song: 'Massa turn poor buckra away oh! But massa can't turn poor neger away oh!', Marly, *op. cit.*, p. 145.

> *When massa go, me no care a dammee,*
> (For how them usy me) – *hey-ho-day !*[1]

Thus even in their exultation of a kind master, the slaves could not resist referring to the brutality of the overseer which was their usual lot. Cooper heard a party of old women, boys and girls singing the following:

> *O massa ! O massa ! One Monday morning*
>   *they lay me down,*
> *And give me thirty-nine on my bare rump,*
> *O massa, O massa !*[2]

On each estate there were one or two slaves who specialized in improvising songs which 'had usually a ludicrous reference to the white people and were generally suggested by some recent occurrence'.[3] The following two songs were recorded by Phillippo:

> *Song A*[3]
> Sarragree kill de captain,
> O dear, he must die;
> New rum kill de sailor,
> O dear he must die;
> Hard work kill de neger,
> O dear, he must die.
> La, la, la, la, etc.

> *Song B*[4]
> One, Two, three,
> All de same,
> Black, White, Brown,
> All de same,
> All de same,
> One, two, three, etc.

The insistent reference to slavery and their oppressed condition in the songs of the Jamaican slaves and their relative absence in those of the slaves of the United States would certainly indicate a

---

[1] Lewis, *op. cit.*   [2] Cooper, *op. cit.*, p. 18.
[3] Phillippo, *op. cit.*, p. 189.   [4] *Ibid.*, p. 190.

greater lack of adjustment and a greater sense of injustice and persecution on the part of the Jamaican slaves.

The dancing and ring tunes were much the same in content.
Sloane was the first to record some of them. It is interesting to
note that at the time he was writing (late seventeenth century) songs
were still being sung by the slaves in African languages. He recorded
three tunes from Angola, Papaw and 'Koromanti'. Words were given
for the first and last. The Angolan song went: 'Hobaognion Haba-
ognion Hoba Hobaognion ognion'. And the Koromanti: 'Meri
Bonbo mich langa meri walanga'.[1] The tone of the dancing songs
apparently differed from those of the digging-songs but the content
remained much the same.[2] The following are three examples of
dancing and ring songs:

Song A

Hipjaw! my deaa! you no do like a me!
You no jig like a me! you no twist like a me!
Hipjaw! my deaa! you no shake like a me!
You no wind like a me! Go yondaa!
Hipjaw! my deaa! you no jig like a me!
You no work him like a me! you no sweet him like a me!

Song B

Tajo, tajo, tajo! tajo, my mackey massa!
O! land, O! tajo, tajo, tajo!
You work him, mackey massa!
You sweet me, mackey massa!
A little more, my mackey massa!

Tajo, tajo, etc.
O! land, etc.
I'll please my mackey massa!
I'll jig to mackey massa!
I'll sweet my mackey massa![3]

The third song is that of a wife whose husband had been 'obeahed'
by another woman because he had rejected her advances:

[1] Sloane, *op. cit.*, introduction.
[2] Edwards, *op. cit.*, Vol. 2, p. 103.
[3] J. B. Moreton, *Manners and Customs*, pp. 156-7.

Song C
Me take my cutacoo (a matting basket)
And follow him to Lucea.
And all for love of my bonny man-O
My bonny man come home, come home!
Doctor no do you good.

When neger fall into neger hands,
Buckra doctor no do him good more.
Come home, my gold ring, come home![1]

Generally speaking, one finds in these songs certain of the basic elements of African musical form and style. First, there is the element of group singing taking the antiphonal or bobbin form which, as a musicologist described it in the 1920s, 'consists in a short refrain taken by one group every now and then, while the rest of the singers follow the leader except when he introduces a new and telling verse to the delight of the participants . . . The repetition of single short musical phrases with the same words is also African'.[2]

The other three basic elements of African music (which also characterize Jamaican folk music) Lubenstein has commented on as follows:

The music is first of all, *occasional*, life rendered vocal, having to do with a wide range of subjects, small and great, as life itself.* This helps to explain why the music is *improvisatory* in character and when a chorus lends its support, or when there is more than one improviser, it assumes *a communal* origin and significance.[3]

He then goes on to show how these three elements, in addition to that of antiphonality, form the basis of the folk-songs of the American Negro. We only have to glance over our own references on

---

[1] Lewis, *op. cit.*, p. 253.
[2] H. H. Roberts, 'Possible Survivals of African Song in Jamaica', in, *The Musical Quarterly*, Vol. 12, 1926.
[3] Lubenstein, *op. cit.*
* Note that both in Jamaica and Africa songs which began by relating some particular incident later lose their meaning, the words then simply forming a basis for the melody. See, Evans-Pritchard, 'The Dance', *Africa*, Vol. 1, No. 4.

the subject to see that these elements were also basic to the folk-songs of the Jamaican Negro, both during slavery and for long afterwards. In the verbal content of their songs, however, and in their social significance, there were marked differences, as we have already indicated.

CHAPTER IX

The Mechanisms of Resistance to Slavery

DESPITE the rigours and severity of slavery, despite the all-embracing nature of the exploitation by the master of his slave and the totality of his domination over him, the latter, nonetheless, was never completely subdued. In one form or another the slave expressed his resentment of his lot, sometimes in a covert, indirect and relatively mild manner, at other times in direct revolt against the object of his oppression. This chapter will attempt to examine the various techniques used by the slave in resisting the total power assumed by the master over him; it will also explore the extent to which such techniques were used and the factors accounting for their success or failure.

There is, however, a more general problem which the subject at issue poses. If – as the former chapters have demonstrated – the authority of the master was so complete, and if the means for exercising this authority were so severe, whence arose the spirit of rebellion in the slave? The ensuing analysis will attempt to give several sociological explanations related to the specific historical situation with which we are concerned. But sociological explanations can only partly explain the persistence of this spirit of rebellion. The ultimate answer to the question we have posed lies – strictly speaking – outside the framework of the sociologist, and, as such, will only be briefly dealt with at the end of this chapter.

There were two basic forms of resistance to slavery, one passive, the other violent. Passive resistance may be further sub-divided into four types: refusal to work, general inefficiency and deliberate laziness or evasion; satire; running away; suicide. Violent resistance may also be divided into two sub-categories: individual violence and collective violence.

PART I

PASSIVE RESISTANCE

(a) *Refusal to Work etc.* The inefficiency of slave labour was recognized by all but the most naïvely pro-slavery of writers.[1] The laziness of the slave, as we have pointed out in an earlier chapter, was notorious. As Adam Smith commented, 'a person who can acquire no property can have no other interest than to eat as much, and to labour as little as possible'.[2]

Sometimes this type of resistance was more extreme and manifested itself in an outright refusal to work. Quite often this refusal appeared to have been almost gratuitous. An entire group of slaves would suddenly decide that they had, for the moment, reached the limit of their endurance and could only be induced to start working again by the application of severe punishment.[3] The most popular form of passive resistance, however, was evasion of work under various pretences, the most common of which was illness. Several writers observed that many slaves went to the extreme lengths of injuring themselves either by re-opening old sores or allowing the 'chigga' worms in their feet to remain there, thus making them limp.[4] Another form of evasion, which had the added function of embarrassing the white supervisor, was the frequency with which permission was asked to 'go a bush' so as to perform basic bodily functions.[5] Women also exploited every opportunity which their feminine complaints offered them. While, for example, long weaning may have been partly a survival of African birth customs, there can be little doubt that it was also prolonged so as to lengthen the time away from work.

(b) *Satire* This form of resistance, the most innocent, but in many ways the most satisfying, has already been discussed in Chapter 8 and needs no further elaboration here.

---

[1] See Adam Smith, *The Wealth of Nations*, pp. 365–6. (Cannan, ed.).
[2] *Ibid.* See also Lewis, *op. cit.*, p. 101.
[3] See the *Jamaica Journal*, Vol. 1, No. 42.
[4] See E. Long, *op. cit.*, Vol. 2, Bk. 3, p. 415; also Lewis, *op. cit.*, p. 204.
[5] Marly, *op. cit.*, pp. 50–51.

(c) *Running away* To run away or 'to pull foot' – to use the jargon of the slaves – was very common throughout the period of slavery, but particularly so during the period before 1740. After this, the existence of the Maroons who had a vested interest in (and were bound by treaty) returning runaways to their masters made this avenue of escape somewhat precarious.[1] A distinction was drawn in the laws between rebellion and running away. The Slave Act of 1696 defined any slave, resident in the island for more than three years, who absconded for less than twelve months as a runaway punishable by severe flogging;[2] and one who absconded from his master for more than twelve months as a rebel, punishable by death or transportation. Slaves who had been imported less than three years before their offence were less severely dealt with.[3] The following table gives an account of runaways in the work-houses of Jamaica in 1794 and 1813.

TABLE I: SLAVES IN THE WORK-HOUSES OF JAMAICA: 1794 & 1813[4]

	Creoles			Africans			Unclassified	
Year	M+	F+	Total	M+	F+	Total		Total
1794	212	56	268	713	94	807	—	1,075
1813	443	177	620	657	167	824	16	1,460

M+ = Males   F+ = Females

It should be noted that the above figures state only the runaways caught. According to Gardner there were, in 1818, 'a total of 2,555 slaves reported to be at large' which would suggest that the total number was almost twice as much as those captured.[5] The figures of Table 1 reveal that the majority of the runaways were Africans. Most of these Africans were described as 'newly arrived'. The

[1] See discussion of Maroons below.
[2] *Acts of the Assembly of Jamaica*, 1691–1737.
[3] *Ibid.*
[4] Calculated from *The Royal Gazette*, 1794 and 1813, in, C.O. 142/1; 2; 3.
[5] Gardner, *History of Jamaica*, p. 254.

difference between the creole and African figures are even more striking when it is realized that by 1794 the creoles outnumbered the Africans by about 4 to 1. Male slaves tended to run away far more than females – obviously, because they were better able to bear the vicissitudes of such an undertaking. Slaves of both sexes tended to hide themselves away on other estates with their lovers.[1] Occasionally a couple would run off together as Prince and Dove did in October 1788.[2] Most of these runaways were described as 'a sly artful fellow' or 'a likely fellow' and it was frequently warned that the culprit would try to 'pass himself off as a freeman'. No doubt the slave Halifax well deserved his description as 'a very artful fellow' for on meeting a party sent out to search for him he boldly produced a false ticket of freedom, then audaciously joined the party in search of himself.[3]

Running away, however, was obviously something 'very artful'. The consequences for newly arrived Africans unacquainted with the country or even creole slaves who lacked the right contacts in other places or the 'art' of deceit, could be disastrous.[4] There is evidence too, that the Maroon Negroes who earned part of their income by capturing runaways sometimes treated their captives quite severely.[5] Quite a few slaves ran away to the neighbouring islands of Hispaniola and Cuba. In 1699 twenty slaves ran off to Cuba in a canoe and successfully appealed to a Spanish law of 1680–82 whereby the Spanish crown protec:ed refugees on its soil.[6] Runaways to Haiti showed a marked increase after the successful slave revolt there at the end of the eighteenth century. One slave, who had returned to the island after running away with a party of eight reported that they were often tempted by Haitian seamen to desert the island and that he saw 'from thirty to forty' Jamaican runaways in Haiti.[7]

Finally, it should be noted that despite the presence of the

---

[1] For example, Slave Venus, advertised in *The Royal Gazette*, No. 18, 1792.
[2] *The Jamaica Gazatte*, No. 81.
[3] *The Royal Gazette*, No. 18, 1792.
[4] For example, the case of the newly arrived African couple taken up on Cabbage Valley estate; *ibid.*
[5] Slave Cyrus, for example was 'very badly chopped by the Maroon party who took him up'. Spanish Town Workhouse, 22/5/1794 – C.O. 142/1.
[6] Beeston to Whitehall, C.O. 138/9.
[7] *Report of a Committee of the . . . House . . . Jamaica*, 1818, App. F.

Maroons many slaves did succeed in running away permanently to the mountains and establish runaway villages. In 1818 'a considerable number' of the 2,555 runaways had settled in villages situated in the hills between Kingston and Old Harbour Bay under a leader called Scipio and often 'descended into the plains to steal cattle and whatever else came handy'.[1] Typical of these runaway villages was that of 'Me-no-sen-You-no-Come' in Trelawney parish which had houses that 'were well built, shingled and floored' and a population of nine men, eight women and four children: the slaves who founded the village had run away in 1812, and in 1824, after an incident in which two whites were shot, six companies of the militia and a party of Maroons amounting in all to 270 armed men, attacked and routed the village.[2]

One curious feature of Jamaican slave society which may be added, was the custom whereby a runaway slave who wished to return to his master asked a neighbouring overseer or slave-owner to plead with his own master on his behalf. Apparently such requests were not infrequently granted and on such occasions the slave 'never fails to obtain the pardon required.'[3]

(d) *Suicide* This, the most extreme form of passive resistance, we have already touched upon in previous chapters. As in the case of runaways, suicide was largely restricted to the African group of slaves. Ibo slaves[4] and those from Angola[5] had a reputation for suicide among the planters because of their timidity, but the evidence suggests that the highly desired Gold Coast slaves had an even greater record of suicide for the very opposite reason, namely, their intractability and stubborn refusal to accept their status as slaves. Dr Harrison, who lived in Jamaica between 1755 and 1765, mentioned two instances 'out of a great many'.[6] William Fitzmaurice, in Jamaica between 1771 and 1788, said that hanging and dirt-eating were the most common forms of suicide:

I lost in one year a dozen new Negroes by dirt eating though

---

[1] Gardner, *op. cit.*, p. 254.
[2] *Account of a Shooting Excursion on the Mts. near Dromily Estate*, Oct. 1824.
[3] See Barclay, *A Practical View*, p. 8; Lewis, *op. cit.*, p. 115.
[4] B. Edwards, *op. cit.*, Vol. 2, p. 89.
[5] Sir H. Sloane, *op. cit.*, introduction.
[6] Evidence of, 1790–91, Select Committee on Slave Trade.

I fed them well – when I remonstrated with them, they constantly told me, that they preferred dying to living; and a great proportion of the new Negroes who go upon sugar plantations, die in this manner.[1]

We have already (in Chapter 7) shown how the belief in a return to Guinea after death induced many to commit suicide which, according to Phillippo, was 'awfully prevalent'.[2] Mass suicides were not uncommon, particularly among slaves from Ghana. A large number of the slaves involved in the unsuccessful slave rebellion of 1760 (mentioned below) committed mass suicide in the woods, sometimes in bodies as large as twenty-five of them.[3] And Henry Coor told the Select Committee of 1790 of fourteen slaves 'who ran away into the woods, and cut their throats together', adding, 'I could relate several other instances'.

PART II

VIOLENT RESISTANCE

(a) *Individual Violence* The legal penalty for a slave 'imagining the death' of a white person or threatening to injure him in any way, except in the defence of his master's property, was death.[4] Despite the severity of this law and the barbarous manner in which it was executed (usually the culprit was burned to death) the incidences of masters dying at the hands of their slaves were not uncommon.[5] The means usually employed for exacting vengeance on the master was poisoning. At this the slaves were extremely expert, especially the African obeah-man from whom most of the poison originally came.[6] Long gives a detailed account of the numerous herbs known to and used by the Negroes, with an impact which could be varied for different lengths of time after application.[7]

---

[1] *Ibid.*
[2] Phillippo, *op. cit.*, pp. 252–3.
[3] See below.
[4] See Chapter on Slave laws.
[5] For example, in Dec. 1775, five slaves were found guilty of beating their master to death. See *Scots Magazine*, Vol. 37, 1775. For other examples, see Marly, *op. cit.*, pp. 225–9; The *Jamaica Journal*, Vol. 2, No. 2. (1824.)
[6] See section on Obeah in Chapter 7.
[7] E. Long, *op. cit.*, Vol. 2, pp. 418–20.

Lewis, who thought that poisoning was the Negroes' greatest vice, cited the following cases:

> A neighbouring gentleman, as I hear, has now three Negroes in prison, all domestics, and one of them grown grey in his service, for poisoning him with corrosive sublimate; his brother was actually killed by similar means . . . Another agent, who appears to be in high favour with the Negroes, whom he now governs, was obliged to quit an estate, from the frequent attempts to poison him; and a person against whom there is no sort of charge alleged for tyranny, after being brought to the doors of death by a cup of coffee, only escaped a second time by his civility, in giving the beverage, prepared for himself, to two young book-keepers, to both of whom it proved fatal.[1]

(b) *Collective Violence* Rebellion, or the threat of it, was an almost permanent feature of Jamaican slave society. A distinction may be made between three types of rebellions in the island. First, there were the purely spontaneous revolts. These were usually hastily conceived affairs restricted to either one estate or to a few neighbouring properties. The immediate occasion of such revolts varied – sometimes it was out of a desire for vengeance, as in the rebellion of 1798; at other times the immediate instigation may simply have come from a favourable opportunity offering itself, as when Captain Duck's estate was cut off from neighbouring whites by the flooding of a river;[2] but in the majority of cases simply out of a desire to escape the terrors of slavery. Secondly, there were planned revolts involving or meant to involve either all the slaves in the island (as in the rebellion of 1831–32) or restricted to one particular group of slaves throughout the island who planned, after the overthrow of the whites, to rule the island themselves, for example, the Coromantee rebellions of 1760 and 1765. The third type of rebellion sometimes developed independently, but more often grew out of the remnants of the first two. These were the revolts involving mainly slaves who had already absconded and who lived in rebel hideouts.

---

[1] Lewis, *op. cit.*, p. 149.
[2] H. Barham, *The Most Correct and Particular Account of the Island of Jamaica, from the time of the Spaniards first Discovery and Settling upon it, 1722*: B.M. Sloane MS. 3918.

The most famous of these revolts was the first Maroon war which lasted for fifteen years beginning about 1725.

In order to demonstrate the frequency of these revolts and the serious and continuous threat which they posed to the very existence of the slave régime, we shall give a summary review of all the revolts that took place in the island between 1655 and 1832. Two basic periods may be distinguished – that between 1655 and 1740 and that after this date. Before 1740 the rebellions tended to have one element in common: they led to the emergence of the Maroons as an independent group within the society and their final legal recognition as freemen by the whites in the treaties of 1738 and 1740. After 1740 with this group already established, a careful distinction has to be drawn between the rebel slaves and the Maroons, the latter, by the terms of their treaty, being opposed to the interests of the former.

1655–1670 During this time the whites were mainly engaged with the ex-slaves of the Spaniards who, at the date of the capture, numbered about 1,500.[1] A section of them, about 150 in number, under their leader Juan de Bolas, was eventually induced to surrender under the condition of pardon,[2] but the remainder, known as the 'Carmahaly' Negroes, continued to plunder, murder and generally harrass the whites until about 1670 – their number being about forty – when they retreated to the north-eastern section of the island and for the next thirty years remained relatively secluded.[3]

1673 The first serious rebellion of the English Negroes took place in this year. Three hundred slaves, mainly from the Gold Coast, murdered their master and thirteen other whites in St Ann's parish then fled to the interior, different sections of them settling in various parishes to the south-centre of the island, 'from whence they never were dislodged'.[4] These rebels formed the nucleus of what later became known as the leeward band of Maroons.

[1] Sedgwick to Whitehall, C.O. 1/14.
[2] C.S.P. 1661–68, No. 411; also census of Jamaica in Journal of the House of Assembly, Vol. I, Appendix.
[3] See C.O. 138/1; also C.S.P. 1661–68, No. 1038; also Barham. MS History, *op. cit.*
[4] Anon. Account of the origins of the Maroons and the first Maroon war, in C. E. Long Papers, B.M. MS 12431.

1678 All the slaves on Captain Duck's estate in St Catherine revolted, killed their mistress and seriously wounded their master. A few were killed and others captured, but the majority escaped to the woods.[1]

1685–1686: Several rebellions – possibly linked together – took place during these years. In August 1685 one hundred and fifty slaves on Grey's estate revolted, seizing all the available arms and killing several whites. Seven of them were killed, thirty captured and fifty later surrendered. Although posses were sent after the rest there is no evidence that they were ever captured.[2] In 1686 Governor Molesworth wrote to the Lords that the rebels in the island were 'now more formidable than ever'. The rebels here referred to had their origin in the survivors of a slave ship containing mainly Madagascar Negroes which had been wrecked on the island about 1670. In 1686 they were divided into two or three villages and numbered between forty and one hundred.[3]

1690 In this year four hundred slaves, almost all from the Gold Coast, on Sutton's estate in Clarendon killed their overseer, fired the plantation, and fled to the interior of the parish. Later seventy of them, mainly women and children, surrendered, but the Governor still feared that 'so many of them remained that they will be very dangerous to the mountain plantations'.[4] Most of these rebels united with those who had previously fled to the hills in the leeward part of the island. Not long after this another group of slaves revolted in St Elizabeth parish, where they killed the wife of their master and her children then fled to the mountains and joined 'the great gang' of leeward rebels.[5]

1700–1722 Hardly a year passed during this period without some conflict between the whites and rebel slaves, although it should be pointed out that most of the trouble came from slaves already in

[1] Barham, *op. cit.*
[2] C.O. 138/5, f. 87.
[3] C.S.P. 1685–88, No. 560; No. 869; No. 445; No. 623, No. 883.
[4] Inchiquin to the Board of Trade, C.O. 138/7; or C.S.P. 1689–92, No. 1041; Barham's account, *op. cit.*, f. 152 seems to have been based largely on this letter.
[5] Anon. *Account*, C.E Long Papers, *op. cit.*

revolt rather than from new uprisings. The eighteenth century opened with an eruption of the small group of Spanish Negroes and their descendants who now began to entice rebel slaves to their village.[1] Beckford wrote in 1702 that the rebels 'have mightily increased in numbers these twelve months past' and expressed the view that if some serious measures were not taken the settlers to the north-east or windward section of the island might have to abandon their estates.[2] By now the main body of the windward rebels had risen to three hundred and in another letter to the Board of Trade Beckford wrote that 'I take this thing to be of as much consequence as any I can think of at present'.[3] In July 1704 forty Gold Coast Negroes rebelled, attacked several places, burned one house, wounded a white, then fled to the hills, leaving the Governor and white population in more apprehension 'of some bloody design from them than any other enemy'.[4] Not long after this another twenty Negroes revolted in the north-eastern section of the island, killed three or four whites and retreated to the hills.[5] Between 1705 and 1720 a large body of slaves absconded from Dan's Valley and formed a rebel village to the leeward of the island not far from the main group of Coromantee rebels. After several conflicts between them, the two groups were finally amalgamated into one great band.[6] An historian writing in 1722 claimed that in that year rebellions were taking place all over the island.[7] It was about this time that the whites attempted to make substantial settlements in the north-eastern section of the island, thus cutting off the rebels there from their vital communication with the sea coast. The latter responded by plundering the white settlers on a large scale – 'murders were daily committed, plantations burnt and deserted, every person settled near the mountains in dread of the Rebels and of mutinies in their own Plantations'.[8] Thus began the first Maroon war.

1725–1740 For fifteen years the whites waged an all-out campaign against the two bodies of insurgents in their interior – who by now were generally designated Maroons – but particularly those to the

---

[1] *Ibid.*   [2] C.S.P. 1702, No. 912.   [3] *Ibid.*
[4] Handasyd to Board of Trade, C.S.P. 1704–5, No. 484.
[5] Barham, *op. cit.*
[6] Anon, *Account*, C. E. Long Papers, *op. cit.*
[7] Barham, *op. cit.*   [8] Anon, *Account*, C. E. Long Papers, *op. cit.*

north-east of the island. Together, they 'amounted to some thousands' in the mid-1720s. In 1730, when conditions really became critical for the whites, the Governor told the Assembly that their frontiers 'are no longer in any Sort of Security (and) must be deserted'.[1] Despite the assistance of two British regiments, the Governor had to report in 1732 of the grave danger the island was in, 'all former attempts against these slaves having been either unsuccessful, or to very little purpose'.[2] In 1734 a planter wrote home that the rebels 'openly appear in Arms and are daily Increasing'.[3] These increases came mainly from among the slaves of the plantations who had begun to desert in great numbers after 1730.[4] Between 1730 and 1734 the whites had spent £100,000 in attempting to suppress the rebellion 'and no benefit received or relief had'.[5] The rebels instead had completely shaken the morale of the whites; by December 1733 one planter wrote to England that 'we are in terrible Circumstances in respect to the rebellious Negroes, they gett the better of all our partys, and our Men are quite dispirited and dare not look them in the face in Open ground or in Equal Numbers'.[6] The rebels were spread all over the island: there was the most aggressive Windward group to the north-east of the island, their two main towns, Nanny and Guy's having three-hundred and two-hundred armed men respectively not including women and children;[7] there was the leeward band under Cudjoe; and there was a third group, formed during the war, in Hanover parish to the north-west of the island.[8]

Eventually, in 1739 the whites were obliged to seek peace with the rebels. They first negotiated a treaty with Cudjoe whose group had played only a secondary part in the war.[9] The rebels were given their freedom and the right to 15,000 acres of land. The other important points of the treaty were Cudjoe's agreement to fight with

[1] Report of Address to Assembly in *The Weekly Ja. Courant*, No. 688, in C.O. 137/18; or see Journals of House, Vol. 2, p. 708.
[2] Hunter to Board of Trade, C.O. 137/18, f. 78. See also, C.O. 137/20, f. 40.
[3] Extract of a letter from Jamaica, C.O. 137/21, f. 57.
[4] C.O. 137/20, f. 67; f. 47; f. 54; also, C.O. 137/21, f. 11.
[5] Ayscough to Board of Trade, C.O. 137/21, ff. 174–5.
[6] A paragraph in a letter from Ja.: *Ibid.* f. 11.
[7] 'The further Examination of Sarra, alias Ned'; C.O. 137/21, f. 42.
[8] C.O. 137/21.
[9] For a copy of this Treaty, see: *Journal of the House of Assembly*, Vol. 3, p. 458.

the whites against the more stubborn Windward rebels in the event that they did not accept the treaty, and also to return all runaways who fell into his hands in future, a reward being granted for such activities. A year later, the Windward body of rebels, under their leader, Quao, signed a slightly less favourable treaty.

There was immediate general dissatisfaction throughout the slave population at the news of the treaty, the main reason being concern over the fact that the only real avenue of escape from slavery – desertion to the hills – was now cut off. Numerous conspiracies were plotted and some were on the verge of breaking out when the whites discovered and crushed them.[1]

1760 This rebellion, which lasted between April and September, was planned in great secrecy among the Coromantee slaves throughout the island who aimed at 'a total massacre of the whites and to make the island a Negro colony'.[2] Well over a thousand slaves were involved[3] and for months they burned, killed and spread terror but the whites eventually managed to subdue them. After their leader, Tackey, was killed, many of them committed mass suicide rather than allow themselves to be re-enslaved.[4] During the course of the rebellion sixty whites were killed and between three-hundred and four-hundred slaves were either killed or committed suicide. The planters obtained their vengeance afterwards, at least six hundred slaves being either executed or transported. According to Long, 'the whole loss sustained by the country, in ruined buildings, cane pieces, cattle, slaves and disbursements, was at least £100,000, to speak within compass'.[5]

1765–1784 In 1765 a planned revolt, again mainly involving Gold Coast slaves, broke out prematurely on seventeen estates. The unpreparedness of the rebels made their subjection by the whites relatively easy; thirteen of them were executed and thirty-three transported.[6] The next year the Coromantees struck again, killing

[1] Anon. *Account*, C. E. Long Papers, *op. cit.*
[2] *Scot's Magazine*, Vol. 22, p. 441.
[3] *Ibid.*
[4] Long, *op. cit.*, Vol. 2, pp. 447–62; also, Letter of H. Moore, C.O. 137/60, f. 294.
[5] Long, *op. cit.*, Vol. 2, p. 462.
[6] *Ibid.*, pp. 465–70.

nineteen whites in Westmoreland, but were soon subdued.[1] Then in 1769 a woman betrayed a plot to burn the city of Kingston and kill all its inhabitants; 'a large body of men were seized in consequence'.[2] Another revolt took place in 1776 in the parishes of Hanover and St James resulting in the execution of thirty slaves and great alarm among the whites.[3] The very next year 'an alarming insurrection' was discovered, involving a large number of slaves who had taken a blood oath to massacre all the whites. Those involved were either burned alive, gibbetted, hanged or transported.[4] Another plot was discovered in 1784, again involving mainly Gold Coast Negroes.[5]

1784–1832 In 1795 the second Maroon war broke out between one section of the Maroon Negroes and the whites, but since this was not, strictly speaking, a servile war, we may pass over it.[6] In 1798 about forty-three slaves formed themselves into a banditi camp and for months created terror among the white population. They were eventually dispersed, although there is no evidence that the whites brought any of them to justice.[7] Toward the end of 1806 a conspiracy was discovered in St George's parish but the whites seemed to have made more of it than it deserved.[8] In 1808, thirty-three Coromantee and Chamba slaves who had been recruited to the West Indian regiment mutinied and killed two of their officers while being drilled; half of them were killed in action and another nine executed.[9] Another conspiracy was discovered in 1815 in which 250 Ibo slaves were supposed to have been involved, but Lewis, who reported the incident, may have been misinformed, as only two slaves were finally executed.[10]

[1] Long, *op cit.*, Vol, 2 p. 471; also Hope Elletson Papers; Oct. 18, 1766 in *Ja. Historical Review*, Vol. 1, No. 3; also *ibid.*, Vol. 2, No. 1, pp. 51–6.

[2] Gardner, *op. cit.*, p. 142.

[3] *Ibid.*, p. 145. Also, Sir Basil Keith to Board of Trade, 2/8/1766; C.O. 138/27.

[4] *Scot's Magazine*, 1777, Vol. 39, p. 449.

[5] *Ibid.*, 1784, Vol. 46, pp. 544–5.

[6] See. B. Edwards, *Proceedings ... Re ... The Maroon War ...*; R. C. Dallas, *The Maroons*, 2 Vols.

[7] Dallas, *Ibid.*, Vol. 2, pp. 293–7.

[8] Gardner, *op. cit.*, pp. 243–4.

[9] *Ibid.*, p. 245.

[10] Lewis, *op. cit.*, p. 237.

Between 1823 and 1824 three conspiracies were discovered, lead-ing almost to panic among the whites. In only one case, however, was there any overt act of violence, that of the Hanover conspiracy, the leader of which, an Ibo, committed suicide when the conspiracy collapsed.[1] The fear of revolt among the slaves had reached such a stage by this time that on several occasions large bodies of militia-men and soldiers went out against imaginary revolts, or as a local pro-slavery newspaper described one of them, on 'a complete wild goose chase'.[2]

The last and most ambitious of all the slave rebellions of the island broke out two days after Christmas 1831, and although it lasted for less than two weeks was the most damaging to the property of the whites and to the institution of slavery. Several thousand slaves – a rough estimate, about 20,000 with a much larger number of sympathisers – were involved; 207 of whom were killed in action and well over 500 executed.[3] Although only fourteen white lives were lost[4] the damage to property was very great – £1,132,440 12s. 6d worth being destroyed and over £161,570 0s. 0d spent on sup-pressing the revolt.[5] More important is the fact that the news of the rebellion strengthened the hand of the abolitionists in England and led to a marked change of attitude on the part of the British government to the whole question of slavery.[6]

The General Causes of Jamaican Slave Revolts

It is clear from the above review that, with the possible exception of Brazil, no other slave society in the New World experienced such continuous and intense servile revolts. During the seventeenth and eighteenth centuries the slaves of Barbados and the Leeward Islands were remarkably docile compared with those of Jamaica, only two mild disturbances taking place in all the latter islands during this time.[7] Aptheker 'found records of approximately 250 revolts and

[1] See copy of all Judicial Proceedings relative to the Trial and Punishment of Rebels ... in ... Ja ... since 1st Jan. 1823 with Previous Informations, the Minutes of Evidence, and the final fate of the Prisoners, in, C.O. 137/157.

[2] The *Jamaica Journal*, Vol. 1, No. 39, Jan. 10, 1824.

[3] See C.O. 137/184; also, 'General Return of Slaves and Whites killed and wounded': C.O. 137/185.   [4] *Ibid.*   [5] *Ibid.*

[6] See 'Papers Rel. to Slave Insurrection', Ja. 137/181, or *Imperial Blue Books*, *Ja.* 1832–53.

[7] Elsa Govea, *Slave Society in the British Leeward Islands, 1780–1800*, Un-published Ph.D. Thesis, p. 6. (University of London).

conspiracies in the history of American Negro slavery'.[1] But his definition of a revolt was rather liberal[2] and in any case, when these two hundred and fifty cases are spread over the much greater slave population of America and over the much longer period of slavery there, the Jamaican record is far more impressive. In addition, the scale of the average Jamaican revolt was far greater and more dangerous than that of the average American. The most serious revolt in the latter country – that of Nat Turner – involved only seventy slaves. The average number of slaves in the Jamaica revolts of the seventeenth and eighteenth centuries was approximately four hundred, and the three most serious revolts of the island – the first Maroon war; the 1760 rebellion; and the 1832 rebellion – each involved over a thousand slaves.

For this greater spirit of rebellion among the Jamaican slaves compared with those of the other British slave societies of the New World several causes may be given. First, there was the ratio of masters to slaves. On average, there were, during the seventeenth and eighteenth centuries over ten slaves to every white person in the island; and in the nineteenth century, over thirteen slaves to every white.[3] In Barbados, on the other hand, the average ratio during the entire period of slavery was very close to four slaves to one white,[4] and although after 1724 the number of slaves increased greatly in the Leeward Islands, with the exception of Antigua, it was never more than eight Negroes to one white. In the case of the American south we find that of the fourteen slave states only two – South Carolina and Mississippi – had slave populations which slightly outnumbered the whites. In nine of the other states the slave population varied between 1·5 and 33 per cent; and in three, between 44 per cent and 47 per cent of the total population.[5] Thus, of all the British slave societies Jamaica had by far the highest ratio of slaves to whites. A brief comparative analysis is enough to demonstrate a positive correlation between the density of the slave population and the frequency of servile revolts. If we take the most famous of the slave revolts of ancient times – that of the Sicilian revolt of 134–132 B.C

[1] Apthaker, *American Negro Slave Revolts*, p. 162.

[2] *Ibid.*, p. 10, A Minimum of ten slaves, etc.

[3] See Chapter 4 on Slave population; also, Pitman, *The Development of the B.W.I.*, pp. 373–4.

[4] *Ibid.*, pp. 372–3.

[5] K. Stampp, *The Peculiar Institution*, p. 41.

– we find that it was that area of the Roman Empire which had the highest proportion of slaves in the population which broke into rebellion, Sicily being, according to Mommsen, 'the chosen land of the plantation system'.[1] In the case of the Leeward Islands we find that the only two serious conspiracies took place in Antigua in 1736[2] and Tortola in 1790[3] both of which had the two highest ratios of slaves to whites in their population.[4] And with regard to the United States Aptheker has noted that 'areas of dense Negro population, particularly areas showing a recent accession, were very frequently the centres of unrest'.[5] It is not unreasonable to conclude therefore, that the greater density of the Jamaican slave population partly accounts for its larger number of slave revolts in comparison with other slave societies of the New World.

The second general cause accounting for the frequency of Jamaican slave revolts is to be found in the ratio between creole and African slaves. Naturally, a slave population which had a higher proportion of slaves who were born freemen and were enslaved only as adults would exhibit a greater tendency to revolt than one in which there was a higher proportion of creoles who were born into the system and socialized in it. It is significant that almost every one of the revolts of the seventeenth and eighteenth centuries was instigated and carried out by African slaves (and their children born in the rebel camps). The agent for Jamaica in England wrote after the 1776 revolt that the planters had been 'more particularly alarmed on Account of many of the Creole Negroes being concerned in it, who never were concerned in former rebellions.'[6] In an earlier chapter we have estimated the African sector of the slave population in the middle of the eighteenth century at about a half; at the end of the eighteenth century at a little more than a quarter; and in the last decade or so of slavery, at about a little less than a quarter. The reason for the persistence of the African sector was the failure of the slave population to reproduce itself in Jamaica. On the other hand, we may infer from the more successful attempts at

---

[1] T. Mommsen, *The History of Rome*, Vol. 3, pp. 306–10; see also W. L. Westermann, *The Slave Systems of Greek and Roman Antiquity*, p. 65.

[2] Pitman, *op. cit.*, pp. 59–60.

[3] Govea, *op. cit.*, p. 247.

[4] Pitman, *op. cit.*, pp. 379–80; 383.

[5] Aptheker, *op. cit.*, p. 114.

[6] Fuller to Board of Trade, 27/10/1776: C.O. 138/27.

reproduction both in Barbados[1] * and the United States[2] that the creole slaves formed a much greater proportion of those populations at a much earlier period than they did in Jamaica. This factor, in turn, partly accounts for the greater frequency of slave revolts in Jamaica.

Thirdly, there was the quality of the slaves bought by the Jamaican planters. It is remarkable that almost every one of the serious rebellions during the seventeenth and eighteenth centuries was instigated and carried out mainly by Akan slaves who came from a highly developed militaristic régime, skilled in jungle warfare.[3] Yet a bill to restrain their entry into the island after the 1765 revolt was defeated.[4] It is significant that modern researches on the descendants of the maroon rebels reveal a marked degree of Akan cultural survivals mong them.[5]

A fourth general cause of these revolts lies in the character of the Jamaican whites – their inefficiency (especially in military matters) and general smugness. Govea explains the absence of any serious slave revolt in the Leewards in terms of the rigid execution of the slave laws which were 'expressly designed to make formal organization virtually impossible'.[6] Jamaica too, had many severe laws in this respect but they were made useless by the planters' lack of vigilance. The planters' attitude toward slave revolts oscillated between extreme hysteria and unbelievable smugness. Corbett wrote near the middle of the eighteenth century that:

> One would imagine that Planters really think that Negroes are not of the same Species with us, but that being of a different Mould and Nature as well as Colour, they were made entirely for our Use, with Instincts proper for that Purpose, having as great a propensity to subjection as we have to command and loving slavery as naturally as we do liberty; and that there is not need for Management, but that of themselves they will most

[1] See Pitman, 'Slavery on British West Indies plantations in the 18th Century', in, *Journal of Negro History*, Vol. 11, pp. 584–668.

[2] Stampp, *op. cit.*, p. 305; the U.S. slave population grew by natural increase at a rate of 23 per cent each decade.

[3] See W. W. Claridge, *A History of the Gold Coast and Ashanti*, Vol. 1, pt. 3–4.

[4] Long, *op. cit.*, Bk. 3, p. 470.

[5] J. J. Williams, *The Maroons of Jamaica*, (1938).

[6] Govea, *op. cit.*, p. 245.

* Thus, in 1817 there were 71,777 creole (345 of them from other islands) and only 5,496 African slaves in Barbados. See BPP, Vol. xvi, 1818, p. 111.

pleasantly to hard labour, hard Usages of all kinds, Cruelties and Injustice at the Caprice of one white man – such one would imagine is the Planter's Way of thinking.[1]

He bemoans the neglect of the slave laws, and on the hysteria of the planters in time of danger he comments: 'As no People are more thoughtless of Danger at a Distance, so I must own they are apprehensive of it enough when it is at hand'.[2] The vacillation of the planters was particularly marked during the nineteenth century. Between 1800 and 1825 – due largely to the successful slave revolt in the neighbouring island of Haiti – the responses and fears of the planters in respect of conspiracies or suspected plots were out of all proportion to what did in fact take place among the slaves which, in the words of the governor, often amounted to little more than 'a very active spirit of enquiry which may be naturally accounted for without attributing to them any criminal intentions'.[3] On the other hand, by 1831 the planters had, to use Corbett's phrase, relating to the mid-18th century 'took T'other Turn and fell quietly flat a-sleep again'. The abolition debate was openly discussed by them in front of their slaves without the slightest awareness of the impact it was having on them. One of them, an Assembly-man, even went so far as to write that 'Our Slave Population have been too long habituated to hear discussed the details of the question of slavery and emancipation, for us to entertain any alarm from their recollections on this subject'.[4] And a visitor to the island during the period of the rebellion wrote that:

> The greater part of the inhabitants of Jamaica had indeed been lulling themselves into a fancied and fatal security, while, in fact, they were sleeping on a mine; and any one who suspected the probability of an insurrection was looked upon as a timid alarmist (even after the preparatory notes of insubordination had been sounded).[5]

It was in vain that the governor pleaded with them to be more

[1] Corbett, *Essay Concerning Slavery*, p. 19.
[2] *Ibid.*
[3] *Report of the Secret C'ttee at Close of Sessions, 1824.*
[4] A. H. Beaumont, 'Compensation-Manumission, etc.' enclosed in C.O. 137/179.
[5] T. Foulks, *Eighteen Months in Jamaica,* etc. (1833).

discreet in their denunciation of the abolitionists.[1] One can well understand then, why the masters had no hint of the widespread rebellion that broke out after Christmas 1831 until a few days before it actually began,[2] although the secrecy with which the slaves kept their plans must be borne in mind.

A fifth cause of slave revolts in the island was to be found in the treatment and maintenance of the slaves. An historian of ancient slavery has noted that 'in any slave system the slave group has definite rights – not legal, but actual, and sanctioned by custom. These rights the slaves both accept and insist upon';[3] and he gives this as 'the primary cause of the first Sicilian slave revolt'[4] It has already been pointed out in our chapter on the slave laws that the Jamaican slave, like his American and Sicilian counterpart, had certain minimum customary rights which he insisted upon. Without becoming involved in the rather tired controversy as to which area of the New World had the most severe form of slavery – a controversy which Professor Harris, has, not unreasonably, dismissed as 'a waste of time'[5] – it may be suggested that there was one feature of Jamaican slave society which may well have encouraged the greater infringement of the minimal customary rights of the slaves. This was the excessive degree of absenteeism which was greater than in any other slave colony in the New World, the effects of which on the treatment of the slave we have discussed in Chapter 1. Pitman makes the cogent observation that the period during which the whites suffered most from the rebels and general desertion from the estates – i.e. between 1730 and 1739 – was that in which the profits from sugar had greatly declined, in which large numbers of whites were leaving the island and those supervising the slaves were making excessive demands on their labour in addition to reducing their supplies of clothing and food.[6]

Another factor explaining the revolts of the island was its geography. The mountainous interior of the country with its intricate,

---

[1] Belmore to Board of Trade, 6/8/1831 in, C.O. 137/179.
[2] Belmore to Board of Trade, Jan. 6, 1832, C.O. 137/181.
[3] W. L. Westermann, 'Slave Maintenence and Slave Revolts', in, *Classical Philology*, Vol. 40, 1945, p. 8.
[4] *Ibid.*, p. 9.
[5] Marvin Harris, *Patterns of Race in the Americas*, p. 72.
[6] Pitman, *op. cit.*, 1917, p. 115.

innumerable ravines, naturally concealed mountain passes, precipices and forests, was ideal for guerrilla warfare. In this respect the African slaves, used to the jungle warfare of their own country, had an insurmountable advantage over their British masters. It was their knowledge of the interior country and the guerrilla tactics they evolved[1] in it which more than compensated for the inferiority of the Maroons in arms and numbers against the whites. The latter sought to redress the balance in their favour by importing Mosquito Indians in the 1720s[2] and specially trained Cuban bloodhounds in 1795,[3] but there is no evidence that either of these measures proved of any use. After 1740, however, with the Maroons on the side of the whites, the opportunities offered by the interior of the country were cut off to future rebels.

Finally, between 1770 and 1832, rebellions in Jamaica were caused partly by the impact of certain social, religious and political forces current at that time, on the slave. The agent for Jamaica in England suggested that the American Revolution may have been partly responsible for the slave revolt of 1776, the first in which the creole slaves played a significant part.[4] And Balcarres, Governor of Jamaica, insisted that the second Maroon war of 1795 was largely instigated by professional revolutionaries from Haiti, France and the United States.[5] So much did the planters fear the contagious revolutionary spirit of the Haitian Negroes who had successfully revolted against their masters, that an entire regiment of soldiers who had been recruited from among the slaves to augment the troops of an ill-fated attack on Haiti was refused re-admittance into the island. They were disbanded in Haiti and 'numbers of them joined the enemy'.[6]

The abolition movement also played its part in inciting the slaves to revolt. Its influence, however, was due largely to the misinterpretation (sometimes deliberately) by the slaves of the debates they heard among their masters and – in a few cases – read in local

---

[1] For a description of these tactics, see Dallas, *op. cit.* Vol. I, pp. 39–40.

[2] *Ibid.*, p. 38; also, Lawes to Board of Trade, C.O. 137/13, f. 93.

[3] Edwards, *Proceedings*, pp. IXV–IXXXI, also Dallas, *op. cit.*, Vol. 2, letters 9–12.

[4] Fuller to Lords, 27/10/1776: C.O. 138/27.

[5] Earl of Balcarres to the Duke of York, 20/5/1795, in *The Maroon War*, p. 7.

[6] Gardner, *op. cit.*, p. 225.

or foreign newspapers.[1] Large numbers of slaves who joined the various conspiracies of the nineteenth century were convinced that the King, or some other benefactor abroad, had sent their 'free-paper' but that the planters were maliciously keeping it from them. When the slave trade was abolished in 1807 it was generally believed among the slaves that they had been emancipated. Related to the abolition movement were the activities of the missionaries who had begun to preach among the slaves with some effect since the last decade of the eighteenth century. While these preachers strenuously denied ever inciting the slaves to revolt, there can be little doubt that the latter saw in the egalitarian aspects of Christianity part of the justification they needed to rebel against their masters. When a popular preacher left for a short stay in England in 1831 his return was anxiously awaited as it was the general opinion that he would be returning with 'the gift' or their 'free paper'.[2] Indeed, the rebellion of 1831–32 was dubbed the 'Baptist war' by the Negroes.[3]

As in Jamaica, the American Revolution,[4] the Haitian slave revolution,[5] the abolition movement,[6] as well as rumours of the King having sent orders to set them free and debates about emancipation all played their part in inciting the American slaves to revolt. The Haitian revolution – the only completely successful slave revolt in the New World – was directly inspired and made possible by the French Revolution. There are also instances in ancient slavery where rumours regarding their emancipation incited agitation among slaves, for example, the possible disturbances created in Asia Minor by the rumour of the emancipation of the slaves in Pergamum during the First Century B.C.[7]

The final question to be answered is why was it that despite the favourable conditions discussed above, the Jamaican slaves failed to overthrow their masters? The first answer is the divisions within

---

[1] See Evidence of Rev T. Stewart, 'Papers Relating to Rebellion 1832': C.O. 137/181; Evidence of Lieut. Col. Codrington, *ibid.*; Viscount Goderich to Earle of Belmore, *ibid.*, Bleby, *op. cit.*, pp. 138–42.

[2] B. M. Senior, *Jamaica, As it was, As it is, and as it May be*, (1835) pp. 183–4.

[3] T. Foulks; *op. cit.*, p. 112.   [4] Aptheker, *op. cit.*, p. 87.

[5] *Ibid.*, pp. 97–100.

[6] *Ibid.*, pp. 79, 81.

[7] Westermann, 'Slave Maintenence and Slave Revolts', *op. cit.*, pp. 9–10.

the slave group itself. These were of two types: firstly, that between the African slaves. Due partly to the deliberate policy of the masters, and, more important, to the nature of the supply of slaves, it was the unusual estate which had all, or even the majority of its slaves from one tribal stock. And it would seem that the different tribal groups hated 'one another so mortally that some of them would rather die by the Hands of the English than join with other Africans in an Attempt to shake off their yoke'.[1] The second major division was that between the creole slaves and the Africans. We have already discussed the animosity which the creoles bore for the Africans and it is inconceivable that any of them would allow themselves to be led in a rebellion by an African.

A second reason for the slaves' lack of success was, paradoxically, their early successes against the whites. The whites, having been obliged to come to terms with the Maroons in 1739, then proceeded to use them to prevent or subdue further uprisings. It was unfortunate for the slaves that Cudjoe – the rebel chief with whom the first treaty was signed – should have been as obsequious in his relation with the whites as he was, since the position from which he negotiated with them was not weak. Several of his commanding officers disagreed with the treaty to the extent of rebelling against his authority and attempting to incite the slaves on the plantations to revolt.[2]

Finally, there was the military strength of the whites. It is true that the militia was an inefficient body but, however incompetent its members were, they had at least some semblance of up-to-date military training and a more than adequate supply of arms. Against these the relatively primitive African rebels could never hope to win in an open engagement, and when the possibility of compensating for their disadvantage by resorting to guerrilla warfare was cut off, the chances of a successful revolt became very thin. This was, of course, as long as the whites remained united. Thus, if we compare the Jamaican situation with that of Haiti it will be found that the crucial difference lies in the hopeless division of the master class during the course of the successful rebellion in the latter country.[3] The French Revolution created fatal divisions between the loyalists,

---

[1] Leslie, *A New History*, p. 311.
[2] See 'Cudjoe's Fidelity', C. E. Long Papers, B.M. *op. cit.*
[3] See C. L. R. James, *The Black Jacobins*, pp. 27–61; 174–98.

radical revolutionaries, and bourgeois revolutionaries among the Haitian planter-class, and, what was worse, the political state of the mother country made it impossible for her to assist the planters until it was too late.

Selfish and incompetent though they were, the Jamaican planters always managed at least to present a united front against the rebels and there was never any question of losing the support of the mother country. Thus, when assistance was asked for during the first Maroon war, two regiments of soldiers from Gibraltar were promptly sent to the island, having an immediate impact on those slaves who were not in revolt.[1] Throughout the remainder of the period of slavery there were always at least two regiments stationed on the island. In addition, Jamaica was a frequent port of call for squadrons of the British navy which, on several occasions (not always to the best effect) offered their services in quelling revolts.[2] It is quite possible too, that the terrible reprisals of the whites after they had subdued a rebellion deterred other slaves from rebelling.[3]

This chapter has attempted to explain the reasons for the frequency and intensity of the resistance of the Jamaican slaves to their exploitation, and the reasons why they did not, like their Haitian neighbours, completely succeed. We have seen that most of this resistance came from among that section of them which had already experienced freedom. But in the last days of slavery even the creole slaves, who had never known what it was to be free, began to organize revolts against their masters, and the last and most damaging of all the rebellions remains a living memory of their struggle for something they had never experienced but for which they felt a need sufficiently strong for which to die.

What then, accounts for the presence of this need which seems to survive under conditions which in every way conspire to smother it? Every rebellion, Camus has written, 'tacitly invokes a value'. This value is something embedded deep in the human soul, a value discovered as soon as a subject begins to reflect on himself[4] through which he inevitably comes to the conclusion that 'I *must* become

---

[1] Hunter to Board of Trade, 13/11/1731: C.O. 137/19.
[2] Hunter to Board of Trade, C.O. 137/20, f. 165; Swanton to Hunter, *ibid.*, f. 184; Extract out of Lieut. Swanton's Journal Rel. to Expedition against the Rebel Negroes, *ibid.*, f. 192–3; Gardner, *op. cit.*, p. 145.
[3] See Review of Rebellions above.
[4] Gabriel Marcel, *The Existential Background of Human Dignity*, p. 87.

free – that is, that my freedom must be won'.[1] In the final analysis it is the discovery of this universal value which justifies and stimulates the most tractable of slaves to rebel. As Camus pointed out: 'Rebellion cannot exist without the feeling that somewhere, in some way you are justified. It is in this way that the rebel slave says yes and no at the same time. He affirms that there are limits and also that he suspects – and wishes to preserve – the existence of certain things beyond those limits. He stubbornly insists that there are certain things in him which "are worth while . . ." and which must be taken into consideration'.[2]

[1] *Ibid.*
[2] Albert Camus, *The Rebel*, p. 19.

CHAPTER X

The Cultural and Social Development of Jamaica 1655-1865

THIS WORK has been primarily a structural analysis of Jamaican slave society. It is now our task to summarize, briefly, the overall social development of the society in the two centuries after it was first occupied by the British. This will not only be of practical historical interest but will present an interesting case study of social and cultural change. We may distinguish four phases in this period of Jamaica's history:

(a) the period of Disintegration between 1655 and 1730,
(b) the period of Adaptation between 1730 and 1780,
(c) the period of Consolidation between 1780 and 1834 and
(d) the period of Disjunction between 1834 and 1865.

(a) *The Period of Disintegration, 1655–1730*

This was the early unsettled period of slavery. Both masters and slaves were largely newcomers to the society and strangers to each other. The early attempts at creating a *colonie de peuplement* failed and with the development of large-scale sugar plantations the exploitation of the slave group by the masters was total. The values of both masters and slaves were in almost complete disorganization and the society existed solely for the pursuit of one goal – that of making vast fortunes as quickly as possible from growing sugar. These factors led to the harsh and inhuman treatment of the slaves and their complete lack of any rights either in law or custom. All that existed were – to use a term of Merton's – purely 'technical' norms. The society approximated to the limiting case of one polar type of Merton's typology of malintegrated cultures. As he wrote:

The cultural emphasis placed upon certain goals varies independently of the degree of emphasis placed upon institutionalized means. There may develop a very heavy, at times a virtually exclusive, stress upon the value of particular goals, involving comparatively little concern with the institutionally prescribed means of striving toward these goals. The limiting case of this type is reached when the range of alternative procedures is governed only by technical rather than institutionalized norms.[1]

(b) *The Period of Adaptation, 1730–80*

During this period both a slave and a white creole society emerged. These creole groups were both numerically superior to their foreign-born counterparts but were, nonetheless, incapable of fully repro-ducing themselves and depended on the latter for augmentation. One demographic difference between the master and slave creole groups which was of major social importance was the fact that the wealthiest and most talented sector of the white creole group con-stantly left the island to take up residence in Britain. The result was that the master group was dominated by men of poor calibre, little able to preserve the most basic elements of their own civilization, let alone mould a new one.

But certain significant changes were discernible during this second period. In the first place, masters and slaves were no longer strangers to each other. The white masters no longer saw their slaves as exotic brutes, with violent, unpredictable passions which had to be kept in check by the constant exercise of harsh, inhuman discipline. By now they had developed certain stereotypes concern-ing 'Quashee's' personality and intellectual capacities which acted both as a system of rationalization for whatever moral problems slavery presented and as a base from which to interact with the stereotyped group. The Negro, in turn, had also come to learn a great deal about his master – he now spoke his language, under-stood his role within the society and, most important, out of the cultural chaos of the early period, had begun to develop patterns of behaviour by which he could best adjust to his thraldom. The slave also developed certain stereotyped views of his master and certain patterns of responses not only to the demands which his master made on him, but also to the expectation of these demands.

[1] R. K. Merton, *Social Theory and Social Structure*, p. 133.

He acted out the stereotype his master had of him since this was always the best path to survival.

Further, the purely technical norms of the early period were now acquiring the force of custom. The laws still left the slave almost completely at the mercy of the master and acts of barbarity were certainly not uncommon. But there is reason to believe that the general trend was toward a less severe treatment of the slave and a recognition of the fact that certain minimal customary rights were due to him. The norms, in short, were becoming less 'technical', more institutionalized; they were acquiring the status of folkways.

(c) *The Period of Consolidation, 1780–1834*

This is what has been designated the period of amelioration. Due largely to pressure from the abolitionists and emancipationists of the mother country, but also to the internal dynamics of change in the colony, the tendencies already manifest in the second period now came into full force. Nowhere was this more evident than in the changes in the slave laws, or 'consolidated slave laws' as the Jamaica Assembly described them. There was not only an improvement in the treatment of the slaves but attention was now being paid to the non-material areas of his life, especially in the matter of religion.

Not only were the laws codified during this period, but also the relation between masters and slaves and the 'proper' treatment of the slaves, in the legion of books and pamphlets which purported to give the last word on the subject. All these changes went hand in hand with the gradual erosion of the economic basis on which the entire system of slavery rested.

Generally speaking, it may be said that the norms of the society had become fully normative: or, to use Sumner's terminology, the folk-ways had become the 'right-ways'.[1]

(d) *The Period of Disjunction, 1834–65*

The emancipation of the slaves in 1834 marked not only the political end of the period of slavery but ushered in an entirely new social and economic order in Jamaica. Strictly, our period ends with the abolition of slavery but the material we have dealt with overlaps so much with the post-emancipation period and has so many implications with respect to it, that it seems natural to end our analysis

---

[1] Quoted in Hoebel, *Primitive Law*, p. 15.

of the development of the society with a few remarks concerning this period. These remarks will also be based on the works of two scholars who have devoted a considerable amount of attention to the social[1] and economic[2] development of this phase of the island's history.

Abolition meant that the enforced ties between ex-master and ex-slave were cut. The Negro, no longer under any compulsion to remain on the plantation, abandoned the scene of his thraldom which he despised so much and lived instead in mountain villages centred partly on their original provision grounds. At first, it appeared as if the ex-slaves were rapidly enculturing the values of their original masters under the influence of the missionary teachers. By 1850, however, there was general disillusionment among those interested in 'civilizing' the Jamaican Negro. On the one hand, attendance to Christian churches rapidly fell off and the almost phenomenal success of missionary schools immediately after slavery had now been replaced by an almost complete lack of interest in education on the part of the Negroes. On the other hand, there was a resurgence of the non-European features of the Negro society which had developed during slavery. It was shown in Chapter VII how revivalism and myalism erupted with great frenzy during the late forties and fifties and finally in the early 1860s when both converged to form the basis of modern Jamaican folk religion. Sociologists of culture change have identified such outbursts of supernatural fervour as being both symptomatic of, and instrumental in, the revitalization of disorganized cultures.[3]

Thus there emerged in the post-emancipation period a dual culture, or as Curtin puts it, 'two Jamaicas'; one was the Afro-Jamaican cultural system, which was largely a consolidation and revitalization of patterns developed during slavery; the other was the European oriented cultural system, which was the revival of British civilization in the island after its disintegration during slavery. It is this dual cultural pattern which still forms the basis of Jamaican society.[4]

[1] P. Curtin, *Two Jamaicas*.
[2] D. Hall, *Free Jamaica*.
[3] For a discussion of such 'revitalization processes' see F. C. Wallace, *Culture and Personality*, pp. 143–6.
[4] See M. Kerr, *Personality and Conflict in Jamaica*, (1952); M. G. Smith, 'A Plural Framework for Ja. Society', B.J.S., Jan. 1962.

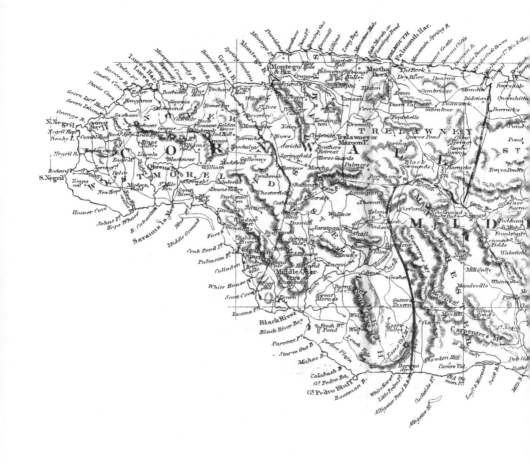

Map of Jamaica: from *The British Colonies* by R. M. Martin, published 1852

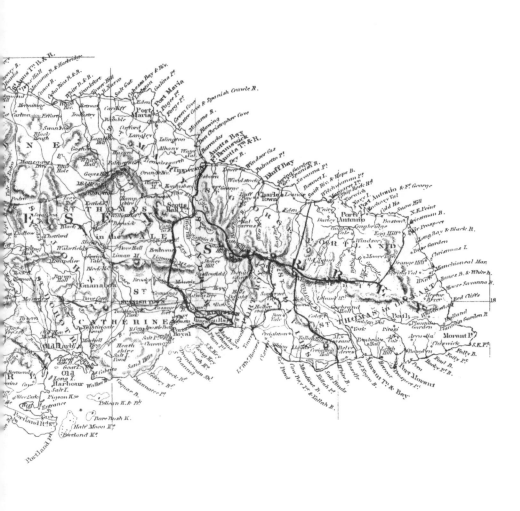

APPENDIX 1

Stephen Fuller's Account of the Number of Negroes imported and exported at Jamaica each year, 1702–75

Year	Number of slave ships	Number of Negroes imported	Number of Negroes exported
1702	5	843	327
1703	14	2,740	481
1704	16	4,120	221
1705	16	3,503	1,669
1706	14	3,804	1,086
1707	15	3,358	807
1708	23	6,627	1,379
1709	10	3,234	1,275
1710	15	3,662	1,191
1711	26	6,724	1,532
1712	15	4,128	1,903
1713	19	4,378	2,712
1714	24	5,769	3,507
1715	10	3,372	1,039
1716	24	6,361	2,872
1717	29	1,775	3,153
1718	25	6,253	2,247
1719	27	5,120	3,161
1720	23	5,064	2,815
1721	17	3,715	1,637
1722	41	3,469	3,263
1723	20	6,624	4,674
1724	25	6,852	3,569
1725	41	10,297	3,368

Year	Number of slave ships	Number of Negroes imported	Number of Negroes exported
1726	50	11,708	4,112
1727	17	3,876	1,555
1728	30	5,350	935
1729	10	10,499	4,820
1730	43	10,104	5,222
1731	45	10,079	5,708
1732	57	13,552	5,288
1733	37	7,413	5,176
1734	20	4,570	1,666
1735	20	4,851	2,260
1736	15	3,943	1,647
1737	35	8,995	2,070
1738	32	7,695	2,070
1739	29	6,787	598
1740	27	5,362	495
1741	19	4,255	562
1742	22	5,067	792
1743	38	8,926	1,368
1744	38	8,755	1,331
1745	18	3,843	1,344
1746	16	4,703	1,502
1747	33	10,898	2,376
1748	9	10,430	2,426
1749	25	6,858	2,123
1750	16	3,587	721
1751	21	4,840	713
1752	27	6,117	1,036
1753	39	7,661	902
1754	47	9,551	1,592
1755	64	12,723	598
1756	46	11,166	1,902
1757	32	7,935	943
1758	11	3,405	411

Year	Number of slave ships	Number of Negroes imported	Number of Negroes exported
1759	18	5,212	681
1760	23	7,573	2,368
1761	29	6,480	642
1762	24	6,279	232
1763	33	10,079	1,582
1764	41	10,213	2,639
1765	41	8,951	2,006
1766	43	10,208	672
1767	19	3,248	375
1768	27	5,940	485
1769	19	3,575	420
1770	25	6,824	836
1771	17	4,183	671
1772	22	5,278	923
1773	49	9,676 (10,729)*	800 (587)*
1774	79	18,448 (17,686)*	2,511 (2,658)*
1775	39	9,292 (17,364)*	1,629 (13,870)*
	2,092	497,736 (sic) 488,865 (correct)	137,114 (sic) 135,619 (correct)
1776		18,400	3,384
1777		5,607	558
1778		5,191	772
1779		3,343	484
1780		3,267	252
1781		7,049	294
1782		6,291	1,868
1783		9,644	64
1784		15,468	4,635
1785		11,046	4,667
1786		5,645	3,764
1787		5,703	2,158

*The alternative figures are derived from source 2 above.

Sources:

For the years 1702–1775: Appendix to the Memorial of Stephen Fuller (Agent for Jamaica) to the Board of Trade, 1788. C.O. 137/38.

Import and Export of Negroes, and Negroes retained in the island, for 49 years, viz, from 1739 to 1787, both inclusive, distinguishing the Years of War from those of Peace: *Minutes of Evidence taken before a Committee of the House of Commons . . . to Consider the Circumstances of the Slave Trade*, 1790, p. 497.

APPENDIX 2

Exports from Jamaica, 1768

Places of Destination	Hhds of sugar of 16 cwts.	Puns. of rum 100 gals.	Bags of Pimento 100 lbs.	Bags of Ginger 70 lbs.	Bags of Cotton 200 lbs.
To Gt. Britain & Ireland	54,181	11,127	13,116	2,551	2,211
To North America	1,580	4,424	738	620	262
Total	55,761	15,551	13,854	3,171	2,463

Bags of Coffee 100 lbs.	Tons of Fustick and Logwood	Feet of Mahogany	Tons of Lignum Vitae	Tons of N woods and Ebony	Gals. of Molasses	Hides
1,491	4,035	443,920	120	26	—	—
2,712	—	424,080	—	—	201,960	2,287
4,203	4,035	868,000	120	26	201,960	2,287

Source: B. Edwards, *The History . . . of the British Colonies in the West Indies*, Vol. I, p. 303.

APPENDIX 3

General Return of Exports from the Island of Jamaica, for 53 Years, ending 31st December, 1836, abstracted from the Journals of the House of Assembly.

Years	Sugar			Rum				Molasses	Ginger		Pimento		Coffee	Remarks
	Hhds.	Trs.	Brls.	Puns.	Hhds.	Casks.	Brls.	Casks.	Casks.	Bags.	Casks.	Bags.	lbs.	
1772	69,451	9,936	270	...	...	...	...	...	...	...	...	...	841,558	
1773	72,996	11,453	849	...	...	...	...	...	...	...	...	...	779,303	
1774	69,579	9,250	278	...	...	...	...	...	...	...	...	...	739,039	
1775	75,291	9,090	425	...	...	...	...	...	...	...	...	...	493,981	
1776	...	...	...	...	...	...	...	...	...	...	...	...	...	
1788	83,036	9,256	1,063	...	...	...	...	...	...	...	...	...	1,035,368	
1789	84,167	10,078	1,077	...	...	...	...	...	...	...	...	...	1,493,282	
1790	84,741	9,284	1,599	...	...	...	...	...	...	...	...	...	1,783,740	
1791	85,447	8,037	1,718	...	...	...	...	...	...	...	...	...	2,299,874	August, destruction of St. Domingo.
1792	...	...	...	...	...	...	...	...	...	...	...	...	...	
1793	77,575	6,722	642	34,755	879	...	...	...	62	8,605	420	9,108	3,983,576	
1794	89,532	11,158	1,224	39,843	1,570	...	...	...	121	10,305	554	22,153	4,911,549	
1795	88,851	9,537	1,225	37,684	1,475	...	...	...	426	14,861	957	20,451	6,318,812	
1796	89,219	10,700	858	40,810	1,364	...	...	...	690	20,275	136	9,820	7,203,539	
1797	78,373	9,963	753	28,014	1,463	...	...	...	259	29,098	328	2,935	7,869,133	
1798	87,896	11,725	1,163	40,823	2,234	...	...	...	119	18,454	1,181	8,961	7,894,306	
1799	101,457	13,538	1,321	37,022	1,981	...	...	...	221	10,358	1,766	28,273	11,745,425	Bourbon Cane introduced.
1800	96,347	13,549	1,631	37,166	1,350	...	...	...	444	3,586	610	12,759	11,116,474	
1801	123,251	18,704	2,692	48,789	1,514	...	...	...	12	239	648	14,084	13,401,468	
1802	129,544	15,403	2,403	45,632	2,073	473	205	366	23	2,079	591	7,793	17,961,923	
1803	107,387	11,825	1,797	43,298	1,416	...	...	461	51	3,287	867	14,875	15,866,291	
1804	103,352	12,802	2,207	42,207	913	...	...	429	1,094	1,854	1,417	19,572	22,063,980	
1805	137,906	17,977	3,689	53,211	1,328	...	167	471	315	2,128	288	7,157	24,137,393	Largest Sugar Crop.
1806	133,996	18,237	3,579	58,191	1,178	133	...	499	485	1,818	1,094	19,534	29,298,036	
1807	123,175	17,344	3,716	51,812	1,998	...	...	699	512	1,411	525	19,224	26,761,188	March 25, Abolition of African Slave Trade.
1808	121,444	15,836	2,625	52,409	2,196	...	...	379	436	1,470	225	6,529	29,528,273	

Years	Sugar				Rum			Mo-lasses	Ginger		Pimento		Coffee	Remarks
	Hhds.	Trs.	Brls.	Puns.	Hhds.	Casks.	Brls.	Casks.	Casks.	Bags.	Casks.	Bags.	lbs.	
1809	104,457	14,596	3,534	43,492	2,717	..	..	230	2,321	572	24,022	1,177	25,586,668	
1809	108,703	4,560	3,719	42,353	1,964	..	..	293	520	1,881	4,276	21,163	25,885,285	
1810	127,751	15,235	3,046	54,093	2,011	..	..	446	1,110	2,072	638	22,074	17,460,068	Storm in October, 1812.
1811	105,283	11,357	2,558	43,346	1,531	..	..	151	804	1,235	598	7,778	18,481,986	Largest Coffee Crop.
1812	97,548	10,029	2,304	44,618	1,345	382	874	208	816	1,428	1,124	14,361	24,623,572	
1813	101,846	10,485	2,575	43,486	1,551	202	1,146	145	884	1,668	394	10,711	34,045,585	
1814	118,767	12,324	2,817	52,996	1,465	574	1,398	242	1,493	1,667	844	27,386	27,362,742	Storm in October, 1815.
1815	93,881	9,332	2,236	35,736	769	281	903	166	2,354	1,118	851	28,047	17,289,393	
1816	116,012	11,094	2,868	47,940	1,094	203	916	254	3,361	1,196	946	15,817	14,793,706	
1817	113,818	11,388	2,786	50,195	1,108	121	191	407	2,526	1,067	941	21,071	25,329,456	
1818	108,305	11,450	3,244	43,946	1,695	602	1,558	253	1,714	718	882	24,500	14,091,983	
1819	115,065	11,332	2,474	45,361	1,783	106	460	252	1,159	316	673	12,880	22,127,444	Extreme drought.
1820	111,512	11,703	1,972	46,802	1,793	153	534	167	984	271	1,224	24,827	16,819,761	
1821	88,551	8,705	1,292	28,728	1,324	9	442	144	891	72	699	18,672	19,773,912	Mr Canning's resolu-
1822	94,905	9,179	1,947	35,242	1,935	20	118	614	1,041	60	1,894	21,481	20,326,445	tions relative to slavery.
1823	99,225	9,651	2,791	37,121	3,261	5	64	910	2,230	52	599	33,306	27,677,239	Severe drought in 1824,
1824	73,813	7,380	2,858	27,630	2,077	101	215	894	3,947	348	537	20,979	21,254,656	the previous year.
1825	99,978	9,514	3,126	35,610	3,098	1,852	..	549	5,724	517	522	16,433	20,352,886	
1826	82,096	7,435	2,770	31,840	2,672	1,573	..	204	4,871	240	3,236	26,691	25,741,529	
1827	94,912	9,428	3,204	38,585	2,793	1,013	..	189	5,382	279	4,003	25,352	22,216,780	
1828	91,364	9,193	3,024	36,285	2,909	563	..	66	4,101	168	3,733	48,933	22,234,640	
1829	93,882	8,739	3,615	33,355	2,657	1,367	..	154	3,494	15	5,609	37,925	22,256,950	
1830														
1831	88,409	9,053	3,492	34,743	2,846	982	..	230	3,224	22	2,844	22,170	14,055,350	Emancipation Act passed.
1832	91,453	9,987	4,600	32,060	2,570	1,362	..	799	4,702	38	3,736	27,936	19,815,101	Seasons favourable.
1833	78,375	9,325	4,074	33,215	3,034	977	..	755	4,818	23	7,741	58,581	9,866,060	Ditto.
1834	77,801	9,860	3,055	30,495	2,588	1,288	..	486	5,925	116	496	29,301	17,725,731	
1835	71,017	8,840	8,455	26,433	1,820	747	..	300	3,985	486	1,115	59,033	10,593,108	
1836	61,644	7,707	2,497	19,938	874	646	..	182	5,224	69	227	46,779	13,446,053	

Source: BPP 1837 (Vol. XLVII) Jamaica, p. 31.

APPENDIX 4

Output, Income and Expenditure in 1832
£'000

	1	2	3	4	5	6	7	8	9	10	11	12	13	14
	Gross Domestic Output	Agricultural Labourers	Small-Settlers	Planters	Plantation Staff	Other Wages and Salaries	Merchants	Professional Workers	Independent Workers	Imports	Exports	Goods and Services Available Domestically	Consumed	Invested
Exports*	2,086·8	458·4	—	1,206·6	381·6	24·9	89·4	—	—	106·6	2,193·4	—	—	—
Food Production*	900·1	62·2	847·1	—	—	88·4	29·4	—	39·0	422·2	—	1,322·3	1,322·3	—
Building and Construction	180·0	—	—	—	—	—	—	—	—	31·3	—	211·3	—	211·3
Manufacturing for Local Consumption*	320·1	—	—	—	—	—	—	—	260·0	615·5	—	935·5	883·1	52·5
Passenger Transport and Communications	—	—	—	—	—	—	—	—	—	—	—	—	—	—
Distribution	286·4	—	—	50·4	—	71·6	164·4	—	—	—	57·7	228·7	228·7	—
Public Administration	322·9	—	—	10·9	10·3	253·4	17·0	2·1	29·2	—	—	322·9	322·9	—
Ownership of Houses	552·9	124·1	—	35·3	69·6	41·4	250·4	5·3	26·8	—	—	552·9	552·9	—
Professional Services	217·5	—	—	—	—	20·4	—	197·1	—	—	—	217·5	217·5	—
Domestic Services	175·2	—	—	—	—	164·8	10·4	—	—	—	—	175·2	175·2	—
Totals	5,041·9	644·7	847·1	1,303·2	461·5	664·9	561·0	204·5	355·0	1,175·6	2,251·1	3,966·4	3,702·6	263·8
Less Income from Abroad	—	—	—	—	—	—	—	—	—	−14·9	—	−14·9	−14·9	—
Plus Payments Abroad	—	—	—	—	—	—	—	—	—	1,090·4	—	1,090·4	—	1,090·4
Foreign Balance	—	—	—	—	—	—	—	—	—	—	—	—	—	—
	5,041·9	644·7	847·1	1,303·2	461·5	664·9	561·0	204·5	355·0	2,251·1	2,251·1	5,041·9	3,687·7	1,354·2

* Incomes shown in columns numbers 2 to 7, row 1, include incomes arising out of the production of retained exports as well as exports, hence columns numbers 2 to 9, row 2 show, only incomes arising out of the production of ground provisions and animal products and columns numbers 2 to 9, row 4, only those arising out of the manufacture of non-export crops and public utilities. The incomes in these three rows thus do not add up individually to give the total under Gross Domestic Product.

Source: G. Eisner, *The Economic Development of Jamaica, 1830–1930*, p. 28.

APPENDIX 5

Manuscripts and Official Publications Consulted

1. *The Public Records Office, London*
(A) Calendar of State Papers (C.S.P.) All references in this work are to the *Colonial* and *America* and *West Indies* series:
(B) Colonial Office Records (C.O.)

C.O.137: Vols. 1–194 (1694–1834): Correspondence, Original – Secretary of State. (Including Despatches Offices and Individuals; Return of Manumissions, 1817–1830; Slave rebellion Trials; Military Papers; etc.)

C.O.138: Vols. 1–11 (1661–1706)
Vol. 21 (1760)   Entry Book of Commissions,
  „ 26 (1766–1771)   Instructions, Correspondence, etc.
  „ 27 (1771–1777)

C.O.139: Vols. 1–73 (1662–1834) Acts of the Council and Assembly of Jamaica. Vols. 1 & 8 Printed; remainder MS.

C.O.141: Vols. 1–12 (1794; 1813–1818) The Royal Gazette (Jamaica)

C.O.142: Vols. 1–2 (1830–1836) The Watchman and Jamaica Free Press.
Vol. 3 (1835–1837) The Kingston Chronicle.

C.O.142: Vols. 13–19 Jamaica Shipping Returns, 1680–1784.

C.O.142: Vol. 31 List of Landholders and their Holdings in Jamaica, 1754

C.O.142: Vol. 33 Memoranda, Military, Barracks, Maroons, Blue Books of Statistics, etc. 1823–1835.

(c) Board of Trade Records to 1837 (B.T.6:)

   B.T.6: Vols. 9–11 Slave Trade Enquiry – Copies of certain of the evidence submitted to the Committee of Council for Trade and Plantations in the course of their enquiry into the State of the African Slave Trade.

   B.T.6:9:– 1788; B.T.6:10:– 1788; B.T.6: 11:–1788–89.

2. *British Museum Manuscripts*

   Abstract of Ships and Vessels, with their Lading, imported into Jamaica, from Dec. 25, 1687, to March 25, 1688: Add. MS. 3984.

   Abstract of Wills Relating to Jamaica, 1625–1792: Add. MS. 34.181.

   Account of Sugar Plantations: The Poll-tax, 1740, etc. MS. 12,434.

   Barham, H., A Most Correct and Particular Account of the Island of Jamaica, From the Time of the Spaniards First Discovery and Settling Upon It, 1722. Sl.MS. 3918.

   Corbett, B., Memorial of What I Observed During My Being at the Island of Jamaica, from 1670 to 1673: Sl.MS. 4020, f.22.

   Ekines, T., Proposals Relating to the Trade of Jamaica, 1724: Sl.MS. 4047, f. 169.

   Long, C.E., Histories of, Papers and Tracts relating to Jamaica, Collected by Charles E. Long: MS. 12402–12440. Sections of particular value to this study were:

   Add: 12407: Miscl. Notes for the history of Jamaica.

   12409: Littleton's Report on Jamaica.

   12411–12414: Papers Relating to History, Trade and Statistics, including *The Essayist No. 4.* Saturday, Jan. 6, 1787, Add. 12.12412: Extract of letter from Bryan Edwards to Mark Davis, 188/4/1774, Add. 12413, f.12.

   12415–21: J. K. Knight, MS. *History of Jamaica,* to 1746.

   12431: Miscl. Letters on Jamaica.

   12434: Account of Jamaica Sugar Plantations, 1739.

   Names of Persons whose Wills are Registered in Jamaica Previous to 1700: Add. MS. 21,931.

Papers Relating to Jamaica, 1670–1688: Sl.MS. 3984, ff.
165–169; 174–183.

Papers Relating to Jamaica, 1677–1681: Sl.MS. 2724.

Papers Relating to the Trade of Jamaica, 1694–1700: Sl.MS.
2902, ff. 151–154.

The State of the Trade to Africa between 1680 and 1707:
MS. 8223 c4.

3. *Manuscripts at the Jamaica Archives* (*Spanish Town*)
St Catherine Vestry Minutes, 1750–1785.
St David Vestry Minutes, 1780–1800.
Radnor Estate Account Book, 1880.
Green Park Estate Journal, 1823.

4. *Institute of Jamaica, Manuscripts.* (*Kingston*)
The Private Letters of the Marquis of Sligo.

5. *Worthy Park Estate:*
MSS. of Account Books, Private Journals and Negro Sermons
kept in the Accounts Office of the Worthy Park Estate,
Jamaica.

Official Publications

British Parliamentary Papers (*BPP*); *Sessional Papers of both*
Houses

i. BPP: Vol. XX, 1831–1832: (a) Report from the Select Commit-
tee on the Extinction of Slavery throughout the British
Dominions; with the Minutes of Evidence, Appendix and
Index, p. 1.

(b) Report from the Select Committee on the Commercial
State of the West Indian Colonies; With the Minutes of
Evidence, Appendix and Index, p. 657.

BPP: Vol. XVII, 1818: Papers Relating to the Treatment of
Slaves in the Colonies.

BPP: Vol. XXVI, 1833: Baptist Missionaries: etc. (540)

BPP: Vol. XLVII, 1837–1838: Reports from Bishop of Jamaica,
1831–32 (481); Slave Manumissions, Jamaica, 1825–1830;
(365); tables of the Revenue, Population; Commerce, etc.

of the United Kingdom and its Dependencies (Supplement to pt. 6)

ii. *House of Commons Sessional Papers*
Papers Respecting the Slave Trade, 1789: Vol. XXVI (646).
Minutes of Evidence of the Slave Trade, 1789: Vol. XXV (635–640).
Minutes of Evidence Relative to the Slave Trade; Select Committee Appointed 29th January, 1790; Vol. XXIX (698).
Minutes of Evidence Relative to the Slave Trade; Select Committee Appointed 23rd April, 1790: Vol. XXX.
Minutes of the Evidence Taken Before a Committee of the House of Commons . . . respecting the African Slave Trade, 1790–1791: Vol. XXXLV.

iii. *House of Lords Sessional Papers*
Manumissions granted in Jamaica in each year, from 1817–1830, distinguishing the gratuitous manumissions from those paid for (254 of 1831–32) CCVIII.
Report from the Select Committee of the House of Lords, in 1832, for enquiring into the Laws and Usages of the several West India Colonies in relation to the Slave Population, etc. and into the distressed condition of those Colonies; with Minutes of Evidence, Appendix, etc. (239 & 127 of 1831–32) CCCVI & CCCVII.

Other Official Publications

Acts of Assembly Passed in the Island of Jamaica from 1681–1769, inclusive. (2 Vols.) St. Jago De La Vega, Jamaica, 1769; 1771.
The Colonization of Jamaica: Proclamations, Commissions, etc. . . . Relating to the Planting and Settling of Jamaica. (No imprint) 1792.
Communications made to the Government by Lord Belmore relative to the Rebellion in Jamaica . . . Return of all Teachers or Preachers . . . connected with Missionary establishments in Jamaica who have been arrested, etc. London, 1832.
The Consolidated Slave Law, passed 22nd December, 1826. Kingston, Jamaica, 1827.

The Debates in Parliament, session 1833, on the resolution and the Bill for the Abolition of Slavery in the British Colonies, London 1834.

Further Proceedings of the Hon. House of Assembly of Jamaica relative to a Bill introduced into the House of Commons for effectually preventing the unlawful importation of slaves, etc. London 1816.

The Laws of Jamaica, passed by the Assembly and confirmed by His Majesty in Council, April 17th, 1684, London, 1684.

The Proceedings of the Hon. House of Assembly of Jamaica . . . in consequence of Mr Bushthorn's Motion on the gradual Abolition of Slavery throughout the Colonies. Kingston, 1811.

The Proceedings of the Governor and Assembly of Jamaica in regard to the Maroon Negroes. (ed. B. Edwards) 1796.

Report of the Trial of Fourteen Negroes of Montego Bay, January 1824, on a charge of Rebellious Conspiracy etc. Montego Bay, Jamaica, 1824.

Report of the Incorporated Society for the Conversion and Religious Instruction and Education of the Negro Slaves in the British West India Islands for the year 1826. London 1827.

Report of the Jamaica Royal Commission of Enquiry respecting certain Disturbances in the Island of Jamaica and the measures taken in the course of their suppression, London 1866.

A Report of the Committee of the House of Assembly of Jamaica relative to the present state of the Island, etc. Jamaica, 1818.

Report of the Royal Commission on the Rebellion of 1865.

The Journals of the House of Assembly, Jamaica, Vols. 1, 2, 3, 5, 10.

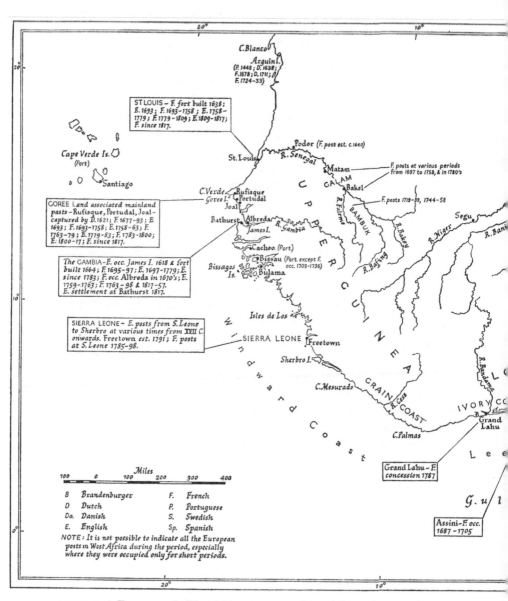

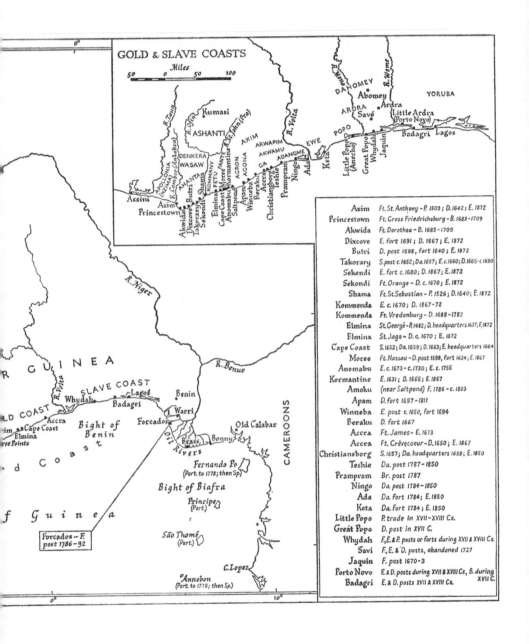

GOLD & SLAVE COASTS

Miles
50   0   50   100

Axim	Ft. St. Anthony – P. 1503; D. 1642; E. 1872
Princestown	Ft. Gross Friedrichsburg – B. 1683-1709
Akwida	Ft. Dorothea – B. 1685-1709
Dixcove	E. fort 1691; D. 1867; E. 1872
Butri	D. post 1598, fort 1640; E. 1872
Takorary	S. post c. 1652; Da. 1657; E. c. 1660; D. 1665-c.1690
Sekondi	E. fort c. 1680; D. 1867; E. 1872
Sekondi	Ft. Orange – D. c. 1670; E. 1872
Shama	Ft. St. Sebastian – P. 1526; D. 1640; E. 1872
Kommenda	E. c. 1670; D. 1867-72
Kommenda	Ft. Vredenburg – D. 1688-1782
Elmina	St. George – P. 1482; D. headquarters 1637; E. 1872
Elmina	St. Jago – D. c. 1670; E. 1872
Cape Coast	S. 1652; Da. 1659; D. 1663; E. headquarters 1664
Moree	Ft. Nassau – D. post 1598, fort 1624; E. 1867
Anomabu	E. c. 1673 – c. 1730; E. c. 1755
Kormantine	E. 1631; D. 1665; E. 1867
Amoku	(near Saltpond) F. 1786 – c. 1803
Apam	D. fort 1697-1811
Winneba	E. post c. 1650, fort 1694
Beraku	D. fort 1667
Accra	Ft. James – E. 1673
Accra	Ft. Crèvecoeur – D. 1650; E. 1867
Christiansborg	S. 1657; Da. headquarters 1659; E. 1850
Teshie	Da. post 1787-1850
Prampram	Br. post 1787
Ningo	Da. post 1784-1850
Ada	Da. fort 1784; E. 1850
Keta	Da. fort 1784; E. 1850
Little Popo	P. trade in XVII-XVIII Cs.
Great Popo	D. post in XVII C.
Whydah	F., E. & P. posts or forts during XVII & XVIII Cs.
Savi	F., E. & D. posts, abandoned 1727
Jaquin	F. post 1670-3
Porto Novo	E. & D. posts during XVII & XVIII Cs., B. during XVII C.
Badagri	E. & D. posts XVII & XVIII Cs.

Forcados – F. post 1786-92

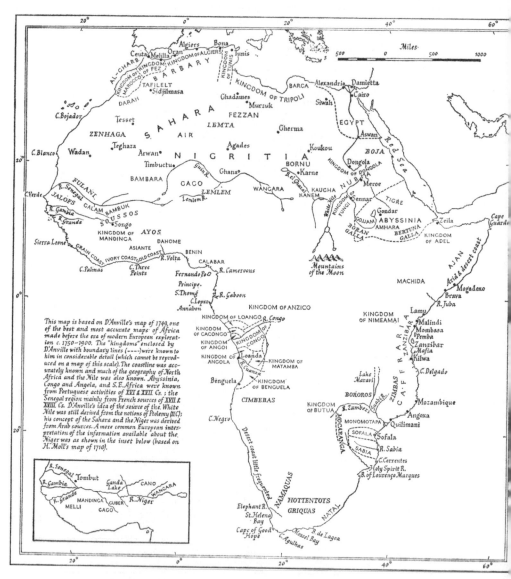

The map contains the following text:

This map is based on D'Anville's map of 1749, one of the best and most accurate maps of Africa made before the era of modern European exploration c. 1750–1900. The "kingdoms" enclosed by D'Anville with boundary lines (----) were known to him in considerable detail (which cannot be reproduced on a map of this scale). The coastline was accurately known and much of the geography of North Africa and the Nile was also known. Abyssinia, Congo and Angola, and S.E. Africa were known from Portuguese activities of XVI & XVII Cs.; the Senegal region mainly from French sources of XVII & XVIII Cs. D'Anville's idea of the source of the White Nile was still derived from the notions of Ptolemy (IIC); his concept of the Sahara and the Niger was derived from Arab sources. A more common European interpretation of the information available about the Niger was as shown in the inset below (based on H. Moll's map of 1710).

APPENDIX 7: Africa as known to Europeans in the mid-eighteenth century. From *Atlas of African History* by J. D. Fage: reproduced by permission of Edward Arnold (Publishers) Ltd.

PLATE CREDITS

Frontispiece. Courtesy of the National Library of Jamaica.
Reproduced in W.P. Livingstone. 1900. Black Jamaica: A Study in Evolution.

1. Source: Captain Canot: Or Twenty Years of an African Slaver, Ed. By Branz Mayer, 1854. p. 94

2. Source: Captain Canot: Or Twenty Years of an African Slaver, Ed. By Branz Mayer, 1854. p. 102.

3. Slavery Images: A Visual Record of the African Slave Trade and Slave Life in the Early African Diaspora. http://www.slaveryimages.org/s/slaveryimages/item/2553

4. A.Chains and Other Instruments Used by Slave Traders, 19th cent.
Source: Slavery Images: A Visual Record of the African Slave Trade & Slave Life in the Early African Diaspora. http://www.slaveryimages.org/s/slavery-images/item/2013

4B. Courtesy of National Library of Jamaica

5. Slavery Images: A Visual Record of the African Slave Trade and Slave Life in the Early African Diaspora http://www.slaveryimages.org/s/slaveryimages/item/2763

6. Courtesy of National Library of Jamaica.

7. Slavery Images: A Visual Record of the African Slave Trade and Slave Life in the Early African Diaspora http://www.slaveryimages.org/s/slaveryimages/item/1103

8 & 9. Slavery Images: A Visual Record of the African Slave Trade and Slave Life in the Early African Diaspora http://www.slaveryimages.org/s/slaveryimages/item/2505

10. Courtesy of the Library of Jamaica

11. Source: I.M. Belisario, Sketches of Character of the Negro Population in the Island of Jamaica, 1837–1838.

12. Courtesy of the National Library of Jamaica.
Quote from: J.Ranston. 2008. Belisario: Sketches of Character. A Historical Biography of a Jamaican Artist. p. 246

13. Courtesy of the National Library of Jamaica

Quote: Douglas Hall, ed. 1989. In Miserable Slavery: Thomas Thistlewood in Jamaica, 1750-86. University of the West Indies Press. pp. 137–138.

14. Carrying the Coffin

Image source & quote: James Phillippo, 1843. Jamaica: Its Past and Present State. Frontispiece and pp. 94–95.

15. Courtesy of the National Library of Jamaica

16. Courtesy; William and Mary Quarterly, OIEAHC

* Chambers, Douglas B., "Jamaica Runaway Slaves: 18th Century" (2013). https://ufdc.ufl.edu/AA00021144/00001; Source: D. Hall. 1989. In Miserable Slavery: Thomas Thistlewood in Jamaica pp. 198–201.

17 & 18. Courtesy of the National Library of Jamaica

* Tom Zoellner. 2020. Island on Fire: The Revolt that Ended Slavery in the British Empire, pp. 176–177.

19. Courtesy of the National Library of Jamaica

*Tom Zoellner. 2020. Island on Fire: The Revolt that Ended Slavery in the British Empire. Pp. 80–82; 207–208; 257–259; 278–279

20. Courtesy of the National Library of Jamaica

Title for Map:

Volume and Direction of the Trans-Atlantic Trade from all African to All American Regions

Source. David Eltis and David Richardson, Atlas of the Transatlantic Slave Trade. Yale University Press, 2010.

INDEX